Digestible Governance

Digestible Governance

Gastrocracy and Spanish Foodways

Edited by Eugenia Afinoguénova,
Lara Anderson,
and Rebecca Ingram

Vanderbilt University Press
NASHVILLE, TENNESSEE

Copyright 2024 Vanderbilt University Press
All rights reserved
First printing 2024

Library of Congress Cataloging-in-Publication Data

Names: Afinoguénova, Eugenia, editor. | Anderson, Lara, Ph. D., editor. | Ingram, Rebecca, 1977- editor.
Title: Digestible governance : gastrocracy and Spanish foodways / edited by Eugenia Afinoguénova, Lara Anderson and Rebecca Ingram.
Description: Nashville, Tennessee : Vanderbilt University Press, [2024] | Includes bibliographical references and index.
Identifiers: LCCN 2024012297 (print) | LCCN 2024012298 (ebook) | ISBN 9780826507082 (paperback) | ISBN 9780826507099 (hardcover) | ISBN 9780826507105 (epub) | ISBN 9780826507112 (pdf)
Subjects: LCSH: Food--Political aspects--Spain--History. | Food--Social aspects--Spain--History. | Gastronomy--Spain. | Food habits--Spain--History.
Classification: LCC TX360.S7 D54 2024 (print) | LCC TX360.S7 (ebook) | DDC 641.01/30946--dc23/eng/20240410
LC record available at https://lccn.loc.gov/2024012297
LC ebook record available at https://lccn.loc.gov/2024012298

Front cover image: *Miralda*. Stomak Digital / El Internacional Tapas Bar Restaurant

HISPANIC ISSUES
Nicholas Spadaccini, Founding Editor
Ana Forcinito, Executive Editor
Luis Martín-Estudillo, Executive Editor
Megan Corbin, Managing Editor
William Viestenz, Associate Managing Editor
Sophia Beal, Osiris A. Gómez, Associate Editors
Carolina Julia Añón Suárez, Ariel Arjona,
Collin Diver, Tim Frye, Javier Zapata Clavería,
Assistant Editors

*ADVISORY BOARD / EDITORIAL BOARD
Rolena Adorno (Yale University)
Román de la Campa (Unversity of Pennsylvania)
David Castillo (University at Buffalo)
Jaime Concha (University of California, San Diego)
Tom Conley (Harvard University)
Estrella de Diego Otero (Universidad Complutense de Madrid)
Nora Domínguez (Universidad de Buenos Aires)
William Egginton (Johns Hopkins University)
Brad Epps (University of Cambridge)
Edward Friedman (Vanderbilt University)
Wlad Godzich (University of California, Santa Cruz)
Antonio Gómez L-Quiñones (Dartmouth College)
Hans Ulrich Gumbrecht (Stanford University)
*Carol A. Klee (University of Minnesota)
Germán Labrador Méndez (Princeton University)
Eukene Lacarra Lanz (Universidad del País Vasco)
Raúl Marrero-Fente (University of Minnesota)
Kelly McDonough (University of Texas at Austin)
Walter D. Mignolo (Duke University)
*Louise Mirrer (The New-York Historical Society)
Mabel Moraña (Washington University in St. Louis)
Alberto Moreiras (Texas A & M University)
Bradley J. Nelson (Concordia University, Montreal)
Michael Nerlich (Université Blaise Pascal)
*Francisco Ocampo (University of Minnesota)
Antonio Ramos-Gascón (University of Minnesota)
Jenaro Talens (Universitat de València)
Miguel Tamen (Universidade de Lisboa)
Noël Valis (Yale University)
Teresa Vilarós (Texas A & M University)
Santos Zunzunegui (Universidad del País Vasco)

CONTENTS

ACKNOWLEDGMENTS ix

INTRODUCTION. *Digestible Governance: Gastrocracy and Spanish Foodways* 1
EUGENIA AFINOGUÉNOVA, LARA ANDERSON, AND REBECCA INGRAM

PART I. GASTROPOLITICS

1. Public Control over Private Trade: Barcelona's Market Hall Food Retailing System 25
MONTSERRAT MILLER

2. Regenerating Catalan Culinary Identity 58
H. ROSI SONG

3. Francoist Food Culture in Post-Authoritarian Spain: Culinary Maps, Centralism, and Food Memories 81
LARA ANDERSON

PART II. INGESTIBLE IDENTITIES

4. Food Fights: Nativism and Culinary Xenophobia in Europe 101
AITANA GUIA

5. *Kashrut* in Spain: Religious Observance, State Tolerance, or Niche Market Entrepreneurship? 128
SILVINA SCHAMMAH GESSER AND SUSY GRUSS

6. Culinary Conflict or *Convivencia*?: *Halal* Food Practices, Perceptions, and Promotion in Spain 153
JESSICA R. BOLL

PART III. GASTROCRATIC INSTITUTIONS

7. The Institutionalization of the Asturian *Espicha* during the Franco Regime   179
LUIS BENITO GARCÍA ÁLVAREZ

8. Cava's Place   198
BOB DAVIDSON

9. Food, Heritage, and Tourism: On the Uses of Food Heritage and Its Relations with Culture, Politics, and Socioeconomic Development   220
F. XAVIER MEDINA

PART IV. HARD TO SWALLOW

10. Ideology "à la Carte": Food Politics in Franco's Spain   239
SUZANNE DUNAI

11. Creating a "Land of Charcuterie": Cured Meat Producers, Culinary Marketing, and the Construction of Gastronationalist Discourses in Twentieth-Century Catalonia   264
ALEJANDRO J. GÓMEZ DEL MORAL

AFTERWORD. *Future Directions on Food Studies and Politics in Spain Today*   293
CAROLYN A. NADEAU

Contributors   303
Index   309

◆ ACKNOWLEDGMENTS

The work for *Digestible Governance* began at the 2019 Association of Spanish and Portuguese Historical Studies conference in Barcelona where we co-editors were joined in a roundtable conversation on politics, Peninsular history, and gastrocracy by Montserrat Miller, Nadia Fava, Jordi Mari, and Mary Nash.

We thank the College of Arts & Sciences at the University of San Diego, specifically Dean Noelle Norton and Assistant Dean Frances Kuhn, as well as Marquette University's Vice President for Research and Innovation, Dr. Jeanne Hossenlopp, whose ongoing support for faculty scholarship during the lean COVID-19 years freed up university funding for editing and formatting expenses. Sean Grattan aided us with his pre-review copyediting and formatting, and Matthew Phillips completed final copyedits and reformatted all chapters into *Chicago* style.

Special thanks go to Luis Martín-Estudillo and the Hispanic Issues board for their support of the volume, in addition to its many peer reviewers. One influential one was Carolyn Nadeau whose lovely afterword concludes our work. Gianna Mosser, Steven Rodriguez, and Alissa Faden were especially patient and generous in ensuring that our vision for the cover could come to be. We offer our sincere gratitude to them and the rest of the Vanderbilt University Press team.

Finally, kudos to Antoni Miralda, whose wit and creativity in exploring the intersections of food, culture, and art have inspired us. We are grateful to Miralda for allowing us to use his *Stomak Digital / El Internacional Tapas Bar Restaurant* for the book cover.

◆ INTRODUCTION
Digestible Governance
Gastrocracy and Spanish Foodways

Eugenia Afinoguénova
Lara Anderson
Rebecca Ingram

Spanish Food Studies, a subset of Spanish Cultural Studies, is a rich and expanding field of inquiry that allows us to address food as a material object, social ritual, cultural practice, and discourse. Contributing to this body of research, our collected volume focuses on those case studies where governance has become inextricably linked to the food system, bringing to the fore the political agendas that are not always visible in discussions surrounding food. Contributors examine public projections of how food is sourced, cooked, consumed, and codified in relation to Spain's political and culinary center, peripheries, and migrant cuisines, as well as how such activity is tied to identity debates and resistance.

The term "gastrocracy" at the center of this volume refers to the power produced and reproduced by appropriating discourses and "foodways," or those practices related to the sourcing, preparation, distribution, and consumption of food. While gastrocracy is often used to translate questions of cultural self-identification, identity, hybridity, assimilation, and differentiation into everyday language, the works collected in this volume examine how gastrocracy is also called on to realize identity-related claims through daily activities and conversations involving food. Unlike other works, the chapters collected here look at how food manages gendered, class, religious, racial, and cultural differences in the interest of the state.

Eliciting wide public participation, coopted for political purposes, regarded as a factor of economic development at any scale, and integrated into every "banal nationalism" (Billig 1995), food, together with the political mobilization of its production, distribution, and consumption, is highly relevant for understanding the idiosyncrasies of Spain's cuisines, as well as its economy, politics, and culture.[1] If scholars have overlooked the link between food and power, this is because food culture itself is still mistaken for a set of unimposing and irreflexive everyday practices. The apparent disconnect between food and politics means that even those who are aware of the political mobilization of food struggle to give it a name. We propose to study gastrocracy to account for such cases when cooking, eating, and thinking about food seem inseparable from politics.

Gastrocracy is usually deployed to support nationalist agendas and promote Spain through the brand of its gastronomy in a global marketplace, as confirmed by the Gastro Marca España project developed by the Royal Academy of Gastronomy with support from a number of government ministries.[2] Whether through branding Spain's gastronomy or applying "design thinking" to projects that seek to educate or circulate the brand beyond state borders, both the state and capital undergird and legitimize Spain's imagined food identity as produced from the center and are often oblivious to the histories and varieties of contemporary local and regional cuisines.[3] For example, food heritage as a gastrocratic phenomenon can make invisible the diversity of foodways and foodscapes actually present in contemporary Spain.

Also of interest is how food, food discourse, and culinary practices are repurposed *against* the state. The everydayness of food offers unique possibilities for resistance. According to Henri Lefebvre, "everyday life is profoundly related to all activities, and encompasses them with all their differences and their conflicts; it is their meeting place, their bond, their common ground."[4] This everydayness means that the political nature of food often goes unnoticed by those in power. Therefore, culinary activity and public projections of food offer unique possibilities for resistance.

The politics of food developed in Spain in the last quarter of the nineteenth century, when debates around nationalism in its different forms took the guise of discussions about not just national food culture but also the role of regional and local cuisines in Spanish culinary nationalism. Unlike French gastronomy, this link between food and governance has been a key feature of Spanish food culture, involving center and periphery debates, in addition to contemporary multicultural realities. Until recently, however, Spain has been treated as an area of peripheral interest in Food Studies circles, which have ignored the considerable insights on the history and the uses of food in Spain from Humanities and Social

Sciences scholars. The absence of interdisciplinary approaches to understanding food in Spain has made it difficult to discuss the intermingling of gastronomy and governance, as well as its potential to empower communities in how they produce, consume, and think about food and its meanings. The responses, it will be argued here, can only be found if the place of Spain in Food Studies is fully acknowledged, as Anderson and Ingram recently argued, and if we study food as part of broader comparative framing inherent in Iberian Studies (Anderson and Ingram; Gimeno Ugalde and Pérez Isasi; Newcomb).[5]

Representing an array of disciplines from History and Anthropology to Literary and Cultural Studies, this volume demonstrates that critical attention to gastrocratic policies, practices, discourses, and representations is key for understanding not only food but also politics. This research focus is particularly important now, as territory-bound, nineteenth-century conceptualizations of food heritage in the service of nation-states clash with the reality of peripheral nationalisms, the influx of refugees that challenge territory-based identities, the growing visibility of diasporic communities, and concomitant questioning of the concepts of citizenship. Amid the news about projects such as refugee-run restaurants or ethnic food recognition, more research is needed to understand what is taken for granted when food is instrumentalized in this way.

By bringing to the fore the ubiquitous, lingering instrumentalization of food and the practices, discourses, and artifacts involved in or resulting from such mobilizations, our usage of the term "gastrocracy" thus uncovers new forms of power. Scholars interested in food and power have used Michel Foucault's notion of biopolitics to account for food-related practices and discourses that can influence citizens' culinary choices.[6] Biopolitics, which assumes the responsibility and control of the vital processes and bodily discipline, is exerted by different official institutions. Still, if government food policy is one way that people are regulated or controlled, another equally important yet less tangible area is cultural practices surrounding food, along with media and textual representations of cooking and eating. While biopower relies upon state efforts to measure and control populations, biopolitical interventions critically involve circulating images of food, cookbooks, food sections in newspapers and descriptions of food in official documents, which some of our contributors discuss.

Why "Gastrocracy"?

We did not invent the term "gastrocracy," which appeared for the first time in a newspaper column by the Spanish philosopher Fernando Savater. Commenting on his compatriots' mysterious fascination with TV cooking shows at a time when the foundations of public life were still crumpling after the economic crash of 2008, Savater writes:

> La única pasión española que puede hoy compararse con el fútbol es la cocina. ¡Somos una gastrocracia! Santa Teresa nos aseguró que Dios también anda entre pucheros, pero no dijo que se dedicase personalmente a deconstruir albóndigas. Ahora resulta que no hay destino más sagrado y los ilusionistas del fogón son los únicos gurús indiscutibles de una asamblea de crédulos y esnobs. En todas las radios predican los fabricantes de recetas y en cada televisión tienen su concurso de potajes. Todo el mundo va disfrazado de cocinero, como en la tamborrada donostiarra, y hasta a los niños les hacen competir en el arte de remover la olla. Y los que tanto denuncian otras corrupciones de menores, calladitos y contentos. Lo peor es el discurso pringoso y altisonante que pretende darle *glamour* estético a la fabricación de tortillas o croquetas: peor que los textos de los catálogos artísticos, con eso se lo digo todo. A este paso, el buen gusto tendrá que desembocar en la anorexia o la huelga de hambre. Si Nietzsche viniese a España, ya no diría "no soy un hombre, soy dinamita", sino "no soy un hombre, soy bicarbonato . . . "[7]

> *The only Spanish passion that can be compared today with soccer is cuisine. We are a gastrocracy! Saint Theresa assured us that God also dwells among the pots, even if she personally neglected deconstructing meatballs. Today there is no calling more sacred, and the magicians of the cooktop are the indisputable gurus among an assembly of the gullible and snobs. Recipe writers preach from all radio stations while each television station features its own cooking competition. People run around dressed up like cooks as if participating in the San Sebastian tamborrada, and even children are compelled to compete in the art of stirring the pot. And those who always denounce other instances of child grooming remain quiet and happy. The worst are the greasy and high-sounding discourses that attempt to give aesthetic glamour to making* tortillas *or croquettes: worse than any art catalog and that says it all. At this rate, good taste must lead to anorexia or a hunger strike. If Nietzsche came to Spain, he wouldn't say "I am not a man, I am dynamite," but "I am not a man, I am baking soda."*

Drawing on Savater's understanding of gastrocracy as a new type of power, this volume makes explicit the political foundations and negotiations behind the popular performances of food-making, be they televised or not. At the same time, the contributions collected here demonstrate that food systems and governance so visible in contemporary foodscape have a long history of connections underpinning Spain's nation-building.

Gastronomy is the fixture of gastrocracy that Spain inherited from France. An intellectual child of the French Revolution, gastronomy was born from an implicit connection between food and society. Its foundational text, *Physiology of Taste* by the French lawyer and writer Jean Anthelme Brillat-Savarin (1826), adapted traditional approaches to food as medicine to satisfy the bourgeois concern with the "common good" resulting from the flourishing of a political body imagined in class-based, gendered, and nationalistic terms. This and other seminal gastronomic texts coming from France acquired currency in Spain, where the quest for autochthonous models of food culture also became a part of a broader push to facilitate national cohesion.[8]

Acknowledging the importance of gastronomic discourses for public projections of food-related activities, this volume, however, challenges the common view that the only publicly relevant food practices are the high-profile activities of famous chefs. By shifting from gastronomy to gastrocracy, our work restores the agency of women and other marginalized subjects who do not achieve status or recognition as "professionals."[9] If, as Daniel Sipe writes, gastronomy was invented as a tool of social improvement—as a biopolitical twin of utopian socialism—this volume's gastrocratic framing examines how food is used to exercise power, articulate civic responses to top-down politics, and, more broadly, make social meaning.[10]

In Spain, the word "gastronomía" is still considered a somewhat foreign term; the intersection of material, social, and medical aspects of food is usually called "alimentación," a concept that combines nutrition and food culture. Mabel Gracia Arnaiz writes:

> Utilizamos el concepto de cultura alimentaria refiriéndonos al conjunto de actividades establecidas por los grupos humanos para obtener del entorno los elementos que posibilitan su subsistencia, abarcando desde el aprovisionamiento, la producción, la distribución, el almacenamiento, la conservación y la preparación de los alimentos hasta su consumo, e incluyendo todos los aspectos simbólicos y materiales que acompañan las diferentes fases de este proceso.[11]

> *We use the concept of nutritional culture to refer to the whole of activities undertaken by humans to obtain elements that make possible their subsistence, including provisioning, production, distribution, storage, preservation, and the preparation of foods until their consumption, and including all symbolic and material aspects that accompany the different phases of this process.*

In English, "nutrition" does not include the cultural aspects of eating. This is why we refer to gastrocracy, rather than "nutrocracy," to account for the intersections between food, culture, and governance, not only in the things people eat, but also in how they talk about foods and the values they attach to their dishes.

Priscilla Parkhurst Ferguson, a pioneer of Food Cultural Studies, explains that "food talk—the ways we talk about and represent food—structures our experience of food, from kitchen to table, from menu to meal. While food as material object is ingested literally into our being, equally important is the way we talk about food to 'craft identities and construct social worlds.'"[12] This system of discourses and representations crosses the writing, oral communication, and visual culture explicitly dedicated to gastronomy, as well as all the references to food made in passing. Attentive to contexts ranging from menus, cookery books, and public discussions of food heritage, in addition to laws, medical literature, and political journalism, this inclusive approach to food talk, which we identify as gastrocratic, influences both collective identities and the uptake of individual subjectivities.

The gastrocracy approach also calls on food scholars to put food-related work back into gastronomic debates. Drawing on Hannah Arendt's distinction between labor (that also includes feeding the body), work, and action, the simultaneous attention to gastronomy and governance better captures the reality of the body politic than a sociology of power that does not take into consideration food and other gendered labor. Arendt famously viewed both work and action as ways of overcoming the pain of "laboring, where the human body . . . is also thrown back on itself, concentrates on nothing but its own being alive, and remains imprisoned in its metabolism with nature without ever transcending or freeing itself from the recurring cycle of its own functioning."[13] The persistent interdependence between the discourses of food and governance suggests, however, that reproductive labor—food labor or foodwork—needs to be better understood as the basis of other activities and as an activity with intrinsic political dimensions.

According to Germán Labrador Méndez, debates around food in democratic Spain transform social practices of nurturing bodies and the physical activity of digestion into "processes" that support capitalism.[14] Engaging labor, land, and money—the three "fictitious commodities" that, according to the economist Karl Polanyi, delineate the limits of capitalism—food systems still rely on the unpaid, underpaid, and erased labor of women, migrants, and racialized others.[15] This is why one of the goals of our focus on gastrocracy is to show that food, cooking, and eating are not merely pre-political, but also political.

Digestible Governance

The gastrocracy framework at the heart of this volume reveals key connections between food and the broader nationalist political project. Discussions surrounding food became particularly influential after the last quarter of the nineteenth century, when forms of Spanish nationalism, regionalism, and localism became subject of public debate. It was a gendered discourse: until the twentieth century, male authors positioned themselves as opinion-makers in the matters of food. Women were distinctly implicated in this work due to the degree to which food provisioning and preparation occupied their daily lives. While women navigated paradoxical messages about the national ties their cooking fomented, the modernity of their practices, and the political consequences of cooking and eating "right," their contributions were for a long time marginalized or ignored.[16]

Spain's male intellectuals at the Institución Libre de Enseñanza, as well as their disciples who came to political power in the early twentieth century, considered food one of the overlooked yet crucial elements of nation-building. In 1877, Spain's first gastronomic treaty, *Letters Exchanged between the Dining Room and the Kitchen* by José de Castro y Serrano and Mariano Pardo de Figueroa, who published under the pen names of "His Majesty's Cook" and "Dr. Thebussem," set the standards of Spain's culinary nationalism.[17] According to both authors, the country's elites had a mission to collect, organize, and popularize local recipes to promote both the mutual recognition among the inhabitants of Spain's disjointed territories and a respect for Spain's cultural identity among its neighbors.[18] Insisting on the importance of freeing the dishes recognized as national from the hegemony of neighboring France's cuisine, these pioneering gastronomes highlighted the importance of discourse to the projects that now would be referred to as culinary nationalism. "Dr. Thebussem" and "His Majesty's Cook" concluded that, for Spain to have a cuisine of its own, a book would need to be written containing recipes from the diverse regions. This would solidify the idea of a regionally diverse national food culture, while helping Spain's citizenry to know more about foodstuffs and recipes from across the country. By the late nineteenth and early twentieth centuries, as Eric Storm writes, food became an essential element of not only national but also regional identity-making in the domestic sphere.[19]

The "digestible governance" that emerged as a response to lackluster nation-building flourished during the Primo de Rivera and Franco's dictatorship, when food discourse partook in the production of unified gastronomic spaces.[20] Importantly, during the Franco regime, texts about food not only taught citizens how to eat, but they also instructed them in the uptake of gendered, nationalist, autarkic identities.[21] Although Francoist food discourse developed against the backdrop of autarky, those who wrote about food at the time were more concerned with codifying national food culture than finding ways of representing scarcity.

In the late 1950s and early 1960s, the regime took the course of ending autarky. The government's plans of economic development relied on the tourism industry as a source of fiscal solvency, and Spanish food acquired new political prominence.

However, feeding tourists was not the only focus of state attention.[22] Franco's debut on the international stage was made possible by the 1953 military agreement with the United States. American military bases on Spanish soil spurred research and assistance programs from the American Interdepartmental Committee on Nutrition for National Defense to ensure that civilians' diets prepared them for military duties. Though the Committee revealed no illnesses triggered specifically by nutrition, it estimated that Spaniards' diet was highly deficient in protein and vitamin A, while surpassing the norm in vitamin C and Tiamine.[23]

The end of autarky thus opened to gastrocracy new geopolitical horizons. At the same time, Spain's own geopolitical unity was coming under pressure. Indeed, it is in some relatively obscure gastronomic texts published from the late 1960s onward that we first glimpse the move away from Franco's ideal of a monolithic cuisine. If gastronomic guides of the 1940s and 1950s all but obliterated regional cuisines, culinary texts such as *El libro de la cocina española* (1970) by Nestor Luján and Juan Perucho, *La Cocina Española* (1970) by Cándido López (Mesonero Mayor de Castilla), *Guía gastronómica de España* (1970) by José Luis Rueda, and *Guía gastronómica de España* (1976) by Gonzalo Sol saw culinary and gastronomic diversity as a source of celebration.[24]

According to Labrador Méndez, the transition to democracy after the dictator's death in 1975 gave rise to "the most rudimentary forms of a trophic politics as: those who eat (or are eaten) what (and how much) or those who go hungry (and how and where)," which linked gastronomies to social engineering and governance.[25] As the state attempted to harness the political power of food to unify a disparate population, so too did Spain's peripheral nationalisms. Both before and after 1975, food was used in Catalonia and the Basque Country to mark these regions' differences from Spain. Since then, these subnations have drawn on food in their rise from unknown cuisines to culinary power houses to promote the idea of gastronomic heritage, as is touched on in this volume. The Generalitat de Catalunya has had systematic recourse to the culinary advances and food history of the region to mark Catalonia's distinctiveness.[26] Contemporaneously, the Basque Country showcases traditional and local food under the banner of Euskadi Gastronoika in its attempts to identify the region's celebrated age-old food culture as a key component of Basque identity and nationalism.

If the public discussion of food has been, from its inception, related to Spain's incomplete and contested territorial integration, it also quickly became a tool of managing regional difference. In the twenty-first century, Spain's multicultural and multiethnic presence also shows up in its foodways, even if hegemonic representations of Spanish or other Iberian gastronomies erase them almost completely. Since the 1980s, immigration to Spain has impacted how people eat, cook, supply provisions to their homes, work for others, and understand their food identities and foodways given these phenomena. Famed cultural commentators, including some well-known gastronomical writers such as Manuel Vázquez Montalbán, did not acknowledge how the waves of immigrants arriving to the country have shaped its foodways.[27] Instead, much of the debate since the '80s and '90s has focused on the diversity represented by Spain's autonomous communities.[28] Racialized Spaniards, citizens who identify as Spanish according to the racial and ethnic identities of their immigrant parents and grandparents, have come to comprise a significant minority population. And yet, as writers like Chenta Tsai Tseng, who self-identifies as "Putochinomaricón," and Quan Zhou Wu illustrate in their autobiographies, food metaphors and discourse allow them to comment on and critique Spain's dominant cultures and how it promotes assimilation as a pathway toward belonging.[29]

Continuing the insight of bell hooks who, as early as 1991, began to warn against "eating the other," scholars of race and migration are especially attentive to the language of acculturation and hybridity that rely on culinary metaphors.[30] Jeroen Dewulf proposes understanding "hybridity as anthropophagy" in order to "liberate" understandings of hybridity from an "obsession with specific minorities or (post-) colonial structures."[31] On her part, Katharyne Mitchell, a sociologist of diasporic communities, writes about a "hype of hybridity" that "seizes upon" the subversive and progressive potential of the term even as it makes abstract the practices of everyday life (cooking and eating) and obscures how diasporic, hybrid subjects are used for economic gain.[32] Bringing together the reactions to the recent wave of migrations and the language of gastronomy deeply engrained in Italian public debate, Gaia Giuliani draws on the work of Fatimah Tobing to distinguish "a digestive model of racialized citizenship." This model "transforms phenotypic differences into nutrients for the Italian body politic that assimilates them, neutralizing their cultural differences and their political subjectivities." Guiliani concludes that "a number of subjects can be assimilated insofar as they are considered absorbable."[33]

The movements of people and foods, as Elizabeth Zanoni has shown, are deeply intertwined and critical to understanding nation-building, globalization, and the formation of migrant marketplaces.[34] The contacts and exchanges of multicultural and multiethnic foodways show up as a "diet that mingles" foods from ancestral homelands with those of others or a desire to "eat a multi-ethnic mix of foods," as Donna Gabaccia demonstrates.[35] Yet, extrapolating Krishnendu Ray's argument and applying it to Spain, migrants and racialized Spaniards are those who often labor as low-prestige care workers or overworked entrepreneurs in spaces that intensify how their foodways remain marginal from discussions about aesthetics or taste more broadly.[36] More research, alongside the studies in this volume, is needed in this area to understand what is coopted or taken for granted when the food and foodways of migrants and racialized Spaniards are instrumentalized or "digested" for the purposes of assimilation.

Gastronomy has always been gastrocracy, occupying itself with the public projection of food while also making invisible the labor of cooking. What happened to the Spanish economy also and first happened to Spanish gastronomy, marking it as a horizon of failed ways of modernization: financialization, reliance on scientific innovation, and invisiblization of care and foodwork at the expense of the public cult of celebrity chefs. The connections between gastronomy and politics, however, are becoming more visible now. Against the backdrop of the 2008 financial crises, as the south of Europe was singled out as an area of flawed industrial development, gastronomy emerged both as a symptom of Spain's desired place in the company of world's most developed nations and as a marker of the Global South, reimagined as a space of authenticity. Unable to compete with the industrialized North, the nations identified as southern began to refashion themselves as the keepers of artisan traditions and "slow food."

Counterintuitively, since the beginning of the twenty-first century, the central and autonomic governments have been investing public funds not in Spain's artisan traditions, but rather in their technologically enhanced versions. The complicity between the industrial food system and the "innovative" cuisine that became an essential part of Spain's national brand was first denounced by chef Santi Santamaría in his 2008 book *La cocina al desnudo*.[37] The Royal Gastronomy Academy, the organizers of MadridFusion (the country's main annual culinary gathering), food journalists, and many celebrity chefs were fast to react by marginalizing Santamaría on the grounds of his grossly misrepresented ideas.[38] The sad fame of this visionary book, which subsequently remained out of print for fifteen years, and the hate campaign against its author serve as reminders of gastrocracy's power to shape society as well as the cuisine itself. Now we must call it by its name.

This Volume: Gastrocracy and Spanish Foodways

Focused on the twentieth and twenty-first centuries and referencing Spain's history extending back to the Middle Ages, the studies in this volume examine some of the most persistent debates that emerge at the intersection of gastronomy and governance. The volume is divided into four sections dedicated to (1) the politics of gastronomy, (2) the ways in which gastronomy articulates identity debates, (3) the institutions of gastronomy, and (4) the political resistance channeled through gastronomy.

Section One, "Gastropolitics" brings to the fore the political agendas that have historically remained implicit in debates concerning food. Gastropolitics is a phenomenon related to nation-states. Yet, as Montserrat Miller demonstrates in "Public Control over Private Trade: Barcelona's Market Hall Food Retailing System," once we shift the scale to municipal power, which kept its relevance through Francoist unification in Spain, food and authority have been united since the Middle Ages. Miller shows how Barcelona's city government manifested its authority through asserting its control over the supply and distribution of food. Beyond their well-known role as the center of the exchange of goods and ideas, public markets thus also must be viewed as institutions encapsulating the idea of the "common good." Importantly, they were places where women vendors gained high visibility, which gave a "feminine character" to the system of power mediated by the provisioning of food.

In "Regenerating Catalan Culinary Identity," H. Rosi Song analyzes Ferran Agulló's cookbook *Llibre de la cuina catalana* (1928). She connects the author to the broader context of early twentieth-century Catalan nationalist political projects, while showing how the eating and cooking practices reflected in the cookbook—ones that evoke loss rather than exaltation—establish an idea of Catalan nationality that continues to resonate in the current political climate.

Rounding out this section, Lara Anderson's contribution "Francoist Food Culture in Post-Authoritarian Spain: Culinary Maps, Centralism, and Food Memories" explores the continued influence of Francoist biopolitics in contemporary Spain through her analysis of how nostalgia for Franco's gastronomical unification is deployed in popular television, media, and in restaurant spaces. This work underscores how Francoist food policies, attitudes, and "food talk" continue to subordinate the diversity of foodways present in Spain to a nationalist ideal of Spanish gastronomy.

Section Two, "Ingestible Identities," explores how gastronomy has been mobilized to resolve the pressing need to negotiate differing and overlapping religious, territorial, and national self-identifications in Spain. The chapters comprising this section cover how gastrocracy is used to articulate both autochthonous and diasporic identities as well as Spain's place in the European Union. The government's insistence on positioning Spain as the world's prime tourist destination—and to raise the profile of the gastronomic tourism industry—makes distinguishing (or "hybridizing") these multiple identities crucial.

The section begins with Aitana Guia's "Food Fights: Nativism and Culinary Xenophobia in Europe," which provides an account of xenophobia in relation to migrant cuisines in Spain and other European countries. Guia shows that these nativist positions have resulted in culinary xenophobia and tensions hindering the rights of minority groups and migrants.

The analysis of the gastronomic discourses and practices and their relevance for understanding the position of religious and ethnic minorities is continued in "*Kashrut* in Spain: Religious Observance, State Tolerance, or Niche Market Entrepreneurship?" by Silvina Schammah Gesser and Susy Gruss. In this analysis, the uneven revival of the dietary practices and infrastructures of *kashrut* in the twentieth and twenty-first centuries not only mirrors the return and a greater recognition of Jewish communities, but also the State's wider geopolitical alliances, international trade interests, and tourism development. This chapter points to parallels between *kashrut*—an ancient practice of belonging rooted in religion and channeled through food—and the growing use of food communities and regulations as vehicles of integration and normalization encouraged by the State.

Gastronomic practices and discourses have been equally present in the discussions of Spain's Arabic past, its present Arab and Muslim diasporas, and its tourism policy. In "Culinary Conflict or *Convivencia*?: *Halal* Food Practices, Perceptions, and Promotion in Spain," Jessica Boll explores how Spain's contemporary foodscapes are grappling with the marked increase of *halal* food products and production, responding to the demand created by Muslim migrants and converts alike. Her review of current scholarship and laws, in addition to the marketing practices of key restaurants, shows that both obfuscations and/or "orientalizations" of *halal* identities persist, even as key stakeholders advance pathways toward new acceptances of how *halal* foods comprise Spain's culinary cultures.

The third section, "Gastrocratic Institutions," explores how state and international power structures shape the codification and perception of food, as well as its consumption. Concomitant with the rise of the "slow food" movement and following the inscription of "Gastronomic Meal of the French" by UNESCO into the list of Intangible Cultural Heritage of Humanity in 2011, public/private associations all around Spain have been established with the goal of achieving recognition by UNESCO for Spanish, Catalan, and other national cuisines. In 2016, Gastro Marca España—an association and a web portal—was launched to raise the profile of food in Spain's national brand. It is therefore significant that two chapters of this section were written by academics who are also involved with the UNESCO Commission on Intangible Cultural Heritage and occupy prominent UNESCO Chairs.

Luis Benito García Álvarez, the Chair in Asturian Cider at the University of Oviedo, traces the impact of Francoist state institutions on the practices of cider consumption—what he calls "institutionalization." His chapter, "The Institutionalization of the Asturian *Espicha* During the Franco Regime," argues that the state intervention into the rituals of tapping the barrel—called *espichas*—

is still affecting the times, places, and ways in which cider is consumed, in Asturias and far beyond.

Dedicated to a no less emblematic drink of a different region, Catalan cava, Bob Davidson's essay "Cava's Place" examines contemporary conflict surrounding the drink. Pushes outside of Catalonia to boycott consumption aligned with pro-independence debates and momentum toward independence referendums. Despite the connections between cava and Catalan terroir, it became imperative for some producers to disassociate the drink from place to maintain its market across Spain and its symbolic connections to the state. Davidson notes the choice to serve cava rather than champagne at a 2014 ceremony headed by monarchs Felipe VI and Leticia Ortiz. In the leadup to the polemic independence debate that divided much of the country, the new monarchs requested not only a menu showcasing traditional Spanish cuisine but also gave place to "Cava Catalana." The special place given to cava was clearly meant to reassure Catalans of their influential position within the Spanish state.[39]

Building on an extensive bibliography, in the chapter "Food, Heritage, and Tourism: On the Uses of Food Heritage and Its Relations with Culture, Politics, and Socioeconomic Development," F. Xavier Medina, the UNESCO Chair in Food, Culture, and Development at the Open University of Catalonia, discusses gastronomy and foodways as constructions of heritage in Spain. He establishes key understandings of the links between heritage projects, tradition, and the past while also indicating how food heritage particularly intersects with tourism.

Finally, Section Four, "Hard to Swallow," focuses on the opportunities for political resistance harbored in the preparation of food and debates about it. Francoism was not exactly a gastrocracy, yet it would be hard to find a clearer case of a state pretending to imbue the daily lives of its subjects with ideological teachings. Still, studies of food practices of everyday Spaniards, under Franco as well as since, demonstrate that nationalistic models were not accepted unquestioningly. In the kitchen or in the supermarket, resistance is more accessible than it sometimes is in the street.

Tracing the differences between the language of ideology, the discourse of policy-making, and Spaniards' real foodways, Suzanne Dunai's chapter "Ideology 'à la Carte': Food Politics in Franco's Spain" examines how gastronomy promotes "soft," rather than dictatorial, power. Dunai reveals how individual agency grew within private homes that resisted the nationalistic model of public life promoted by Francoist ideologues and policymakers.

Alex Gómez del Moral's contribution, "Creating a 'Land of Charcuterie': Cured Meat Producers, Culinary Marketing, and the Construction of Gastronationalist Discourses in Twentieth-Century Catalonia," uncovers the cured meat's potential for resistance that flourished in Catalonia in the context of the debates around self-determination. His chapter provides an in-depth account of how twentieth-century Catalonian cured meat producers and culinary marketing participate in nation-building.

Future research will undoubtedly expand the question of gastrocratic policies and discourses to the parts of Spain's territory not covered in this volume. It is important to note, for instance, how restaurant owners are called on to invent the culinary traditions for branding and blending the identities of different Roads of St. James, from Andalucía and La Mancha all the way to Galicia. It is also crucial to compare the food traditions developed for Spain's seventeen Autonomous Communities, on the one hand, and the local and regional forms of culinary self-identification, on the other. Extremadura, the Basque Country, Galicia, the Canary Islands, and every other part of Spain's territory should become a focus of gastrocratic inquiry.

The production and distribution of food also need to be further examined in the context of gastrocracy, especially given the growing concern for the environmental impacts of Spain's leadership as a provider of fresh produce, meat, and seafood in Europe. From pig urine in the water supply in Catalonia, overuse of pesticides, and increasing reliance on genetically modified crops in Spain, all the way to the untenable conditions of migrant farm and food workers, topics invisibilized in most recent research narrowly focused on gastronomy need significant scrutiny. This volume offers a framework for dialogue between Humanities research and activism involving food sovereignty, food gentrification, cooperative agricultural movements, and the fight for animal rights. Work on bringing together food, governance, and Environmental Cultural Studies that has already begun will undoubtedly receive a boost from a gastrocratic focus.40

It is important to point out that Spain has recently begun exporting its gastrocratic models, especially since 2018, when the imminent bursting of the "restaurant bubble" became a popular topic of discussion among food writers and journalists.[41] Whether real or perceived, the crisis brought thinking about gastronomy back again into the planning of social improvement and the quest for postindustrial alternatives to late capitalist exploitation. Thus, Dani Laso, who was trained as a chef in the Mugaritz restaurant in the Basque Country, recently founded Imago, a social innovation lab offering gastronomic solutions to social conflict. At present, Imago is contributing to the United Nations' effort to combat poverty and appease political tensions in Southern Thailand. The vision, as

Laso remarked speaking at the 2021 Madrid Fusion, is derived from his thinking about how food is used in the Basque Country as a matter that unites people in the market, at the table, and in their memories. "And what if gastronomy could be a key to alternative politics?" he asked. More than anything, these words reflect the attitudes to food hitherto invisible. The time is ripe to make them apparent and begin understanding them.

NOTES

1. Michael Billig, *Banal Nationalism* (London: SAGE Publications, 1995).
2. Rebecca Ingram, "From the Mediterranean Diet to Gastronationalism: Cultural Studies and Spanish Foodways," in *Routledge Companion to Twentieth and Twenty-First Century Spain: Ideas, Practices, Imaginings*, eds. L. Elena Delgado and Eduardo Ledesma (New York: Routledge, 2025). See also the website for Gastro Marca España.
3. Fabio Parasecoli and F. Xavier Medina, "Patrimonio gastronómico y diseño: Nuevas herramientas para la puesta en valor del patrimonio gastronómico español en el exterior," NYU Fundación Rey Juan Carlos I. Fundación Ramón Areces, Madrid, June 13, 2023.
4. Henri Lefebvre, *Critique of Everyday Life: Volume I, Introduction*, trans. John Moore (New York: Verso, 1991), 97.
5. Lara Anderson and Rebecca Ingram, "Transhispanic Food Cultural Studies: Defining the Subfield," *Bulletin of Spanish Studies* 97, no. 7 (2020): 471–83; Esther Gimeno Ugalde and Santiago Pérez Isasi, "Lo "ibérico" en los Estudios Ibéricos: meta-análisis del campo a través de sus publicaciones (2000-)," in *Iberian Studies: Reflections Across Borders and Disciplines*, eds. Núria Codina Solà and Teresa Pinheiro, 23–48 (New York: Peter Lang, 2019); Robert Patrick Newcomb, "Theorizing Iberian Studies," *Hispania* 98, no. 2 (2015): 196–97.
6. Nir Avieli, *Food and Power: A Culinary Ethnography of Israel* (Berkeley: University of California Press, 2017); Lara Anderson, *Control and Resistance: Food Discourse in Franco Spain* (Toronto: University of Toronto Press, 2020); Katharina Vester, *A Taste of Power: Food and American Identities* (Berkeley: University of California Press, 2015).
7. Fernando Savater, "Empeoría: Los recortes en educación y la piratería avanzan, mientras tenemos los futbolistas más caros," *El País*, January 20, 2014.
8. Lara Anderson, *Cooking Up the Nation: Spanish Culinary Texts and Culinary Nationalization in the Late Nineteenth and Early Twentieth Century* (Rochester, NY: Tamesis, 2013).
9. See Jennifer Davis, *Defining Culinary Authority: The Transformation of Cooking in France, 1650–1830* (Baton Rouge: Louisiana State University Press, 2013); and Rachel Black, *Cheffes de Cuisine: Women and Work in the Professional French Kitchen* (Champaign: University of Illinois Press, 2021).
10. Daniel Sipe, "Social Gastronomy: Fourier and Brillat-Savarin," *French Cultural Studies* 20, no. 3, (Aug. 2009): 219–36.

11. Mabel Gracia Arnaiz, "La alimentación en el umbral del siglo XXI: una agenda para la investigación sociocultural en España," *Somos lo que comemos: estudios de alimentación y cultura en España* (Barcelona: Ariel, 2002), 17.
12. Priscilla Parkhurst Ferguson, *Word of Mouth: What We Talk About When We Talk About Food* (Berkeley: University of California Press, 2014), xvii. Parkhurst Ferguson distinguishes the activities that surround cooking and eating as "culinarity," which offers "privileged entry into the social order" (8). Culinary discourse, then, affixes the gestures of culinary practice and converts them into the narratives that generate social meaning.
13. Hannah Arendt, *The Human Condition* (Chicago: University of Chicago Press, 1958), 115.
14. Germán Labrador Méndez, "The Cannibal Wave: The Cultural Logic of Spain's Temporality of Crisis (Revolution, Biopolitics, Hunger and Memory)," *Journal of Spanish Cultural Studies* 15, nos. 1–2 (2014): 246, 248
15. Karl Polanyi, *The Great Transformation: The Political and Economic Origins of Our Time* (Boston, MA: Beacon Press, 1944), 68–77.
16. Rebecca Ingram, *Women's Work: How Culinary Cultures Shaped Modern Spain* (Nashville, TN: Vanderbilt University Press, 2022).
17. Originally published in 1877 as articles in *Ilustración española y americana*, these imaginary letters were later collected in an anonymous book *La mesa moderna, cartas sobre el comedor y la cocina, cambiadas entre el Doctor Thebussem y un cocinero de S. M.* (Madrid, 1888). Castro y Serrano acted under the alias of "un cocinero de S. M." and Pardo de Figueroa used the identity of an imaginary German scholar, "Doctor Thebussem."
18. See Eugenia Afinoguénova, "An Organic Nation: State-Run Tourism, Regionalism, and Food in Spain, 1905–1931," *The Journal of Modern History* 86, no. 4 (December 2014): 743–79; Anderson, *Cooking Up the Nation*; Ingram, *Women's Work*.
19. Eric Storm, "Hasta en la sopa: nacionalismo y regionalismo en la esfera doméstica, 1890–1936," in *Vivir la nación: Nuevos debates sobre el nacionalismo español*, ed. Xavier Andreu Miralles (Granada: Comares, 2019), 29–55.
20. Lara Anderson, "A Recipe for a Modern Nation: Miguel Primo de Rivera and Spanish Food Culture," *Revista de Estudios Hispánicos* 52, no. 1 (2018): 75–99; Anderson, *Control and Resistance*.
21. Anderson, *Control and Resistance*.
22. Eugenia Afinoguénova, "De la carta a la papeleta: el 'menú del día' entre la dictadura y la democracia en España, 1964–1981," *Bulletin of Spanish Studies* 97, no. 4 (2020): 515–38.
23. See Pedro Fatjó Gómez, Francisco Muñoz Pradas, Roser Nicolau Nos, "The Nutritional Condition of the Spanish Soldier: 'Spain. Nutrition Survey of the Armed Forces, a Report by the Interdepartmental Committee on Nutrition for National Defence 1958,'" *Int. J. Environ. Res. Public Health* 18, no. 23 (2021): 12623, especially Table 10.
24. Juan Perucho and Nestor Luján, *El libro de la cocina española: gastronomía e historia* (Barcelona: Ediciones Danae, 1972); Cándido (Mesonero Mayor de Castillo) López,

La cocina española: El libro de la gastronomía (Barcelona: Plaza and Janés, 1970); José Luis Rueda, *Guía gastronómica de España* (Barcelona: El Mueble, 1970); Gonzalo Sol, *Guía gastronómica de España* (Madrid: Sol de Liaño, 1976).
25. Labrador Méndez, "The Cannibal Wave," 245.
26. See Leigh H. Mercer and H. Rosi Song, "*Catalanidad* in the Kitchen: Tourism, Gastronomy and Identity in Modern and Contemporary Barcelona," *Bulletin of Spanish Studies* 97, no. 4 (2020): 659–80; and H. Rosi Song and Anna Riera, *A Taste of Barcelona: The History of Catalan Cooking and Eating* (Lanham, MD: Roman and Littlefield, 2019).
27. Manuel Vázquez Montalbán, *Contra los gourmets* (Barcelona: Muchnik Editor, 1990).
28. Lara Anderson, "El multiculturalismo culinario en España: De la asimilación a la diversidad," in *Fronteras y migraciones en ámbito mediterráneo*, eds. Enric Bou and Julieta Zarco (Venice: Edizioni Ca' Foscari, 2017), 29–30, citing Bou and Taberna.
29. Chenta Tsai Tseng (Putochinomaricón), *Arroz Tres Delicias: Sexo, raza y género* (Barcelona: Plan B, 2019); Quan Zhou Wu, *Gazpacho agridulce* (Bilbao: Sillón Orejero, 2021).
30. bell hooks, "Eating the Other: Desire and Resistance," *Black Looks: Race and Representation* (Boston, MA: South End Press, 1992), 21–39. See also Lisa Heldke, "'Let's Eat Chinese!': Reflections on Cultural Food Colonialism," *Gastronomica* 1, no. 2 (2001): 76–79; and *Exotic Appetites* (New York: Routledge, 2015).
31. Jeroen Dewulf, "As a Tupi-Indian, Playing the Lute: Hybridity as Anthropophagy," in *Reconstructing Hybridity: Postcolonial Studies in Transition*, eds. Joel Kuortti and Jopi Nyman (Amsterdam: Rodopi, 2007), 81.
32. Katharyne Mitchell, "Different Diasporas and the Hype of Hybridity," *Environment and Planning D: Society and Space* 15, no. 5 (Oct. 1997): 533–53.
33. Gaia Giuliani, "Gender, Race, and the Colonial Archive: Sexualized Exoticism and Gendered Racism in Contemporary Italy," *Italian Studies* 71, no. 4 (2016): 550–67.
34. Elizabeth Zanoni, "Migrant Marketplaces: Globalizing Histories of Migrant Foodways," *Global Food History* 4, no. 1 (2018): 3–21.
35. Donna R. Gabaccia, *We are What We Eat: Ethnic Food and the Making of Americans* (Cambridge, MA: Harvard University Press, 1998), 227
36. Krishnendu Ray, *The Ethnic Restaurateur* (New York: Bloomsbury, 2016).
37. Santi Santamaría, *La cocina al desnudo* (Barcelona: Ediciones Península, 2023), 152–62 et passim.
38. Ibid., 263–96.
39. Reflecting the fact that cava is not rooted in a specific geographical location, the authors of this volume do not capitalize "cava."
40. See Jorge Marí, "Cierra La Boca y Abre Los Ojos: Gastronomy, Environmental Awareness, and Contemporary Spanish Cinema," *Arizona Journal of Hispanic Cultural Studies* 23 (2019): 197–208; Glen S. Close, "Intensive Industrial Livestock Production: Envisioning the Burden on Animals and the Environment," in *A Companion to Spanish Environmental Cultural Studies*, ed. Luis I. Prádanos (Rochester, NY: Tamesis, 2023), 146–56; Matthew I. Feinberg and Susan Larson, "Madrid Río, El Matadero and the

Nature of Urbanization," *Arizona Journal of Hispanic Cultural Studies* 23 (2019): 175–90; Luis I. Prádanos, ed., *A Companion to Spanish Environmental Cultural Studies* (Rochester, NY: Tamesis, 2023); Luis I. Prádanos, *Postgrowth Imaginaries: New Ecologies and Counterhegemonic Culture in Post-2008 Spain* (Liverpool, UK: Liverpool University Press, 2019); and Sainath Suryanarayanan and Katarzyna Beilin, "Still Different? Biotechnology, Politics, and Culture in Contemporary Spain," in *Ethics of Life: Contemporary Iberian Debates*, eds. Katarzina Olga Beilin and William Viestenz (Nashville, TN: Vanderbilt University Press, 2016), 203–28.

41. See Óscar Brock, "Los peligros de la burbuja de los restaurantes," *El País*, May 12, 2018, https://elpais.com/gastronomia/el-comidista/2018/05/02/articulo/1525283552_891417.html; Laura Del Valle, "Ferrán Adriá: 'Cerré El Bulli porque alcancé mi perfección, no iba a hacer nada major,'" *La Voz de Galicia*, July 29, 2021, https://www.lavozdegalicia.es/noticia/gastronomia/2018/11/17/cerre-bulli-alcance-perfeccion-iba-mejor/0003_201811G17P30991.htm.

WORKS CITED

Afinoguénova, Eugenia. "De la carta a la papeleta: el 'menú del día' entre la dictadura y la democracia en España, 1964–1981." *Bulletin of Spanish Studies* 97, no. 4 (2020): 515–38.

———. "An Organic Nation: State-Run Tourism, Regionalism, and Food in Spain, 1905–1931." *The Journal of Modern History* 86, no. 4 (December 2014): 743–79.

Anderson, Lara. *Control and Resistance: Food Discourse in Franco Spain.* Toronto: University of Toronto Press, 2020.

———. *Cooking up the Nation: Spanish Culinary Texts and Culinary Nationalization in the Late Nineteenth and Early Twentieth Century.* Rochester, NY: Tamesis, 2013.

———. "El multiculturalismo culinario en España: De la asimilación a la diversidad." In *Fronteras y migraciones en ámbito mediterráneo*, edited by Enric Bou and Julieta Zarco, 29–42. Venice: Edizioni Ca' Foscari, 2017.

———. "A Recipe for a Modern Nation: Miguel Primo de Rivera and Spanish Food Culture." *Revista de Estudios Hispánicos* 52, no. 1 (2018): 75–99.

Anderson, Lara, and Rebecca Ingram. "Transhispanic Food Cultural Studies: Defining the Subfield." *Bulletin of Spanish Studies* 97, no. 7 (2020): 471–83.

Arendt, Hannah. *The Human Condition.* Chicago: University of Chicago Press, 1958.

Avieli, Nir. *Food and Power: A Culinary Ethnography of Israel.* Berkeley: University of California Press, 2017.

Black, Rachel. *Cheffes de Cuisine: Women and Work in the Professional French Kitchen.* Champaign: University of Illinois Press, 2021.

Brillat-Savarin, Jean Anthelme. *Physiologie du Goût ou, Méditations de Gastronomie Transcendante.* Paris: A. Sautelet, 1826.

Brock, Óscar. "Los peligros de la burbuja de los restaurantes." *El País*, May 12, 2018. https://elpais.com/gastronomia/el-comidista/2018/05/02/articulo/1525283552_891417.html.

Close, Glen S. "Intensive Industrial Livestock Production: Envisioning the Burden on Animals and the Environment." In *A Companion to Spanish Environmental Cultural Studies*, edited by Luis I. Prádanos, 146–56. Rochester, NY: Tamesis, 2023.

Davis, Jennifer. *Defining Culinary Authority: The Transformation of Cooking in France, 1650–1830*. Baton Rouge: Louisiana State University Press, 2013.

Del Valle, Laura. "Ferrán Adriá: 'Cerré El Bulli porque alcancé mi perfección, no iba a hacer nada major.'" *La Voz de Galicia*, July 29, 2021. https://www.lavozdegalicia.es/noticia/gastronomia/2018/11/17/cerre-bulli-alcance-perfeccion-iba-mejor/0003_201811G17P30991.htm.

Dewulf, Jeroen. "As a Tupi-Indian, Playing the Lute: Hybridity as Anthropophagy." In *Reconstructing Hybridity: Postcolonial Studies in Transition*, edited by Joel Kuortti and Jopi Nyman, 81–97. Amsterdam: Rodopi, 2007.

Fatjó Gómez, Pedro, Francisco Muñoz Pradas, Roser Nicolau Nos. "The Nutritional Condition of the Spanish Soldier: '*Spain. Nutrition Survey of the Armed Forces, a Report by the Interdepartmental Committee on Nutrition for National Defence 1958*.'" *Int. J. Environ. Res. Public Health* 18, no. 23 (2021): 12623.

Feinberg, Matthew I., and Susan Larson. "Madrid Río, El Matadero and the Nature of Urbanization." *Arizona Journal of Hispanic Cultural Studies* 23 (2019): 175–90.

Foucault, Michel. *The Birth of Biopolitics: Lectures at the College de France. (1978–1979)*. Edited by Michel Sennellart, translated by Graham Burchell. New York: Palgrave Macmillian, 2008.

Gabaccia, Donna R. *We are What We Eat: Ethnic Food and the Making of Americans*. Cambridge, MA: Harvard University Press, 1998.

Gimeno Ugalde, Esther, and Santiago Pérez Isasi. "Lo "ibérico" en los Estudios Ibéricos: meta-análisis del campo a través de sus publicaciones (2000-)." *Iberian Studies: Reflections Across Borders and Disciplines*, edited by Núria Codina Solà and Teresa Pinheiro, 23–48. New York: Peter Lang, 2019.

Giuliani, Gaia. "Gender, Race, and the Colonial Archive: Sexualized Exoticism and Gendered Racism in Contemporary Italy." *Italian Studies* 71, no. 4 (2016): 550–67.

Gracia Arnaiz, Mabel. "La alimentación en el umbral del siglo XXI: una agenda para la investigación sociocultural en España." *Somos lo que comemos: estudios de alimentación y cultura en España*, 15–38. Barcelona: Ariel, 2002.

Heldke, Lisa. *Exotic Appetites*. New York: Routledge, 2015.

———. "'Let's Eat Chinese!': Reflections on Cultural Food Colonialism." *Gastronomica* 1, no. 2 (2001): 76–79.

hooks, bell. "Eating the Other: Desire and Resistance." *Black Looks: Race and Representation*, 21–39. Boston, MA: South End Press, 1992.

Ingram, Rebecca. "From the Mediterranean Diet to Gastronationalism: Cultural Studies and Spanish Foodways." In *Routledge Companion to Twentieth and Twenty-First Century Spain: Ideas, Practices, Imaginings*, edited by L. Elena Delgado and Eduardo Ledesma. New York: Routledge, 2025.

———. *Women's Work: How Culinary Cultures Shaped Modern Spain*. Nashville, TN: Vanderbilt University Press, 2022.

Labrador Méndez, Germán. "The Cannibal Wave: The Cultural Logic of Spain's Temporality of Crisis (Revolution, Biopolitics, Hunger and Memory)." *Journal of Spanish Cultural Studies* 15, nos. 1–2 (2014): 241–71.
Lefebvre, Henri. *Critique of Everyday Life: Volume I, Introduction*. Translated by John Moore. New York: Verso, 1991.
Lopez, Cándido (Mesonero Mayor de Castillo). *La cocina española: El libro de la gastronomía*. Barcelona: Plaza and Janés, 1970.
Marí, Jorge. "Cierra La Boca y Abre Los Ojos: Gastronomy, Environmental Awareness, and Contemporary Spanish Cinema." *Arizona Journal of Hispanic Cultural Studies* 23 (2019): 197–208.
Mercer, Leigh H., and H. Rosi Song. "*Catalanidad* in the Kitchen: Tourism, Gastronomy and Identity in Modern and Contemporary Barcelona." *Bulletin of Spanish Studies* 97, no. 4 (2020): 659–80.
Mitchell, Katharyne. "Different Diasporas and the Hype of Hybridity." *Environment and Planning D: Society and Space* 15, no. 5 (Oct. 1997): 533–53.
Newcomb, Robert Patrick. "Theorizing Iberian Studies." *Hispania* 98, no. 2 (2015): 196–97.
Parasecoli, Fabio, and F. Xavier Medina. "Patrimonio gastronómico y diseño: Nuevas herramientas para la puesta en valor del patrimonio gastronómico español en el exterior." NYU Fundación Rey Juan Carlos I. Fundación Ramón Areces, Madrid, June 13, 2023.
Pardo de Figueroa, Mariano, and José de Castro y Serrano. *La mesa moderna, cartas sobre el comedor y la cocina, cambiadas entre el Doctor Thebussem y un cocinero de S. M.* Madrid: Librerías de Fernando Fé, 1888.
Parkhurst Ferguson, Priscilla. *Word of Mouth: What We Talk About When We Talk About Food*. Berkeley: University of California Press, 2014.
Perucho, Juan, and Nestor Luján. *El libro de la cocina española: gastronomía e historia*. Barcelona: Ediciones Danae, 1972.
Polanyi, Karl. *The Great Transformation: The Political and Economic Origins of Our Time*. Boston, MA: Beacon Press, 1944.
Prádanos, Luis I., ed. *A Companion to Spanish Environmental Cultural Studies*. Rochester, NY: Tamesis, 2023.
———. *Postgrowth Imaginaries: New Ecologies and Counterhegemonic Culture in Post-2008 Spain*. Liverpool, UK: Liverpool University Press, 2019.
Ray, Krishnendu. *The Ethnic Restaurateur*. New York: Bloomsbury, 2016.
Rueda, José Luis. *Guía gastronómica de España*. Barcelona: El Mueble, 1970.
Santamaría, Santi. *La cocina al desnudo*. Barcelona: Ediciones Península, 2023.
Savater, Fernando. "Empeoría: Los recortes en educación y la piratería avanzan, mientras tenemos los futbolistas más caros." *El País*, January 20, 2014.
Sipe, Daniel. "Social Gastronomy: Fourier and Brillat-Savarin." *French Cultural Studies* 20, no. 3 (Aug. 2009): 219–36.
Sol, Gonzalo. *Guía gastronómica de España*. Madrid: Sol de Liaño, 1976.
Song, H. Rosi, and Anna Riera. *A Taste of Barcelona: The History of Catalan Cooking and Eating*. Lanham, MD: Roman and Littlefield, 2019.

Storm, Eric (H. J.). "Hasta en la sopa: nacionalismo y regionalismo en la esfera doméstica, 1890–1936." In *Vivir la nación: Nuevos debates sobre el nacionalismo español*, edited by Xavier Andreu Miralles, 29–55. Granada: Comares, 2019.

Suryanarayanan, Sainath, and Katarzyna Beilin, "Still Different? Biotechnology, Politics, and Culture in Contemporary Spain." In *Ethics of Life: Contemporary Iberian Debates*, edited by Katarzina Olga Beilin and William Viestenz, 203–28. Nashville, TN: Vanderbilt University Press, 2016.

Tsai Tseng, Chenta (Putochinomaricón). *Arroz Tres Delicias: Sexo, raza y género*. Barcelona: Plan B, 2019.

[United States] Interdepartmental Committee on Nutrition for National Defense. Nutrition Survey of the Armed Forces. Spain. November 1958.

Vázquez Montalbán, Manuel. *Contra los gourmets*. Barcelona: Muchnik Editor, 1990.

Vester, Katharina. *A Taste of Power: Food and American Identities*. Berkeley: University of California Press, 2015.

Zanoni, Elizabeth. "Migrant Marketplaces: Globalizing Histories of Migrant Foodways." *Global Food History* 4, no. 1 (2018): 3–21.

Zhou Wu, Quan. *Gazpacho agridulce*. Bilbao: Sillón Orejero, 2021.

Part I: Gastropolitics

◆ CHAPTER 1

Public Control over Private Trade
Barcelona's Market Hall Food Retailing System

Montserrat Miller

After serving as the backbone of urban life for thousands of years, many open-air food markets underwent a process of transformation in the nineteenth century. In responding to the challenges associated with industrialization, governing authorities in most European cities built large scale public market halls to contain and control private retail food vendors and to clear streets of the congestion and disorder they caused. Offering greater year-round stability in food supply and upping the ante in terms of sanitation standards, many of the new halls that enclosed market trade were veritable monuments to modernity in their day.[1] (Guàrdia and Oyón 11). Though market halls were generally eclipsed by other forms of food retailing in the mid-twentieth century, some Mediterranean cities such as Barcelona followed a different trajectory. On the eve of the 1992 Summer Olympic Games, the Catalan capital was still served by forty-one retail food market halls, each municipally owned and managed, open to the public six days a week. With one for every 44,000 inhabitants, late twentieth-century Barcelona had more such structures per capita than any other city in Europe.[2] To understand why, this chapter first examines the historical significance of public control over private trade in Barcelona's food markets through the medieval, early modern, and modern centuries.[3] It then illustrates the importance of markets to maintaining urban social order, traces the process through which Barcelona's markets underwent modernization, and explores long-term social and cultural patterns related to widespread female participation in market-based trade.

Premodern Background

The success of urban polities has long been predicated upon the existence of significant levels of agricultural surplus and the operation of an effective system for reallocating those supplies from points of production to concentrated sites of consumption. In towns and cities the world over, open-air, market-based trade in locally produced agricultural commodities has historically operated to permit urban residents who did not grow food—or enough food—to access the alimentary supplies upon which life depended. Yet, not even the oldest such urban food systems functioned on the basis of the pure and unfettered laws of supply and demand. Rather, food markets invariably involved forms of control—state, temple, etc.—over trade in staple crops and other vital commodities.[4] While arrangements and degrees of complexity varied over time and place, some form of regulatory power over private food trade remains one of the oldest and most enduring elements of urban life. In many parts of the world, including the west, women played a vital role in these urban food systems, working in large numbers as market vendors and constituting the majority of market clientele.

After centuries of decline and disruption following the collapse of Rome, the economic dynamism underpinning Western Europe's eleventh-century urban revival was principally driven by dramatic increases in local agricultural output.[5] Surging food production beginning in the tenth century stimulated local market exchange and drew producers to nascent urban centers where growing numbers of people converged. As new food markets took shape, villages grew into towns. Where towns expanded, growth drove the extension of defensive walls to encircle and annex peripheral areas where thriving food markets and other forms of commerce had become established.

Through the twelfth and thirteenth centuries, open-air market trade in Western Europe intensified to meet the alimentary needs of growing urban centers. Yet, here too the laws of supply and demand operated within political, cultural, and other institutional constraints. Though some trade was spontaneous and unregulated, virtually all markets were controlled by ecclesiastic, seignorial, or royal authorities. In some European cities such as Barcelona, these gradually ceded power over the course of the Middle Ages to emerging municipal governments, which set and enforced details of market operation such as hours, stall rentals, prices, and mark-up rates. Municipal authorities pursued multiple aims through such efforts. As arbiters of community standards of fairness, they sought to bolster popular support and to dampen urban unrest. But pecuniary interests also served as an impetus for public control over private trade; the revenues generated by food markets fattened municipal coffers, underwriting other projects and concerns. In England and parts of France, seigneurial control over market trade eroded more slowly, with nobles holding such privileges hard-pressed to forgo the potential income they could represent.

Feeding the Medieval City

Barcelona resembled any number of other Western European walled enclaves during the Middle Ages in terms of its open-air food markets. The classical Mediterranean city's medieval revival had involved an influx of people from the countryside seeking, among other pursuits, to trade in surplus agricultural goods. In the tenth century, demographic pressure led to the formation of a new seaside settlement just outside the northern wall marking what had been the old Roman urb. Known as the Ribera, this area included a vibrant open-air food market called the Born, which operated alongside churches, workshops, and other vital commercial and manufacturing concerns. The agglomeration of people, both inside Barcelona's defensive walls and just beyond them in the Ribera, had grown by the eleventh century to some fifteen thousand souls.[6]

A second, less densely populated extra-mural settlement, known as the Raval, took shape in the 1200s outside the southern end of the city's walls. It included a thriving open-air market along what eventually became known as the Ramblas, as peasant women congregated near the Pla de la Boqueria to sell produce and other food. Butchers' stalls, authorized by royal patent in the early thirteenth century, and the concentration of additional vendor groups nearby, eventually led to the Boqueria's rise as rival to the Born market in the Ribera.[7] Continued growth in these two areas led to their annexation when defensive walls were extended to surround them. By the fifteenth century, the newest set of fortifications encircled some twenty-five thousand people in what is known today as Barcelona's Ciutat Vella, its pre-modern core.

In addition to shaping the city's physical form, the complexities involved in managing food supply through market trade were driving forces in the formation of Barcelona's municipal system of government. The twelfth-century royal authority to charge indirect taxes on grain entering the city, to license bread ovens, and to issue permits for certain types of market stalls was gradually ceded in the thirteenth century to the urban oligarchy. The 1249 and 1265 royal decrees establishing Barcelona's Consell de Cent—a town council comprised of one hundred representatives—asserted the new body's control over people and supplies moving through the city's gates and extended its powers to regulate open-air market trade.[8] The Consell thereafter sought to rationalize meat and wheat sales, as well as the production of flour. A century later, it increased indirect taxation on cereals and other foodstuff, creating the office of *Mostassaf* to govern food market trade more directly.[9] A key development was the 1329 *vi vel gratis* concession by Alfons III, which gave the Consell the right to seize grain transports moving though the city or on ships in transit through its jurisdictional waters.[10]

This was a period of great vibrancy for Barcelona and the larger political structures to which its fortunes were tied. A series of successful conquests and dynastic unions had transformed the Catalan-Aragonese confederation—political germ of the Crown of Aragon—into a composite monarchy and a major Mediterranean power. Its late medieval holdings came to include Roussillon, the Kingdoms of Valencia, Mallorca, and Naples, plus Sardinia and Sicily—and for about sixty years, the Duchy of Athens.[11] Even after Barcelona lost its privileged place as administrative capital of the Crown of Aragon in the early fifteenth century, it remained cosmopolitan in its orientation and economically powerful within the western Mediterranean urban system. One definitive advantage in terms of provisioning was Barcelona's access to overseas grain supplies from Sicilian, Sardinian, and southern French ports.[12] While grain trade had largely been handled by private merchants until the late fourteenth century, Barcelona's Consell became increasingly active thereafter, concentrating more efforts on acquiring strategic supplies and supervising their sale as part of the city's broader fifteenth-century efforts to extend further control over its food system.[13]

Maintaining alimentary supplies and regulating commerce in food as a fiscal strategy were vital governing concerns.[14] Yet the system of public control over private trade periodically broke down, as occurred from 1349 to 1410, when plague and provisioning crises caused demographic contraction and generated significant unrest; or in the early 1600s, when a mob of some 4,000 bread rioters wreaked havoc on various parts of the city, including the Ribera residence of a high-ranking municipal provisioning official.[15] Such episodes drove further steps in the extension of municipal control. One measure adopted in 1752 extended the city's reach over the disposition of agricultural surplus to a distance of seven leagues into the Catalan hinterland; all victuals produced there were barred from export. Special exceptions for commodities destined for the Americas notwithstanding, oil, wine, vinegar, fruits, vegetables, fish, pork, and poultry could only be exported beyond the city's hinterland when supplies exceeded demand.[16] These new rules further limiting private trade in a manner that favored urban consumers over rural producers serve as evidence of the growing control that Barcelona's municipal authorities exerted within the provisioning sector.

While public control over private food retailing tightened in response to crises and upheavals, corollary marketplace activities associated with the performance of gender roles proved more elusive to regulation. Barcelona's markets remained key sites for social and cultural exchange by serving as meeting places for women engaged in the work of provisioning their households. Indeed, market-based trade itself exhibited a tangible feminine character.[17] Though family economic arrangements were commonplace in marketplace business enterprises, women often worked the retail end of such operations alone, a practice that afforded them a modicum of independence within what was otherwise a male-dominated political economy. We can see this in various market ordinances, which suggest that a range of stall types—especially those selling fruits, vegetables, poultry, and fish—were all but monopolized by women.[18]

In writing about the northern Iberian peninsula, James Casey has observed that there was a real distance between the gender ideology of the period, which recommended household isolation for even the unmarried daughters of peasants, and the lived experience of the many women populating the "chronicles of Spanish cities of the Golden Age as market vendors and bakers and servants in inns—a wide variety of trades where they were constantly in touch with the public."[19] Casey also cites Pedro de Medina, who travelled from his native Andalusia toward the north in 1548. Medina observed that women were tougher in the north in the sense that they could be frequently observed going to market to sell their wares, a pattern less common in the south.

As in other cities of northern Spain, high rates of female participation in market trade, whether independent or embedded within family economy systems, persisted as a long-term continuity in Barcelona. Likewise, women's widespread participation in markets, both as vendors and as consumers, was common in other parts of Western Europe, including France. In this regard, as well as in the pre-modern physical and regulatory evolution of its food markets, Barcelona's history of public control over private trade was not significantly exceptional.

Early-Modern Challenges

The eighteenth century deserves particular attention in the history of Barcelona's public control over private trade in food. As elsewhere, in the prelude to industrialization, the motor of economic expansion was in the agricultural sector, where increasing exports of cash crops generated capital for investment in textile production. Though its full industrial revolution was still a century down the road, Barcelona was physically and socially transformed by these developments. Crowding within the walled confines of the city intensified as short-distance migration caused population to swell from some 58,000 in 1717 to 100,000 in 1787.[20] With no buildable space remaining inside the new Bourbon fortifications, Barcelona expanded vertically.[21] Most construction in the final quarter of the eighteenth century consisted of adding new floors to old buildings and chopping up existing floors to add new rooms.[22] Intensifying demographic pressure caused open air markets to explode in size and number, increasing cacophony, and impeding foot and carriage traffic alike. Public management of the city's markets became an even more urgent challenge. Significant parts of the city had become lined with market stalls, extending along narrow streets emanating from the Born, the Boqueria, and six other key points.[23]

Overcrowding in the eighteenth century magnified the importance of the city's food markets, which had come to rival churches and public squares as the most-frequented sites for women's popular social exchange. In addition to the large number of women who worked selling food, women also made up the bulk of market customers shopping daily in these venues as part of their domestic chores. Yet women frequented these public spaces for more than just provisions. "Anar al la plaça" (going to market) was a form of entertainment. The commercial exchanges that took place there could involve news and gossip, mutual aid, and even social capital.[24] Markets were venues where status could be displayed and affirmed, but also spaces where women sought help from one another, disseminated survival strategies, and found employment as clerks. They were sites wherein that which was understood to constitute fairness could be asserted and where women's collective concerns could be aired.

Municipal policies with respect to markets remained focused on the generation of income and fiscal dependence, which, in turn, lent additional urgency to issues of market control. The city sought through regulation to underpin popular concerns about fairness by guaranteeing equal public access to all that was for sale in the markets, setting reasonable mark-up rates, imposing more rigorous and systematic inspections of weights and measures, and policing a growing range of other details relating to the mechanics of food trade. These municipal controls were meant to uphold what the popular classes in Barcelona understood to be the "*el bé comú*" (the common good).[25] On occasions when the collective sense of fairness was breached, tumult, billingsgatry, or worse could result. Restoring order depended upon the ability of municipal authorities to make both real and symbolic concessions to the aggrieved. Indeed, the eighteenth century's most intense bout of food rioting in Barcelona, the 1789 *Rebomboris del Pa*, illustrates this process. While the episode shook urban elites, it also re-affirmed popular expectations about the obligation of governing authorities to regulate food access and to act as final arbiters of the common good.[26]

Part of a series of popular upheavals that took place in Spain and elsewhere in Western Europe in connection with rising cereal prices, Barcelona's 1789 food riots were sparked by price increases in the cost of all bread and by shortages in the darkest and cheapest form consumed by the popular classes.[27] The uprising began among women in the markets of the city on a crowded Saturday morning, February 28.[28] The popular ire spread quickly as men were alerted to the perceived injustice and joined the cause. Soon a mob of some eight thousand converged on the municipal bread ovens and attacked the residences of the city's main grain contractor and other municipal officials.[29] Violent clashes with troops and a series of arrests succeeded in quieting the uprising just before midnight.

The next morning, Sunday, March 1, rioting resumed, involving even larger numbers of people clashing with authorities. Mounted troops wielding sabers fought irate men and women armed with stones. One group of rioters broke through the doors of the cathedral and, after hurling a series of insults at the Bishop, took control of the campanile, sounding the bells to alert others to join in. This further stoked the fires of protest. What had begun on the day before as isolated disputes over the price and availability of bread in the open-air marketplaces morphed into an unwieldy conflagration that spread from Barcelona to other Catalan cities, including Vic, Sabadell, and Mataró.[30]

The scale of the 1789 uprising was unprecedented. Yet the rioters' demands were limited and specific. They sought a return to the previous years' bread prices and the release of all who had been arrested in the course of the outbreak. Eager to re-assert their commitment to the common good, municipal authorities quickly made concessions by lowering the prices market vendors and shopkeepers could charge for bread, meat, oil, and wine, and intervening to increase the city's supply of grain.[31] The announcement of such measures on Sunday afternoon effectively ended the riot and sales resumed in the markets by noon the next day. There were no mass arrests, though several dozen people were detained, and four men and one woman went to the gallows for their part in the upheaval.[32] Taking a conciliatory attitude, Barcelona's elites generally denounced the repression and intensified their contribution to charity efforts designed to forestall a repetition of the episode. Unlike what resulted from the bread rioting that set off the French Revolution six months later, in this instance, the pre-riot social order survived the popular uprising.

Spurred by the stressors of economic transformation and urban overcrowding, Barcelona's 1789 food riots were also a consequence of administrative changes resulting from the imposition of Bourbon rule.[33] In forcibly annexing the Principality of Catalonia to Spain in 1714, Philip V (1700–1724) had suspended a set of 500-year-old charters and self-governing institutions. The bans included Barcelona's ruling Consell de Cent, which had grown into a body comprised of representatives from the nobility, the military, honored citizens, merchants, shopkeepers, artisans, and artists. The new Bourbon political system shut out all these constituencies save the nobility. The Consell was replaced with what came to be known as the Ajuntament, which ruled the city through a military Corregidor and twenty-four aldermen appointed directly by the king. The introduction of new more extensive market regulations in 1752 reflect Barcelona's intensifying food supply challenges. This, in turn, encouraged Bourbon authorities in Madrid to reform the city's governing structures.[34] In 1766, they created a bicameral system to govern the city through the addition of a body comprised of guild representatives charged with helping to oversee markets and provisioning. Only a year later, Spain's "enlightened" despot Carlos III (1766–1788) abruptly declared freedom of commerce for bakers and bread makers, forcing Barcelona's authorities to give up their controls over the production and sale of the most vital of all foods.[35] These changes undercut popular trust in the commitment of authorities to the common good, fueling the ire that was expressed in the 1789 uprising and demonstrating the explosive impact that could result from disputes among buyers and sellers of food in the markets of the city.

After the 1789 *Rebomboris* had been put down, Barcelona's ruling Ajuntament took a series of emergency measures to further extend public control over private trade in food. During the first week of March, it appointed a charity board of nobles and others who could help maintain order by subsidizing the purchase of grain to bolster the city's supply. It also organized guild members to patrol the streets after nightfall.[36] The wholesale wheat market was closed from March 4 to June 15 while strategic grain reserves were restocked. Any parties storing wheat in the city had to register with the municipal government. Bakers were subjected to new levels of suspicion for having abundant bread to sell to the moneyed, yet little for sale to the poor.[37] The pre-riot mixed economy in grain was gradually restored until the 1793 outbreak of war with France and subsequent bread crises at the end of the century brought the municipality back into de facto, if not de jure, control.[38] At various intervals during the French Revolutionary Wars and Napoleonic invasion of Spain, Barcelona's municipal authorities took charge of baking and distributing bread made from a mixture of wheat combined with ground maize, fava bean flour, and barley. Only the infirm, by medical prescription, could legally acquire white bread.[39] Here we see why the liberalization of commercial activities in Spain that ultimately took place in 1834 allowed free trade in food, drink, and fuel—*with the exception of bread*, the single commodity deemed too central to the diet and too closely linked to the maintenance of urban social order to relegate to the unfettered laws of supply and demand.

The demographic pressures of the eighteenth-century had combined with wheat shortages and erratic shifts in bread pricing policies to produce the 1789 crisis and upheaval. An additional stressor was the spread of consumerist value systems, whose origins were decisively pre-industrial. Consumerism dramatically spread acquisitiveness beyond elite groups and bound personal identity much more intimately to that which one could purchase.[40] As elsewhere in Western Europe, eighteenth-century consumerism in Barcelona involved skyrocketing demand among the popular classes for colorful clothing, costume jewelry, and other household goods, as well as the eager embrace of sugar-sweetened foods, chocolate, coffee, and tobacco. The boom in demand for confectionary goods, chocolate, and coffee reshaped urban street culture while also supercharging demand for bread.[41] These developments had heightened consumers' sense of social injustice as they were reflected in the inequalities associated with access to the most basic foods in the markets of the city.

Nineteenth-Century Modernization

Long-standing concerns over food supply and popular perceptions of fairness thereto laid the groundwork for the modernization of the city's nineteenth-century markets. Full industrialization and dramatic urban densification had paired to further transform Barcelona by the 1830s. Social tensions mounted as the rapidly burgeoning working class struggled in the face of long hours, low wages, poor housing, and unhygienic conditions. Virulent political debates over the merits of Liberalism, and the extent and nature of control to be exercised by the central government in Madrid, contributed to a period of tremendous political instability through the entirety of Isabel II's reign (1833–1868) and the failed revolution that followed it, known as the Sexenio Democratico (1868–1874). This forty-year period marked the beginning of a new era of public control over private trade in food in Barcelona. From the reign of Isabel II forward, Barcelona's governing authorities—irrespective of ideological orientation—embraced a program, adopted and adapted from Britain and France, of consolidating control over open-air market trade by moving stalls into a set of enclosed spaces and structures. The first of these market modernization projects involved re-appropriating church properties destroyed in a round of anticlerical mob violence that had broken out in Barcelona during the summer of 1835.

The fact that popular upheaval became more frequent and more intense as industrialization unfolded led Friedrich Engels to assert that Barcelona had "seen more barricade fighting than any other city in the world."[42] A constellation of issues associated with the plight of labor underpinned discontent. Urban overcrowding dwarfed earlier levels, with population density inside the walled city in the mid-nineteenth century reaching ten times that of London and more than twice that of Paris and Madrid.[43] Anticlerical resentment was also significant, inasmuch as the church remained in control of extensive urban terrain that could have been used for housing in the horribly crowded city. Furthering popular resentment, the most conservative Catholics formed what was known as the Carlist movement, an armed insurrection opposed to Isabeline rule. The Carlists' aim was to force a return to absolutist rule in Spain. Two key issues brought groups with disparate interests together to contest the power of Barcelona's governing authorities in this period. One was opposition to centralized control of municipal government from Madrid. The other was the Spanish state's imposition of *consumo* taxes on food, which exacerbated the chronic problem of hunger for a significant swath of the urban population. These, combined with a heat wave in Catalonia during the summer of 1835, set off an explosive uprising.

The crisis began on July 25 in the bullring when the audience became outraged over a matador's poor performance. By the time the riot ended two days later, anticlerical and Luddite-inspired violence had resulted in the incineration of seven major convents and monasteries, along with the state-of-the-art Bonaplata steam-powered textile factory. Barcelona's military governor, General Pere Nolasc de Bassa, after being shot, defenestrated, and dragged through the streets of the city, had been immolated on a heap of files from the commissariat of police.[44] Such violence, dwarfing the 1789 bread riots, presaged new levels of unrest that, while driven by a range of issues, were triggered by food taxes, price hikes, and shortages in the markets of the city.

The food-related uprisings of the nineteenth century in Barcelona continued to generate municipal responses involving both repression and concession. Following the 1835 violence, official concern for the problem of hunger among the urban masses began to find expression in forms of municipal pageantry that cast new public market hall construction as a bellwether of progress and commitment to common good. Market halls, serving as physical enclosures that segregated food trade from street life, became symbols of progress and municipal commitment to public well-being. Groundbreaking and inauguration ceremonies for such projects brought political, religious, and military authorities together to trumpet their commitment to modernizing the city's food system. The scripts followed at these public events illustrate how authorities sought to harness the new market halls as symbolic capital in their quest for popular legitimacy in what was fast becoming one of Europe's most revolutionary cities.

We see this strategy employed when the city moved to purchase church properties destroyed in the 1835 uprising. The sixteenth-century Sant Josep Convent, located near the sprawling Boqueria open-air market, was one of these. Repurposed to serve as a new, semi-enclosed market for those vendors, the anticlerical nature of the violence that had opened up the space ascribed great urgency to groundbreaking ceremonies for the project. The events began with a procession from town hall designed to legitimize the public appropriation of church property for secular use and to exalt the benefits to the popular classes that would accrue from liberal commitments to modernizing the city's food supply system.[45] Among the symbolic gestures, authorities buried a cache of coins, including Mexican gold pesetas, meant to link the new semi-enclosed market to Spain's imperial past and to forecast the future riches that it would generate for the city.[46]

The symbolic power of market modernization is also observable in the second, larger and fully enclosed construction project designed to rehouse vendors in the Ribera neighborhood on the ground where the Santa Caterina Convent had gone up in flames in the 1835 uprising. Here, once more, market ceremonies took place in the wake of yet another round of popular upheaval. Revolutionary violence in the early 1840s was again triggered by the rising price of food and by worker distress in response to mechanization, low wages, and urban crowding. *La Jamáncia*, one particular phase of this upheaval, began in the summer of 1843. It was known as such for the enthusiasm with which the hungry swelled the ranks of the popular militia as a desperate act to gain access to food rations.[47] The revolutionaries' numbers were such that by September 2, they seized control of the streets, causing Barcelona's ruling Ajuntament to flee in retreat to the nearby village of Gràcia. Though the military rained bombs down from its nearby fortress on Montjuïc, the revolutionary mob held on for eighty-one days before fresh troops arrived from Madrid to re-subjugate the city.[48]

Less than a year later, authorities organized ceremonies to lay the foundation stone at the site of the former Santa Caterina Convent where a new, modern market hall, named in honor of Spanish Queen Isabel II, was to be constructed. Set for October 10, 1844, to coincide with the young queen's fourteenth birthday, the rituals were attended by the highest-ranking political, religious, and military authorities, as well as all the foreign consuls to the city. The ceremony ended with the customary shouting of *Vivas!* to Her Majesty, the Spanish constitution, and the queen mother, who had been a specific target of strident revolutionary rhetoric. The occasion may well have been the only time that a royal birthday celebration was held at the site of a convent that had been burned to a crisp in a fit of popular anticlerical rage. Rather than commemorating the victims, what was venerated instead was the promise of a modernized food system in which new retail market halls structures would serve as centerpieces. Food market modernization was directly harnessed to build popular support for the young Queen and her moderate Liberal regime. At inaugural ceremonies held for Santa Caterina's actual opening four years later, Barcelona's Mayor Domènec Portefaitx emphasized the benefits that the market represented for the popular classes of the city, adding that "the public should not lose sight of either the aesthetic or the practical concerns that had been embodied in its construction."[49] Similar ritualization accompanied food market modernization projects in Barcelona through the course of the nineteenth century.

The Public Market Hall System

Purposefully built market halls were not new to the industrial era per se. Many European towns and cities in the Middle Ages had built specialized structures for wholesale trade in grain, cloth, glass, and other goods. Barcelona itself had the Llotja de Mar trading house where cereals and a range of other commodities had been wholesaled since the fourteenth century. It was not the concept of the market hall but rather the idea of building such structures for food retailing on a scale capable of meeting industrial demand that represented an administrative, infrastructural, and commercial innovation.[50]

Barcelona's first two market modernization projects, La Boqueria and Santa Caterina, set the stage for a plethora of others. The key turning point was the mid-nineteenth-century demolition of the Bourbon fortifications encircling the city's pre-modern core and the construction of the vast *Eixample* residential district that fanned out dramatically into the hinterland. The vanguard in European food market halls in the second half of the nineteenth century involved monumental iron-framed structures reminiscent of train stations and world's fair pavilions.[51] It was to this architectural paradigm that Barcelona's municipal authorities turned in the next phase of its market modernization program. Under both the Liberal and Conservative governments alternating in power during Spain's Bourbon Restoration in the last quarter of the nineteenth century, Barcelona's Ajuntaments built a series of large-scale metal market halls to serve its burgeoning and restive urban population.[52]

The boom in metal market hall construction began near the outer edges of the Ciutat Vella with construction of El Born, which opened to 1876. Sant Antoni market was inaugurated two years later.[53] La Barceloneta followed in 1884. Thereafter,

Hostafrancs and La Concepció market halls were completed in time for the city's 1888 Exposición Universal, which showcased Catalan modernity through its industrial and monumental artistic achievements. These five, grand iron-framed structures, along with their older Boqueria and Santa Caterina counterparts, vested the city with the beginnings of a modern, Parisian-styled polynuclear public market hall system. It was not just the structural and aesthetic bases of these new markets that riffed on Victor Baltard's innovative design for Les Halles, but also the locational strategy followed in Paris that Barcelona's municipal government sought to adopt and adapt. Rather than building markets along a centrally located main street and drawing consumers in to shop from surrounding residential areas—a locational strategy more common to British towns and cities—the Parisian system involved situating new market halls across the urban landscape where they could serve specific neighborhood clienteles. This polynuclear market hall system first devised in Paris and imitated in Barcelona, was designed to provide all urban districts, rich and poor alike, with the basic infrastructure of food retailing proximity. It was a goal embraced by successive nineteenth- and twentieth-century municipal regimes in Barcelona, irrespective of their ideological orientation.

Social and Cultural Patterns

Municipal investment in market halls was tied to the politics of public health and food safety and reflected the growing power of the state. One aim of the design of such structures had been to improve the hygiene of food retailing by shielding stalls from the mud and filth of nineteenth-century streetscapes. Market hall roof and window designs facilitated the circulation of fresh air and permitted natural light to illuminate cavernous indoor spaces; vendor access to potable water was key to new sanitary standards. Conceived as vital components of the urban infrastructure, the new markets were integrated with the expansion of sewage systems, gas lighting, and electrification, forming part of the larger system of municipal public services.

The concentration of vendors in these vast spaces facilitated multiple forms of inspection and policing, subjecting female vendors (as in Paris and elsewhere) to new levels of social control.[54] Because women dominated numerically as the legal holders of market stall titles in this period, the daily practice of selling food to what was mainly a female clientele created bonds of friendship and dependency that often linked one generation to the next.[55] What was to be cooked in home kitchens and served at family meals were among the issues discussed and negotiated daily among women in the markets. The ability of female vendors to dispense culinary advice was a key commercial advantage. The dexterity through which vendors built and maintained the loyalty of their clientele determined the success or failure of their businesses, along with the well-being of their families who depended on the income they generated through market sales. The enclosure of markets in the new structures of the nineteenth century and the concentration of women working therein only intensified the gendered subculture that had developed in this sector of the economy. In the transition from open air to enclosed space, public food markets remained crucial social venues.

Any temptation to view Barcelona's market hall system of provisioning through rose colored glasses should be tempered. The nineteenth century modernization of Barcelona's markets was, as in Paris, designed to achieve various ends. Among them was dampening the embers of popular unrest so easily sparked by food shortages and price hikes. The economic and political advantages of public ownership and management, as well as the utility of using such institutions for purposes of extending efforts related to social control, contributed to their survival over the long run.[56]

Management was tied to policing, and the nineteenth-century market halls bore some similarities to modern prisons.[57] Versions of the panopticon were included in numerous metal market hall designs. These located municipal offices at the physical epicenter so that surveillance of transactions could be maximized.[58] Public health concerns drove some of the need to exercise control over food sales. The long history of uprisings incentivized the deployment of uniformed guards and inspectors who roamed the markets' aisles and departments, watching, listening, confronting, reporting, and citing infractions of municipal market codes. For all the merriment and the intensely personal sociability that could characterize market hall trade, there was certainly a darker side to the system, wherein fear and intimidation were lorded over vendors and customers alike by their municipal masters.[59] This observation raises the question of why market vendors merited such surveillance and regulation. Other incentives notwithstanding, one part of the answer has to do with gender, the female body, and how social exchanges among women remained elusive to the state's imperative for control. In writing about the nineteenth-century market halls of Paris, historian Victoria Thompson emphasizes the extent to which female vendors were suspected of sexual improprieties, including prostitution.[60] Market women everywhere, by virtue of their independent commercial activities in the public sphere, defied nineteenth-century, Western gender ideologies emphasizing domesticity and submission. And their resistance to dominant gender norms invited increasing prurience. As the city and the market hall system continued to expand over time, the female body assumed a more visible place in both public symbolism and popular iconography.

Twentieth-Century Continuity and Change

By the turn of the century, Barcelona's food supply challenges had become less related to density than they were to scale. Having demolished the walls and built up the *Eixample*, municipal authorities set their gaze beyond. Between 1897 and 1921, they pursued a deliberate program of metropolitanism that involved annexing a series of surrounding industrial towns. In so doing, the Ajuntament assumed ownership of four pre-existing market halls; and with the addition of five more structures, built or acquired by virtue of further annexation, Barcelona's system had expanded to include sixteen retail food market halls by 1930.[61] Within these, a total of more than 7,000 individual stall enterprises operated to feed a population that, by dint of migration and annexation, had surpassed the one million mark.[62]

Of course, public control over private trade in Barcelona was not limited to the market halls. Retail shops and stores selling food were also regulated through municipal licensing, which permitted the opening of new establishments only in areas underserved by the existing market system. Shop licensing thus shielded market vendors to some degree from competition. Still, a great many market stalls and shops operated in symbiotic relationship to one another.[63] Successful shopkeepers sometimes acquired market stall titles for daughters coming of age to operate on their own or with other family members.[64] Likewise, the owners of highly profitable stall enterprises established some of the city's most prosperous shop chains, using both horizontal and vertical integration to meet the demand of consumers in the burgeoning twentieth-century metropolis.[65]

Food market modernization efforts continued in the early decades of the twentieth century. Vendors combined age-old commercial practices with efforts to capitalize on new consumerist trends. This is evidenced through a range of strategies, including an embrace of novelty and stall infrastructure updates.[66] Market vendors, like shopkeepers, pushed new products, dispensed nutritional advice, and contributed to the embrace of dietary shifts resulting from industrial farming, mechanical refrigeration, pre-packaging, processing, and branding. Such changes were also driven by municipal market administrators, who offered short-term stall permits to food processing firms for the purposes of distributing samples of branded products, including condensed milk, bouillon cubes, and flan powders.[67] Regular long-term vendors, especially those holding grocer's licenses, updated their product lines in response.[68] The use of telephones to place orders, home deliveries, and newspaper advertisement for market stall firms were all common by the 1930s. Barcelona's modern market halls, like those of other major European cities, must therefore be understood as large-scale consumerist institutions related in design and function to department stores. In advance of the emergence of supermarkets, they were commercial spaces, fully adapted to modernity, where pleasure and necessity could felicitously be joined to define consumer experiences.

Municipal investment in Barcelona's market hall food-retailing infrastructure in the early twentieth century continued to be tied to the politics of public health, food safety, and emerging science of nutrition, which emphasized the need for male industrial workers to consume greater levels of protein in their diets.[69] Butchers were closely policed for the use of banned preservatives or anything other than clean, white paper for packaging, while new hygiene standards mandated fish stalls be constructed of tile and brick rather than wood.[70] Concern that working-class diets were alarmingly low in protein led to calls for higher levels of egg and dairy consumption. The extension of municipal control over meat slaughtering and the creation of more direct and efficient systems for supplying butcher's stalls became key policy thrusts.[71] Under the Primo de Rivera Dictatorship (1923–1930) meat slaughtering was monopolized and centralized by the Ajuntament and all private concerns in that sector forcibly shut down.

Female market vendors in the first decades of the twentieth century benefitted from expanded legal rights to their commercial operations but were also targets of consternation about the general erosion of more rigidly defined gender roles. The Ajuntament issued a new uniform regulatory code for the food markets in 1898 that recognized women's right to enter into contracts without the permission of husbands and fathers.[72] As of 1928, women could legally bequeath their stall titles to daughters and other designated heirs.[73] Such provisions aided female entrepreneurs by enhancing conditions of stability that encouraged entrepreneurial investment and expansion. These developments occurred amidst the heady political atmosphere of early twentieth-century Barcelona, wherein feminist calls for the expansion of women's rights from anarchists and other groups on the left intensified. Conservatives, for their part, viewed the spread of such ideas as a catastrophic. Their efforts to publish and disseminate prescriptive discourses setting forth idealized versions of womanhood increased as a result.[74]

Women's consumer protest was not new in early twentieth-century Spain, though it became a more important feature of mass politics.[75] Significant instances of female mobilization against price hikes and shortages of food and fuel erupted in Barcelona in 1895 and 1905 but were quickly resolved through the intervention of municipal authorities.[76] The subsistence crises associated with World War I inflation were another matter, ultimately requiring force of arms to quell.

In January 1918, a strike against the high cost of food, fuel, and rent in Barcelona widened to include more than 24,000 women and as many as 1,800 men.[77] Some 280 factories concentrated in both the Sants and Poble Nou districts were idled by the work stoppage and the uprising caused serious alarm. Led and dominated by women, thousands converged in mass protest gatherings on the afternoons of the January 24 and 25. On both days, there were physical altercations between women and the Guardia Civil, along with angry confrontations with shop owners throughout the city, incidents of looting, and seizures aimed at forcing retailers to sell provisions at pre-World War I levels.[78] One important theme of the protest was criticism of male authorities for failing to fulfill their roles as protectors.[79] As such, there were reports that "more than one policeman or civil guard was given a spanking and thrashing and sent home without his pants and with his alleged manhood exposed in the street."[80]

The 1918 tumult, which lasted for more than two weeks, spread to other Catalan cities, such as Sabadell, ending only after a state of siege was declared on the entire Province of Barcelona on January 26. In restoring order, authorities were forced to cap retail prices on cooking fuel, salt cod, and other foods. Significantly, while some conflict took place inside the city's covered markets, markets themselves did not constitute the main targets of consumer ire in the food crisis. Though the protesters converged at markets, they mainly used them, like cabarets and department stores, as points from which to launch their female mobilization efforts.[81]

Market women found themselves caught between growing working-class consumer protest and the state's use of force as a countermeasure. This mirrored their place in the urban social order, which was neither proletariat nor properly bourgeois. They owned very little capital and rarely employed labor from beyond family and kinship networks, belonging, like shopkeepers, to the lower-middle class, or what some would term the *petite bourgeoisie*. Yet all evidence indicates that women who worked in markets suffered more social derision than did their sisters working in proper shops, whether as owners or as clerks. Their unique place in the social order underpinned their reputations as iconic urban figures, known for their sharp tongues and volatile tempers. Market women frequently appeared as stock types in popular theatrical productions. The plot lines featuring them involved an ongoing struggle with honor and sexual reputation, fending off the advances of moneyed men and abusive market directors alike.[82] Concern with market women's propriety was reflected in new regulatory measures. The 1928 market code, for example, included new provisions seeking to tame female vendors' speech and attire.[83]

While the first market hall inaugural ceremonies in the 1840s signaled the birth of a particular form of civic ritual focused on the rationalization of urban space through architecture, by the early twentieth century, authorities had broadened the symbolic appropriation to include market women's bodies, presenting them in sanitized, virginal forms. Annual springtime civic celebrations, including those held in June 1930, featured beauty pageants wherein each of the markets elected a "Queen" from amongst the ranks of its most nubile young female vendors. Paraded through the streets of the city, the pulchritude of the queens was judged in determining the "Queen of all the Queens." The winner of that particular competition, young Lola Capdevila, a humble vegetable vendor representing Horta's market, was honored at a grand ball by a dance with no less than the still-reigning King of Spain, Alfonso XIII.[84] In life, as in the theatre, market women were both reviled for their purported bawdiness and reified as prototypes of desire.

Disruption and Dictatorship

The decade that followed the 1930 market queen cavalcade and ball featured jarring, violent political change. Under the auspices of the Second Spanish Republic (1931–1939), Barcelona's municipal regimes introduced new measures to shield the network of public market halls from unfettered competition. There were crackdowns on the growing numbers of unlicensed street sellers, along with concerted efforts to strictly enforce the details of provisioning regulations.[85] During the difficult years of the Spanish Civil War (1936–1939), Barcelona's food markets—initially targeted by anarcho-syndicalists as symbols of bourgeois tyranny—proved crucial as distribution points for food rations and other emergency aid. Revolutionary efforts to collectivize the supply and distribution of provisions through the market halls ultimately failed.[86] In a context characterized by internecine conflict, it was not just the physical structures that survived, but also the market hall *system*, which Republican authorities, having re-asserted power, found expedient in the struggle to feed a population under siege. Public control over private trade in food survived throughout and beyond the Spanish Civil War.

The fall of Barcelona to Franco's Nationalist forces in January 1939 involved sweeping purges, tens of thousands of executions, but no immediate or significant shift away from the market hall food retailing paradigm that had taken shape over the course of the previous century. The imposition of fascist-inspired policies of economic autarky ushered in an extended period of hunger and starvation in Spain. The return to prewar food supply and per-capita alimentary consumption levels took more than a decade. In the interim, consumers had to look beyond the state, the public markets, and private shops for the survival of their families. The personal testimonies of men and women working stalls in Barcelona's markets during Franco's dictatorship recount how black market trade in food intensified personal relations between retailers and consumers because it was clandestine and dependent upon familiarity and trust.[87] Public derision notwithstanding, engaging in black market trade was often a daring and desperate act, carried out on a mass basis by individuals coping with the regime's untenable food policies.[88] The discourses of control and resistance that Lara Anderson has analyzed in food texts of this period had corollaries in everyday practices inside Barcelona's market halls, where vendors skirted the rules on a daily basis.[89] Dealing with the intensification of graft and corruption on the part of market directors and inspectors proved particularly vexing for vendors and consumers alike.[90]

Barcelona's municipal governments under Franco's dictatorship never abandoned public market hall construction and administration as the principal means through which to feed the city's burgeoning population.[91] Markets were lucrative sources of public funds through taxes and fees. And they retained symbolic value for the regime's efforts to legitimate its rule among the popular classes. New market hall construction thus resumed in the 1940s and continued as a vigorous program throughout the nearly four decades of the dictatorship. Twenty-four retail food market halls were inaugurated under Franco's rule in Barcelona by 1974; none of the seventeen older markets were closed.[92] The new markets were mostly located in emerging neighborhoods formed along the periphery of the city, serving immigrant populations drawn to Barcelona's dramatic post-war industrial expansion. Building on the nineteenth-century ideal of maintaining a Parisian-inspired polynuclear market system that assured food retailing proximity to all residents irrespective of class, the state—here under a new corporatist ideological guise—used such projects as symbolic capital in its effort to legitimize rule on a neighborhood level.[93] Inauguration ceremonies for the new market halls were replete with assertions of the state's commitment to the common good. The fact that stall auctions generated more than seven million pesetas for municipal coffers from just the first of the new markets could hardly have served as a disincentive for further such undertakings.[94]

While the municipal market hall system proved useful to the dictatorship, there were important ways in which Barcelona's markets continued to remain elusive to the regime's cultural and social dictates. One had to do with the ongoing use of the Catalan language—alongside Spanish—by vendors and customers alike. Bilingualism was widespread and persisted in food retailing spaces even where market officials admonished vendors for "speaking like dogs" when communicating with customers in Catalan.[95] The ubiquitous presence of married women working as market vendors was another feature standing in seeming contradiction to Franco-era social policies. In a reversal of the Second Republic's social reforms, women's domestic roles were re-affirmed under the dictatorship through the ideology of True Catholic Womanhood.[96] Early on, the regime prohibited women's access to many professions, restricted married women's participation in the workforce, and legalized gender-based pay.[97] Even after the 1961 law that prohibited workplace discrimination on the basis of sex, women were still required to secure their husband's permission to work outside the home. Yet Franco-era market codes in Barcelona explicitly recognized the pre-existing rights of married women to sign contracts for market stall titles without the permission of their husbands.[98] Women's presence among the ranks of market vendors remained ubiquitous. From 1937 to 1960, over half of all regular stall titles in the city's markets went to women, typically continuing to work full-time in the markets even after their children were born.[99] The tradition of passing stall licenses on to daughters or other family members persisted. The vast and complicated familial networks that had come to characterize Barcelona's market vendor population survived the disruption of the Civil War and the imposition of the Franco dictatorship, continuing to flourish through the return of prosperity and the reinvigoration of consumer culture associated with the abandonment of autarky in the second half of the 1950s and the boom years that followed.

Economic recovery and demographic expansion caused demand for food to soar in Barcelona during the 1950s. The city's population reached 1.74 million in 1955, a more-than-70-percent increase in just twenty-five years. Though the late nineteenth-century city had been vested with one market hall for every 37,500 persons, by the mid-1950s, the ratio had risen to one for every 59,000 residents.[100] Demand for food skyrocketed and, without straying from its commitment to municipally owned and operated market halls, the city moved in 1956 to authorize smaller-scale, privately developed indoor food markets termed *galerías comerciales* (commercial galleries). The aim was to provide one market for every 25,000 inhabitants.[101] Rather than free-standing structures, these new markets were typically carved out of the ground floors of existing apartment buildings and included no more than a few dozen stalls, a small fraction of the numbers that comprised some of the city's largest market halls. Boqueria market, for example, housed 1,468 food stalls in 1955, Sant Antoni had 752, and Santa Caterina 737.[102]

A further step toward the decentralization of food retailing geography, *galerias comerciales* proliferated in residential areas of the city through the second-half of the twentieth century. They were certainly not exceptions to the well-established pattern of public control over private trade in the food retailing sector of the political economy but were highly regulated by municipal authorities, which reserved the right to revoke individual stall licenses and mandated that they feature entrances from two public streets and include modern refrigeration.[103] This effort to expand the infrastructure of retail distribution did nothing, of course, to arrest the alarming inflationary trend as the cost of living in Barcelona increased between 1956 and 1958 by 27.85 percent.[104]

The more significant innovation embraced to address the problem of rising food costs was the American-style self-service supermarket, first appearing in Barcelona in 1958. A great leap forward in terms of economies of scale, branding, and pre-packaging, the downside was that supermarkets introduced new levels of anonymity in the relationship between food retailers and consumers. While lower prices and ample offerings mostly offset concerns about quality and social relations, the Spanish state, through its Comisaría General de Abastacimientos y Transportes (Commisary-General for Supply and Transports) undertook to convince housewives of the advantages of shopping in these newest venues of modern food retailing.[105] When fifteen new supermarkets were announced for Barcelona in early 1959, the trade organization representing the city's 5,000 retail grocers sounded the alarm. They gathered on March 12 to assert that such a development could lead to the complete disappearance of traditional food shops.[106] Their worst fears, however, would take time to materialize. In 1987, almost four decades later, 92 percent of consumers in Catalonia were still relying on small neighborhood grocery shops for food, while 56 percent still regularly acquired their provisions from the region's market halls. Concurrently, just over half of Catalan consumers had by then come to regularly depend upon self-service supermarkets for some portion of that which they consumed.[107] Such data show that one form of retailing did not immediately eclipse another in the second half of the twentieth century.

Crucial to the history of public control over private trade is the fact that supermarkets had not come to Spain as a consequence of free market forces, an organizational innovation responding organically to unmet demand. Rather, their spread was very deliberately state-led as a policy response designed to address the extended food shortages characterizing the first decades of Franco's rule. Food supply issues constituted a vexing problem that had not been adequately resolved with the return of prosperity that began in the mid-1950s.[108] Perhaps unsurprisingly, the inaugural events held to commemorate supermarket openings often bore remarkable similarities to those long held for new market halls, with municipal and religious officials coming together in rituals that involved scripts touting public commitment to the common good through the embrace of modern organizations borrowed from beyond Spain's borders.

Contemporary Patterns

Through the transition to democracy, firm commitment to market hall food retailing in Barcelona persisted alongside growth in the supermarket sector. Four new public market hall structures were added to the system by the early 2000s and significant investment in dramatic renovation schemes continued from the 1960s to the present. The ubiquitous inclusion of supermarket space within market hall renovation designs only served to institutionalize the long history of adaptation to change. While new forms of food retailing spread widely, they did so largely alongside, in addition to, and within municipal market halls rather than instead of them. Indeed, Barcelona's contemporary food retailing sector—like that of many other Spanish cities—features small-scale and large-scale enterprises operating in symbiotic relationship to one another, mutually engaging in selective borrowing of commercial tactics, symbols, and strategies. While the overall number of neighborhood food shops and market stalls has fallen since the 1980s, those that remain are typically larger and more highly capitalized enterprises that reflect the modernizing provisioning policy thrusts of varying municipal governments since the 1980s.

In recent decades, Barcelona's municipal regimes intensified symbolic appropriation of the market hall system, continuing reliance upon the funds generated through operation but shifting expenses related to renovation and modernization to vendors and their organizational representatives. The era of market queen pageantry having passed, the focus of municipal propaganda with respect to markets now emphasizes sustainability, healthfulness, abundance, and culturally pluralist attitudes toward immigrant communities. The Institut de Mercats Municipals de Barcelona, which governs markets on behalf of the Ajuntament, continues to set forth strong didactic messages through the city's food market halls. The extensive publicity and propaganda campaigns surrounding Barcelona's market system remain central in the municipality's claim to advancing the common good.[109]

Significance

Though the exercise of public control over private trade in food is not unique to Barcelona's history, the city's market halls do constitute an interesting case study of its historical significance. Initially inspired by British and French models, market halls were built in many Spanish cities between 1840 and 1930. Concentrated in northern and coastal regions, along with Madrid and some other cities such as Valladolid, numerous such structures have survived as viable neighborhood food shopping venues.[110]

Yet Barcelona's market system deserves particular attention, both for its scale and the extent of its durability. While the city's markets were largely unremarkable through the pre-modern period, the virtually unprecedented nature of its industrial era food-related protest lent special levels of urgency to the exercise of municipal control. High population density, coupled with the compact nature of urban growth, both within and then beyond the walled confines, underpinned continued municipal commitment to market hall construction in the twentieth century. While in most of post-World War II Western Europe, market halls were razed or converted to other purposes as food retailing gave way to more highly capitalized forms of commerce, such as self-service shops, chain stores, and supermarkets, Barcelona is one of the Mediterranean cities that followed a different pattern. Neither Franco-era nor post-Franco urban authorities chose to abandon the market hall provisioning system, even as supermarkets and other even larger scale forms of retail commerce spread. As a consequence, Barcelona entered the twenty-first century with more markets per capita than any other city in Europe, including a series of monumental iron structures of great architectural and historical significance.[111]

Examining Barcelona's long-term history through the lens of its food markets also reveals social and cultural patterns that are otherwise easily ignored. One of these is the gender and sociability practices that connected putatively private domestic obligations to the very public act of food shopping at municipal markets, where the bulk of the enterprises were owned and operated by women under the direct supervision of municipal authorities charged with regulating food trade. These interpersonal lived experiences have also contributed to the persistent success of Barcelona's public food markets as beloved neighborhood institutions and as sites of everyday social exchange.

NOTES

1. Manuel Guàrdia and José Luis Oyón, eds., *Making Cities through Market Halls. Europe, 19th and 20th Centuries* (Barcelona: Museu d'Història de Barcelona, 2010), 11.
2. For a late twentieth-century celebration of retail market halls as monuments glorifying public commitment to the common good, see Arxiu Històric de la Ciutat de Barcelona (AHCB), "Més mercats que a cap ciutat Europea," *Diario de Barcelona*, Fascile 28, October 16, 1988.
3. The ability of the state to exert control over the distribution of food is never absolute. Some power is always wielded by otherwise marginalized groups acting within the culinary sphere. See Nir Avieli, *Food and Power: A Culinary Ethnography of Israel* (University of California Press, 2017).
4. Garett Dale, "'Marketless Trading in Hammurabi's Time': A Re-appraisal," *Journal of the Economic and Social History of the Orient* 56 (2013): 182–83.
5. One of the many studies undermining the "Pirenne Thesis" is Guy Bois, *The Transformation of the Year One Thousand: The Village of Lournand from Antiquity to Feudalism* (New York: St. Martin's Press, 1992). See also Guàrdia and Oyón, *Making Cities*, 14.

6. Jaume Sobrequés Callicó, *Barcelona. Aproximació a Vint Segles d'Història* (Barcelona: La Busca, 1999), 19.
7. Ramon Grau, "Gènesi del mercat actual," in *Boqueria: 150 Aniversari*, eds. Xavier Olivé and Llorenç Torrado (Barcelona: Ajuntament de Barcelona, 1986), 5.
8. Guàrdia and Oyón, *Making Cities*, 14.
9. Pere Ortí Gost, "Protegir i controlar el mercat alimentary: De la fiscalitat reial a la municipal (selgles XII-XIC)," *Alimentar la Ciutat. El proveïment de Barcelona del segle XIII al segle XX* (Barcelona: Ajuntament de Barcelona, Institut Municipal de Mercats, Museu d'Història de Barcelona, Institut de Cultura, 2013), 12.
10. Pere Benito Montclús, "Crisis de subsistència I polítiques frumentàntaries a la Barcelona medieval," in *Proveir Barcelona. El municipi i l'alimentació de la ciutat, 1329-1930*, ed. Mercè Renom (Barcelona: Museu d'Història de Barcelona, 2016), 23-34.
11. Josep R. Llobera, *Foundations of National Identity: From Catalonia to Europe* (New York: Berghahn Books, 2004), 68.
12. James Amelang, *Honored Citizens of Barcelona: Patrician Culture and Class Relations, 1490-1714* (Princeton, NJ: Princeton University Press, 1986), 8-9.
13. Juanjo Cáceres Nevot, "El Consell municipal i el proveïment de cereals a la Baixa edat Mitjana," in *Proveir Barcelona. El municipi i l'alimentació de la ciutat, 1329-1930*, ed. Mercè Renom (Barcelona: Museu d'Història de Barcelona, 2016), 85.
14. Pere Verdés-Pijuan, "Fiscalitat municipal i proveïment urbà: Dues cares de la mateixa moneda?" in *Proveir Barcelona. El municipi i l'alimentació de la ciutat, 1329-1930*, ed. Mercè Renom (Barcelona: Museu d'Història de Barcelona, 2016), 47-58.
15. James Amelang, "People of the Ribera: Popular Politics and Neighborhood Identity in Early Modern Barcelona," in *Culture and Identity in Early Modern Europe (1500-1800): Essays in Honor of Natalie Zemon Davis*, eds. Barbara B. Diefindorf and Carla Hesse (Ann Arbor: University of Michigan Press, 1993), 127.
16. Arxiu del Gremi d'Empresaris Carnissers i Xarcuters de Barcelona i Provincia (AGCB), *Ordenanzas de el Marqués de las Amarillas*, June 30, 1752.
17. Montserrat Miller, *Feeding Barcelona, 1714-1975: Public Market Halls, Social Networks, and Consumer Culture* (Baton Rouge: Louisiana State University Press, 2015), 49.
18. Marta Vicente, "Mujeres Artesanas en la Barcelona Moderna," in *Las Mujeres en el Antiguo Régimen: Imagen y Realidad*, eds. Isabel Pérez Molina, Marta Vicente Valentín, Alba Ibero, Eva Carrasco de la Fuente, Antonio Gil (Barcelona: Icaria Editorial, 1994), 74-80. See also Arxiu Històric de la Ciutat de Barcelona (AHCB), "Curiosidades Históricas: Reglamento de la Pescaderia en el siglo XIV [1375]," *Gaceta Municipal de Barcelona* 1 (1914); and AGCB, *Ordenanzas*, Articles 28, 80, 83, and 85.
19. James Casey, *Early Modern Spain: A Social History* (New York: Routledge, 1999), 204-5.
20. Joan Busquets, *Barcelona: The Evolution of a Compact City* (San Francisco: Applied Research + Design Publishing, 2005), 83; Sobrequés Callicó, *Barcelona*, 61.
21. Barcelona's defeat by the armies of Philip V in the War of the Spanish Succession (1701-14) led to the construction of a new set of fortifications and a Citadel, that, in following the lines of the older walls they replaced, added little territory for civilian use. See Martin Wynn, "Spain," in *Planning and Urban Growth in Southern Europe*, ed. Martin Wynn (London: Mansell Publishing, 1984), 112.

22. Wynn, "Spain," 113.
23. Other open-air food markets were located in the Plaça Nova, Plaça del Pi, Plaça del Pedró, Plaça de Sant Augustí Vell, Plaça dels Àngels, and along Carrer de la Peixeteria.
24. Clifford Geertz, "The Bazaar Economy: Information and Search in Peasant Marketing," *American Economic Review* 68, no. 2 (May 1978): 28–32.
25. See Luis Corteguera, *For the Common Good: Popular Politics in Barcelona, 1580–1640* (Ithaca, NY: Cornell University Press, 2002). Corteguera outlines the centrality of this concept within early modern Catalan culture.
26. Gaspar Feliu, "El pa el segle XVIII: continuïutats i canvis," in *Proveir Barcelona. El municipi i l'alimentació de la ciutat, 1329–1930*, ed. Mercè Renom (Barcelona: Museu d'Història de Barcelona, 2016), 222.
27. Irene Castells, "Els Rebomboris del Pa de 1789 a Barcelona," *Recerques: Història, Economia, Cultura* 1 (1970): 54; María de los Ángeles Pérez Samper, "El pan nuestro de cada día en la Barcelona moderna," *Pedralbes* 22 (2002): 29–72; Gabriel Tortella, *The Development of Modern Spain: An Economic History of the Nineteenth and Twentieth Centuries* (Cambridge, MA: Harvard University Press, 2000), 26.
28. Mercè Renom, "Les formes i el lèxic de la protesta a la fi de l'Antic Règim," *Recerques* 55 (2007): 23.
29. E. Moreu-Rey, *Revolució a Barcelona el 1789* (Catalan: Institut d'Estudis Catalans, 1967), 23.
30. Castells, "Els Rebomboris del Pa de 1789 a Barcelona," 54–70; Mercè Renom, *Conflictes socials i revolució: Sabadell, 1718–1823* (Vic: Eumo Editorial, 2009).
31. Castells, "Els Rebomboris del Pa de 1789 a Barcelona," 69.
32. Ibid., 71.
33. Marina López Guallar, "El proveïment del pa a Barcelona sota el règim de Nova Planta," in *Proveir Barcelona. El municipi i l'alimentació de la ciutat, 1329–1930*, ed. Mercè Renom (Barcelona: Museu d'Història de Barcelona, 2016), 201–12.
34. Ibid.
35. Ibid.
36. Castells, "Els Rebomboris del Pa de 1789 a Barcelona," 73.
37. Ibid., 75–76.
38. López Guallar, "El proveïment del pa."
39. María Rosa Bultó Blajot, "Dificultades para la abactecimiento de pan en el siglo XVIII," in *Los Abastecimientos de la ciudad: Oficios y Técnicas, Índice Analítico de los Tomos I-XII textos del Boletín Semanal radiado desde la emisora "Radio Barcelona" por el Instituto Municipal de Historia de la Ciudad*, ed. Pedro Voltes Bou, vol. 12 of *Divulgación histórica de Barcelona* (Barcelona: Ayuntamiento de Barcelona, Instituto Municipal de Historia, 1965), 12.
40. Peter N. Stearns, *Consumerism in World History: The Global Transformation of Desire*, 2nd ed. (New York: Routledge, 2006).
41. Albert García Espuche, "Una ciutat d'adroguers," in *Drogues, Dolços i Tabac: Barcelona 1700*, ed. Albert García Espuche et al. (Barcelona: Ajuntament de Barcelona, Institut de Cultura, 2010), 21–107.
42. Karl Marx and Friedrich Engels, *Collected Works*, vol. 23 (New York: International Publishers, 1988), 586.

43. Busquets, *Barcelona*, 117; Albert Serratosa et al., *Semiòtica de l'Eixample Cerdà* (Barcelona: Edicions Proa, 1995), 133.
44. Raymond Carr, *Spain, 1808–1975*, 2nd ed. (Oxford, UK: Clarendon Press, 1982), 166; Felipe Fernández-Armesto, *Barcelona: A Thousand Years of the City's Past* (New York: Oxford University Press, 1992), 143.
45. Arxiu Històric de la Ciutat de Barcelona (AHCB), "Nuestros Centros de Abastos: El Mercado de San José," *Gaceta Municipal de Barcelona*, October 17, 1949, 1218.
46. Montserrat Miller, "Mercats Nou-Centistes a Barcelona: Una Interpretació del seus Orígens i significat cultural," *Revista del l'Alguer* 6, no. 4 (December 1993): 100. See also Arxiu Històric de la Ciutat de Barcelona (AHCB), *Barcelona Antigua y Moderna: El Mercado de La Boquería, 1840–1944. Recuerdos, Evocaciones, Perspectivas* (Publicidad Gabernet, 1944).
47. Gabriel Cardona, *A Golpes de Sable. Los Grandes Militares que han Marcado la Historia de España* (Barcelona: Editorial Ariel, 2008), 160
48. Fernandez-Armesto, *Barcelona*, 169.
49. For an account of the resonance of these ceremonies a century later, see Arxiu Històric de la Ciutat de Barcelona (AHCB), "Mercado de Santa Caterina: Breve historial con motive a la celebración de su primer centenario," *Gaceta Municipal de Barcelona*, April 26, 1948, 256.
50. Busquets, *Barcelona*, 108.
51. Manuel Guàrdia, José Luis Oyón, and Nadia Fava, "The Barcelona Market System," in *Making Cities Through Market Halls. Europe, 19th and 20th Centuries*, eds. Manuel Guàrdia and José Luis Oyón (Barcelona: Museu d'Història de Barcelona, 2010), 264; Bertrand Lemoine, "Market Halls in France," in *Making Cities Through Market Halls. Europe, 19th and 20th Centuries*, eds. Manuel Guàrdia and José Luis Oyón (Barcelona: Museu d'Història de Barcelona, 2010), 103–38.
52. Mercè Renom, "La construcción de mercats a la segona mietat del segle XIX: un resposta a diversos reptes," in *Proveir Barcelona. El municipi i l'alimentació de la ciutat, 1329–1930*, ed. Mercè Renom (Barcelona: Museu d'Història de Barcelona, 2016), 295–308.
53. Wrought and cast iron in market hall construction dates to late eighteenth-century Britain. It was further developed technologically and aesthetically in France, most notably by Baltard in the famed Les Halles of Paris. See Esteban Castañer, "Iron Markets in Spain," in *Making Cities through Market Halls. Europe, 19th and 20th Centuries*, ed. Manuel Guàrdia and José Luis Oyón (Barcelona: Museu d'Història de Barcelona, 2010), 255.
54. Victoria E. Thompson, *The Virtuous Marketplace: Women and Men, Money and Politics in Paris, 1830–1870* (Baltimore, MD: The Johns Hopkins University Press, 2000).
55. Miller, *Feeding Barcelona*, 158–60.
56. For a discussion of other factors, see Guàrdia, Oyón and Fava, "The Barcelona Market System," 261.
57. See Guàrdia, Oyón and Fava, "The Barcelona Market System," 266, note 11, which cites Municipal Minutes from July 29, 1870, in which the Public Works Committee noted that among the "most meaningful pieces of information regarding the prosperity, the

progress, and even the culture of a town is undoubtedly the state of its police force, and consequently, the state of its most frequented public places, including markets."
58. Castañer, "Iron Markets in Spain," 244.
59. Miller, *Feeding Barcelona*, 168–71; 185–86.
60. Thompson, *The Virtuous Marketplace*, 86–118.
61. Market halls inherited from annexed municipalities include: Llibertat (1875), Abaceria Central (1892), Clot (1889), and Unió (1889). Market halls inaugurated in the early twentieth century included: Sarrià (1911), Sant Gervasi (1912), Sants (1913), Sant Andreu (1923), Galvany (1927), and Ninot (1933). The designs of the newest structures followed European trends in shifting to reliance upon reinforced concrete and Modern Movement-inspired styles.
62. Arxiu Històric de la Ciutat de Barcelona (AHCB), "Presupuestos Ordinarios de Gastos," *Gazeta Municipal de Barcelona*, 1931, 27–134.
63. Miller, *Feeding Barcelona*, 171–81.
64. Ibid., 142.
65. Ibid., 231.
66. Ibid., 80–108.
67. Ibid., 90–103.
68. Ibid., 101–3.
69. Cristina Borderías, "Nutrició i gènere a la Barcelona obrera," in *Proveir Barcelona. El municipi i l'alimentació de la ciutat, 1329–1930*, ed. Mercè Renom (Barcelona: Museu d'Història de Barcelona, 2016), 401–14.
70. Administrative Records, Sant Antoni Market, Barcelona (ARSAM), document dated October 27, 1911.
71. Miller, *Feeding Barcelona*, 117–18.
72. Arxiu Històric de la Ciutat de Barcelona (AHCB), *Reglamento para el régimen de los mercados*, 1898, Article 11.
73. Arxiu Històric de la Ciutat de Barcelona (AHCB), *Reglamentos de los mercados en general*, 1928, Articles 9, 24, 42 and 43, section E.
74. See Isabel Segura and Marta Selva, *Revistes de Dones, 1846–1935* (Barcelona: Edhasa, 1984), 289–90. Published by the Institut Cultural i Biblioteca Popular de la Dona, *La Dona Catalana* (1925–1938), which was aligned ideologically with the conservative Catalan Lliga Regionalista party, was one of these.
75. Pamela Beth Radcliff, "The Emerging Challenge of Mass Politics," *Spanish History since 1808*, eds. José Alvarez Junco and Adrian Shubert (London: Arnold, 2000), 152.
76. María Luz Arriero, "Los motines de subsistencias en España, 1895–1905," *Estudios de Historia Social* 30 (1984): 199–250.
77. Arxiu Històric de la Ciutat de Barcelona (AHCB), "Las subsistencias," *Diario de Barcelona*, January 23–25, 1918.
78. Ibid.
79. Radcliff, "The Emerging Challenge of Mass Politics," 303.
80. Manent i Peses, qtd. in Lester Golden, "The Women in Command: The Barcelona Consumer War of 1918," *UCLA Historical Journal* 6 (1985): 20.

81. Ibid., 13, 20.
82. Miller, *Feeding Barcelona*, 168–71.
83. AHCB, *Reglamentos de los mercados en general*, 1928, Articles 24, 42, and 43.
84. Miller, *Feeding Barcelona*, 1–26.
85. Ibid., 147–48.
86. Ibid., 181–200.
87. Semi Colominas Aluja, oral history interview by Montserrat Miller, May 11, 1992.
88. Michael Seidman, *Republic of Egos: A Social History of the Spanish Civil War* (Madison: The University of Wisconsin Press, 2002).
89. Lara Anderson, *Control and Resistance: Food Discourse in Franco Spain* (Toronto: University of Toronto Press, 2020).
90. Miller, *Feeding Barcelona*, 210–13.
91. Arxiu Històric de la Ciutat de Barcelona (AHCB), "Los mercados de Barcelona serán objeto de importantes reformas," *El Noticiero Universal*, January 12, 1944.
92. Market halls inaugured under Franco-era municipal regimes include: Sagrada Família (1944), Carme (1950), Horta (1951), Vallvidrera (1953), Guinardó (1954), Sagrera (1955), L'Estrella (1957), Les Tres Torres (1958), Bon Pastor (1960), Montserrat (1960), Les Corts (1961), Mercè (1961), Guineueta (1965), Ciutat Meridiana (1966), Núria (1966), Felip II (1966), Sant Martí (1966), Besòs (1968), Sant Gervasi (1968), Vall d'Hebron (1969), Carmel (1969), Port (1973), Provençals (1974), and Lesseps (1974)
93. Arxiu Històric de la Ciutat de Barcelona (AHCB), "Un Año de vida Municipal," *Diario de Barcelona*, December 31, 1944.
94. Arxiu Històric de la Ciutat de Barcelona (AHCB), "La obra constructiva del Ayuntamiento," *Gaceta Municipal de Barcelona*, April 12, 1948, 211.
95. María Cararach Vernet, Oral history interview by Montserrat Miller, May 5, 1992. The regime initially pursued a set of policies designed to effect de-Catalanization through banning the teaching of the language, its publication, and its use in public space. Catalan linguists were among those executed in the post-war purges.
96. Aurora G. Morcillo, *True Catholic Womanhood: Gender Ideology in Franco's Spain* (Dekalb: Northern Illinois University Press, 2000).
97. Lina Gálvez Muñoz and Paloma Fernández Pérez, "Female Entrepreneurship in Spain during the Nineteenth and Twentieth Centuries," *Business History Review* 81, no. 3 (2007): 495–515
98. Arxiu Històric de la Ciutat de Barcelona (AHCB), *Reglamentos de los Mercados en General y de los especiales del de pescado y de frutas y verduras, al por mayor, y de los encantos*, 1942, Article 9, Section E.
99. Miller, *Feeding Barcelona*, 213–35. Between 1937 and 1949, 58.41 percent of all fixed-title market stall permits in Barcelona were conveyed to women; from 1950 to 1960, 57.42 were conveyed to women. Administrative Records Area de Proveïments i Consum (now Institut Municipal de Mercats de Barcelona), Llibres de Registre, and Administrative Records Santa Caterina, L'Abaceria Central, and Sant Antoni Markets. Data collected by author. The only market not included in the analysis is La Boqueria.
100. Arxiu Històric de la Ciutat de Barcelona (AHCB), "Déficit de Mercados de Abastos," *Barcelona Revista*, 1955.

101. Arxiu Històric de la Ciutat de Barcelona (AHCB), "Los mercados de Barcelona y el aumento constante de la ciudad," *Solidaridad Nacional*, June 14, 1956.
102. Arxiu Històric de la Ciutat de Barcelona (AHCB), "Barcelona en cifras. Mercados y puestos," *El Destino*, October 22, 1955.
103. Arxiu Històric de la Ciutat de Barcelona (AHCB), "Fomento de la construcción de mercados particulares," *La Prensa*, August 1, 1958.
104. See Arxiu Històric de la Ciutat de Barcelona (AHCB), "A comprar en los supermercados," *Diario de Barcelona*, July 15, 1958; AHCB, "Quince nuevos supermercados serán instalados en Barcelona," *El Noticiero Universal*, March 13, 1959.
105. Alejandro J. Gómez del Moral, *Buying into Change: Mass Consumption, Dictatorship, and Democratization in Franco's Spain, 1939–1982* (Lincoln: University of Nebraska Press, 2021), 127.
106. AHCB, "Quince nuevos supermercados serán instalados en Barcelona."
107. Guillermo Burriel, "Función Comercial de un Mercado Municipal," *Jornades Sobre el Futuro de los Mercados Municipales*, 57; Adolf Cabruja, "La Revitalización de los mercados a través de la gestión municipal," *Jornades Sobre el Futuro de los Mercados Municipales*, 24.
108. Gómez del Moral, *Buying into Change*, 127.
109. Guàrdia, Oyón, and Fava, "The Barcelona Market System," 261.
110. Castañer, "Iron Markets in Spain," 234.
111. AHCB, "Més mercats que a cap ciutat Europea."

WORKS CITED

Administrative Records, Sant Antoni Market, Barcelona (ARSAM), document dated October 27, 1911.

Amelang, James. *Honored Citizens of Barcelona: Patrician Culture and Class Relations, 1490–1714*. Princeton, NJ: Princeton University Press, 1986.

———. "People of the Ribera: Popular Politics and Neighborhood Identity in Early Modern Barcelona." In *Culture and Identity in Early Modern Europe (1500–1800): Essays in Honor of Natalie Zemon Davis*, edited by Barbara B. Diefindorf and Carla Hesse, 119–37. Ann Arbor: University of Michigan Press, 1993.

Anderson, Lara. *Control and Resistance: Food Discourse in Franco Spain*. Toronto: University of Toronto Press, 2020.

Arxiu del Gremi d'Empresaris Carnissers i Xarcuters de Barcelona i Provincia (AGCB). *Ordenanzas de el Marqués de las Amarillas*. June 30, 1752.

Arxiu Històric de la Ciutat de Barcelona (AHCB). *Barcelona Antigua y Moderna: El Mercado de La Boquería, 1840–1944. Recuerdos, Evocaciones, Perspectivas*. Publicidad Gabernet, 1944.

———. *Barcelona Revista*. "Déficit de Mercados de Abastos," 1955.

———. "Curiosidades Históricas: Reglamento de la Pescadería en el siglo XIV [1375]." *Gaceta Municipal de Barcelona* 1, 1914.

———. *El Destino*. "Barcelona en cifras. Mercados y puestos." October 22, 1955.

———. *Diario de Barcelona*. "Las subsistencias," January 23–25, 1918; "Un año de vida Municipal," December 31, 1944; "A comprar en los supermercados," July 15, 1958; "Més mercats que a cap ciutat Europea," Fascile 28, October 16, 1988.

———. "Mercado de Santa Caterina: Breve historial con motivo a la celebración de su primer centenario." *Gaceta Municipal de Barcelona*, April 26, 1948, 256.

———. *El Noticiero Universal*. "Los mercados de Barcelona serán objeto de importantes reformas," January 12, 1944; "Quince nuevos supermercados serán instalados en Barcelona," March 13, 1959.

———. "Nuestros Centros de Abastos: El Mercado de San José." *Gaceta Municipal de Barcelona*, October 17, 1949, 1218.

———. "La obra constructiva del Ayuntamiento. El Mercado de la Sagrada Familia." *Gaceta Municipal de Barcelona*, April 12, 1948, 211.

———. *La Prensa*. "Fomento de la construcción de mercados particulares," August 1, 1958.

———. "Presupuestos Ordinarios de Gastos." *Gazeta Municipal de Barcelona*, 1931, 27–134.

———. *Reglamento para el régimen de los mercados*. 1898. Article 11.

———. *Reglamentos de los mercados en general*. 1928. Articles 9, 24, 42, and 43, Section E.

———. *Reglamentos de los Mercados en General y de los especiales del de pescado y de frutas y verduras, al por mayor, y de los encantos*. 1942. Article 9, Section E.

———. *Solidaridad Nacional*. "Los mercados de Barcelona y el aumento constante de la ciudad." June 14, 1956; "Superservis. Un nuevo supermercado Barcelonés en el corazón de la ciudad," December 20, 1959.

Avieli, Nir. *Food and Power: A Culinary Ethnography of Israel*. Berkeley: University of California Press, 2017.

Benito Montclús, Pere. "Crisis de subsistència I polítiques frumentàntaries a la Barcelona medieval." In *Proveir Barcelona. El municipi i l'alimentació de la ciutat, 1329–1930*, edited by Mercè Renom, 23–34. Barcelona: Museu d'Història de Barcelona, 2016.

Billig, Michael. *Banal Nationalism*. London: SAGE Publications, 1995.

Bois, Guy. *The Transformation of the Year One Thousand: The Village of Lournand from Antiquity to Feudalism*. New York: St. Martin's Press, 1992.

Borderías, Cristina. "Nutrició i gènere a la Barcelona obrera." In *Proveir Barcelona. El municipi i l'alimentació de la ciutat, 1329–1930*, edited by Mercè Renom, 401–14. Barcelona: Museu d'Història de Barcelona, 2016.

Bourdieu, Pierre. *Outline of a Theory of Practice*, trans. Richard Nice. Cambridge University Press, 1977.

Bultó Blajot, María Rosa. "Dificultades para la abactecimiento de pan en el siglo XVIII." In *Los Abastecimientos de la ciudad: Oficios y Técnicas, Índice Analítico de los Tomos I-XII textos del Boletín Semanal radiado desde la emisora "Radio Barcelona" por el Instituto Municipal de Historia de la Ciudad*, edited by Pedro Voltes Bou. Vol. 12 of *Divulgación histórica de Barcelona*. Barcelona: Ayuntamiento de Barcelona, Instituto Municipal de Historia, 1965.

Burriel, Guillermo. "Función Comercial de un Mercado Municipal." *Jornades Sobre el Futuro de los Mercados Municipales*, 22 junio 1988 (Vitoria, Gobierno Vasco, Departamento de Indústria y Comercio), 47–59.

Busquets, Joan. *Barcelona: The Evolution of a Compact City*. San Francisco: Applied Research + Design Publishing, 2005.

Cabruja, Adolf. "La Revitalización de los mercados a través de la gestion municipal." *Jornades Sobre el Futuro de los Mercados Municipales*, 22 junio 1988 (Vitoria, Gobierno Vasco, Departamento de Indústria y Comercio), 19–35.

Cáceres Nevot, Juanjo. "El Consell municipal i el proveïment de cereals a la Baixa edat Mitjana." In *Proveir Barcelona. El municipi i l'alimentació de la ciutat, 1329–1930*, edited by Mercè Renom, 85–96. Barcelona: Museu d'Història de Barcelona, 2016.

Cararach Vernet, María. Oral history interview by Montserrat Miller, May 5, 1992.

Cardona, Gabriel. *A Golpes de Sable. Los Grandes Militares que han Marcado la Historia de España*. Barcelona: Editorial Ariel, 2008.

Carr, Raymond. *Spain, 1808–1975*. 2nd edition. Oxford, UK: Clarendon Press, 1982.

Casey, James. *Early Modern Spain: A Social History*. New York: Routledge, 1999.

Castañer, Esteban. "Iron Markets in Spain." In *Making Cities through Market Halls. Europe, 19th and 20th Centuries*, edited by Manuel Guàrdia and José Luis Oyón, 231–60. Barcelona: Museu d'Història de Barcelona, 2010.

Castells, Irene. "Els Rebomboris del Pa de 1789 a Barcelona." *Recerques: Història, Economia, Cultura* 1 (1970): 51–81.

Colominas Aluja, Semi. Oral history interview by Montserrat Miller, May 11, 1992.

Corteguera, Luis. *For the Common Good: Popular Politics in Barcelona, 1580–1640*. Ithaca, NY: Cornell University Press, 2002.

Dale, Garett. "'Marketless Trading in Hammurabi's Time': A Re-appraisal." *Journal of the Economic and Social History of the Orient* 56 (2013): 159–88.

Feliu, Gaspar. "El pa el segle XVIII: continuïutats i canvis." In *Proveir Barcelona. El municipi i l'alimentació de la ciutat, 1329–1930*, edited by Mercè Renom, 213–24. Barcelona: Museu d'Història de Barcelona, 2016.

Fernández-Armesto, Felipe. *Barcelona: A Thousand Years of the City's Past*. New York: Oxford University Press, 1992.

Gálvez Muñoz, Lina, and Paloma Fernández Pérez. "Female Entrepreneurship in Spain during the Nineteenth and Twentieth Centuries." *Business History Review* 81, no. 3 (2007): 495–515.

García Espuche, Albert. "Una ciutat d'adroguers." In *Drogues, Dolços i Tabac: Barcelona 1700*, edited by Albert García Espuche et al., 21–107. Barcelona: Ajuntament de Barcelona, Institut de Cultura, 2010.

Geertz, Clifford. "The Bazaar Economy: Information and Search in Peasant Marketing." *American Economic Review* 68, no. 2 (May 1978): 28–32.

Golden, Lester. "The Women in Command: The Barcelona Consumer War of 1918." *UCLA Historical Journal* 6 (1985): 5–32.

Gómez del Moral, Alejandro J. *Buying into Change: Mass Consumption, Dictatorship, and Democratization in Franco's Spain, 1939–1982*. Lincoln: University of Nebraska Press, 2021.

Grau, Ramon. "Gènesi del mercat actual." In *Boqueria: 150 Aniversari*, edited by Xavier Olivé and Llorenç Torrado, 5–6. Barcelona: Ajuntament de Barcelona, 1986.

Guàrdia, Manuel, and José Luis Oyón, eds. *Making Cities Through Market Halls. Europe, 19th and 20th Centuries*. Barcelona: Museu d'Història de Barcelona, 2010.

Guàrdia, Manuel, José Luis Oyón, and Nadia Fava. "The Barcelona Market System." In *Making Cities Through Market Halls. Europe, 19th and 20th Centuries*, edited by Manuel Guàrdia and José Luis Oyón, 261–96. Barcelona: Museu d'Història de Barcelona, 2010.

Lemoine, Bertrand. "Market Halls in France." In *Making Cities Through Market Halls. Europe, 19th and 20th Centuries*, edited by Manuel Guàrdia and José Luis Oyón, 139–66. Barcelona: Museu d'Història de Barcelona, 2010.

Llobera, Josep R. *Foundations of National Identity: From Catalonia to Europe*. New York: Berghahn Books, 2004.

López Guallar, Marina. "El proveïment del pa a Barcelona sota el règim de Nova Planta." In *Proveir Barcelona. El municipi i l'alimentació de la ciutat, 1329–1930*, edited by Mercè Renom, 201–12. Barcelona: Museu d'Història de Barcelona, 2016.

Luz Arriero, María. "Los motines de subsistencias en España, 1895–1905." *Estudios de Historia Social* 30 (1984): 199–250.

Marx, Karl, and Friedrich Engels. *Collected Works*, Volume 23. New York: International Publishers, 1988.

Miller, Montserrat. *Feeding Barcelona, 1714–1975: Public Market Halls, Social Networks, and Consumer Culture*. Baton Rouge: Louisiana State University Press, 2015.

———. "Mercats Nou-Centistes a Barcelona: Una Interpretació del seus Orígens i significat cultural." *Revista del l'Alguer* 6, no. 4 (December 1993): 93–106.

Morcillo, Aurora G. *True Catholic Womanhood: Gender Ideology in Franco's Spain*. Dekalb: Northern Illinois University Press, 2000.

Moreu-Rey, E. *Revolució a Barcelona el 1789*. Catalan: Institut d'Estudis Catalans, 1967.

Ortí Gost, Pere. "Protegir i controlar el mercat alimentary: De la fiscalitat reial a la municipal (selgles XII-XIC)." *Alimentar la Ciutat. El proveïment de Barcelona del segle XIII al segle XX*, 12–13. Barcelona: Ajuntament de Barcelona, Institut Municipal de Mercats, Museu d'Història de Barcelona, Institut de Cultura, 2013.

Pérez Samper, María de los Ángeles. "El pan nuestro de cada día en la Barcelona moderna." *Pedralbes* 22 (2002): 29–72.

Pirenne, Henri. *Medieval Cities: The Origins and Revival of Trade*. Princeton University Press, 1980.

Radcliff, Pamela Beth. "The Emerging Challenge of Mass Politics." *Spanish History since 1808*, edited by José Alvarez Junco and Adrian Shubert, 137–54. London: Arnold, 2000.

Renom, Mercè. *Conflictes socials i revolució: Sabadell, 1718–1823*. Vic: Eumo Editorial, 2009.

———. "La construcción de mercats a la segona mietat del segle XIX: un resposta a diversos reptes." In *Proveir Barcelona. El municipi i l'alimentació de la ciutat, 1329–1930*, edited by Mercè Renom, 295–308. Barcelona: Museu d'Història de Barcelona, 2016.

———. "Les formes i el lèxic de la protesta a la fi de l'Antic Règim." *Recerques* 55 (2007): 5–33.

Segura, Isabel, and Marta Selva, *Revistes de Dones, 1846–1935*. Barcelona: Edhasa, 1984.

Seidman, Michael. *Republic of Egos: A Social History of the Spanish Civil War*. Madison: The University of Wisconsin Press, 2002.

Serratosa, Albert, et al. *Semiòtica de l'Eixample Cerdà*. Barcelona: Edicions Proa, 1995.

Sobrequés Callicó, Jaume. *Barcelona. Aproximació a Vint Segles d'Història*. Barcelona: La Busca, 1999.
Stearns, Peter N. *Consumerism in World History: The Global Transformation of Desire*. 2nd edition. New York: Routledge, 2006.
Thompson, Victoria E. *The Virtuous Marketplace: Women and Men, Money and Politics in Paris, 1830-1870*. Baltimore, MD: The Johns Hopkins University Press, 2000.
Tortella, Gabriel. *The Development of Modern Spain: An Economic History of the Nineteenth and Twentieth Centuries*. Cambridge, MA: Harvard University Press, 2000.
Verdés-Pijuan, Pere. "Fiscalitat municipal i proveïment urbà: Dues cares de la mateixa moneda?" In *Proveir Barcelona. El municipi i l'alimentació de la ciutat, 1329-1930*, edited by Mercè Renom, 47-58. Barcelona: Museu d'Història de Barcelona, 2016.
Vicente, Marta. "Mujeres Artesenas en la Barcelona Moderna." In *Las Mujeres en el Antiguo Régimen: Imagen y Realidad*, edited Isabel Pérez Molina, Marta Vicente Valentín, Alba Ibero, Eva Carrasco de la Fuente, Antonio Gil, 59-90. Barcelona: Icaria Editorial, 1994.
Wynn, Martin, "Spain." In *Planning and Urban Growth in Southern Europe*, edited by Martin Wynn, 111-63. London: Mansell Publishing, 1984.

◆ CHAPTER 2

Regenerating Catalan Culinary Identity

H. Rosi Song

The recent political mobilization in Catalonia leading to its failed effort to hold a referendum on its independence from Spain in 2017 has resulted in a resurgence in examinations of the region's nationalistic discourses, from historicizing its origins to paying attention to its connection to present-day political activism. Catalan gastronomy has been part of this examination as the region's culinary prestige has helped to identify this area of the Iberian Peninsula as a distinct place with its own cooking and eating traditions. Cookbooks are important to our understanding of nation-building narratives, as they identify culinary traditions or the significance of its particularities. They are also able to "tell unusual cultural tales."[1] (Appadurai 3). In this essay, I examine a cookbook that could be characterized as telling such a story, Ferran Agulló's 1928 *Llibre de la cuina catalana*, which turns out, has a lot to do with the way we talk about the region's food and its culinary identity today.

Agulló's work is very present in the writing of contemporary Catalan gastronomy because it contains an explicit statement about Catalan cuisine. First published in 1928 and reprinted in a second edition in 1933, it gained much popularity and is still available today. The paragraph contained in the book's prologue is repeated by many, including Néstor Luján, Manuel Vázquez Montalbán, and Jaume Fàbrega, three writers who have contributed the most to narrating the culinary history of the region in the second half of the twentieth century. Vázquez Montalbán highlights these words in the introduction to his seminal *L'art del menjar a Catalunya* (1977):

> Catalunya, com té una llengua, un dret, uns costums, una història pròpia i un ideal polític, té una cuina. Hi ha regions, nacionalitats, pobles que tenen un plat especial,

característic, però no una cuina. Catalunya la té, i té més encara: té un gran poder d'assimilació de plats d'altres cuines com la francesa i la italiana; fa seus els plats d'aquelles cuines e els modifica segons el seu estil i el seu gust.

Catalonia, just as it has a language, its own laws and traditions, its own history and political thought, it has a cuisine. There are regions, nationalities, people who have a special dish, a typical one, but not a cuisine. Catalunya has it and has even more: it has a great power of assimilation of dishes from other cuisines, like the French or the Italian; it makes its own dishes from these cuisines adapting it to its own style and taste.[2]

The writers quote this paragraph in order to assert the existence of a Catalan cuisine, as it is easy to identify it as an example of an early exaltation of Catalan nationalism that resonates in the region's current political climate.[3] But, if we consider this statement in the context of the cultural and political enterprise of late nineteenth-century Catalonia, we are better able to understand the significance of this cookbook and how its origin hinges on loss rather than exaltation, as well as how the idea of the "nationalitat catalana" (Catalan nationality) is intimately linked with eating and cooking practices.

The Food Loving Catalanist Secretary

Ferran Agulló i Vidal was born in Girona in 1863 and died in Santa Coloma de Farners in 1933. He was a minor figure closely linked with the *Lliga Regionalista* (Regionalist League), the political party founded in 1901, which came together as conservatives in the area decided to get organized to bring their own interests to the Liberal ruling class in Madrid.[4] He served as secretary of the party since the early years of its formation and came to be regarded as a devoted *Catalanist* and a relentless advocate for the Catalan language. This political party, born from the combination of the *Unió Regionalista* and the *Centre National Català*, was the first one that was specifically "Catalanist, modern, reformist, conservative and bourgeois," supported by an impressive list of public figures who "represented the aspirations of the industrial bourgeoisie and the upper and middle classes of Catalonia."[5] It was also the party connected with the artistic movement of the *Noucentisme*, which sought to provide the idealism required for building the ambitious project of the "proto-governmental structures in a society that was devoid of political power," with a commitment from cultural producers to create "an organized, efficient modern society with an expansive culture."[6] The link between politics and culture was already established by the earlier movement of the *Renaixença*, which considered the development and revival of Catalan language and cultural awareness a key component of political mobilization.[7] While *Modernisme*, the third cultural movement of the period connected to the revival of Catalan culture, looked up to Northern European cultures as models, the artists of the *Noucentisme* privileged the Mediterranean world, inspired by the memory of Catalonia's medieval power.[8]

Among his contributions, Agulló wrote the daily column "Al Dia" under the pseudonym "Pol" for the daily *La Veu de Catalunya*, the mouthpiece of the *Lliga*, for about three decades until his death.[9] Josep M. Figueres describes his columns as personal, incisive comments on some current topic that always reflected the "pensament profund del diari" (the deep thinking of the newspaper).[10] His writing is described as elegant and persuasive, expressing profound love for Catalonia and contributing to the normalization of the Catalan language.[11] He was also a poet and a playwright, having won prizes at the *Jocs Florals*, and was even once proclaimed *Mestre en Gai Saber* in 1893.[12] Today his public service as well as most of his writings have been forgotten, yet he remains a referent in Catalan gastronomy thanks to his cookbook. Curiously and perhaps more generally, he is mentioned for the role he played in naming the northeast coast of Catalonia as "Costa Brava."[13]

While mostly forgotten, the few literary sketches of Agulló's character that still exist point to his cultural significance during his lifetime. After his death, Josep Maria de Sagarra (1894–1961) described him as representative of the most realist and authentic *catalanisme* and a true romantic when it came to anything that had to do with Catalonia. He wrote in his column "L'aperitiu" in *Mirador*:

> Si Prat, si Cambó, i Duran i Ventosa representen els moments gloriosos i patètics de la Lliga, Ferran Agulló representa el treball constant, la feina difícil i dolenta de fer, la continuïtat abnegada, representa aquesta feina del secretari, de l'home que està entre bastidors, que no porta mai la corona de llorer al cap, però que amb la traça, la malícia, el seny i l'experiència, és ell qui moltes vegades evita que la corona de llorer no voli del cap dels altres.

> *If Prat, Cambó and Duran i Ventosa represent the glorious and pathetic moments of the Lliga, Ferran Agulló represents the constant work, the difficult and unpleasant tasks that needed to be done, the dedicated constancy, he represents the work of the secretary, the man behind the curtains, who never wears the laurel wreath, but who with skills, slyness, wisdom and experience, is the one who many times avoids that the laurel wreath flies off the head of others.*[14]

Sagarra also identified him as a gourmand and someone knowledgeable about good cooking, a member of a disappearing group, "les autèntiques senyores del nostre país que ja s'han acabat per sempre" (the authentic elders of our country, who no longer exist).[15] There is a sense that, in the passing of this minor politician and intellectual, a particular moment in Catalan cultural and social life passed with him.

But not everyone was so admiring of Agulló's character. Josep Pla (1897–1981), the well-known essayist and journalist, was not very fond of our author and spent some time trying to debunk the idea that Agulló had baptized the Catalan coast. Perhaps as someone who later wrote extensively about the coast as well as its food, Pla had complicated feelings toward this literary and political figure.[16] To be fair, Agulló himself recognized that the name belonged to the title of a poem by Gabriel Alomar referring to the coastline of Majorca. But later it came to be generally accepted that it was through the journalist's first use in his column "Per la Costa Brava" in "Al Dia" in 1908 that the term came to be officially used to designate the Catalan coastline. Pla has argued that this was not the case and that it was another person, the owner of the hotel Paradís de Fornells, Bonaventura Sabaté, who used the term for the first time during a dinner attended by Agulló who simply repeated it later in his column.[17] Pla's antipathy is clearly expressed in the following sketch:

> Ferran Agulló, "Pol", era un senyor petit, devastat (per la bona cuina y probablement per les dones), d'un erotisme dissimulat permanent, sempre disposat a fer un qualsevol sacrifici per menjar mitja llagosta a la brasa. Completament escèptic, amb un accentuat aspecte d'estar de tornada de tot, tenia un horror total de la política, i el senyor Cambó li feia una por cerval. Només s'enriolava quan parlava dels escenaris de teatres, de les actrius i dels artistes. Ell llibre de cuina que havia publicat, el considerava molt bo. Havia inventat la truita electoral com a dinar per als interventors de les meses. L'invent havia estat genial, havia evitat moltes tupinades, perquè l'atracció de la truita i les quatre atmelles torrades, el vi, el cafè i la copa, feia que els interventors no abandonessin la mesa.

> *Ferran Agulló, "Pol," was a small man, wrecked (by good food and probably by women too), of a great erotism that was permanently veiled, always ready to make any sacrifice to eat half a grilled lobster. Completely skeptic, with a look of having been through it all, he had a complete aversion to politics, and Mr. Cambó paralyzed him with fear. He only loosened up when talking about theater stages, actresses and artists. The cookbook he published, he thought it was very good. He*

> *invented the electoral omelet as a meal for poll workers. The invention was brilliant because it avoided voter fraud as the appeal of the omelet and a handful of roasted almonds, wine, coffee, and drink, made sure that the poll workers did not abandon their table.*[18]

A rather cynical description of someone so closely involved with the *Lliga*, Agulló's cooking ability didn't seem to have impressed Pla much, which contradicts the way the secretary saw his own culinary capabilities. In an untitled interview from 1928, Agulló adamantly stated, "'De mi, que diguin que faig articles, versos o drames dolents, no m'enfadaré; però si algú prova un arròs o un peix a la marinera o un 'stockfish' amb patates i all-i-oli, cuinat per mi, i no li agrada, que no em mirin més la cara'" (They can say about me that I write bad articles, verses or plays, I won't get upset; but if anyone tastes my rice or my fish with marinera sauce or a stockfish with potatoes and oil and garlic sauce prepared by me and doesn't like it, I would say don't look at me anymore).[19] What is interesting about Pla's sketch is that Agulló is described as someone more interested in the arts (or cooking) than in politics, pointing to the close relationship that existed between Catalan politics and culture at the time.

Landscape and Catalanism through Food

Jaume Subirana has explained well in his *Construir con palabras: escritores, literatura e identidad en Cataluña (1839–2019)* how the rhetorical and symbolic space of literature played an important role in the configuration of Catalan identity.[20] While the cultural imagination enabled by writers and their writing in the language of the region was fundamental to the cultural enterprise undertaken by the *Lliga*, clearly the "nationalitat catalana" (Catalan nationality) needed to encompass more than just words. For the purposes of this essay, I am interested in the party's notion of *catalanitat* as laid out in Prat de la Riba's essay-cum-political manifesto from 1906, *La nationalitat catalana*, and how this identity, expressed in terms of culture, reflects a sense of territory that could also be summoned by its physical landscape and the everyday customs that are determined by its natural characteristics. From this perspective, cooking and eating were not only important but an essential aspect of this identity, shaped by the bounties contained in the area. This interest in connecting territory with national identity resonates with the way the Spanish government, as examined by Eugenia Afinoguénova, used tourism in the early twentieth century as a political tool to "craft, from the center, regional identities that could fit together and form a renewed competitive nation."[21] The program to integrate Spanish territories relied on the daily activities of peripheral rural communities. In a similar way, Catalans appealed to the interior of the region to rediscover and embrace their regional identity.

While the ambition of the young leaders of the party, Francesc Cambó i Batlle, the abovementioned Enric Prat de la Riba i Sarrà, and Lluís Duran i Ventosa, all in their twenties in 1900, was to actively intervene and dominate Spanish politics for the greater good of Spain, it is interesting to examine how they made culture the bedrock of their political program.[22] Prat de la Riba's essay could be interpreted as a call to recognize, value, recover and build on what Catalans have had in their history.[23] The starting point was to acknowledge a moment of deficiency that allowed the impoverishment of the region and its subjugation to Castilians:

> Catalunya pobra, sense comers, sense industrial, Catalunya sense direcció política autònoma, va quedar també sense cultura propia, subjecta a la cultura de la Cort, tributaria de la cultura castellana. [. . .] Pobra, sense acció política, sense cultura propia, sotmesa al govern, a la llengua, a la direcció social d'un altre poble, Catalunya va perdre la noció de la propia personalitat, va devenir *provincia*.
>
> *Poor Catalonia, without commerce, without industry, Catalonia without an autonomous political orientation, was also left without its own culture, subjected to the Court's culture which belonged to Castile [. . .] Poor, without political action, without its own culture, subjugated to the government, to the language, to the social orientation of other people, Catalonia lost its own personality, it became a province.*[24]

A way to counteract this bankrupt state was to vindicate a sentiment for the fatherland, the *patria*, which existed because there was a language, law, art, spirit, character, and thought that belonged to a concrete geographical area.[25] The term *nació* (nation), used interchangeably with *patria* (fatherland), denotes, above all, a feeling, as well as a status that equals them to Castile and Castilians. Becoming "lesser," in this context, means to be considered *provincial*, just another part of an administrative division of Spain's territory. It is important to note the difference between this feeling and contemporary manifestations of the region's desire for independence. However connected they may be, sovereignty from central government was not the goal, as Prat articulated a national feeling for the region. What was of importance was the collective and unnamed feeling, the "sentir inconscient de la massa" (the subconscious feeling of the people) and its source.[26] The author places this feeling at the territorial core of the region, which, in turn, is firmly linked to its local traditions. In Chapter VI, where he articulates the idea of *nationalitat* (nationality) along the lines of a sense of being of and from a place, Prat de la Riba lists territory as one of the elements that contributes to this sentiment. In this writing, land is not a passive element, rather it constantly shapes the people who inhabit it:

> la terra obra sobre'ls homes y'ls pasta a semblança seva; representa una acció contínua exercida per les impresions que entren pels ulls, pels productes que restauren les forces físiques, pels flagells que congria, pels esforços que gasta, per les necessitats que engendra, pel tremp que dóna al cos y al esperit.
>
> *the land works over men and makes them bear its resemblance; it represents a continued form of action that works by the vision that enters their eyes, the products that restore their physical strength, the flagellations it lashes, the efforts it makes, the needs it creates, the firmness it gives to body and spirit.*[27]

Paradoxically, despite this statement, we should remember that the politician privileged language and local laws as the fundamental elements behind the origin and the existence of an *esperit nacional*, a national spirit. Yet his explanation of what makes the Catalan *poble*—people—refers to a spirituality that results from intangible influences—"una mena d'ambient moral, que s'apodera dels homes y'ls penetra y'ls enmotlla" (a form of moral environment that takes over men and penetrates and shapes them—and, what is more, is that this spirituality needs to be physically contained somewhere).[28] As he himself concludes, the national spirit would not exist "si la estructura o la situació del territori no hagués sotmés sos pobladors a les meteixes influencies" (if the structure or the situation of the land would have not subjected its inhabitants to the same influences).[29] I would argue that the material importance of the land and the customs its inhabitants forge can engender a national spirit, which can be extended to the food they consume, as people need to adjust their diets to the physical realities of their surroundings. It is not surprising, from this perspective, to discover in Agulló's cookbook an almost fixation with the landscape of Catalonia. What his recipes collect and remember are not only instructions on how to prepare dishes but a testament to the way people lived in this region through its history.

Advocating for the Costa Brava

That Agulló's name is linked to the concept of Costa Brava is perhaps a fitting legacy for his role in connecting the landscape of the region to its food. The reason his name has not been entirely forgotten is because the controversy surrounding the naming of the coastline.[30] Considering the fame this geographic area has achieved among local and international visitors and its transformation into a gastronomic mecca for food lovers in the latter part of the twentieth century thanks to the reputation of, among others, Ferran Adrià and his now-closed elBulli, it is necessary that we revisit Agulló's writing on food and landscape and discover how it expresses, above all, a sense of loss. In his cookbook, the author longs to recover a form of Catalan cooking based on simplicity. He does so by compiling genuine dishes that he has taken from their original sources, from the places he visited and the people with whom he interacted. As Llorenç Torrado explains in his 1999 edition of the book, Agulló's approach to the topic is intellectual and political, as his intentions are to establish the boundaries of a national cuisine, emphasizing its simplicity and naturalness: "vol configurar una cuina nacional, al costat d'una política nacionalista o d'un art i una llengua nacionals" (he wants to establish a national cuisine, next to a nationalist politics or a national art or language].[31] Similarly, Venetia Johannes observes that Agulló's discussion of food for daily meals and festive occasions "has an 'anthropological' feel to it, of a writer who has researched the facts, and set them down for readers."[32] He was interested in writing them down because these celebrations were no longer being practiced in the city: "Això és la tradició. Si a ciutat no es conserva gaire, regeix molt, encara, en els pobles, viles i pagesies" (That's the tradition. Even if these practices are no longer current in the city, they still remain in villages, towns, and estates).[33] At the same time, the collected recipes, even if aiming for simplicity, don't simply describe known dishes, such as grilled rabbit (*conill a la brasa*), but do so with what Agulló calls "gràcia" (flair). He interprets Catalan simplicity as coming from a basic form of cooking, defined by its environment, sometimes by scarcity or the lack of ingredients or utensils. For example, he explains that the hunter cooks a pheasant buried in soil because he doesn't have a cooking vessel or provides a description for ingredients of a dish that needs to be modified to what is available in the patch of cultivated land. With very few ingredients, without much complexity, and with products that might not be of top quality but seasonal (or preserved), the resulting dishes can achieve refinement with the help of people's imagination and good taste.[34] This culinary knowledge, articulated as a return to the origins of Catalan cooking, is the result of the many travels taken by Agulló, a city dweller, around Girona and the coast between the Mediterranean Sea and the Pyrenes.[35]

It is worth remembering that Agulló's article "Per la Costa Brava" was written almost two decades before his cookbook. The first installment was published on Saturday, September 12, 1908, in the midnight edition of *La Veu de Catalunya*. It was meant to be a response to a column written by Lluís Duran i Ventosa and published in the morning edition of the same paper entitled "Tornem a parlar-ne. Les costes catalanes" (Let's talk about it again. The Catalan Coasts). This first column, written under his pseudonym "Pol," became the first of several installments that allowed Agulló to express his admiration for the landscape but also his early advocacy for tourism. Perhaps what he envisioned was not the mass tourism of the late twentieth century, but the reason behind his desire to colonize and domesticate this area was connected to how he saw this space, as the remnant of a lost past, with its disappeared activities and from which only his picturesque words remain.[36] Agulló offered in his initial article a meditative piece exalting the qualities of the wild coastal landscape and insisted on the unique way in which it needed to be seen: "la nostra s'ha de veure seguint-la a peu, baixant a les cales, vorejant en bot o llagut les roques, ... acariciant-la tota com amb manyagueries d'enamorat que acarona a l'estimada" (ours must be seen by following on foot, going down the creeks, bordering the rocks by fishing boats... caressing it all with the tender gesture of a lover toward his beloved).[37] His desire for visitors to get to know this area meant that he was aware of the lack of infrastructure to support travelers. Agulló became an early proponent of tourism in the area and encouraged local governments to think about building hotels, allowing the arrival of ships, considering the need to organize fishing trips and excursions, maintaining the roads, etc. He tried to convince them that, for each peseta spent, visitors would leave tens or hundreds behind.[38] Because the coast was poor, hurt by phylloxera and the dying fishing industry, he believed that what the region needed was collective action to make the beautiful villages accessible and visible.[39] Agulló also criticized the rich *americanos*, the Catalan emigrants who returned to the coast wealthy after years of working abroad but who remained disconnected from the general needs of their surrounding.[40] He argued that, while outsiders are perceived by many as the enemy—they drive up the price for provisions, demand festivities and diversion, and expect public services that force neighborhood expenditures— given the economic deterioration of the area and its abandonment by younger generations, the locals needed to understand that the salvation of many was "la indústria dels forasters" (the industry of foreigners).[41]

His goal was to make the Costa Brava a desirable destination for travelers, not only from Barcelona, but also from the interior of Spain and abroad. As Pagès Jordà points out, the naming of Costa Brava included the "invocació al turisme" (the invocation to tourism) as a savior for all evils, even if the term "tourism" was yet not used.[42] Mass tourism might not have been what Agulló desired as a transformative force for his beloved landscape, but his conclusion then, following the thinking of the *noucentistas*, was that the Costa Brava needed to change. The coast had everything nature could offer, and while the exaltation of its qualities and propaganda for the region might alter these small villages, it had to be a positive change, as it would be "en benefici llur i honra de Catalunya" (for the benefit and honor of Catalonia).[43]

Joan Nogué and Joan Vicente have discussed the importance of landscapes in the process of forming the Catalan nation in the late nineteenth century and how it became "a fundamental element in the creation process of a national identity."[44] While the initial geographical focus was the mountainous landscape of Catalonia, the concept of landscape evolves to designate a cultural one, "a social product, the cultural projection of a society on a specific space."[45] The significance of geographical territories rose from the assumption that people who live in the same space must share commonalities, and as their landscapes are imbued with values, they intervene in shaping existing imaginaries.[46] Part of the process of consolidating this imaginary and identity took the form of excursions, where Catalans were encouraged to travel to get to know their own territory. As Venetia Johannes writes, *excursionisme* was a way of getting to know Catalonia "through travel, physically experiencing the nation by visiting its different regions."[47] Under *Noucentisme*, the value of nature was integrated into national identity, as adherents saw the Mediterranean as the setting to materialize it, simultaneously exalting the national myths but also wanting to deploy modern equipment and infrastructure.[48] This sentiment is not far from Agulló's own: when writing about the Catalan coast, he praises its qualities while hoping for its modernization. Interestingly, Nogué and Willbrand have concluded that, from the two archetypes of landscape generated by the cultural movements, "the green, moist Catalonia, with the Pyrenean Mountains, driven by *modernisme*, and the Mediterranean Catalonia, classic, maritime, sunny and intensely humanized, generated by *noucentisme*," the one that prevails in today's politics is the mountain landscape.[49] In terms of Catalan gastronomy, however, we could argue that it is the Mediterranean that is favored as a landscape, not only because of its contemporary culinary prestige but also because the region connects with the cultures of other nation-states as equals despite its own lack of sovereignty. In the case of Agulló's cookbook, his collection of recipes ties both landscapes through eating practices, creating a culinary imaginary for the entire region. More significantly, his recipes share an intimate connection with Catalonia's landscape because they were collected through Agulló's many excursions, ones that he himself organized or participated in, pointing out his own culinary interventions during these outings. As Venetia Congdon documents, even today "Catalans use specific food maps to travel and eat on their way through Catalonia."[50]

Authentic Cooking and Terroir

Considering the Costa Brava's transformation into a destination for tourism and gastronomic adventures (using the city of Barcelona as a gateway to this world), it is surprising to detect the nostalgia and fear or loss that underpins the texts written by Agulló—especially his cookbook, which was presented as an effort to preserve what he understood to be a Catalan cuisine on the verge of disappearance, along with the small villages in rural Catalonia. His quest for culinary preservation went beyond this published book, as he talked, perhaps in jest, about other (unfinished) culinary projects, such as the tracing of the history of Catalan cuisine. He also wanted to demonstrate how French cuisine originated in Catalonia, as its best dishes come from the area of Languedoc and its bests chefs from Provence.[51] Tracing the history of Catalan cuisine was important to establish its existence, and his desire to link it to a more prestigious culinary tradition aided the effort of preserving and continuing this regional cuisine. Contrary to the present reputation of Catalan gastronomy, Agulló's own perception of this cuisine was not as strong as his writing seems to suggest. If we look closely, it is telling how he focuses on its assimilation of other cuisines or how it has traveled to other geographic points to become part of other culinary traditions:

> La cuina catalana representada per alguns dels seus plats, ha sortit de les fronteres, conquerint Amèrica del Sud i del Nord, Austràlia, Itàlia i bona part de les regions ibèriques. Han estat instrument d'expansió, amb la bondat dels plats, els cuiners catalans dels vaixells de vela, que en el decaïment de la marina catalana, s'instal·laren en les cinc parts del món.
>
> *Catalan cuisine, represented by some of its dishes, has traveled beyond its borders, conquered South and North America, Australia, Italy and a good portion of Iberian regions. The virtues of these dishes served as tools of expansion for Catalan chefs on board sailing ships as they established themselves all over the world as the Catalan merchant shipping deteriorated.*[52]

Agulló's underlying rhetoric, again, is about decay and loss, a moment of crisis that echoes Prat de la Riba's text. And while renewal and glory can be found through its language and literature, what is clear is that the path for its future is through its material existence, that is, its territory and landscape. Culinary practices seem to fit the role well, as cooking and eating can work as cultural projects dedicated to specific spaces. After all, what makes Catalan cuisine national is the use of local ingredients rather than the type of dishes that exists in its repertoire ("elements propis, tant en els aliments com en els condiments" [their own ingredients, in products as well as in condiments]), which, again, expresses above all a geographical link.[53]

The connection between landscape and food brings us to concepts associated with tradition, heritage, and authenticity, and even more so with the idea of *terroir*. Let's remember that Agulló's intention was preservation, as the recipes, meticulously described, were classic ones that were known to everyone and did not need to be taught. What is valuable about these recipes is their provenance, as Agulló made clear that he got them directly from their source, from the farmer to the fisherman throughout the Empordà region.[54] The effort to safeguard culinary practices can be linked to our current understanding of concepts like "heritage" or "authenticity," which, as Gfeller explains, are cultural and social practices "through which objects, places, or practices rooted in the past are endowed with meaning."[55] From this perspective, cooking and eating acquire importance and purpose, as they become vehicles to connect with the past. In Agulló's case, his cookbook reveals an effort to connect Catalan identity with its geographic territory. His cookbook, rather than evidence for the existence of a Catalan cuisine, is relevant as a document of the political context that produced it, linking cooking practices and culinary culture to the idea of territoriality, expressing both a longing for the past and a desire for the future.

Amy Trubek, discussing taste and place, writes about the importance of *terroir*, especially as it can be seen as a reaction to our increasingly global food system.[56] From this perspective, *terroir* can be linked to a desire to pay attention to and value authenticity and heritage as safeguard measures from the processes of modernization.[57] While Agulló does not explicitly link place with taste, his emphasis on the origin of the recipes captures his preoccupation with the future of the region. Even if modernization was not to be rejected, as a *noucentista*, he expressed anguish at the possibility of losing certain ways of life. As Bob Davidson examines in his essay about *terroir* and winemaking in Catalonia, the later articulation between Catalan national identity and its landscape is not unexpected.[58] Today, the cookbook, read alongside the author's other texts on the Costa Brava, reveals the way territoriality worked as a founding principle of Catalan identity and how this thinking may have (unintentionally?) paved a way for developing its geography. The writer's recipe collection also reveals that the haute cuisine prestige that Catalan gastronomy enjoys in the present is a far cry from the way it was once understood as simple and easy cooking, connected to small villages and eating venues for the working class or home cooking, and, paradoxically, culinarily distant from the celebratory banquets organized to pay homage to and celebrate the region's language and literary tradition.[59]

Cookbooks, Culinary Taste, and Social Change

Catalonia as a region boasts an impressive number of cookbooks dedicated to its culinary tradition. Written by locals and foreigners, they tend to emphasize its unique particularities. We know that cookbooks play a role in nation-building narratives; they are not just a compilation or a collection of recipes. As Abigal Dennis argues, cookbooks can serve a multitude of functions, "they can be didactic, informative, boasting, instructional, patriotic/propagandist; they can act as an ideological advertisement, an economic guide, or an aid to social mobility."[60] María Paz Moreno and Lara Anderson have highlighted, for instance, how they can be valuable historical and cultural documents. Moreno's *De la página al plato* (2012) demonstrates the intersection between cookbooks, gender, literature and writing, while Anderson's *Cooking Up a Nation* (2013) considers the link between the idea of a nation, its discourses, and foodwriting in the Iberian Peninsula.[61]

More recently, Eric Storm has written about the relationship between national identity and the domestic sphere in Spain.[62] Drawing on research on French cooking and how the practices of the middle classes became identified as national cuisine, he examined how conscious nation-building played a role in the rise of national cuisines in Spain.[63] While many Spanish culinary authors propagated a model of cosmopolitan cuisine well into the twentieth century, Storm points out how, in the late nineteenth century, the writer Mariano Pardo de Figueroa (who published under the pseudonym of Doctor Thebussen), was worried about the lack of gastronomic unity in Spain and "suggested that a repository should be compiled of the 'most illustrious Spanish dishes.'"[64] For Storm, the 1913 cookbook published by Emilia Pardo Bazán was the first inventory of Spanish recipes, and it shows how the writer, "as a convinced nationalist . . . argued that Spanish cuisine did already exist and that she just wanted to salvage the old recipes that were about to disappear," and later, even more radicalized, "argued that Spanish cuisine should recover its positions, not only among the poor . . . but also among the middle and upper classes."[65]

When Agulló published his cookbook about fifteen years after Pardo Bazán's, Catalonia already had a few well-known cookbooks. *La cuynera catalana*, for instance, published in 1835, was linked to the emerging cultural movement of the *Renaixença* and noteworthy for its use of Catalan and clearly stated didactic purpose. Pep Vila mentions that, between 1907 and the start of the Spanish Civil

War in 1936, in addition to Agulló's cook, there were a good number of published compilations of Catalan recipes, such as *La cuyna catalana* (1907) by Josep Cunill del Bosch (pseudonym of Francesc Puig i Alfonso), *L'art de ben menjar* (1923) by Marta Sàlvia (pseudonym of Adrianna Aldavert i Sara Aldavert), *La Teca: la veritable cuina casolana de Catalunya* (1924) by Ignasi Domènech i Puigcercós, and, from Menorca, *De re cibaria* (1923) by Pere Ballester, a book much esteemed by Josep Pla.[66] For Vila, these books, which incorporate international dishes, represented a moment that revolutionized the roots of Catalan cooking knowledge. While they all share a didactic intention, they don't communicate the sense of loss or nostalgia as is present in Agulló's work. While some of these books have the term "Catalan" in their title, the cookbooks offer a mix of recipes. For example, in Domènech's books, one can find the chef's own creations and recipes for dishes that could be considered *haute cuisine*. As Torrado explains, the cooking style for these recipes was rather Baroque, edited by a trained chef or adapted to the taste of the more cosmopolitan dwellers of Barcelona: dishes with sauces and condiments.[67] In turn, Agulló's cookbook offered only a small selection of what he called "plats universalitzats de vàries cuines" (universalized dishes from various cuisines), mainly focused on local ingredients and, above all, simplicity.[68] Perhaps, from this perspective, his intentions for the book were closer to those of Pardo Bazán when she compiled recipes for her Spanish cookbook.

A final piece of information about Agulló's cookbook, not often mentioned, is that it was dedicated to the founder of the *Institut i Biblioteca de la Dona* in Barcelona, Francesca Bonnemaison i Farriols (1872–1949). A private institution dedicated to the education and promotion of women that functioned from 1909 to 1937, the *Institut* offered vocational training to thousands of women in Barcelona, a city that had become home to a new mobilizing urban working class.[69] The institute also offered more leisurely, organized cooking lessons for middle- and upper-class women. The fact that Agulló seemed to recognize the importance of the *Institut* suggests that he also understood the crucial role that women from the middle and working classes played in preserving the cooking practices that they had to be taught to value. However, Agulló's desire to preserve Catalan cooking through a conservative and gendered understanding of foodwork contradicted the very culinary taste of its citizens. In Barcelona and beyond, women were more inclined and exposed to cosmopolitan tastes, the same way Storm documented it in his study about the relationship between cookbooks and nationalism in Spain.[70] For example, in their study of a private recipe collection of a Catalan bourgeois family in Girona dated around the time of Agulló's publication, Rosa Maria Gil Tort and Pep Vila observe that not many dishes could be recognized as specifically "Catalan."[71]

Given the scientific approach to the teaching of cooking that seems to have characterized the courses offered at the *Institut*, it might be surprising to read Agulló's dedication of his book to Bonnemaison. But she was a close ally to the *Lliga*: she was married to Narcís Verdaguer Callís (1863–1918), a Catalanist lawyer and politician close to the party, a relative of the famed poet of the *Renaixença*, Jacint Verdaguer. After the death of her husband, she became an even closer collaborator, eventually overseeing the feminine section of the *Lliga* during the Spanish Second Republic. Her work in the *Institut* clearly followed the modernizing tenets of *Noucentisme* but also taught housewives how to maintain a Catalan cultural doctrine. Agulló explains how he wrote his book for housewives ("mestresses de casa") because he wanted to honor and to recover the simplicity of Catalan cooking and couldn't think of a better candidate than Bonnemaison to open its pages.[72] He hoped that her name, one with ancestral and cultural signification, would shelter and protect his book. His dedication highlights the two different realities that coexist in the teaching of the *Institut*: a vocational program geared toward working-class women who made cooking a way of earning their keep in their households or elsewhere, and another dedicated to middle- and upper-class housewives and single, young women who, while they might not have been cooking themselves, were expected to have culinary knowledge as part of their traditional female education. As Gil Tort and Vila write, education for these women was mainly based on three pillars: abnegation, religious devotion, and adherence to strict social customs.[73] They represented the traditional values that Agulló shared as member of the conservative *Lliga Regionalista*. He probably thought of these housewives as the ideal guardians for his traditional recipes, but, unfortunately, these were not the people who would have been interested in them. Torrado points out that these women, belonging to the upper and middle classes of Barcelona's bourgeoisie, were probably not attracted to Agulló's recipes. They already ate in a simple manner every day, and when it was time to prepare a meal for guests or for a special occasion, they wouldn't find much use for Agulló's recipes.[74] A quick look at the recipes taught at the *Institut* points to a more sophisticated palate and a preference for dishes by other cuisines. Women were taught to prepare or to taste dishes such as "bavaresa Bristol, consomé Celestina, puré Longchamps, maionesa de salmó a la russa, rosbif a l'inglesa, etc." (Bristol cream, Celestina consommé, Longchamps puree, Russian salmon mayonnaise, English roastbeef, etc.), and only in rare occasions would a local or regional dish appear among the recipes.[75]

In addition to its cosmopolitanism, the work in the *Institut* also reflects the ongoing social changes of its time. Rebecca Ingram has studied the *Institut*'s archives to highlight how its program of educating women contributed to the process of modernizing the city and how its popular cooking classes helped link an activity connected to women and domesticity to issues of broader social relevance.[76] Learning to cook, for instance, became a pathway for illiterate women to learn how to read and write.[77] In 1921, the Italian chef Josep Rondissoni started teaching at the *Institut*, and his cooking lessons were very popular among the working- and middle-class women who attended the courses. A veritable star chef of his time, even though not much was known about his origin except that he trained with the French chef August Escoffier (1846–1935), Rondissoni became well known through his culinary activities and publications, including the magazine *Ménage* (and, much later, his cookbook *Culinaria*, published after the war in 1945). During his tenure, he offered different types of classes, one on popular cuisine (the first one to be offered consisted of daily lessons from Monday to Saturday, when a dish per class would be prepared), another on practical cookery (offered once a week and, depending on the difficulty of the recipe, could last up to three hours), and, finally, a session on home cooking (also once week, usually on Sunday afternoons).[78] It is noteworthy that Rondissoni's classes were not only geared toward how to prepare a dish or follow a recipe but also how to develop a more complete culinary knowledge, including nutrition, putting together meal plans that paid attention to dietary as well as economic needs, shopping in markets, visiting food factories, etc.[79] While, at first sight the Rondissoni's teaching and Agulló's desire for Catalan cooking might appear to be in conflict, perhaps they should be examined as contributing to the awareness about cooking and eating practices. If culinary knowledge and training were important for working-class woman who needed them to find employment, so were the meals that comprised the daily menus of most of the Catalan families. The qualities of the latter may be later idealized, yet they still provide insight about the everyday experience in the region.[80]

The fact that Agulló's cookbook is today considered a classic in Catalan gastronomy tells a long story of how popular culture and knowledge is romanticized and preserved. A quest for the authentic, it reminds us of how folklore works as an escape from modernity and as "fundamentally an emotional and moral quest."[81] It also tells the story of how his idealized view of the past generated feelings of national identity that could then be used to justify its preservation. In the case of Agulló's cookbook, couched in the cultural movement of the *noucentistas*, it reflected social practices that pulled in opposite directions: while forward-looking and embracing change, it expresses a longing for a traditional and simple form of existence. The contradiction is present in his other texts: aware of the need to transform the interior and coastline of the region of Catalonia to assure its economic survival, the changes he supports would probably only manage to preserve an idealized version of this tradition.

In the end, Agulló's writing about Catalan foodways can be read in two ways: as establishing a link between territory and culinary tradition and as an effort to preserve and remember a way of life. While it is not surprising that Agulló's statement about Catalan cuisine continues to gather attention because of its explicit articulation of a distinct Catalan entity that reflects the current political interests of the region, his work is not about exalting the region but rather preserving it from an impending loss. The statement in his prologue about the undidactic nature of the book reveals its real purpose: to demonstrate the existence of a Catalan cuisine through a compilation of recipes directed to someone who already knows how to cook. A form of witnessing a way of life, it also recognizes the social changes that Catalan society was experiencing during those years. The final words of the introduction are revealing from this perspective, as they acknowledge that life had become costly, and everyone, from working to middle classes, needed to be careful with household expenditures. The return to simple cooking is a response to financial necessity as it is to the value of the region's tradition. Ironically, almost a century later, Agulló's call to preserve simple Catalan cooking has been hailed as an example of the region's authentic cuisine and considered to have played a key role in the creation and preservation of a national repertoire of culinary dishes.

NOTES

1. Arjun Appadurai, "How to Make a National Cuisine: Cookbooks in Contemporary India," *Comparative Studies in Society and History* 30, no. 1 (January 1988): 3.
2. Agulló, qtd. in Manuel Vázquez Montalbán, *L'art del menjar a Catalunya. El llibre roig de la identitat gastronómica catalana* (Barcelona: Salsa Books, 2004), 18. Translations from the Catalan in the essay, unless otherwise noted, are mine.
3. Several recent publications have examined the role food has played in Catalan identity politics. See: Montserrat Roser i Puig, "What's Cooking in Catalonia?" in *A Companion to Catalan Culture*, ed. Dominic Keown (Suffolk, UK: Tamesis, 2011), 229–52; Leigh K. Mercer and H. Rosi Song, "Catalanidad in the Kitchen: Tourism, Gastronomy and Identity in Modern and Contemporary Barcelona," *Bulletin of Spanish Studies* 97, no. 4 (2020): 659–80; and Venetia Johannes, *Nourishing the Nation: Food as National Identity in Catalonia* (New York: Berghahn, 2020). These works document instances in which food writing and culinary practices have been used to bolster Catalan nationalism.
4. Charles E. Enrlich, "The Lliga Regionalista and the Catalan Industrial Bourgeoisie," *Journal of Contemporary History* 33, no. 3 (July 1998): 400.
5. Antoni Segura i Mas and Elisenda Barbé i Pou, "Catalonia: From Industrialization to the Present Day," in *A Companion to Catalan Culture*, ed. Dominic Keown (Suffolk, UK: Tamesis, 2011), 76.

6. Joan Ramon Resina, "*Noucentisme*," in *The Cambridge History of Spanish Literature*, ed. David T. Gies (Cambridge, UK: Cambridge University Press, 2004), 532–33.
7. John Etherington, "Nationalism, Nation and Territoy: Jacint Verdaguer and the Catalan *Renaixença*," *Ethnic and Racial Studies* 33, no. 10 (2010): 1814. Etherington studies the role played by the poet Jacint Verdaguer (1845–1902), considered by many the most representative poet of the *Renaixença*, in constructing a geographical narrative that links the idea of nation and territory. He argues that his epic *Canigó*, a poem about a mountain located in the Pyrenees, represents "the greatest contribution to the process of the territorial construction of national identity" (1823).
8. Resina, "*Noucentisme*," 534.
9. For a comprehensive study of the role played by this publication in Catalan politics, see Josep M. Figueres, *La Veu de Catalunya (1899–1937)* (Barcelona: Editorial Base, 2014). While recovering the political significance or the role played by Agulló might be of interest to historians or political scientists, for the purpose of this essay he will be considered a minor figure who is best remembered for authoring a cookbook that remains current today.
10. Ibid., 404.
11. Ibid., 404–5.
12. The *Jocs Florals*, medieval poetry competitions, were revived during the *Renaixença* in 1859. The winner in three categories of competition was declared *Mestre en Gai Saber*. For a discussion of the significance of the competition see Josep M. Domingo, "The *Jocs Florals* in Contemporary Catalan Literature," *Catalan Historical Review* 6 (2013): 73–83.
13. There are many newspaper articles that mention or refer to Agulló as the person who first called the Catalan coastline the Costa Brava. A useful and more recent overview of the story behind the name and its aftermath is: Vicenç Pagès Jordà, "Ferran Agulló, Inventor de La Costa Brava," *Revista de Girona*, no. 287 (2015): 66–68. In 2014, a selection of Agulló's essays on this geographic area as well as other topics was published in an edited collection by Pep Vila entitled *Marines*, including the original newspaper column. Ferran Agulló, "Per la Costa Brava," *Marines. El text fundacional de la Costa Brava*, ed. Pep Vila (Girona, Spain: Curbet Edicions, 2014), 109–20.
14. Qtd. in Ferran Agulló, *Llibre de la cuina catalana*, ed. Llorenç Torrado, 9th ed. (Barcelona: Editorial Alta Fulla, 1999), xiii–xiv.
15. Qtd. in Agulló, *Llibre*, xvi.
16. Josep Pla, whose writing on food was later published in the collection of essays entitled *El que hem menjat* (1972) [What We Have Eaten], is another author who linked eating with the past. His reflective essays on the dishes he used to eat as a child or the cooking and eating practices of the coastal region of Catalonia are very different from Agulló's collection of recipes but serve as an interesting point of comparison between how Catalan culinary practices are narrated or collected and how both share a sense of loss when it comes to food practices. Josep Pla, *El que hem menjat*, vol. 22, *Obra completa* (Barcelona: Destino, 1980).

17. Pagès Jordà, "Ferran Agulló," 67.
18. Qtd. in Agulló, *Marines*, 15.
19. Qtd. in Agulló, *Marines*, 169.
20. Jaume Subirana, *Construir con palabras: escritores, literatura e identidad en Cataluña (1859–2019)* (Madrid: Cátedra, 2018).
21. Eugenia Afinoguénova, "An Organic Nation: State-Run Tourism, Regionalism and Food in Spain, 1905–1931," *The Journal of Modern History* 86, no. 4 (December 2014): 744.
22. Enrlich, "The Lliga Regionalista," 401.
23. The obsession with the past in Catalonia during this time has to do with the glory of its medieval period and the Catalan-Aragonese crown. In contrast, historian Josep M. Figueres explains that the current obsession with the past in Catalonia has to do with the year 1714, the loss suffered during the War of Spanish Succession. See also Víctor Farradellas, "La Mancomunitat no hauria pogut existir sense 'La Veu de Catalunya,'" *Sàpiens*, no. 140 (March 2014).
24. Enric Prat de la Riba, *La nacionalitat catalana* (Barcelona: Les Ales Esteses, 1930), 12–13.
25. Ibid., 45.
26. Ibid., 14.
27. Ibid., 81.
28. Ibid., 84.
29. Ibid., 85.
30. Pagès Jordà, "Ferran Agulló," 67.
31. Torrado, in Agulló, *Llibre*, viii.
32. Johannes, *Nourishing*, 53.
33. Agulló, *Llibre*, 21. Johannes talks about the idealization of the rural as a "common feature of nationalist movements" (*Nourishing*, 53).
34. Torrado, in Agulló, *Llibre*, ix.
35. Ibid., x.
36. Pagès Jordà, "Ferran Agulló," 67.
37. Agulló, *Marines*, 113.
38. Ibid., 114.
39. Ibid., 116–17.
40. Ibid., 118.
41. Ibid., 119.
42. Pagès Jordà, "Ferran Agulló," 67.
43. Agulló, *Marines*, 114. In her study about state run tourism, regionalism, and food in Spain, Afinoguénova writes about the fate of these coasts under the dictatorship of Francisco Franco, when tourism was mobilized to counter peripheral nationalisms in the 1960s. The Registry of National Geo-Touristic Destination, created in 1964 by the Ministry of Information and Tourism under Manuel Fraga Iribarne, "launched the process of renaming and reconfiguring large part of Spanish territory by 'coasts': Costa Brava, Costa del Sol, Cosa de la Luz and so on. [. . .] The era of coastal tourism transformed Spain into a 'paella nation' in the eyes of foreigners." Afinoguénova, "An Organic Nation," 779.

44. Joan Nogué and Joan Vicente, "Landscape and National Identity in Catalonia," *Political Geography*, no. 23 (2004): 113. Nogué and Vicente discuss the importance of the mountainous landscape in the formative process of the Catalan nation and its link to the cultural discourses of the late nineteenth century. They argue that, while the interpretation and use of landscape can be connected to the romantic *Modernisme*, the transformation of the territory can be linked to the more pragmatic *Noucentisme* (113).
45. Ibid., 116.
46. Ibid., 116; Joan Nogué and Stephanie M. Wilbrand, "Landscape Identities in Catalonia," *Landscape Research* 32, no. 3 (2018): 443.
47. Venetia Johannes, "Catalan Culinary Nationalism: A Contemporary Case Study," in *The Emergence of National Food: The Dynamics of Food and Nationalism*, eds. Atsuko Ichijo, Venetia Johannes, and Ronald Ranta (London: Bloomsbury Publishing, 2019), 92.
48. Nogué and Vicente, "Landscape and National Identity," 124–25.
49. Nogué and Wilbrand, "Landscape Identities," 447.
50. Venetia Congdon, "Regionalists and *Excursionistes*. Catalan 'Regions' and National Identity," in *Reanimating Regions: Culture, Politics and Performance*, eds. James Riding and Martin Jones (Abingdon, UK: Routledge, 2017), 80.
51. Agulló, *Marines*, 170–71.
52. Agulló, *Llibre*, 11–12.
53. Ibid., 11.
54. Torrado, in Agulló, *Llibre*, x.
55. Aurélie Élisa Gfeller, "The Authenticity of Heritage: Global Norm-Making at the Crossroads of Cultures," *American Historical Review* 122, no. 3 (June 2017): 762.
56. Amy B. Trubek, *The Taste of Place: A Cultural Journey into Terroir* (Berkeley: University of California Press, 2008), 12.
57. Valdimar Tr. Hafstein, "Intangible Heritage as a Festival; or, Folklorization Revisited," *Journal of American Folkore* 131, no. 520 (2018): 128.
58. Bob Davidson, "Terroir and Catalonia," *Journal of Catalan Studies* 10 (2007): 40.
59. Jaume Fàbrega discusses the difference in the eating habits of the working class and the Catalan bourgeoisie. See Jaume Fàbrega, *El gust d'un poble. Els plats més famosos de la cuina catalana* (Valls, Spain: Cossetània Edicions, 2002); and *La cuina modernista. Obrers, menestrals, burgesos i indians* (Barcelona: Viena Edicions, 2015).
60. Abigail Dennis, "From Apicius to Gastroporn: Form, Function, and Ideology in the History of Cookery Books," *Studies in Popular Culture* 31, no. 1 (Fall 2008): 1.
61. María Paz Moreno, *De la página al plato: El libro de cocina en España* (Gijón, Spain: Ediciones Trea, S. L., 2011); Lara Anderson, *Cooking up the Nation: Spanish Culinary Texts and Culinary Nationalization in the Late Nineteenth and Early Twentieth Century* (Woodbridge, UK: Tamesis, 2013).
62. Building on Michael Billig's work on "banal nationalism," Storm examines how national identities are internalized in all sorts of spaces, objects, or daily practices and, perhaps, more importantly for this essay, how this identity formation can manifest at the level of stateless-nations, regions, or cities. Eric Storm, "When Did Nationalism Become Banal? The Nationalization of the Domestic Sphere in Spain," *European History Quarterly* 50, no. 2 (2020): 205–7.

63. Ibid., 211.
64. Ibid., 212.
65. Ibid., 212–13.
66. Rosa Maria Gil Tort and Pep Vila, "Del plat a la pàgina escrita. Els receptaris i les notes de cuina, rebosteria, conserves i adrogueria de la família Masó-Aragó de Girona," *Annals de l'Institut d'Estudis Gironins* LIX (2018): 507.
67. Torrado, in Agulló, *Llibre*, viii.
68. Torrado, in Agulló, *Llibre*, xxiii.
69. Gil Tort and Vila, "Del plat," 506.
70. Storm, "When Did Nationalism Become Banal?" 211.
71. Gil Tort and Vila, "Del plat." The carefully annotated recipes from the 1920s belonged to Maria de la Bonanova Masó Valentí. They are mostly simple dishes for everyday consumption that reflect seasonal ingredients in the form of soups, rice and pasta dishes, veal, and salt cod dishes, which can be described as traditional but not specifically Catalan. Alongside these dishes, there are those with a more international flair, such as galantine, English-style beef, English-style tuna, potato pudding, German-style meatballs, etc. (509). The authors observe how women like the owner of this collection, educated under strict traditional tenets centered in religion and service, found an outlet in the space of the kitchen and its administration, a small space for their own taste and creativity (503). It would not be hard to imagine that she knew of or even attended some of the *Institut*'s events.
72. Agulló, *Llibre*, 9.
73. Gil Tort and Vila, "Del plat," 503.
74. Torrado, in Agulló, *Llibre*, vvii.
75. Ibid., vii.
76. Ingram examines the fascinating story of the *Institut* and the education program for working-class women that intersected with the process of modernization of the city, as well as its roots in progressive feminist values. I thank the author for sharing a draft of her chapter on the *Institut* before the publication of the book. Rebecca Ingram, *Women's Work: How Culinary Cultures Shaped Modern Spain* (Nashville, TN: Vanderbilt University Press, 2022).
77. Gil Tort and Vila, "Del plat," 506.
78. Manel Guirado, *El llegat de Rondissoni. Història i receptes del xef més influent de la Catalunya del segle xx* (Barcelona: Ara Llibres, 2017), 15.
79. Ibid., 15–16.
80. Perhaps a future work could take a closer look at the differences between Agulló's collected recipes and those taught by Rondissoni to better examine the different versions of Catalan cuisine that existed during this period in the city and in the rest of Catalonia.
81. Regina Bendix, *In Search of Authenticity: The Formation of Folklore Studies* (Madison: University of Wisconsin Press, 1997), 7.

WORKS CITED

Afinoguénova, Eugenia. "An Organic Nation: State-Run Tourism, Regionalism and Food in Spain, 1905–1931." *The Journal of Modern History* 86, no. 4 (December 2014): 743–79.

Agulló, Ferran. *Llibre de la cuina catalana*. Edited by Llorenç Torrado. 9th edition. Barcelona: Editorial Alta Fulla, 1999.

———. *Marines. El text fundacional de la Costa Brava*. Edited by Pep Vila. Girona, Spain: Curbet Edicions, 2014.

Anderson, Lara. *Cooking up the Nation: Spanish Culinary Texts and Culinary Nationalization in the Late Nineteenth and Early Twentieth Century*. Woodbridge, UK: Tamesis, 2013.

Appadurai, Arjun. "How to Make a National Cuisine: Cookbooks in Contemporary India." *Comparative Studies in Society and History* 30, no. 1 (January 1988): 3–24.

Bendix, Regina. *In Search of Authenticity: The Formation of Folklore Studies*. Madison: The University of Wisconsin Press, 1997.

Congdon, Venetia. See Johannes (Congdon), Venetia.

Davidson, Bob. "Terroir and Catalonia." *Journal of Catalan Studies* 10 (2007): 39–53.

Dennis, Abigail. "From Apicius to Gastroporn: Form, Function, and Ideology in the History of Cookery Books." *Studies in Popular Culture* 31, no. 1 (Fall 2008): 1–17.

Domingo, Josep M. "The *Jocs Florals* in Contemporary Catalan Literature." *Catalan Historical Review* 6 (2013): 73–83.

Enrlich, Charles E. "The Lliga Regionalista and the Catalan Industrial Bourgeoisie." *Journal of Contemporary History* 33, no. 3 (July 1998): 299–417.

Etherington, John. "Nationalism, Nation and Territory: Jacint Verdaguer and the Catalan Renaixença." *Ethnic and Racial Studies* 33, no. 10 (2010): 1814–32.

Fábrega, Jaume. *La cuina modernista. Obrers, menestrals, burgesos i indians*. Barcelona: Viena Edicions, 2015.

———. *El gust d'un poble. Els plats més famosos de la cuina catalana*. Valls, Spain: Cossetània Edicions, 2002.

Farradellas, Víctor. "La Mancomunitat no hauria pogut existir sense 'La Veu de Catalunya.'" *Sàpiens*, no. 140 (March 2014).

Figueres, Josep M. *La Veu de Catalunya (1899–1937)*. Barcelona: Editorial Base, 2014.

Gfeller, Aurélie Élisa. "The Authenticity of Heritage: Global Norm-Making at the Crossroads of Cultures." *American Historical Review* 122, no. 3 (June 2017): 758–91.

Gil Tort, Rosa Maria, and Pep Vila. "Del plat a la pàgina escrita. Els receptaris i les notes de cuina, rebosteria, conserves i adrogueria de la família Masó-Aragó de Girona." *Annals de l'Institut d'Estudis Gironins* LIX (2018): 493–568.

Guirado, Manel. *El llegat de Rondissoni. Història i receptes del xef més influent de la Catalunya del segle xx*. Barcelona: Ara Llibres, 2017.

Hafstein, Valdimar Tr. "Intangible Heritage as a Festival; or, Folklorization Revisited." *Journal of American Folkore* 131, no. 520 (2018): 127–49.

Ingram, Rebecca. *Women's Work: How Culinary Cultures Shaped Modern Spain*. Nashville, TN: Vanderbilt University Press, 2022.

Johannes (Congdon), Venetia. "Catalan Culinary Nationalism: A Contemporary Case Study." In *The Emergence of National Food: The Dynamics of Food and Nationalism*, edited by Atsuko Ichijo, Venetia Johannes, and Ronald Ranta, 85–95. London: Bloomsbury Publishing, 2019.

———. *Nourishing the Nation: Food as National Identity in Catalonia*. New York: Berghahn, 2020.

———. "Regionalists and *Excursionistes*. Catalan 'Regions' and National Identity." In *Reanimating Regions: Culture, Politics and Performance*, edited by James Riding and Martin Jones, 79–94. Abingdon, UK: Routledge, 2017.

Mercer, Leigh K., and H. Rosi Song. "Catalanidad in the Kitchen: Tourism, Gastronomy and Identity in Modern and Contemporary Barcelona." *Bulletin of Spanish Studies* 97, no. 4 (2020): 659–80.

Moreno, María Paz. *De la página al plato: El libro de cocina en España*. Gijón, Spain: Ediciones Trea, S. L., 2011.

Nogué, Joan, and Joan Vicente. "Landscape and National Identity in Catalonia." *Political Geography*, no. 23 (2004): 113–32.

Nogué, Joan, and Stephanie M. Wilbrand. "Landscape Identities in Catalonia." *Landscape Research* 32, no. 3 (2018): 443–54.

Pagès Jordà, Vicenç. "Ferran Agulló, Inventor de La Costa Brava." *Revista de Girona*, no. 287 (2015): 66–68.

Pla, Josep. *El que hem menjat*. Volume 22 of *Obra completa*. Barcelona: Destino, 1980.

Prat de la Riba, Enric. *La nacionalitat catalana*. Barcelona: Les Ales Esteses, 1930.

Resina, Joan Ramon. "Noucentisme." In *The Cambridge History of Spanish Literature*, edited by David T. Gies, 532–37. Cambridge, UK: Cambridge University Press, 2004.

Roser i Puig, Montserrat. "What's Cooking in Catalonia?" In *A Companion to Catalan Culture*, edited by Dominic Keown, 229–52. Suffolk, UK: Tamesis, 2011.

Segura i Mas, Antoni and Elisenda Barbé i Pou. "Catalonia: From Industrialization to the Present Day." In *A Companion to Catalan Culture*, edited by Dominic Keown, 71–96. Suffolk, UK: Tamesis, 2011.

Storm, Eric. "When Did Nationalism Become Banal? The Nationalization of the Domestic Sphere in Spain." *European History Quarterly* 50, no. 2 (2020): 204–25.

Subirana, Jaume. *Construir con palabras: escritores, literatura e identidad en Cataluña (1859–2019)*. Madrid: Cátedra, 2018.

Trubek, Amy B. *The Taste of Place: A Cultural Journey into Terroir*. Berkeley: University of California Press, 2008.

Vázquez Montalbán, Manuel. *L'art del menjar a Catalunya. El llibre roig de la identitat gastronómica catalana*. Barcelona: Salsa Books, 2004.

◆ CHAPTER 3

Francoist Food Culture in Post-Authoritarian Spain

Culinary Maps, Centralism, and Food Memories

Lara Anderson

Of interest to this chapter is how aspects of Francoist food culture continue to act as points of reference for many present-day Spaniards. From neo-Francoist restaurants to the royal family and television shows promoting the idea of a unified Spanish culinary nationalism, remnants of food discourse from those years still have an impact on present-day subjectivities and food culture. The restaurants paying homage to Francoism and fascism make clear that Franco's legacy lives on for many and that, although nominally having ended in 1975, the repressive climate of authoritarian rule has persisted in Spain since the transition to democracy. Tellingly, these food memories speak to a public debate that still rages over the past and the role of statues, street names, and *La Fundación Francisco Franco* (The Francisco Franco Foundation) in preserving or promoting fascism. Equally instructive is the continued relevance of the Francoist notion of a unified Spanish gastronomy, at a time when regional food cultures couldn't be stronger. In television shows and royal banquets, culinary maps and food discourse are used to reinforce the notion of regional cuisines or regions as smaller parts of the much greater, incomparable whole that is Spanish cuisine or Spanish national identity. Importantly, these visual and discursive representations of food instruct us not just in the right way to eat or think about food, but also how to think about our identity.

The fact that so much of the Franco's "talk of food" remains influential for many Spaniards speaks to the continued legacy of the Franco regime.[1] The emergence of neo-Francoism—which includes the widespread circulation and popularity of symbols and images of Franco—is a reminder that a large percentage of the mainstream right is pro-Franco. The polemic over neo-Franco culture and food culture speaks to how divided Spain is when it comes to memories of the Dictatorship. For some Spaniards, the regime would have been experienced as fascist only in the early years, but for many others, the experience of repression and violence would have been a constant even during the transition to democracy.[2]

Theoretical Underpinnings: Food and Power

As I have shown in relation to the first two decades of the Franco regime, the analysis of food and food discourse is important for what it tells us about subjectivity and the material everyday conditions of life under dictatorship.[3] In previous research, I have examined instruction and advice about food issued by political leaders, government officials, teachers, food writers, and medical professionals. Harnessing the political potential of food or food discourse is of particular importance at times of social, political, and economic change.[4] During the Franco regime, food discourse was an integral part of the fabric of Spanish society and food instructions, preparation procedure, domestic manuals, descriptions of meals in literature and media, and accounts of national or regional food habits made explicit to Spaniards what was expected of them in a totalitarian and ultra-conservative Spain. The focus of my scholarship on the biopolitics of food is based on the premise that what people eat or how they approach food is not just the result of individual choice, but is also influenced by other primarily political factors, such as "economic trade, national security, and population health."[5]

My focus on the biopolitics of food and the continued influence of Francoist biopolitics on present-day Spain is a reminder that state control of individual bodies and populations does not just happen during times of totalitarian rule but is also a feature of democratic societies. Biopolitics also fits well with the notion of "gastrocracy" that is at the center of this issue. Exploring the political dimension of food and intersections of gastronomy and governance, this volume provides examples of how food and food discourse is frequently harnessed for political purposes. If my examples in this chapter relate to present-day Spain and the Franco era, in other research, I have shown how late nineteenth-century food and food discourse became part of an elite, top-down nation building project.[6] This synergy between governance and gastronomy is particularly important to Spain, where not just centralist but also regional governments have had recourse to food culture and food discourse to influence individual bodies and societal responses to centralist and peripheral sub-nationalist movements.

During parts of the Franco regime, violence and terror were used to control the population. Independent, however, of the experience of repression and or violence, all Spaniards were subject to the same ideological control, though some would have experienced it more positively than others. Discussing this control, Helen Graham writes that: "The Franco regime had free reign to shape public discourse in Spain, entirely unchallenged from abroad and uncontested in the domestic public sphere: through terror, censorship and total control of education and the print and broadcast media the dictatorship confined other memories... to exiles communities."[7] The physical and discursive control Franco wielded, or attempted to wield, has been discussed in terms of biopolitics. Foucault's writing on biopolitics sheds light on how the Franco regime achieved unprecedented management of the population and "institutional stability and political hegemony through strict physical and psychological repression."[8] Of course, as just mentioned, the biopolitics of food is also apparent during times of democracy.

According to Michel Foucault, Western governments since the late eighteenth century have attempted to administer and regulate human behavior and control the body and mind to achieve the general acceptance of social and legal norms.[9] Biopolitics, which assumes the responsibility and control of the vital processes and bodily discipline, is exerted by different official institutions. Foucault's original discussion of biopolitics looked at the way that modern political power managed individual bodies and populations. In totalitarian states, this control reaches unprecedented dimensions, as governments invade all aspects of daily life and subjectivity. In the area of food studies, the term biopolitics has also been fruitful, providing us with a better understanding of how cultural representations of food can push citizens and consumers into different subject positions.

If government food policy is one of the ways in which people are regulated or controlled through official government organizations and institutions, another equally important yet less tangible area is cultural practices surrounding food, along with media and textual representations of food. Food media comprises a multitude of circulating images and texts telling us what to eat and how to think about food, which have an impact on subject formation. While biopower relies upon food policy and state efforts to measure and control populations, equally as powerful are circulating images of food, cookbooks, food sections in newspapers, and descriptions of food in both official and private cultural texts. The examples of food and representations of food that I discuss in this chapter point to the continued influence of Francoist food discourse and biopolitics on contemporary

Spain, also showing how private organizations, texts, and individuals become part of official policy and discourse.

Theoretical Underpinnings: Food and Resistance

Although my focus in this chapter is not on resistance, discussions of food and power must consider resistance. Food studies scholars argue that more attention needs to be paid to the multiple ways in which food functions as a form of resistance, with some going as far as to argue that hegemonic power and resistance go hand in hand.[10] Existing research in food studies has demonstrated compellingly in other national settings the interface between food, hegemony, and resistance. Significantly, not just hegemony, but also resistance sits well with biopolitics. Foucault writes about the possibilities for resistance, "we have to promote new forms of subjectivity."[11] A complete exit from social reality is not, according to Foucault, possible, yet he does mention the possibility of "not being governed quite so much."[12] It is not only the food ingested that can challenge hegemonic practices; how food is represented can also offer a counterpoint to hegemonic discourse.

The everydayness of food means that food discourse, food culture, or the national diet is not registered or surveyed and therefore not subject to the same level of censorship or control as other aspects of life.[13] This means, as I have shown in relation to the Franco regime, that food texts have not been subject to the same degree of control as other forms of culture and have therefore disrupted official discourse in ways that made possible slightly altered identities and subjectivities. The fact that Francoist food culture still remains so relevant in times of democracy, when Spain's pluralistic foodscape is often pointed to as a symbol of the country's successful transition to democracy, that antiquated notions of Spanish cuisine as a monolithic entity continue to have such visibility, is of great interest. This is not just because of Spain's incomplete break with the dictatorship at the time of Spain's transition to democracy, but also on account of food's slippery, elusory quality, which means that food can be politically loaded yet somehow invisible on account of purported apoliticalness. Also telling in this regard are the restaurants paying explicit homage to Spain's fascist or totalitarian past at times of democracy. These restaurants do in part reflect the continued popularity of the figure of Franco; however, the culinary nature of these Francoist symbols means that they are seen as separate from politics and therefore not subject to the same Historical Memory legislation as other symbols, street names, and statues that pay homage to the figure of Franco.

The Transition: Incomplete Break with Past

As Graham explains, the transition to democracy "was a process entirely supervised by a reformist Francoist elite without any policy of lustration (the removal of a regime's political class and officials from power), thus ensuring a virtually total continuity of state and political personal to the new democratic system."[14] The peaceful transition to democracy was only possible because of a de facto "pact of silence" "that avoided confrontation with those responsible for the dictatorship and denied public recognition of its victims."[15] This idea of a unified Spanish cuisine or a unified monolithic nation is also present in some of the restaurants that pay homage to the Franco regime. Although these restaurants are popular amongst parts of Spanish society, there is also a great deal of polemic over such explicit and public adoration of Spain's most recent dictator. This comes as little surprise given the past, public memory, and the role of La Fundación Francisco Franco (The Francisco Franco Foundation) in preserving history or promoting fascism. Significantly, this lingering taste for the food culture of Spain's Francoist past speaks to what Graham describes as a much broader neo-Francoist, ultranationalist influence in present-day Spain, as well as a "nostalgia for a past of apparent certainty and security."[16] Considered one of the most "contentious issues in present-day Spain," the relationship between centralist Spanish and peripheral sub-state nationalisms is the subject of much political and cultural debate.[17] Yet if this discussion (including scholarship on it) has been particularly alive to the nationalist projects of Spain's "aspirant-nation states," very little has been said about present-day centralist Spanish nationalism. Describing Spanish nationalism as a disavowed yet potent project, Brad Epps makes a strong case for its inclusion in any discussions about the relationships between Spain's center and its peripheries. The tendency at the time of Franco's death to represent the Transition as a break with the past has often meant that Spain's right wing has needed to underplay any continuity with Francoism. Yet Epps identifies similarities, for instance, in the views of conservative groups on the Spanish whole and its peripheral parts: Franco's "unitarian conception of the State has rather perversely morphed ... into the threat of popularly asserted self-determination by whatever part (say, the Basque Country or Catalonia) of the whole that would dare to see itself as a different sort, even as a whole apart."[18] The disavowal of centralist nationalism identified by Epps means that any study of present-day nationalism in Spain needs to be alert to a centralizing discourse that is often implicit or misrepresented. This feature of Spanish nationalism is reflected in the fact that the Royal Family uses symbols of the Spanish food nation to impose its view of a unified yet diverse nation state. Also of importance to the presence of culinary nationalist symbols is the way *Un país para comérselo* (A Country Good Enough to Eat) can present as the bastion of Spain's regional and/or peripheral foodscapes (and has been unanimously received as such) whilst asserting a centralizing view of the relationship between the Spanish whole and its parts. By showing that a delegitimizing Spanish nationalist perspective can coexist with a celebration of regional difference, this chapter makes a strong case for the often hidden or misrepresented nature of centralizing nationalist discourse in present-day Spain. If the disavowal of Spanish nationalism means that this discourse is unlikely to be explicit, and that its deployment of national symbols will be comparatively subtler than that of Spain's sub-nationalisms, this certainly says nothing, as Epps and others insist, of its potency.

Culinary Nationalism and The Royal Family

During the Franco regime, food discourse partook in the production of a unified gastronomic space, and regional cuisines were not only subsumed into the national culinary whole, but also co-opted for the purpose of centralist nationalism. Significantly, the term "a la española" (Spanish) was used in some of Franco's earliest menus. An example of one of these from 1939 shows not only a relatively modest menu, but also a desire to use food to bolster national unity: "MENU – Almuerzo – (Plato único) Sopa al cuarto de hora – Cocido a la Española – POSTRES – Monte nevado – Queso y fruta – I-VI-1939 Año de la Victoria" (Menu – Lunch- [Single Dish] Quarter of an hour Soup – Spanish Stew – Desserts – Spanish ham – Cheese and fruit – June 1st Year of the Victory).

This reference to a Spanish style food culture represents just one of myriad efforts made by the Francoist State and associated food writers to create or impose a unified gastronomic space. This aspect of official discourse shaped food discourse during the first two decades of the regime. In line with official discourse, most of these cookbooks and gastronomic texts diminished or co-opted regional cuisines, whilst apparently promoting them.

Importantly this aspect of Francoist food culture has currency today and continues to determine how food is represented. A relatively recent example of the use of food discourse to reinforce the notion of Spanish national identity can be found in the food served at Felipe VI and Letizia Ortiz's wedding banquet in 2004. The descriptions of the wedding menu in the press, social media, and television coverage are constitutive of food discourse. Importantly, this discourse does not just aim to create ways of viewing Spanish food culture, it also attempts to influence thinking about Spanish national identity. Certainly, the then-future monarch's decision to serve a mix of wine and food from all of Spain's regions, described as typical of Spain's "gastronomía clásica española" (traditional Spanish gastronomy), evinces a clear appreciation of the symbolic value of food.[19] In offering up food from every region of the country—presented under the umbrella term "Spanish gastronomy"—the newlyweds declared their intention to serve all these same regions. They also, significantly, used the occasion of their wedding to reinforce the belief inherent to centralist Spanish nationalism that the category of Spanishness—or, in this case, Spanish gastronomy—is the greater whole of Spain's different regional cuisines. The food discourse surrounding this important public event informed viewers and citizens not just how they should think about Spanish food culture, but also how they must understand their often competing regional and national identities.

Making the most of the occasion of their wedding to affirm this view of Spanish gastronomy and national identity, the incoming "Reyes" (monarchs) hosted their first banquet a decade later, during which Felipe and Leticia gave a special nod to Catalonia. In the lead up to the polemic independence debate that has divided much of the country, the new monarchs requested not only a menu showcasing traditional Spanish cuisine, but also one that gave pride of place to "cava catalana" (Catalan champagne) instead of "el champán habitual de este tipo de ceremonias" (the usual champagne at these types of ceremonies).[20] The special place reserved for cava at this state ceremony was clearly meant to reassure the Catalans of their very influential position within the Spanish state compared to other, less visible regions of the Iberian Peninsula. Several scholars have argued that cuisine is often more instrumental to the spread of politics or nationalism than political addresses or ratified documents.[21] The importance placed on serving the right food and drink at the royal wedding and the later official banquet certainly evinces this, demonstrating an awareness amongst Spain's ruling class of the power of food to influence support for the monarchy and centralist Spanish nationalism.

Culinary Nationalism and Popular Culture

These official attempts to discursively create a national culinary culture for Spain or create a culinary whole that is made up of much smaller regional parts can be seen also in the television show *Un pais para comerselo* (A Country Good Enough to Eat), which has achieved both critical and ratings success. It has won several national gastronomy and tourism prizes, including the "Premio Nacional de Gastronomía" (National Gastronomy Prize) in 2010, and in its first season attracted more than 3 million viewers per episode. It is this wholly positive view of the show's service to Spain's gastronomic sector, especially its rural and regional foodscapes, that I discuss here. Although it purports to celebrate regional diversity, the show in fact plates up a version Spain that is primarily imagined as a singular, unified whole. In focusing on *Un país para comérselo* and its centralizing agenda, I would like to consider how Spanish centralist nationalism, inadvertently or otherwise, also uses culinary texts to imagine and assert its view of Spain and Spanish food culture.

Thinking about the possible centralizing agenda of *Un país para comérselo* and its gastro-tour of Spain's highly diverse regional foodscape also recalls not just Franco's monolithic nationalism but also Miguel Primo de Rivera's centralist program of reform of the 1920s, with its emphasis on national regeneration and economic and social modernization. To make Spain a "must do" tourist destination for national and international travelers, the Patronato Nacional de Turismo (The National Patron of Tourism) commissioned Dionisio Pérez to write *Guia del Buen Comer Español* (Guide of Good Spanish Food). The book was published under the penname of "Post-Thebussem." Inviting readers to join him on "un viaje gastronomico" (a gastronomic tour) through "las gloriosas cocinas de las regiones españolas" (the glorious cuisines of Spain's regions), Pérez's mandate was to correct the low opinion both foreign travelers and many Spaniards had of Spanish cuisine.[22] Moreover, in line with Primo de Rivera's centralizing agenda, Pérez was also concerned to promote national culinary cohesion, believing that Spanish cuisine should be seen as the sum of the country's regional parts.

The Primo de Rivera dictatorship and its use of food discourse to control consumer behavior and shape the contours of Spanish food culture would influence not just the Franco regime but also present-day Spain's own recourse to such discourse. Primo de Rivera, though failing to realize many of his ambitions, "inaugurated policies that were to become corner-stones of the Spanish right and eventually of the Francoist state."[23] This is certainly true for Spanish food culture. During the final stages of Primo de Rivera's dictatorship, official institutions commissioned food texts that would remain all-but-canonical throughout most of the Franco regime. Indeed, many food writers in Franco's Spain, such as Enrique Sordo, Luis Antonio de Vega, and La sección femenina treated Post-Thebussem (the most well-known and prolific food writer from the Primo de Rivera era) as an absolute authority on Spanish cuisine, constantly invoking his patriotic codification of Spanish cuisine.

Culinary Nationalism and Maps

Also, of interest to our discussion of *Un país para comérselo* is the ubiquity of maps, not just in the show itself, but also on its accompanying homepage. Indeed, these are featured so extensively in the show that the outline of the map of Spain functions as a pseudo-emblem for this show. The centrality of maps and mapmaking in the imperial projects of conquest is well-established, as maps at this time played a crucial role in transforming/representing land into territory.[24] The notion of a map waiting "to be filled out" is applicable also to the map featured on the accompanying homepage. Empty at the show's inception, this map is filled out with different colored trees marking "todos los destinos de *Un país para comérselo*" (All of the destinations of A Country Good Enough to Eat). If one of the functions of colonial mapping is to plot out all future tours, then the map here can be seen in a similar light. By clicking on the trees to access more information about the destination and its corresponding episode of the show, the viewer has his/her own gastro-tourism guide to Spain.

Maps are, as we know, highly subjective and fulfill many different functions depending on what cartographers (or other interests) deem worthy of inclusion. If maps were traditionally seen as some sort of objective depiction of reality, then we know now that they offer no less than "a way of thinking about the world. . . . [A] set of assertions about the world itself."[25] Whilst the different maps that appear in the show and its accompanying website have not been produced by a mapmaker per se, viewing them for the role they can play in forming our view of a place is an important step in any consideration of the underlying discourses evidenced in this apparently apolitical show. If "[e]very map is someone's way of getting you to look at the world his or her way," then what sort of view of Spain do the maps in the show or on the one that features on the website present?[26] Of most interest about the map on the website is that, unlike the official maps of the country, it is not divided in any way into Spain's seventeen autonomous regions. Even if some of the less detailed maps of Spain use different colors to mark out these communities, it is noteworthy that this map does not even make recourse to this level of differentiation. Instead, just one color—a sandy (neutral) cream—is used for the whole of the peninsula. The only markings on the map are trees, either green or yellow, that can be clicked on to access more information about the title and details of the episode. It is certainly one country—as opposed to discrete autonomous regions—that is plated up for consumption in *Un país para comérselo*.

From viewing this map, we are meant to form first and foremost a vision of the Iberian Peninsula as homogeneous and unified. Implicit in this map's erasure of, or "silence on," Spain's autonomous-regions is the belief that the country should be seen—to once again use Epp's terminology—as a whole rather than made up of different parts. With the show's focus on Spain's celebrated food culture, one has the impression that *Un país para comérselo* tries to unify Spain's disparate parts by downplaying territorial divisions and presenting Spaniards as first and foremost unified by their nation's unparalleled cuisine. And if the comments posted on the website at the end of each episode are anything to go by, the show's directors have been nothing but successful in fulfilling TVE's mandate to promote territorial cohesion. About the episode on Barcelona discussed in this article, for instance, one viewer writes: "Me encanta 'Un país para comérselo'! Que gastronomía tan rica tenemos en esta ESPAÑA nuestra" (I love A Country Good Enough to Eat! What delicious food we have in this Spain of ours). And, brought to tears watching the show, another viewer admits: "Cada capitulo que veo no sé lo que me pasa que me emociono y me se caen las lagrima digo yo que será de lo bonito que es mi país y lo rico que es culturalmente y que conste que mi provincia no a salido que es Sevilla" (Each episode that I see and I am not sure how makes me so emotional and I am brought to tears. How beautiful and culturally rich is my country and I haven't even left my province of origin, Sevilla). As these comments suggest, *Un país para comérselo* encourages viewers to think of and talk about Spain as a singular, unified whole, rather than a series of distinct parts.

Historical Memory and Francoist Restaurants

Culinary nostalgia or food memories can also be thought about in terms of the ongoing presence of Francoist food culture, especially in relation to the restaurants, still open today, that pay explicit homage to the figure of the dictator, rather than just implicitly endorse the notion of a unified cuisine. Not passed until 2007, the Historical Memory Law gives rights to the victims of the Civil War and ensuing dictatorship. Hundreds of graves have been opened since 2000, and there has been an effort to eliminate the Francisco Franco Foundation. The bill also seeks to teach about Franco's repression in the context of democracy and about the importance of removing Francoist symbols and exhuming Franco's remains. Indeed, the Fundación de Franco is legal, despite its glorification of the figure of Franco and attempts to show the greatness of Franco to Spaniards and tourists to Spain. Carmen Franco, the granddaughter, has also taken an active role in trying to improve her grandfather's brutal image. It is the acceptance of such symbols and homages to Franco that leads many Spaniards to be critical of nostalgia or memory in post-Franco Spain. On this point, Caragh Wells writes that, "since the end of the Franco regime, there has been a marked resistance to the process of remembering, and one criticism that has been levelled against pressure groups, organizations, and individuals who are involved the project of historical memory is that they are suffering from nostalgia and have an overly sentimental view of the past."[27]

Scholarship on culinary nostalgia explains why food memories are so frequently found in present-day acts of remembering, not just in Spain, but also in other parts of the globe. In addition to the role played by culinary reminiscences in sustaining the fiction of a happy past, scholars consider that the sensuality of food makes it a particularly intense and compelling medium for memory.[28] This is because food memories speak through our senses; they are performed physically through our bodies, and they reflect a visceral self-awareness. Our experience of food is a physical, sensual, shared human experience. As Jon Holtzman writes: "The experience of food evokes recollection, which is not simply cognitive, but also emotional and physical, paralleling notions such as Bourdieu's habitus, Connerton's notion of bodily memory and Stoller's emphasis on embodied memories. Indeed, varied examples show food to be an important engine for the construction of intense bodily memories."[29] If, as Holtzman's explanation of bodily memory explains, food evokes memories that are particularly powerful because they involve so much more than just cognition, then it stands to reason that culinary nostalgia will be such an important feature of present-day Spain's remembrance of the Franco regime. In addition to the broader Historical Memory context, this more universal aspect of food memories means that culinary nostalgia takes up an important place in Spain.

This restaurant trend has attracted the attention of the international and national press. Journalists have been critical, with one article in a Spanish newspaper decrying "una ruta por los bares franquistas que incumplen la Ley de la Memoria Histórica" (a route through Francoist bars which breach the Historical Memory Law) and arguing that, while it is illegal to have any plaques, commemorative medals, or other paraphernalia that pay homage to Franco Spain, there are restaurants in Spain that fail to adhere to the historical memory laws by being turned into "templos de adulación del franquismo" (temples of adulation to Francoism).[30] The most well-known of these locales is Casa Pepe (Pepe's House), a restaurant in the very small town of Almuradiel in Castile La Mancha, which attracts up to one hundred visitors a day. Visitors can purchase bottles of wine honoring General Francisco Franco on their labels, as well as typical foodstuffs such as *jamón* (ham) and olive oil bearing the national flag used during Franco's reign. One English newspaper reports on an interview with the owner of the restaurant, in which he explained his positive memories of Franco: "We support Franco. We are proud to honor him and what he did for our country, because it was a prosperous period in Spain's history."[31]

The owners answer the phone "Arriba España, dígame" (Long Live Spain, hello) and serve dishes dedicated to Francisco Franco. Food served at such premises is frequently labeled using the descriptor "a la española" (Spanish-style), which, as we have seen, came to refer to the ideal of a monolithic, standard Spanish cuisine. When Spaniards visit these restaurants or read about *comida a la española* (Spanish-style food), they perhaps imagine a sense of national unity that offers continuity with the past and a sense of stability in the face of ongoing economic problems and a constitutional crisis in relation to Catalonia.

Another such restaurant is El Cangrejo (The Crab) in Ciudad Real. The owner of the restaurant, José, explains that, sick of present-day politicians that do nothing for such a big percentage of the population, he decided to open his homage to Franco. He points out that visitors are told up front about what kind of restaurant it is with signage at the door reading, "Aviso – Entras en zona nacional si no te gusta Vuelve por donde viniste Arriba Espana" (Beware, you are entering in national territory, if you don't like it go back where you came from Long Live Spain). "Cara al Sol" (Facing the Sun) role of Francoism in Spain and is racist, sexist, and ultra-nationalist and borders on fascist. Members of the party talk of Spain's indissoluble national unity and have concrete policies aimed at imposing such a view of Spanish national identity.[32] True to this vision for Spain, José complains about the taxes that he must pay and how he thinks that Spain would be stronger as "una, grande y libre" (One, Great and Free).

Whilst there have been calls from Spain's Left for these neo-Francoist restaurants to be closed, they remain open to this day. One such restaurant, which was denounced to no avail to Spanish authorities, is Casa Eladio in Avila. This example goes as far as to invoke the Spanish Nationalist Victory during the Spanish Civil War in its culinary offerings. Describing itself as a "Rincón Nacional" (National nook), Casa Eladio serves up dishes with evocative names such as "bacalao grande y libre" (great and free cod), "patatas revolconas amargadas 36" (mashed potatoes of the 1936 bitter defeat), "chuletillas del Valle [de los Caídos]" (Little lamb chops from the Valley [de los Caídos]),[33] "huevos rotos fusilados" (scrambled eggs of the executed), and "chorizos rojos" (red chorizo sausages of the crooks).[34] To understand this phenomenon, we might turn to the work of Julian Casanova, who writes of the unique situation in Spain's post-dictatorship society (compared to the case of Germany) where "it was Spain's antifascist resistance groups which bore the brunt of the violence. Also in Spain, and crucially unlike elsewhere, the vengefulness of 'victorious' social groups could count on full state backing."[35] If the violence against Spain's antifascist groups is ongoing, then Casa Eladio's invocation of the defeat of the Republicans in the Civil War can be seen not just as a reminder of past violence, but also as a warning of the possibility of continued violence.

This chapter has shown the ongoing impact of the Franco regime and Francoist food culture on contemporary Spain. From culinary maps, television shows promoting the ideal of a monolithic culinary whole, and food memories allowing for segments of Spanish society to pay homage to the figure of Francisco Franco, there are many examples of the continued influence of Franco and Francoist food culture on Spain's way of life and identity. The transition to democracy in Spain did not represent a break with the past, and the continued relevance of Francoism on Spain's identity and Spanish foodways asks us to think about influence of the dictatorship as ongoing, even nearly five decades on from the transition. Individual food choices or ways of approaching food culture are often linked to official organizations, which aim to manage and control both the individual and collective bodies. Importantly, this control transcends food as a material object and instructs people in the uptake of different subject positions. Notwithstanding the multiple ways food can be used to govern people, gastronomy and governance are not unidirectional, and people find ways of not being governed so much. Because of its everydayness, food has a very real capacity to divide people, as we have seen here, and this has been overlooked. We must find new ways of thinking about food that alert us to its inherently political nature and capacity to bring us together over a meal or the memory of a meal.

NOTES

1. Lara Anderson, *Control and Resistance: Food Discourse in Franco Spain* (Toronto: University of Toronto Press, 2020); Priscilla Parkhurst Ferguson, *Word of Mouth: What We Talk about When We Talk about Food* (Berkeley: University of California Press, 2014).
2. Sandie Holguin emphasizes continuity over change, asking us to consider "the thousands of babies, stolen from women between 1939 and 1950 and the continuation of that practice against 'social undesirables' until fifteen years after Franco's death." Sandie Holguín, "How Did the Spanish Civil War End? . . . Not So Well," *American Historical Review* 120, no. 5 (2015): 1768.
3. Anderson, *Control and Resistance*.
4. Megan Elias, *Food on the Page: Cookbooks and American Culture* (Philadelphia: University of Pennsylvania Press, 2017); Parkhurst Ferguson, *Word of Mouth*; Katharina

Vester, *A Taste of Power: Food and American Identities* (Berkeley: University of California Press, 2015).
5. Christopher Mayes, *The Biopolitics of Lifestyle: Foucault, Ethics and Healthy Choices* (Abingdon, UK: Routledge, 2016), 13.
6. Lara Anderson, *Cooking up the Nation: Spanish Culinary Texts and Culinary Nationalization in the Late Nineteenth and Early Twentieth Century* (Woodbridge, UK: Tamesis, 2013).
7. Helen Graham, "Introduction," in *Interrogating Francoism: History and Dictatorship in Twentieth-Century Spain*, ed. Helen Graham (New York: Bloomsbury Academic, 2016), 6.
8. Iván Iglesias, "Performing the anti-Spanish Body: Jazz and Biopolitics in the Early Franco Regime (1939–1957)," in *Jazz and Totalitarianism*, eds. Bruce Johnson, Pedro Cravinho, and Heli Reimann (New York: Routledge, 2017), 162.
9. Michel Foucault, "The Subject and Power," *Critical Inquiry* 4, no. 8 (1982): 777–95.
10. See Nir Avieli, *Food and Power: A Culinary Ethnography of Israel* (Berkeley: University of California Press, 2017); Vester, *A Taste of Power*.
11. Foucaut, "The Subject and Power," 785.
12. Mayes, *The Biopolitics of Lifestyle*, 10.
13. Michael Gardiner, "Everyday Utopianism: Lefebvre and His Critics," *Cultural Studies* 18, no. 2 (2004): 228–54; Henri Lefebvre, *Critique of Everyday Life*, trans. John Moore (New York: Verso, 1991).
14. Graham, "Introduction," 7.
15. Carolyn Boyd, "The Politics of History and Memory in Democratic Spain," *The Annals of the American Academy of Political and Social Science* (2008): 135.
16. Graham, "Introduction," 10.
17. Brad Epps, "To be (a Part) of a Whole: Constitutional Patriotism and the Paradox of Democracy in the Wake of the Spanish Constitution of 1978," *Revista de Estudios Hispánicos* 44 (2010): 544–68.
18. Ibid, 563.
19. "Cocina tradicional española para un banquete histórico," *Hola*, May 22, 2004.
20. Javier G. Negre, "Catering de Mallorca y cava catalán en la proclamación real," *El Mundo*, June 18, 2014.
21. See Takeda Hiroko, "Delicious Food in a Beautiful Country: Nationhood and Nationalism in Discourses on Food in Contemporary Japan," *Studies in Ethnicity and Nationalism* 8, no. 1 (2008): 5–30; Nancy Siegel, "Cooking Up American Politics," *Gastronomica: The Journal of Critical Food Studies* 8, no. 3 (2008): 5361; and Vester, *A Taste of Power*.
22. Dionisio Pérez, *Guía del buen comer español: inventario y loa de la cocina clásica de España y de sus regiones* (Madrid: Suces. de Rivadeneyra, 1929), 40, 39.
23. Sholomo Ben-Ami, *Fascism from Above: The Dictatorship of Primo de Rivera in Spain, 1923–1930* (Oxford, UK: Oxford University Press), x.
24. Rob Kitchin, "Re-thinking Maps," *Progress in Human Geography* 31 (2007): 331–44.
25. Ibid., 332.
26. Ibid., 335.

27. Caragh Wells, "The Case for Nostalgia and Sentimentality in the Detective Fiction of Manuel Vázquez Montalbán," *Hispanic Review* 76 (2008): 208.
28. See, for example, David E. Sutton, *Remembrance of Repasts: An Anthropology of Food and Memory* (Oxford, UK: Bloomsbury Academic, 2001).
29. Jon D. Holtzman, "Food and Memory," *Annual Review of Anthropology* 35 (2006): 363.
30. "Ruta por los bares franquistas que incumplen la Ley de Memoria Histórica." *El plural*, March 11, 2017.
31. Ángel Martínez Cantera, "This Restaurant Is Nostalgic for Fascist Spain: Do You Miss General Franco? Then Head to Casa Pepe," *Vice*, August 14, 2014.
32. These discussions include suspending Catalonia's self-government "until the defeat of the coup plotters" behind the bid for regional independence and the "outlawing of parties, associations and NGOs that strive for the destruction of the sovereignty and territorial unity of the nation."
33. In addition to being evocative, the names of these dishes also echo Franco-ist propaganda. The Valley mentioned is the Valle de los Caídos (Valle de Cuelgamuros since 2022), a monument constructed with the labor of Republican political prisoners by the Franco regime between 1940 and 1958. Falange founder José Antonio Primo de Rivera is interred there as was Franco until his exhumation in 2019.
34. "IU denuncia a un bar que ofrece 'bacalao grande y libre' o 'huevos rotos fusilados,'" *El plural*, June 16, 2017.
35. Julian Casanova, "Disremembering Francoism: What Is at Stake in Spain's Memory Wars?" in *Interrogating Francoism: History and Dictatorship in Twentieth-Century Spain*, ed. Helen Graham (New York: Bloomsbury Academic, 2016), 205.

WORKS CITED

Anderson, Lara. *Control and Resistance: Food Discourse in Franco Spain*. Toronto: University of Toronto Press, 2020.

———. *Cooking up the Nation: Spanish Culinary Texts and Culinary Nationalization in the Late Nineteenth and Early Twentieth Century*. Woodbridge, UK: Tamesis, 2013.

Avieli, Nir. Food and Power: *A Culinary Ethnography of Israel*. Berkeley: University of California Press, 2017.

Ben-Ami, Sholomo. *Fascism from Above: The Dictatorship of Primo de Rivera in Spain, 1923–1930*. Oxford, UK: Oxford University Press.

Boyd, Carolyn. "The Politics of History and Memory in Democratic Spain." *Annals of the American Academy of Political and Social Science* (2008): 133–48.

Casanova, Julian. "Disremembering Francoism: What Is at Stake in Spain's Memory Wars?" In *Interrogating Francoism: History and Dictatorship in Twentieth-Century Spain*, edited by Helen Graham, 203–22. New York: Bloomsbury Academic, 2016.

Elias, Megan. *Food on the Page: Cookbooks and American Culture*. Philadelphia: University of Pennsylvania Press, 2017.

Epps, Brad. "To be (a Part) of a Whole: Constitutional Patriotism and the Paradox of Democracy in the Wake of the Spanish Constitution of 1978." *Revista de Estudios Hispánicos* 44 (2010): 544–68.

Foucault, Michel. "The Subject and Power." *Critical Inquiry* 4, no. 8 (1982): 777–95.

Gardiner, Michael. "Everyday Utopianism: Lefebvre and His Critics." *Cultural Studies* 18, no. 2 (2004): 228–54.

Graham, Helen. "Introduction." In *Interrogating Francoism: History and Dictatorship in Twentieth-Century Spain*, edited by Helen Graham, 1–24. New York: Bloomsbury Academic, 2016.

Hiroko, Takeda. "Delicious Food in a Beautiful Country: Nationhood and Nationalism in Discourses on Food in Contemporary Japan." *Studies in Ethnicity and Nationalism* 8, no. 1 (2008): 5–30.

Holguín, Sandie. "How Did the Spanish Civil War End? . . . Not So Well." *American Historical Review* 120, no. 5 (2015): 1767–83.

Holtzman, Jon D. "Food and Memory." *Annual Review of Anthropology* 35 (2006): 361–78.

Iglesias, Iván. "Performing the anti-Spanish Body: Jazz and Biopolitics in the Early Franco Regime (1939–1957)." In *Jazz and Totalitarianism*, edited by Bruce Johnson, Pedro Cravinho, and Heli Reimann, 157–73. New York: Routledge, 2017.

Kitchin, Rob. "Re-thinking Maps." *Progress in Human Geography* 31 (2007): 331–44.

Lefebvre, Henri. *Critique of Everyday Life*. Translated by John Moore. New York: Verso, 1991.

Martínez Cantera, Ángel. "This Restaurant Is Nostalgic for Fascist Spain: Do You Miss General Franco? Then Head to Casa Pepe." *Vice*, August 14, 2014.

Mayes, Christopher. *The Biopolitics of Lifestyle: Foucault, Ethics and Healthy Choices*. Abingdon, UK: Routledge, 2016.

Negre, Javier G. "Catering de Mallorca y cava catalán en la proclamación real." *El Mundo*, June 18, 2014.

Parkhurst Ferguson, Priscilla. *Word of Mouth: What We Talk about When We Talk about Food*. Berkeley: University of California Press, 2014.

Pérez, Dionisio (Post-Thebussem). *Guía del buen comer español: inventario y loa de la cocina clásica de España y de sus regiones*. Madrid: Suces. de Rivadeneyra, 1929.

El plural. "IU denuncia a un bar que ofrece 'bacalao grande y libre' o 'huevos rotos fusilados.'" June 16, 2017.

———. "Ruta por los bares franquistas que incumplen la Ley de Memoria Histórica." March 11, 2017.

Un país para comérselo. TVE and Grupo Ganga Producciones. TVE, 2010–2013.

Siegel, Nancy. "Cooking Up American Politics." *Gastronomica: Journal of Critical Food Studies* 8, no. 3 (2008): 5361.

Sutton, David E. *Remembrance of Repasts: An Anthropology of Food and Memory*. Oxford, UK: Bloomsbury Academic, 2001.

Vester, Katharina. *A Taste of Power: Food and American Identities*. Berkeley: University of California Press, 2015.

Wells, Caragh. "The Case for Nostalgia and Sentimentality in the Detective Fiction of Manuel Vázquez Montalbán." *Hispanic Review* 76 (2008): 281–97.

Part II: Ingestible Identities

◆ CHAPTER 4

Food Fights
Nativism and Culinary Xenophobia in Europe

Aitana Guia

"Born in Spain. Admired in the World" was the slogan of a European campaign launched by the Asociación Interprofesional del Cerdo Ibérico (Interprofessional Association of the Iberian Pig, ASICI) and the Spanish Ministry of Agriculture, Food, and Environment in 2015. ASICI partnered with world-renowned Spanish tennis player Rafael Nadal to promote the expensive delicacy *jamón ibérico* (cured pork ham) in various tennis tournaments, such as the Italian Open in Rome.[1] Half of one printed ad was a photograph of two round platters of *jamón ibérico* thinly sliced and elegantly displayed in a swirl design. The other half was a photograph of Nadal with a rural background of gall oaks and three Black Iberian breed pigs freely roaming around—two of Spain's most prized and admired offerings to the world.[2] Even though the ad campaign was not limited to ham—Nadal also promoted Spanish wine and olive oil—the implication was obvious: *jamón* (ham) is one of the greatest products of Spanish cuisine, a gift to the world.

This chapter analyses fights over whose culture shapes the public sphere in Europe and how much foreign influences are tolerated. It focuses on the ideological uses of pork in the public sphere, but, rather than looking at the criminal and intimidatory actions of extreme-right parties, I explore how nativists have used pork and "native cuisine" in mainstream politics, turning public schools and historical city centers into battlefields. I argue that nativist positions have successfully determined what are the acceptable tastes, smells, and looks in European schools and cities. The nativist political use of food has effectively mobilized an emotionally charged daily ritual to undermine the rights of religious minorities to receive accommodation for their dietary needs in public institutions. It has also hindered the public appreciation of immigrant cuisines as European and the possibility to set up ethnic businesses in European downtowns.

To build my argument, I explore three debates on food and national values that have received significant media attention. I chose these because of the role they have had in advancing cultural wars over food consumption and availability in Europe. Most but not all the agents pursuing nativist positions are populist radical right parties. Center-left and center-right parties have also occasionally advocated policies defending "native" cuisines. First, I explore debates over the availability of pork and pork alternatives in school menus in Spain, France, and Denmark. The next section focuses on native smells and how various Italian cities have banned Kebab shops and other restaurants deemed foreign from their historical centers. The final section returns to Spain to discuss an anti-Chinese controversy in what was supposed to be Spain's first Chinatown.

An Unsavory History

The Spanish Inquisition thought highly of pork consumption. After the Christian conquest of Islamic Spain was completed in 1492, leaving large segments of Muslims in Christian-controlled territory, eating pork products became a symbol of true allegiance to Christianity for New Christians, Muslims, and Jews forced to convert. Moriscos (converted Muslims) and Conversos or Marranos (the derogatory term for converted Jews, which means filthy in Spanish), were suspected of continuing their religious beliefs and rituals in secrecy, including their dietary restrictions and food practices, and they were often persecuted for being crypto-Jews or crypto-Muslims. As Jodi Campbell argues, "food became one of the most visible signifiers of religious identity, to the extent that it became more a metaphor than a simile—food was religion."[3] After the fall of the last Muslim Kingdom of Granada, there was a long period of religious persecution and homogeneity, during which "la ignorancia de la imaginación triunfante" (the ignorance of triumphant imagination) dominated popular culture.[4]

Despite efforts to the contrary by the National-Catholic dictator General Francisco Franco from 1939 to 1975, Spain today embraces religious pluralism both *de jure* and *de facto*. While the Jewish community remains small, practicing Muslims in Spain may number over two million.[5] Most religious minorities are also recent immigrants, which hinders their ability to practice their religion publicly and have their rituals and food practices accommodated and valued in the public sphere and by public institutions.[6] An important feature of Judaism and Islam are the dietary requirements and other ritual practices their adherents must follow. As a result, food and food practices are ripe for becoming, yet again, a battleground.

Jamón (ham) and pork are not neutral features of Spanish cuisine. They were politicized in the medieval and early modern periods, and this longstanding association between eating pork and belonging to the rightful community remains. While a majority of contemporary Spaniards do not think of themselves in terms of old Christianity or the purity of blood, and are more culturally Catholic rather than practicing Catholics, they nevertheless are acculturated into an environment in which *jamón* and pork are not just normal and delicious, but Spanish and admired.

Nativism and Food Studies

Food and eating traditions have always been complex insofar as they have the ability to build, define, and separate communities. Connecting nationalism and food studies has become a fruitful field of inquiry.[7] Most studies follow one dish, type of food, or national cuisine in order to better understand the origins and characteristics of nationalism.[8] Theoretically, the field is developing fast, with some scholars favoring the notion of gastronationalism, others siding with national food or foodways, and yet others problematizing the notion of cuisine.[9]

Gastronationalism refers to a mechanism mostly deployed by the state to defend violations or threats to the symbolic boundaries of national food. According to Michaela De Soucey, gastronationalism "signals the use of food production, distribution, and consumption to demarcate and sustain the emotive power of national attachment, as well as the use of national sentiments to produce and market food."[10] Gastronationalism works at the state and national levels against internal challengers and other national cuisines. Many scholars have found that limiting our analysis of the politics of food to state (national, regional, or local) actors was unnecessarily limiting our understanding of these phenomena. By adding to the analysis what Michael Billig called "banal nationalism"—that is, the everyday manifestations of national belonging we don't even recognize as such because we take these inherited rituals for granted, such as eating paella every Sunday for Valencian households or *jamón* (ham), *chorizo*, and *sobrasada* (salami) for casual tapas—many scholars were able to develop more nuanced understandings of how food and foodways are shaped and reshaped for nationalist purposes.[11]

The uses of food as a mechanism to shape nationalism is contingent upon the stage in which this ideology is situated. They are not as important during the nation-building project as they are during its period of normalization, and this is where the study of gastronationalism is particularly useful. The political uses of food can also become a crucial feature when nationalism turns into nativism, a philosophical outlook that redefines who the "real" people of a political unit are. "Natives" abrogate for themselves more rights and decision-making power to determine the characteristics of that society vis-à-vis a group considered exogenous and incapable of assimilating.[12] Nativism is a concept first theorized by John Higham in his seminal 1955 *Strangers in the Land: Patterns of American Nativism, 1860–1925* to explain the anti-Catholic, anti-radical, anti-Black, and anti-foreign ideologies that emerged in the United States in the mid-nineteenth century.[13]

Gastronativism—a term coined by Fabio Parasecoli, professor of food studies at New York University, in his recently published book *Gastronativism: Food, Identity, Politics*—refers to the ideological use of food to advance ideas about who belongs to a community and who does not.[14] I understand gastronativism as a phenomenon within a state deployed by those actors who claim to represent the "native stock" against those foods, cultures, and people perceived to be threatening aliens. Gastronationalism turns into gastronativism when a variety of actors use food for the purpose of demarcating "native" food in opposition to alternatives that are perceived as foreign and threatening. Gastronativism has also been called culinary xenophobia.[15] Both concepts are useful. I prefer gastronativism because it places a higher emphasis on how actors prioritize a defense of what is "native," rather than attacking what is foreign *per se*. Studies on halal hamburgers in France, for example, have focused on gastronativism, even when they do not use the term.[16]

In a context of cultural pluralism, when a group self-identifies itself as the native group, food takes on new meaning to sharpen the lines between those who belong to the native group and those who are excluded from it. In Europe at the end of the twentieth and beginning of the twenty-first centuries, the populist radical right parties are the ones who have chosen to politicize food to mark the national/native community vis-à-vis immigrant communities and religious minorities.

Pork is their chosen weapon. As linguistics professor Martha Sif Karrebaek reminds us, "the use and meaning of pork is often based on ideological and moral considerations."[17] When an extreme-right group roasts a pig in front of a mosque in the Netherlands or anonymous actors leave pig carcasses at sites where mosques or asylum centers are to be built, the ideological use of pork to denigrate European Muslims is clear.[18] Ideological uses of pork, however, are only one of their multiple signifiers: "the contemporary meaning, or meaning potential, of pork is more nuanced: pork indexes, for example, class positions, religious and ethnic identities, political and environmental stances, all of which intersect in various ways."[19]

Native Tastes: Halal Meat in Spanish Public Schools

In fall 2014, parents whose children attended Painter Teodoro Andreu Primary School in Alzira, a mid-size agricultural town in the province of Valencia in Spain, removed their children from the school lunch program because it did not offer a halal menu.[20] The conflict escalated, and the Valencian Ministry of Education responded that current regulations already included various options for religious minorities and children with allergies or alternative diets. There was a menu without pork, as well as the option of substituting non-halal meat for fish or eggs. Anabel Juárez, local councilor for education, wished that parents desisted from withdrawing their children from school meals: "Me sabe mal porque están quedándose sin comer y se ha generado una crispación ciudadana innecesaria" (I feel bad, because they [the children] don't get to eat and this has created an unnecessary polarization among residents).[21]

The school had offered a pork-free (but not halal) lunch menu for nine years and Muslim families had been sending their children to the school cafeteria. Non-Muslim parents and teachers in the Alzira school blamed the influence of the local imam on Muslim parents for the controversy. In their minds, if a menu without pork had worked for nine years, why not now?

Demand for a halal menu in school cafeterias was not new. The previous year, various parents in the neighboring region of Zaragoza had asked for it.[22] According to the regional newspaper *Levante-EMV*, imams in various regions of Spain were pushing for halal meat to be offered in school cafeterias. The president of the Cultural Islamic Centre of Alzira, Rachid Gharbi, argued that "Somos españoles y nuestros hijos también lo son. Tienen los mismos derechos que sus compañeros de escuela a recibir una beca del comedor, pero tienen que respetar nuestras costumbres y ritos" (We are Spanish and our children are as well. They have the same rights as their classmates to be eligible for free lunches, but they [school administrators] must respect our customs and rites).[23] Gharbi called for the implementation of the legal requirement to respect the dietary needs of Muslim students who requested it, both in public and semi-private schools, as offered by the 1992 Cooperation Agreement between the Spanish State and the Islamic Community of Spain.[24]

The conflict subsided after the winter holidays because the school threatened parents with the loss of their meal subsidy if they persisted in withholding their children from the school cafeteria. All children resumed eating a menu without pork, but not halal, at the school cafeteria shortly after.[25]

While Spanish schools are legally required to ask whether students have any food intolerances or allergies, which must be justified with a medical note, they do not ask about the dietary needs of religious minorities or those who adopt alternative diets (vegans or vegetarians, for instance). These groups are left to negotiate for accommodations with each school's principal.[26]

Students with allergies, food intolerances, obesity, diabetes, or high cholesterol must receive accommodations by Spanish law. In the Basque region, catering companies calculate that eight percent of students have some sort of dietary need. A small school usually offers half a dozen different menus; a school with over a thousand students could range between twenty and over sixty different menus each day.[27] But these offerings vary by region, as education is managed by the various regional governments. The most common menu offerings are those prepared for students who are gluten-intolerant, low-fat for overweight children, low-cholesterol for those with high blood-pressure, a menu with limited sugar for diabetics, a vegetarian menu (with eggs and milk), and a menu without pork for the large Muslim student population in Spain. Individual offerings for children with allergies are also available. These are prepared on a separate work bench, are highly controlled, served in individual trays with different colors, and labelled with the students' names to protect them from having allergic reactions that in some cases could be fatal. In a public school in Loiu in the Basque region, with more than 2,000 students, "tenemos 140 alumnos con alergias e intolerancias y servimos a diario 67 dietas diferentes" (we have 140 students with various allergies and food intolerances, and we serve every day 67 different menus). A simple accommodation would entail a menu "bajo en colesterol-no yogur-no zumo" (low cholesterol-no yogurt-no juice). A complex one would be "no huevo-no frutos secos-no tomate-no moluscos-no crustáceos-no melocotón-no plátano-no kiwi" (no eggs-no nuts-no tomato-no shellfish-no peach-no banana-no kiwi).[28]

The issue of halal menus in school cafeterias has not been settled and will probably require regulatory change before it can accommodate the needs of religious minorities. In 2018, various pro-immigrant associations, such as Valencia Acoge (Valencia Welcomes), Movimiento contra la Intolerancia (Movement Against Intolerance), and the Islamic Cultural Centre of Valencia, accused the Valencian Ministry of Education of "dejadez" (neglect) for not ensuring that Muslim students have access to halal menus in school cafeterias or, at least, alternatives to dishes that contain pork. The pro-immigrant organizations were particularly offended because some school catering businesses were able to offer halal menus, but various school principals had decided not to request them. They argued the lack of accommodation for Muslim children amounted to "una discriminación indirecta" (indirect discrimination) that left them "en una situación de vulnerabilidad" (in a position of vulnerability).[29]

Amparo Sánchez, a Valencian who converted to Islam in 1996 and has been a prominent activist in Spanish Islamic associations and a spokesperson for the Platform against Islamophobia since 2013, explained: "El argumento siempre es que los musulmanes no nos queremos integrar. Eso es falso. La realidad es que todo son problemas. Por ir a clase con velo, por los cementerios, por un nuevo oratorio, por los menús de los colegios . . . ¿No queremos o no nos dejan ejercer libremente nuestra ciudadanía y nuestra opción religiosa?" (The argument is always that we, Muslims, do not want to assimilate. That is false. The reality is that everything is a problem. If we go to school wearing a headscarf, our cemeteries, new prayer sites, the menus in school cafeterias . . . We don't want to or we aren't allowed to freely exercise our citizenship rights and our religious beliefs?). For Sánchez, the solution is new legislation mandating school cafeterias to offer halal menus.[30]

Considering that some school cafeterias offer up to sixty-seven menu options, and that halal meat is easily available and inexpensive all over Spain, not offering halal menus to Muslim children seems at best an unnecessary oversight, more akin to institutional neglect, and at worst intentional discrimination. It also goes against best practices recommended by public policy studies, including the public institute Observatorio del Pluralismo Religioso en España (Spain's Religious Pluralism Observatory) in their 2011 "Guidelines for Public Policy Management Regarding Religious Diversity and Food." Some of their recommendations involved regional governments asking public-school catering contractors to offer religiously acceptable menus where needed as part of their contractual obligations, particularly in schools with large and stable Muslim, Jewish, or Seventh-Day Adventist student populations. For Muslims, these menus would avoid forbidden foods and include halal meats. In schools with few religious minority students, the Guide suggests offering alternative menus without forbidden foods, such as vegetarian options, that are good for Muslims, Jews, Adventists, but also Buddhists, Hindus, Sikhs, etc.[31]

Pork or Nothing

So far in Spain, not even the populist far-right party VOX has questioned the right of Muslim children not to eat pork in school cafeterias. Whether these children are entitled to alternative menus, vegetarian or halal, is a more contentious matter left to the discretion of school administrators. In France, however, the debate centers on whether French republican values permit religious minority students to skip weekly pork offerings in favor of what they call "substitution meals." Controversies between French Muslims and non-Muslims were not always about pork. For decades, since the first headscarf conflict emerged in 1989, French schools have debated banning ostentatious religious symbols to protect secular spaces. However, in the wake of the *Charlie Hebdo* terrorist attack in 2015, pork became the next battleground in France's uneasy debate over Islam and national identity. It is unclear whether the Spanish populist far-right will follow the French roadmap, but it is a striking possibility.

Controversies about headscarves or pork do not appear overnight. They are composed of scattered events that, over years, amount to a challenge to the status quo that may lead to regulatory change. The headscarf affair started in 1989 and led to the 2004 Conseil d'État ban on ostentatious religious symbols in primary and secondary public institutions.[32] The debate continued and led to the 2010 ban on full veiling in all public institutions and on French streets. As I write, Muslim girls have also been expelled from schools for wearing long black skirts that were considered a symbol of their religious affiliation.

Similarly, pork has not become politicized overnight. In France, far-right politics usually start at the local level and then make it onto the national arena. In 2010, extreme-right groups tried to organize "pork and wine aperitifs" near Muslim places of worship. Authorities banned them, but a "republican aperitif" did take place in central Paris. They placed tables filled with wine and salami with the stated goal of fostering rejection of halal meat and defending secularism.[33] From local controversies, halal meat escalated onto the national stage during the 2012 presidential campaign. Marine Le Pen, then-president of the National Front, falsely claimed that all the meat sold in the Paris region was halal. Nicolas Sarkozy, who was battling to remain president but falling behind the Socialist contender, tried to lure Le Pen's voters by stroking fears that halal meat was being sold to unsuspecting customers and defending that halal options should not be available in state school cafeterias.[34]

Pork became politicized in French school cafeterias despite the absence of the sorts of vocal demands for halal or kosher meat in school cafeterias that occurred in Spain or the United Kingdom (UK). Children who eat only halal or kosher meat either attend private faith schools or go home to eat.

Since the presidential election in 2012, mayors of the National Front (today known as National Rally), as well as other parties on the right, have banned alternative offerings for religious minorities in their towns' public-school cafeterias. For thirty years, Chilly-Mazarin, a small town south of Paris, provided non-pork alternatives to Muslim and Jewish children. But in 2015, the new mayor of Nicolas Sarkozy's right-wing Les Républicains party announced that it was scrapping pork-free options in school cafeterias in the name of secularism and "neutrality." For him, it was a necessary measure in the interests of "living together." He felt that it was important that everyone be served "the same" food and not be set apart by being offered a different meal.³⁵ He equated secularism with sameness. The National Front mayor of the small town of Beaucaire in Southern France, Julien Sanchez, outlawed alternatives to pork in local schools in 2018, arguing that "My decision is for the Republic to win, that in France the Republic has priority and not religion."³⁶ By creating a handful of local conflicts like these, right-wing parties achieved a long-lasting politicization of meat.

Not everybody agrees that secularism in France requires eliminating alternative diets from school menus. A school principal in Chilly-Mazarin explained: "Secularism is not about pork. It is about respecting others' religion; it is not about saying 'no more religion'. The ban on pork-free meals is extremely difficult for me and my teachers. School is about teaching children to respect each other, regardless of their differences. This [the mayor's decision to remove pork-free options] has demolished our teaching of that in class."³⁷

Ideology on a Plate: The Search for a Universal Menu

To reduce expenses by limiting the number of menu offerings in schools, a universal menu could be a vegetarian or halal menu for all students except those with medical conditions. Wherever these options have been tried, parents' organizations have voiced their opposition to feeding halal meat to their children or going meat-free, and the attempt to introduce a universal menu has been abandoned or revoked. When a school with a large Muslim student population in the Catalan town of Mataró announced it was adopting a single halal menu, some parents contacted the far-right xenophobic Plataforma per Catalunya (Platform for Catalonia) to force the school to revoke the measure. After the backlash, the school backtracked, said that there had been a misunderstanding and that it never intended to offer a single halal menu. Parents not only opposed that the meat on the menu be halal and their kids not be offered pork, but also rejected the introduction of North African dishes into the menu. A mother explained that "nos encontramos un menú para niños musulmanes, ya que contenía cuscús, falafel, fajol, cúrcuma o tabulé, y mis hijos no saben ni qué es todo eso" (we found out that it was a menu for Muslim children, because it had cuscus, falafel, buckwheat, turmeric or Tabbouleh, and my children do not even know what all of that is).³⁸

The same reaction against a universal halal menu occurred ten years earlier in Rose Hill Primary School, The Oval, Oxford, UK. The principal announced in a letter that because halal meat was not forbidden by any religion or culture, its use would allow everyone to choose a meat dish for lunch, and thus all the meat served in the cafeteria was going to be halal from then on. She proposed to adopt halal meat as a common denominator. Parents opposed it and the proposal did not go through.[39] Nine years later, in Croydon, near London, New Addington Primary School's principal proposed a universal halal menu for all students. A parents' petition opposed it with the following arguments: "If you are against the school attempting to introduce halal foods on the menu and forcing our children to conform to Islamic beliefs, then please sign this petition and say NO to forced halal . . . Tell them, by signing, you DO NOT agree with the inhumane slaughter of animals in the name of one religion's god over others' freedom and beliefs. Stop the forced introduction of halal foods on our school kids."[40] And here we encounter the main argument to oppose halal meat as a universal staple in the UK: animal rights. While many Muslims consider halal meat a "better meat" because it requires animals to have been raised humanely and killed in a ritual way, opponents of halal meat ignore inhumane industrial farming for human consumption and focus exclusively on challenging the ritual slaughtering of animals as cruel and thus reprehensible.

As for a vegetarian option as a universal menu, the Green party mayor of the French city of Lyon, Gregory Doucet, implemented a meat-free menu as way to streamline school lunch services while social distancing remained necessary during the coronavirus pandemic. He was accused of harming the health of school children, even though the mayor argued that the menus were still nutritionally balanced because fish and egg products remained on offer. Agriculture minister Julien Denormandie charged Doucet with "putting ideology on our children's plates."[41] Interior minister Gerald Darmanin joined in by saying that the measure was an "unacceptable insult" to French farmers and butchers. He then accused Doucet of being an elitist politician oblivious to the needs of the popular classes: "Many children often only get to eat meat at the school canteen."[42] Mayor Doucet responded that the measure was solely due to the pandemic and that his right-wing predecessor had done the same thing without controversy.

Pork Nation

Controversy over the removal of pork from school and hospital menus emerged in Denmark in the summer of 2013. They were labelled "meatball wars," as meatballs are made with minced pork in Denmark. As with France, debates over the place of pork in Danish diets followed other controversies that had already placed Muslim Danes at odds with their non-Muslim neighbors. France had the headscarf affair starting in 1989; Denmark, the controversy over cartoons of Prophet Mohamed in 2005. The far-right magazine *Jyllands-Posten* invited Danish cartoonists to test the strength of freedom of expression in Denmark by daring to draw and publish cartoons of Prophet Mohammed, despite prohibitions against visual depictions of Muhammed among some Islamic sects. Twelve cartoonists submitted originals images and triggered predictable protests from practicing Muslims in Denmark and abroad. One of the main effects of this controversy was to sharpen the lines between Muslim and non-Muslim Danes and reinforce the nativist discourse of the radical right Danish People's Party (DPP-*Dansk Folkeparti*).[43]

During the meatball wars, *Jyllands-Posten* suggested that DPP establish a "pork quota" of "*at least* 20 percent pig" in menus served in public institutions, such as schools, hospitals, and seniors' homes. While the DPP did not include such a measure in their electoral platform, the magazine encouraged local mayors to "write into the municipalities' food policies that dishes from other lands should be offered as supplements to, but never instead of, traditional Danish foods."[44]

Unsurprisingly, in 2016, Randers, a former industrial town of about sixty thousand inhabitants in central Denmark, led by a DPP mayor, voted to require public daycare centers and kindergartens to include pork in their lunch menus, because serving traditional Danish food such as pork was essential to help preserve Danish national identity. "We will ensure that Danish children and youth can have pork in the future," said Randers town councilor Frank Norgaard. DPP spokesman Martin Henriksen wrote in a social media post, "It is unacceptable to ban Danish food culture, including dishes with pork, in Danish child care institutions. What will be next?! The DPP is working nationally and locally for Danish culture, including Danish food culture, and consequently we also fight against Islamic rules and misguided considerations dictating what Danish children eat."[45]

What is considered a national dish offers a window into a country's collective self-image. British foreign secretary Robin Cook claimed in 2001 that chicken tikka masala (CTM, with its own acronym now) had replaced fish and chips as the United Kingdom's national dish.[46] For the United States, it's the hamburger—hardly a stereotype, when Americans consumed the equivalent of 2.4 burgers per day or 58 pounds of beef per capita for 2020.[47] Italy's national dishes are pasta and pizza, which are daily staples of Italian homes, restaurants, and schools.

"National dishes" that can accommodate religious and alternative diets offer a better buffer against instrumentalization by nativist parties. CTM and fish and chips do not present dietary difficulties for most religious minorities and omnivores. Vegetarians may replace chicken with tofu and batter vegetables instead of fish to go along with their chips and still be part of the national culinary community. Neither the burger nor pasta and pizza exclude religious minorities *prima facie* because, even though they may include pork or combine milk with meat, they do not require any of those combinations. Plant-based alternatives to the beef patty are so common nowadays that nobody has to feel deprived of the American "national dish." Likewise, pasta and pizza are universal dishes that can accommodate vegetarians and vegans.

Spanish and Danish national dishes, meanwhile, are more difficult to reconcile with the dietary requirements of religious minorities and people with alternative diets. In 2014, Danes voted crispy pork with parsley sauce and potatoes as Denmark's national dish. Not only does the country self-identify with pork, but Denmark is also among the world's largest pig meat exporters.[48] Karrebæk argues that "pork is acquiring the meaning of Danishness" in the sense that pork and Danishness "have become so closely associated that pork invites the current exclusionary, nationalist sense of Danishness to enter the social space" whenever it is being served or consumed.[49]

Spain has not voted on a national dish, but *paella*, *jamón* (ham), and *tortilla española* (Spanish omelet, with potato, eggs, and sometimes onion) are the most likely contenders. All these options are problematic for one group or another. *Jamón* was, however, irredeemable for Jews and Muslims until a Tunisian-Spanish entrepreneur began to produce halal beef and lamb *jamón* in Andalusia.[50] Paella, if it does not include seafood or pork, can be modified to accommodate religious minorities and is also versatile enough to become a vegetarian and vegan dish. A vegan paella is probably the most universal dish, but most Spaniards would reject it as inauthentic or of lesser quality than a paella with meat or fish—the traditional Valencian paella, for example, is made with chicken and rabbit, with optional snails. The Spanish omelet, served in every bar, broadly cooked in households, and booming as prepared food, is good for religious minorities and vegetarians. Because only vegans are left out, it is probably the most universal national dish Spanish cuisine has nowadays.[51]

Both Denmark and Spain have a strong pork culture, and pork dishes are crucial components of national and regional cuisines. The conditions for equating national identity with pork exists in both countries, but the DPP has moved to politicize the consumption and serving of pork to a higher degree than the Spanish radical right populist party VOX has done. So far, the leader of VOX, Santiago Abascal, has only responded to pork controversies abroad, but his party has not actively tried to legislate on the matter at home. In 2018, Abascal said: "eso no lo queremos para España, porque aquí queremos libertad, queremos comer jamón en los colegios, y que no venga nadie a decirnos lo que tenemos que hacer en nuestra tierra . . . Porque si queremos comer jamón lo haremos, les moleste a los islamistas o les moleste a los animalistas" (we don't want that [eliminating pork from school menus] for Spain, because we want freedom here, we want to eat *jamón* in schools, and nobody should tell us what we must do in our land . . . Because if we want to eat *jamón*, we will do it, whether it bothers Islamists and animal rights activists).[52]

Abascal speaks from a position of fictitious victimisation, as if a horde of animal rights activists or Islamists were successfully stopping Spaniards from eating *jamón*. Everyday pressures actually take place in an inverse direction. Writers such as Najat El Hachmi and Igiaba Scego have documented the pressures that immigrants from Muslim-majority countries face in Spain and Italy by ethnic Europeans who do not accept and trust Muslims until they see them eating pork. The protagonist in Scego's short story "Salsicce," a young Sunni-Muslim Somalian woman, wonders, "If I swallow these sausages one by one, will people understand that I am Italian just like them? Exactly the same as them?" and "Would I be more Italian with a sausage in my stomach? Would I be less Somali?"[53] In Najat El Hachmi's *The Last Patriarch*, the immigrant male protagonist does not get hired for manual odd jobs until native employers see him eating a pork sandwich; only then he can be trusted.[54] In his memoir, Mohammed Chaib, a member of the Catalan parliament from 2003 to 2010 and a member of the Spanish Congress from 2018 to 2019, echoes the discomfort that those who do not eat pork feel in Spain. Chaib also glorifies the virtues of the Spanish omelet as a dish that Muslims and non-Muslim Spaniards can savor together.[55]

Native Smells

During the holiday break before the COVID-19 pandemic closed borders, on an evening stroll around the Valencian Colón Boulevard, the main downtown commercial artery, I noticed the aroma of recently made waffles spread for a block in every direction. It was an unmissable, pungent, and "foreign" scent. Waffles, made from leavened dough cooked between two patterned plates, are mostly associated with Belgium and have become a common staple in American breakfasts. Even though in other Spanish cities they are common, waffles are exotic for Valencians. When Valencians think of comfort food to snack on, they gravitate toward savory empanadillas or sweet croissants. The introduction of waffles as a snack food to eat on the go during a break from shopping is new. Whether one is tempted or not by the sweet treat, the change in how the city smells is profound. For a second, I thought I was in Brussels. The usual smell of Christmas holidays in Valencia is of roasted chestnuts and sweet potato or *churros* and *buñuelos* (donuts). Times change. Smells too.

But when they do, nativists sniff of danger and mobilize to return their cities to native, familiar, and comfortable aromas. The Italian city of Prato, near Florence in Tuscany, with a large Chinese population, passed a regulation banning all non-traditional food offerings from its historical center in 2005. Bussolengo, near Verona, banned in 2007 the opening of new kebab restaurants in the historical center and mandated they be located at least 150 meters away from religious sites, hospitals, and schools. The suggestion here is that foreign food is dangerous and the city had the obligation to protect vulnerable populations. Lucca, near Florence, banned ethnic food offerings in 2008. In Lombardy, regional regulations banned eating kebabs on the street, outside of kebab stores.[56] Altopascio, Genoa, Bergamo, Vicenza... the list keeps growing.[57] Daily Italian newspaper *La Stampa* called it the new Lombard crusade against the Saracens: An anti-kebab crusade.[58]

In the small Venetian Italian town of Cittadella, Massimo Bitonci, the mayor from the populist radical right party Lega Nord (Northern League, today La Lega, or The League), made headlines in 2011 when he passed a ban on new kebab, takeaway, and fast-food restaurants in his town. The reasons given by the mayor were various, but one of them was that they spread "cattivi e sgradevoli odori" (foul and unpleasant smells). First, he argued, kebab is not a food that represents the Venetian culinary tradition. Second, kebab and other foreign restaurants do not respect hygiene and health regulations. Third, kebab restaurants could become a gathering place for people who consume Middle Eastern food, as it had in Padua, and thus transform the character of the city. Fourth, this was a necessary measure considering "le numerose segnalazioni e lamentele da parte di cittadini e associazioni di categoria sull'insorgere di cattivi e sgradevoli odori che possono essere causati dall'apertura di tali attivita' e che di certo non si addicono ad una citta' con caratteristiche storiche e medioevali qual e' la nostra" (the numerous reports and complaints by residents and trustworthy associations regarding bad and unpleasant odors that would be triggered by the opening of such restaurants and that do not befit the historic and medieval features of a city such as ours).[59] While the city approved his proposal, its implementation was uneven.[60]

Bitonci, however, did not ease up on his anti-kebab crusade; rather he just pursued more palatable legislation to achieve the same results. He became mayor of the larger nearby city of Padua and, in 2015, introduced a curfew targeting kebab shops and other takeaways near the city's main train station. In 2016, he proposed that at least sixty percent of the food offered in new takeaway restaurants be Venetian products.[61] The bill defines as local products those that are produced and distributed in the Veneto region. The stated aim of the bill is to safeguard the cultural, historic, artistic, and environmental characteristics and image of Padua. And, to leave no doubt about the nature of the bill, Elonora Mosco, Padua's vice-mayor, explained that these were "anti-kebab" measures.[62]

Bitonci and other Lega mayors aim to hinder the appearance of ethnic neighborhoods in their cities. Ethnic neighborhoods are a common feature in modern cities. They are not only a natural product of immigration waves, but also an effective mechanism of immigrant integration. Toronto, Canada, a city that has had immigration waves since the 1850s and where 46.1 percent of the population was foreign-born in 2016, has Little India, Greektown, Chinatown, Little Italy, Koreatown, Little Portugal, and Little Poland.[63] All these neighborhoods are vibrant immigrant hubs and also entryways into that culture for everybody else. Toronto's ethnic names are neutral geographic indicators of where the immigrant community comes from. In many European towns, in contrast, ethnic neighborhoods have negative connotations. In Barcelona, for instance, Ravalistán, the moniker for the Raval neighborhood where Pakistani immigrants have settled for decades now, is a derogatory rather than neutral name.[64]

The defense of native products and traditional cuisine is not the sole purview of the radical populist right. The center-left local government in Florence moved simultaneously in the same direction and with the same results, albeit with slightly less unsavory arguments. Matteo Renzi, then-mayor of Florence, passed in 2011 new regulations for commercial activity in the downtown, a designated UNESCO cultural heritage site, that banned the opening of new fast-food restaurants, internet, money transfer, money exchange, and wholesale retail, as well as vending machines for drinks and snacks. It was called "operation quality." Dario Nardella, vice-mayor at the time, argued that their regulations were different from the anti-kebab moves of the Lega Nord because in Florence there was no discrimination based on "criteri etnici e culturali legati al prodotto alimentare" (ethnic or cultural criteria related to food). There was "solo al discrimine della qualità" (discrimination based on quality alone).[65]

The following center-left government of Florence, led by now-mayor Nardella, was the first city in Italy to introduce legislation favoring local produce. Nardella's law mandated that, for new businesses in the historic downtown, seventy percent of their food must have either a short distribution chain or be officially recognized as being from the Tuscan region.[66] The law accepts any product that has undergone a maximum of two commercial intermediaries between the producer and the consumer or that falls under the European *denominazione di origine protetta* (Protected Designation of Origin), *indicazione geografica protetta* (Protected Geographical Designation), or the catalogue of *prodotti agroalimentari tradizionali* (Traditional Food products) for the Tuscan region.[67]

With these laws, immigrants would not be able to open new corner stores or ethnic restaurants in the downtown touristic cores of Cittadella, Padua, or Florence. All laws, however, had a provision allowing exemptions for "quality projects." This exemption was put to the test in 2016 by the American burger chain McDonalds, who requested to open a franchise at Florence's Duomo (Cathedral) square. McDonald's did not take lightly mayor Nardella's rejection of its proposal and sued the city, seeking $20 million in damages. As I write, McDonald's lawsuit is still pending.[68]

The concerns of Italian mayors to protect their cities from being overrun by international franchises are perhaps more warranted than the anti-kebab crusade of the Lega because of the greater purchasing and lobbying power international franchises have over small ethnic businesses. Without any legislation, the free market allows international franchises to take over all prime real estate in downtown European towns. As a case in point, most restaurants in the City Hall Square in Valencia are international franchises.[69]

Native Looks

While the smell of waffle is accepted without argument at Valencia's commercial core, the proposal to mark the Roquetes neighborhood with two Chinese arches, which could have inaugurated Spain's first Chinatown neighborhood, became stalled in controversy and nativist backlash.

In 2020, Joan Ribó, the left-wing mayor of Valencia, following similar popular budget initiatives elsewhere in Spain, allocated eight million euros to local projects proposed and voted on by Valencian residents. A young Valencian, Joan Hornos, proposed to install two Chinese arches to the east of the downtown train station.[70] The area is full of Chinese stores and restaurants and the arches would have marked it as Valencia's Chinatown. The original proposal located the arches a quarter mile from City Hall, where Xàtiva boulevard meets Pelai and Convent Jerusalem streets. It explained that all of the world's great cities (London, Los Angeles, Toronto, New York) "existe al menos un arco de entrada al barrio chino ('Chinatown')" (have at least one arch to mark the entrance of Chinatown), arguing that the beautiful arches "siempre atraen turistas y son sitios emblemáticos de la ciudad para hacerse fotos y selfies" (attract tourists and become emblematic locations for photos and selfies).[71] The proposal also suggested that the arches be commissioned to local *Falles* artists. When voters ranked the arches third among the projects proposed, the local Chinese community and the Valencia Confucius Institute celebrated the initiative.[72]

In many large European cities, it is still common for neighborhoods near train stations to be degraded and attract irregular activities, such as prostitution and drug dealing. Often, when immigrants arrive in a city, they look for the cheapest real estate and that happens to be in "undesirable" locations for natives. When Chinese immigrants began to arrive in Valencia in the 1980s and opened restaurants and corner stores, they concentrated on both sides of the train tracks: small retail shops near downtown and wholesale warehouses in the Russafa neighborhood.[73]

The location of the proposed arches made sense, but as soon as it was publicly released, some neighbors and "native"-run businesses rapidly collected 800 residents' signatures against the project.[74] Neighbors were concerned that marking the area as Valencia's Chinatown would cast a shadow over the other Valencian activities in the area: *Falles* and Valencian *pilota*.

Falles is a week-long celebration during which neighbors pay for and install on the streets over four hundred large sculptures made of Styrofoam on wooden structures. It was added to UNESCO's intangible cultural heritage of humanity list in 2016. Three *falles* associations to the east of the train station opposed the construction of the Chinese arches. The original proposal included an arch on Convent Jerusalem street, where the main *falla* in the area is located. Convent Jerusalem's *falla* is part of the top-quality league and regularly wins top prizes. This *falla*, however, welcomed the arches once the arch that was originally proposed to go on its street was moved to another street a block north, where it would be less visible than if it was on Convent Jerusalem and Xàtiva boulevard.

Neighbors also questioned the second arch on Pelai street on the grounds of protecting another Valencian tradition: *pilota* (ball), a handball sport related to the various ballgames played in the Iberian Peninsula. The most famous Valencian *pilota trinquet* (court) is on Pelai street. As soon as the arches proposal became public, the Valencian Federation of Valencian Pilota opposed the arch because it would involve "desnaturalizar" (denaturing) the Valencian *pilota* court, a 150-year sport complex that has been a cultural referent for Valencians. A *Levante-Emv* article called the court "la Catedral del deporte autóctono" (the Cathedral of the autochthonous sport). The President of the Valencian Pilota (Ball) Federation asked that the Pelai arch be moved from the intersection of the Xàtiva boulevard and Pelai street to further north, beyond the *trinquet* (court), so the court would not be included in the area marked as Chinatown.[75] The Federation also reminded Valencia City Hall that they had requested to dedicate that street to celebrate Valencian *Pilota* before the arches' proposal was approved. Their counter-idea was to make a Valencian *Pilota* Walk of Fame on Pelai Street by pedestrianizing the street and decorating it with sculptures and bas-reliefs of the hands of famous *pilotaires* (handball players).[76]

Chen Jui, president of the Association of Chinese Businesses of the Valencian Region, explained that the Chinese arches were a good initiative to promote the integration and rootedness of Chinese immigrants in Valencia. The neighborhood is home to around 200 businesses operated by Chinese immigrants and has become the main location to celebrate the Chinese New Year in Valencia. In the same radio program, Blanca Blanquer, General Director for Urbanism under the regional socialist government in the 1980s, opposed the arches' construction because, in her view, "auténticos barrios chinos" (an authentic Chinatown) should be where businesses sell "productos típicamente, típicamente chinos" (typical, typical Chinese products) and the businesses in the area did not qualify, as there are "un par de supermercados, hay peluquerías, y unas tiendas como las antiguas todo a cien" (a couple of grocery stores, hair salons, and some shops like the old dollar stores).[77] Moreover, the neighborhood also has Russians, Pakistanis, and Peruvians, Blanquer continued, so Chinese are not the main group and thus should not be particularly celebrated. Finally, Blanquer argued, a Chinatown is not about integration, but rather about "colonización" (colonization). It would be akin to accepting that Chinese "nos han colonizado y nos han ocupado este barrio" (have colonized us and have occupied our neighborhood).[78]

Blanquer's three arguments exemplify a nativist zero-sum game understanding of culture. In her view, only "typical Chinese products," as opposed to real products from China and Spanish-Chinese food cooked by Chinese residents, are worthy of respect and protection. Secondly, for Blanquer, only the dominant group, that is, "native" Valencians, are worth celebrating. All other groups are merely one of many. This is cultural diversity seen from the lens of native entitlement. Finally, her understanding of culture is narrow and traditionalist at the same time. According to Blanquer, a neighborhood cannot be both Valencian and Chinese. Non-Valencian indicators, such as the proposed Chinese arches, thus become symbols of cultural colonization.

Mayor Ribó and his coalition team addressed the controversy, saying that they supported the arches, but to make them compatible with the *Pilota* Walk of Fame and the designation of the downtown area as a culturally preserved zone, they were willing to find alternative locations for them. The difficulty for the mayor is that all alternative locations lose visibility and thus purpose.

Opposition parties were not content with this conciliatory tone and demanded to kill the project altogether. The local conservative Partido Popular (Popular Party) asked City Hall to halt the project due to the opposition it had triggered among certain residents, retail owners, and some cultural associations in town, such as the centenarian Real Academia de Cultura Valenciana (Royal Academy of Valencian Culture) and the Valencia Federation of Neighborhood Associations.[79] Manuel Muñoz, President of the Real Academia de Bellas Artes de San Carlos (San Carlos Royal Art Academy), opposed the proposal as "un proyecto anglosajón" (an Anglo-Saxon project) that threatened to transform a popular urban neighborhood into "un espacio (parque) temático" (a theme-park space) destined to replicate a foreign initiative. Instead of being proof of integration, it would become "una muestra efectista, antigua y, además, copiada" (an old, copied, and gimmicky measure).[80]

The opposition successfully delayed that project and will likely kill it altogether. A few months later, the vice-mayor asserted that she was reconsidering the idea of installing Chinese arches and asked her advisers to develop an alternative proposal that was "elegant and well-integrated with the landscape."[81] That proposal materialized a year later. An arch is planned in the area, but it will not be a Chinese arch, and it will not celebrate Spain's first Chinatown. It will be "un pórtico de 7 metros de alto" (a 7-meter-tall gateway) dedicated to the Valencian *pilota*.[82]

Conclusion: Food that Brings Us Together. Food that Sets Us Apart.

This chapter has argued that culinary xenophobia has become a feature of nativism in many Western European countries in the twenty-first century. I have explored three controversies that exemplify the dynamics at work: native tastes, smells, and looks.

My first section, "Native Tastes," documented how the populist radical right has politicized school menus in France and Denmark, in some cases eliminating pork-free menus for religious minority students. Controversies in Spanish schools are of a different nature, as Spanish Muslims, backed by their 1992 Cooperation Agreement with the Spanish State, are pushing for public school cafeterias to offer halal menus, with uneven results so far. The overall effect of these cultural wars over food and food offerings in public institutions is twofold: first, it has politicized pork in ways Europe has not seen since the medieval and early-modern periods. Identity and belonging are, once again, defined by what one eats or refuses to eat. Pork has joined the headscarf as a new cultural battlefield in Europe. Second, it has undermined the rights of religious minorities to equal treatment and accommodation for their needs in the public sphere.

My second section, "Native Smells," argued that the politicization of food is not limited to school menus, but has extended to the type of restaurants, food, and smells welcome in European cities. I focus on Italy, where the populist radical right has engaged in an "anti-kebab" crusade and the center-left has inaugurated campaigns to limit food offerings in historical towns to only "quality" local cuisine. This nativist backlash against foreign smells and foods, and the foreigners who cook, serve, and eat them, undermines immigrants' ability to establish small businesses and settle in Italy.

My last section, "Native Looks," discussed the proposal to erect two Chinese arches in the downtown area of the Spanish city of Valencia, where hundreds of Chinese-run small businesses are located. This would have been the first designated and celebrated Chinatown in Spain. Nativist backlash managed to delay and probably kill the project by demanding that, instead of celebrating a deemed foreign culture, the City Hall should highlight two exclusively Valencian cultural traditions: *falles* and Valencian *pilota*. Native culture was pitched against "foreign" and immigrant cultures in a zero-sum logic that prevented celebrating all of them simultaneously.

Jamón or Spanish omelet? Which should be celebrated as the Spanish national dish? The former excludes more people than the latter. Consumers, following general trends that favor diets with less meat and more plants, are leaning toward the latter. How European are döner kebab or French tacos? It seems very much so. The döner kebab has become the "laborer's meal of choice and the quintessential midnight snack" in Germany, the UK, and France. More recently, the popularity of French tacos, a fast-food immigrant invention, cannot be understated either.[83] Despite turning pork into a battlefield, nativism in Europe is limited by the emergence and popularity of fusion cuisine. The UK's example to toss fish and chips to embrace chicken tikka masala as their favorite dish can only be the beginning of a new culinary journey. In the meantime, however, nativist appetites are still setting the menu.

NOTES

1. *Jamón ibérico* is the dry-cured ham produced from livestock of Black Iberian breed pigs. Translations from Spanish and Italian into English are the author's unless otherwise noted.
2. The ad can be found at "ASICI y Rafa Nadal promocionan el Jamón Ibérico en el Torneo de Tenis de Hamburgo," *Cárnica Association Newsletter*, July 17, 2015.
3. Jodi Campbell, *At the First Table: Food and Social Identity in Early Modern Spain* (Lincoln: University of Nebraska Press, 2017), 76.
4. Juan Goytisolo, *Crónicas Sarracinas* (Barcelona: Ibérica de Ediciones y Publicaciones, 1982), 9, citing R. W. Southern.
5. Observatorio Andalusí and UCIDE, "2019 Estudio demográfico de la población musulmana" (Madrid: Unión de Comunidades Islámicas de España, 2020).
6. Law 26/1992, of 10 November, Approving the Agreement of Cooperation between the State and the Islamic Commission of Spain (BOE N1 272, of November 12, 1992).
7. See Marianne Lien and Brigitte Nerlich, eds., *The Politics of Food* (Oxford, UK: Berg, 2004); Atsuko Ichijo and Ronald Ranta, *Food, National Identity and Nationalism: From Everyday to Global Politics* (New York: Palgrave Macmillan, 2016).

8. See Priscilla Parkhurst Ferguson, *Accounting for Taste: The Triumph of French Cuisine* (Chicago: University of Chicago Press, 2004); Lara Anderson, "The Unity and Diversity of *La olla podrida*: An Autochthonous Model of Spanish Culinary Nationalism," *Journal of Spanish Cultural Studies* 14 (2013): 400–414; Atsuko Ichijo, Venetia Johannes, and Ronald Ranta, eds., *The Emergence of National Food: The Dynamics of Food and Nationalism* (London: Bloomsbury Academic, 2019).
9. See Michaela DeSoucey, "Gastronationalism: Food Traditions and Authenticity Politics in the European Union," *American Sociological Review* 75, no. 3 (2010): 432–55; Atsuko Ichijo, "Food and Nationalism: Gastronationalism Revisited," *Nationalities Papers* 42, no. 2 (2020): 215–23; Ichijo, Johannes, and Ranta, *The Emergence of National Food*.
10. DeSoucey, "Gastronationalism," 433.
11. Wynee Wright and Alexis Annes, "Halal on the Menu? Contested Food Politics and French Identity in Fast-Food," *Journal of Rural Studies* 32 (2013): 388–99.
12. Aitana Guia, *The Muslim Struggle for Civil Rights: Promoting Democracy through Migrant Engagement, 1985–2010* (Chicago: Sussex Academic Press, 2014), 11.
13. John Higham, *Strangers in the Land: Patterns of American Nativism, 1860–1925* (New Brunswick, NJ: Rutgers University Press, 1988).
14. Fabio Parasecoli, *Gastronativism: Food, Identity, Politics* (New York: Columbia University Press, 2022).
15. Lara Anderson, Heather Benbow, and Gregoria Manzin, "Europe on a Plate: Food, Identity and Cultural Diversity in Contemporary Europe," *Australian and New Zealand Journal of European Studies* 8, no. 1 (2016): 2–15.
16. See Wright and Annes, "Halal on the Menu?"
17. See Martha Sif Karrebæk, "Pigs and Pork in Denmark: Meaning Change, Ideology, and Traditional Foods," *Signs and Society* 9, no. 1 (Winter 2021).
18. Es, Margaretha A. van. "Roasting a Pig in Front of a Mosque: How Pork Matters in Pegida's Anti-Islam Protest in Eindhoven." *Religions* 11, no. 7 (2020).
19. See Karrebæk, "Pigs and Pork in Denmark."
20. Meat is halal when the animal's raising and slaughtering follow religious precepts. School cafeteria food in Spain is a large meal for lunch consisting of first and second courses, as well as desert. It constitutes the main daily meal for many children.
21. Salva Vives, "Educación afirma que los menús de Alzira respetan los derechos de los musulmanes," *Levante-EMV*, December 11, 2014.
22. "Once familias musulmanas renuncian a la beca de comedor en Zaragoza por no disponer de menú halal," *AlertaDigital.com*, October 9, 2013.
23. "Los musulmanes del Pintor Andreu de Alzira reciben el menú sin cerdo desde hace 9 años," *RiberaExpress.es*, December 9, 2014.
24. Art. 14.4 of the Cooperation Agreement, however, is ambiguous. It states that "La alimentación . . . de los alumnos musulmanes de los centros docentes públicos y privados concertados que lo soliciten, se procurará adecuar a los preceptos religiosos islámicos, así como el horario de comidas durante el mes de ayuno (Ramadán)" (If requested, the food offered to . . . Muslim students in public and subsidized private schools will attempt to adjust to Islamic religious tenets, as well as the schedule of meals will take

fasting during Ramadan into account). Some scholars have read "se procurará" (will attempt to) as an obligation and others as a voluntary recommendation.

25. Salva Vives, "El colegio Pintor Andreu de Alzira «nunca» proporcionó a los musulmanes el menú halal," *Levante-EMV*, January 10, 2015.
26. Law 17 of July 2011. Food Safety and Nutrition Law. BOE 160, 6 July 2011.
27. Marta Fernández Vallejo, "Los colegios multiplican sus menús: para alérgicos, vegetarianos, musulmanes...," *El Correo*, February 18, 2018.
28. Ibid.
29. "Denuncian que Educación no garantiza menús halal en tres comedores escolares," *Levante-EMV*, April 24, 2018.
30. "Musulmanes piden fin de la discriminación en los comedores escolares de Valencia," *MundoIslam.com*, August 18, 2018.
31. Rita Gomes Faria and Miguel Hernando de Larramendi, "Guía de apoyo a la gestión pública de la diversidad religiosa en el ámbito de la alimentación" (Madrid: Observatorio del Pluralismo Religioso en España, 2011), 42–43.
32. See Joan Wallach Scott, *The Politics of the Veil* (Princeton, NJ: Princeton University Press, 2007).
33. Angelique Chrisafis, "Nicolas Sarkozy: There Are too Many Foreigners in France," *The Guardian*, March 7, 2012.
34. Ibid.
35. Ibid.
36. James McAuley, "Why Halal Meat Generates so much Controversy in Europe," *The Washington Post*, October 9, 2018.
37. Ibid.
38. Manuel Arenas, "Polémica en Mataró por la implantación de un menú único musulmán en un comedor escolar," *El Periódico*, September 18, 2017.
39. "Parents Protest Against School's Decision to Serve Halal Meat to ALL Children," *Daily Mail*, January 9, 2008.
40. Sam Truelove, "Parents Outraged after New Addington Primary School Proposes Only Serving Halal Meat," *Croydon Advertiser*, September 26, 2017.
41. Kate Ng, "'Ideology on a Plate': Row after French City Takes Meat off Menu for Schoolchildren," *Independent*, February 22, 2021.
42. Ibid.
43. Simon Weaver, "Liquid Racism and the Danish Prophet Muhammad Cartoons," *Current Sociology* 58, no. 5 (2010): 675–92; Jytte Klausen, *The Cartoons that Shook the World* (New Haven, CT: Yale University Press, 2009).
44. Sidsel Overgaard, "Pork Politics: Why Some Danes Want Pig Meat Required on Menus," *NPR*, September 23, 2013.
45. Jimmy King, "Danish Town's Meat Policy Sparks Controversy in Muslim Community," *OpposingViews*, January 13, 2016.
46. Marlena Spieler, "The Fancy of Britain: Tikka Masala's more Popular than Fish 'n' Chips," *SFGATE*, May 30, 2001.

47. Emily Rella, "Americans Consume an Average of 2.4 Hamburgers per Day—and more Meaty Facts," *YahooLife.com*, May 28, 2020.
48. Dan Bilefsky, "Denmark's New Front in Debate Over Immigrants: Children's Lunches," *The New York Times*, January 20, 2016.
49. Karrebæk, "Pigs and Pork in Denmark."
50. Lauren Frayer, "At Last, Muslims Can Savor a Halal Spin on Spain's Famous Jamón," *NPR*, December 16, 2014; Cristina Pita and Irene Larraz, "¿Por qué comemos cada vez menos jamón serrano si nos gusta tanto?" *Newtral*, May 3, 2021.
51. "Se dispara el consumo de tortilla de patatas en el hogar," *RevistaInfoRetail*, May 25, 2021.
52. "Santiago Abascal defiende la libertad para comer jamón . . . y así lo manipulan algunos," Contando Estrellas Blog, November 18, 2018.
53. Igiaba Scego, "Salsicce," trans. Giovanna Bellesia and Victoria Offredi Poletto, *Warscapes.com*.
54. Najat El Hachmi, *The Last Patriarch* (London: Serpent's Tail, 2010).
55. Mohammed Chaib, *Enlloc com a Catalunya. Una vida guanyada dia a dia* (Barcelona: Empúries, 2005), 108–10.
56. Lorella Franci, "Renzi vs tutti. Il sindaco di Firenze litiga con la Cgil e rottama i fast food," *Scatti di Gusto*, April 23, 2011.
57. Anderson, Benbow, and Mazin, "Europe on a Plate," 9–11.
58. "In Praise of . . . the Kebab," *The Guardian*, November 16, 2009.
59. "Cittadella, il sindaco leghista vieta kebab, fast food e take away: 'Cattivi odori, i cittadini si lamentano,'" *Quotidiano Nazionale*, August 6, 2011.
60. Patrizia Messina and Fred Paxton, "Strong Localism, Weak Regionalism: The Strengths and Weaknesses of Lega Nord Governance of the Veneto Region," paper presented at the RSA Annual Conference, June 4–7, 2017, Dublin, Ireland.
61. Alberto Nardelli, "A Right-Wing Italian Mayor is Introducing an 'Anti-Kebab' Law," *BuzzFeed.News*, October 14, 2016.
62. Luca Preziusi, "Bitonci: licenza solo ai take away che vendano il 60% di prodotti veneti," *Il Mattino di Padova*, October 12, 2016.
63. Ontario Ministry of Finance, "2016 Census Highlights: Fact Sheet 8, Immigration," 2016.
64. Jordi Moreras, "¿Ravalistán? Islam y configuración comunitaria entre los paquistaníes en Barcelona," *Revista CIDOB d'Afers Internacionals* 68 (2005): 119–32; Guia, *The Muslim Struggle for Civil Rights*.
65. Franci, "Renzi vs tutti."
66. The concept "di filiera corta" (short supply chain) is well established within the local and slow food movement in Italy, akin to the "100-mile food source" movement.
67. Ernesto Ferrara, "Firenze, ok a nuovi ristoranti solo se vendono il 70% di prodotti toscani," *La Repubblica*, March 8, 2016.
68. "McDonald's Claims $20m from Florence over Piazza Restaurant Rebuff," *The Guardian*, November 7, 2016.

69. Taco Bell, Five Guys, Subway, Foster's Hollywood, Burger King, and Yogurtlandia are established offerings on the square. Even restaurants that offer Spanish food, such as Beher: Tienda del Jamón Ibérico and Lizarrán: Casa de Pinchos, are franchises.
70. J.M. Vigara, "València tendrá su propio Chinatown tras instalar 2 arcos en Pelayo," *Levante-EMV*, March 12, 2021.
71. J. M. Vigara, "Joan Hornos, el verdadero autor de la idea de convertir Pelayo en el Chinatown Valenciano," *Levante-EMV*, March 21, 2021.
72. J. M. Vigara, "València será la primera ciudad de España en tener su propio 'Chinatown,'" *Levante-EMV*, March 12, 2021.
73. Francisco Torres Pérez, *Nous veïns a la ciutat: els immigrants a València i Russafa* (València: Universitat de València, 2007).
74. J. M. Vigara, "Los vecinos se organizan contra el Chinatown y preparan movilizaciones," *Levante-EMV*, April 20, 2021.
75. Vigara, "El Trinquet."
76. J. M. Vigara, "El Ayuntamiento ve compatible el Chinatown con el de Pelayo," *Levante-EMV*, March 18, 2021.
77. Hoy por hoy. Locos por Valencia, "Controversia por los arcos del Chinatown Valenciano," *Cadena Ser*, April 9, 2021, 6:15–6:55.
78. Ibid., 8:20–8:28.
79. Vigara, "Los vecinos."
80. Manuel Muñoz, "Chinatown," *Levante-EMV*, April 15, 2021.
81. Paco Moreno, "Los arcos chinos se difuminan," *Las Provincias*, May 3, 2021.
82. J. M. Vigara, "La calle Pelayo será un parque temático de la pelota con un pórtico de 7 metros de alto," *Levante-EMV*, February 6, 2022.
83. Pierre Raffard, "The Doner Kebab, an Unlikely Symbol of European Identity," *The Conversation*, May 13, 2019; Lauren Collins, "The Unlikely Rise of the French Tacos: How an Upstart Fast Food Became Essential Dining in the Home of Haute Cuisine," *New Yorker*, April 12, 2021.

WORKS CITED

Anderson, Lara. "The Unity and Diversity of *La olla podrida*: An Autochthonous Model of Spanish Culinary Nationalism." *Journal of Spanish Cultural Studies* 14 (2013): 400–414.
Anderson, Lara, Heather Benbow, and Gregoria Manzin. "Europe on a Plate: Food, Identity and Cultural Diversity in Contemporary Europe." *Australian and New Zealand Journal of European Studies* 8, no. 1 (2016): 2–15.
Arenas, Manuel. "Polémica en Mataró por la implantación de un menú único musulmán en un comedor escolar." *El Periódico*, September 18, 2017.
Bilefsky, Dan. "Denmark's New Front in Debate Over Immigrants: Children's Lunches." *The New York Times*, January 20, 2016.
Billig, Michael. *Banal Nationalism*. London: SAGE Publications, 1995.

Campbell, Jodi. *At the First Table: Food and Social Identity in Early Modern Spain.* Lincoln: University of Nebraska Press, 2017.
Chaib, Mohammed. *Enlloc com a Catalunya. Una vida guanyada dia a dia.* Barcelona: Empúries, 2005.
Chrisafis, Angelique. "Nicolas Sarkozy: There Are too Many Foreigners in France." *The Guardian*, March 7, 2012.
———. "Pork or Nothing: How School Dinners are Dividing France." *The Guardian*, October 13, 2015.
"Cittadella, il sindaco leghista vieta kebab, fast food e take away: 'Cattivi odori, i cittadini si lamentano.'" *Quotidiano Nazionale*, August 6, 2011.
Collins, Lauren. "The Unlikely Rise of the French Tacos: How an Upstart Fast Food Became Essential Dining in the Home of Haute Cuisine." *New Yorker*, April 12, 2021.
"Denuncian que Educación no garantiza menús halal en tres comedores escolares." *Levante-EMV*, April 24, 2018.
DeSoucey, Michaela. "Gastronationalism: Food Traditions and Authenticity Politics in the European Union." *American Sociological Review* 75, no. 3 (2010): 432–55.
El Hachmi, Najat. *The Last Patriarch.* London: Serpent's Tail, 2010.
"El jamón ibérico llega a Roma de la mano de Rafa Nadal." *EurocarneDigital*, May 9, 2016.
Es, Margaretha A. van. "Roasting a Pig in Front of a Mosque: How Pork Matters in Pegida's Anti-Islam Protest in Eindhoven." *Religions* 11, no. 7 (2020): 359.
Fernández Vallejo, Marta. "Los colegios multiplican sus menús: para alérgicos, vegetarianos, musulmanes…" *El Correo*, February 18, 2018.
Ferrara, Ernesto. "Firenze, ok a nuovi ristoranti solo se vendono il 70% di prodotti toscani." *La Repubblica*, March 8, 2016.
Franci, Lorella. "Renzi vs tutti. Il sindaco di Firenze litiga con la Cgil e rottama i fast food." *Scatti di Gusto*, April 23, 2011.
Frayer, Lauren. "At Last, Muslims Can Savor a Halal Spin on Spain's Famous Jamón." *NPR*, December 16, 2014.
Gomes Faria, Rita, and Miguel Hernando de Larramendi. "Guía de apoyo a la gestión pública de la diversidad religiosa en el ámbito de la alimentación." Madrid: Observatorio del Pluralismo Religioso en España, 2011.
Goytisolo, Juan. *Crónicas Sarracinas.* Barcelona: Ibérica de Ediciones y Publicaciones, 1982.
Guia, Aitana. "The Concept of Nativism and Anti-Immigrant Sentiments in Europe." EUI Working Paper MWP 2016/20. European University Institute, Robert Schuman Centre for Advanced Studies, Max Weber Postdoctoral Program, September 2016.
———. *The Muslim Struggle for Civil Rights: Promoting Democracy through Migrant Engagement, 1985–2010.* Chicago: Sussex Academic Press, 2014.
Higham, John. *Strangers in the Land: Patterns of American Nativism, 1860–1925.* New Brunswick, NJ: Rutgers University Press, 1988.
Hoy por hoy. Locos por Valencia. "Controversia por los arcos del Chinatown valenciano." *Cadena Ser*, April 9, 2021.
Ichijo, Atsuko. "Food and Nationalism: Gastronationalism Revisited." *Nationalities Papers* 42, no. 2 (2020): 215–23.

Ichijo, Atsuko, and Ronald Ranta. *Food, National Identity and Nationalism: From Everyday to Global Politics.* New York: Palgrave Macmillan, 2016.

Ichijo, Atsuko, Venetia Johannes, and Ronald Ranta, eds. *The Emergence of National Food: The Dynamics of Food and Nationalism.* London: Bloomsbury Academic, 2019.

Karrebæk, Martha Sif. "Pigs and Pork in Denmark: Meaning Change, Ideology, and Traditional Foods." *Signs and Society* 9, no. 1 (Winter 2021).

King, Jimmy. "Danish Town's Meat Policy Sparks Controversy in Muslim Community." *OpposingViews*, January 13, 2016.

Klausen, Jytte. *The Cartoons that Shook the World.* New Haven, CT: Yale University Press, 2009.

Lien, Marianne, and Brigitte Nerlich, eds. *The Politics of Food.* Oxford, UK: Berg, 2004.

McAuley, James. "Why Halal Meat Generates so much Controversy in Europe." *The Washington Post*, October 9, 2018.

"McDonald's Claims $20m from Florence over Piazza Restaurant Rebuff." *The Guardian*, November 7, 2016.

Messina, Patrizia, and Fred Paxton. "Strong Localism, Weak Regionalism: The Strengths and Weaknesses of Lega Nord Governance of the Veneto Region." Paper presented at the RSA Annual Conference, June 4–7, 2017. Dublin, Ireland.

Moreno, Paco. "Los arcos chinos se difuminan." *Las Provincias*, May 3, 2021.

Moreras, Jordi. "¿Ravalistán? Islam y configuración comunitaria entre los paquistaníes en Barcelona." *Revista CIDOB d'Afers Internacionals* 68 (2005): 119–32.

Muñoz, Manuel. "Chinatown." *Levante-EMV*, April 15, 2021.

"Los musulmanes del Pintor Andreu de Alzira reciben el menú sin cerdo desde hace 9 años." *RiberaExpress.es*, December 9, 2014.

"Musulmanes piden fin de la discriminación en los comedores escolares de Valencia." *MundoIslam.com*, August 18, 2018.

Nardelli, Alberto. "A Right-Wing Italian Mayor is Introducing an 'Anti-Kebab' Law." *BuzzFeed. News*, October 14, 2016.

Ng, Kate. "'Ideology on a Plate': Row after French City Takes Meat off Menu for Schoolchildren." *Independent*, February 22, 2021.

Observatorio Andalusí and UCIDE. "2019 Estudio demográfico de la población musulmana." Madrid: Unión de Comunidades Islámicas de España, 2020.

"Once familias musulmanas renuncian a la beca de comedor en Zaragoza por no disponer de menú halal." *AlertaDigital.com*, October 9, 2013.

Ontario Ministry of Finance. "2016 Census Highlights: Fact Sheet 8, Immigration." 2016.

Overgaard, Sidsel. "Pork Politics: Why Some Danes Want Pig Meat Required on Menus." *NPR*, September 23, 2013.

Parasecoli, Fabio. *Gastronativism: Food, Identity, Politics.* New York: Columbia University Press, 2022.

"Parents Protest Against School's Decision to Serve Halal Meat to ALL Children." *Daily Mail*, January 9, 2008.

Parkhurst Ferguson, Priscilla. *Accounting for Taste: The Triumph of French Cuisine.* Chicago: University of Chicago Press, 2004.

Pita, Cristina, and Irene Larraz. "¿Por qué comemos cada vez menos jamón serrano si nos gusta tanto?" *Newtral*, May 3, 2021.

Preziusi, Luca. "Bitonci: licenza solo ai take away che vendano il 60% di prodotti veneti." *Il Mattino di Padova*, October 12, 2016.

Raffard, Pierre. "The Doner Kebab, an Unlikely Symbol of European Identity." *The Conversation*, May 13, 2019.

Rella, Emily. "Americans Consume an Average of 2.4 Hamburgers per Day—and more Meaty Facts." *YahooLife.com*, May 28, 2020.

"Santiago Abascal defiende la libertad para comer jamón ... y así lo manipulan algunos." Contando Estrellas Blog, November 18, 2018.

Scego, Igiaba. "Salsicce." Translated by Giovanna Bellesia and Victoria Offredi Poletto. *Warscapes.com*. Web. 10 February 2022.

Scott, Joan Wallach. *The Politics of the Veil*. Princeton, NJ: Princeton University Press, 2007.

"Se dispara el consumo de tortilla de patatas en el hogar." *RevistaInfoRetail*, May 25, 2021.

Spieler, Marlena. "The Fancy of Britain: Tikka Masala's more Popular than Fish 'n' Chips." *SFGATE*, May 30, 2001.

Torres Pérez, Francisco. *Nous veïns a la ciutat: els immigrants a València i Russafa*. València: Universitat de València, 2007.

Truelove, Sam. "Parents Outraged after New Addington Primary School Proposes Only Serving Halal Meat." *Croydon Advertiser*, September 26, 2017.

Vigara, JM. "El Ayuntamiento ve compatible el Chinatown con el de Pelayo." *Levante-EMV*, March 18, 2021.

———. "La calle Pelayo será un parque temático de la pelota con un pórtico de 7 metros de alto." *Levante-EMV*, February 6, 2022.

———. "Joan Hornos, el verdadero autor de la idea de convertir Pelayo en el Chinatown valenciano." *Levante-EMV*, March 21, 2021.

———. "El Trinquet de Pelayo rechaza ser incluido en el Chinatown de València." *Levante-EMV*, 16 March 2021.

———. "València tendrá su propio Chinatown tras instalar 2 arcos en Pelayo." *Levante-EMV*, March 12, 2021.

———. "València será la primera ciudad de España en tener su propio 'Chinatown.'" *Levante-EMV*, March 12, 2021.

———. "Los vecinos se organizan contra el Chinatown y preparan movilizaciones." *Levante-EMV*, April 20, 2021.

Vives, Salva. "Educación afirma que los menús de Alzira respetan los derechos de los musulmanes." *Levante-EMV*, December 11, 2014.

———. "El colegio Pintor Andreu de Alzira «nunca» proporcionó a los musulmanes el menú halal." *Levante-EMV*, January 10, 2015.

Weaver, Simon. "Liquid Racism and the Danish Prophet Muhammad Cartoons." *Current Sociology* 58, no. 5 (2010): 675–92.

Wright, Wynee, and Alexis Annes. "Halal on the Menu? Contested Food Politics and French Identity in Fast-Food." *Journal of Rural Studies* 32 (2013): 388–99.

◆ CHAPTER 5

Kashrut in Spain

Religious Observance, State Tolerance, or Niche Market Entrepreneurship?

Silvina Schammah Gesser and Susy Gruss

Kashrut dietary laws as they appear in the Hebrew scriptures do not match the label of "ethnonational" cuisine.[1] Far from it, *kashrut* dietary laws and practices in Judaism constitute a different kind of phenomena. Indeed, the laws of *kashrut*, together with the observance of Shabbat and the laws of "family purity" (pertaining to the relations of husband and wife), are the three basic pillars of Orthodox Judaism. In other words, the world of *kashrut* (*kosher* food, eating rules, and cooking practices) pertains to a religious, prescriptive domain.[2] The word *Kasher* כשר in Hebrew means "appropriate," that is, complying with the *Torah* laws.[3] Even more so, *kashrut* prescriptions and *kosher* food ways mark differences not only between Jews and non-Jews but also, and most interestingly, among Jews themselves.[4] Thus, *kashrut* observance turns into a complex set of rules and commandments that unites Jews as a community while separating them into different groups and scales.[5]

Kashrut laws have always provoked an enduring search for explanation. Among Jewish believers, the need to provide answers that elucidate *kashrut* rules seeks, for the most part, to reinforce Jews in their religious creed. Conversely, the need to provide clarifications of *kashrut* laws to non-Jews, especially in the contemporary era, functions as a practical manual for gentiles who help produce *kosher* food and products.[6]

Matters related to *kashrut* dietary in Spain in the twentieth and twenty-first centuries respond to the re-initiation of Jewish life in the country. The latter was conditioned by the interests and developments at stake in the Peninsula, by the initiatives and trajectories of individual Jews or affluent families in some cases, by small waves of Jewish migrants or even larger Jewish conglomerates in others, as well as by the always changing international circumstances.[7] Likewise, *kashrut* practices in Spain have always reflected major regional differences—between continental Spain and the Spanish Protectorate in North Africa until 1956, between the Spanish enclaves of Ceuta and Melilla and Madrid and Barcelona, and between these two and smaller Jewish communities, such as Torremolinos, Málaga, or Alicante.[8] This diversity reflects transformations within regional Jewish communities as well as changes taking place in Spanish politics and society.[9] Hence, addressing the changing nature of *kosher* practices and infrastructure in Spain and its territories in the last century can shed light on the changing status of Jews in the country. The sections that follow focus on these issues by analyzing in-depth interviews with members of the Jewish communities in Spain and Melilla, community publications, Jewish cuisine booklets, *kosher* food and wine flyers, together with a close analysis of commercial videos and trade information supplied by the Spanish Embassy in Tel Aviv. This primary data is critically discussed against the backdrop of religious liberty, which, timidly initiated toward the last stages of Francoism, reaches a peak in democratic Spain.

Jews and Kashrut in Spain: A Difficult Puzzle

The study of food provides insights into how socio-political and cultural power relations are distributed among different groups in society.[10] Because food is "not just food" but a medium for the assertion of cultural characteristics and of one's sense of place, the study of the world of *kashrut* and its eating practices offers an unexplored area to study Jewish life in Spain. Given that the formation of the Jewish communities in continental Spain in the early twentieth century resulted from different waves of migration, which underwent processes of de-territorialization, we argue that maintaining *kashrut* among Jews (mainly observant and traditionalist ones) was a way of relating to their original reference group while they struggled to establish themselves in the host society. It is precisely the viability of maintaining *kashrut* practices that provides a new lens through which to examine their self-assertion, degree of acculturation and assimilation, insecurities, or, at best, sense of belonging and acceptance as they struggled to become an "integrated" non-Catholic ethnic minority in a highly Catholic environment.

It is worth mentioning that, as opposed to major Jewish communities in Poland, Germany, France, Austria, or Hungary, which had a highly significant

Jewish presence and infrastructure until the outburst of WWII, there was no organized Jewish life in continental Spain up until the late 1950s. Hence, until then, the Jewish presence constituted a rather sporadic, and at times, *sui generis* model characterized by private initiatives, family and neighborhood arrangements, and rather limited communitarian proposals.

Not only the migrants' origins, their small size, and the host society's regional differences, autonomous enclaves, and colonies, but also Spain's socio-political vicissitudes throughout the twentieth century were crucial factors in determining the prosperity or the ebb and deterioration of Jewish community life and conditioned the possibilities of *kashrut* observance and practices. In this respect, four stages can be roughly delineated—even if they do not always run parallel in the Iberian Peninsula as opposed to Spanish enclaves and the Protectorate in North Africa. First, there was an initial establishment of Jewish communities in continental Spain since the late 1910s up until the Civil War in 1936. Second, these communities were disrupted between 1936–1939 and the Jewish presence was secretly re-initiated after the end of the war and until the late 1940s. Third, there was a slow normalization of a new modus vivendi for Jews in Francoist Spain, which, in the mid-1950s, opened its doors to the arrival of North African Sephardic Jews. This momentum reached a point of no return with the legalization of the Jewish communities in 1965 and the drafting of 1978 Spanish Constitution. Fourth, we conclude with the era initiated by Spanish democracy.

Broadly speaking, Jews began to arrive in continental Spain in the second half of the nineteenth century.[11] (Garzón, *Los judíos 1789–1902*). By the 1910s and early 1920s, the scarce Jewish presence in Madrid and Barcelona was of mixed composition, with Sephardic and Ashkenazi Jews coming from a variety of European, North African, and Asian regions.[12] The Balkan Wars in 1912–1913, as well as the disintegration of the Ottoman, Austro-Hungarian, and Czarist Empires following WWI, brought about various waves of Jewish migration from East to West. Small contingents came to Spain, adding new migrants and refugees to the exiting Jewish presence, which remained fragmentary and small.

In the case of Madrid, Ignacio Bauer, a well-off and highly educated Spanish Jew sufficiently "integrated" within the Spanish elites, aided by other two major non-Spanish Jewish figures, Abraham Shalom Yehuda and Max Nordau, established the first pillars of the Jewish community in the capital.[13] While the group succeeded in organizing a small network of institutions, it is not clear whether *kashrut* observance was a major priority among its members.[14] Jacobo Israel Garzón (b. Tetouan,1942), President of the Jewish Community of Madrid (2001–2008), Head of the Federación de Comunidades Judías de España (2003–2011), and a major researcher of Jewish life in Spain, assesses that "there was no *kashrut* in Spain at the time of WWI, and this was not thought about when creating the synagogues. I remember reading in a magazine of the Community of Madrid, Hakesher, of a refugee, named Halpern or Halphen, who only ate kosher. He was recommended to go to Lisbon, where kashrut facilities were plenty."[15]

While we may assume that the mixed group of local and migrant Jews in Madrid were, for the most part, non-observant Jews, they most probably kept *kashrut* laws (e.g., abstaining from non-*kosher* meat, wine) in their celebration of rites, prayers, and ceremonies. Despite the fact that the Jewish community was developing in Madrid, it was Barcelona of the early decades of the twentieth century that was much more economically attractive to Jewish newcomers, who soon outnumbered their counterparts in the Castilian capital.[16]

Together with the Jews who had gathered around Sant Antoni Market in the early 1920s, other Jewish migrants coming from France (albeit originally from the Ottoman Empire) settled in Barcelona.[17] Mediterranean Jews hailing from Izmir, Istanbul, and Thessalonica were, for the most part, very respectful of *kashrut* observance and had to make do as best they could in a foreign environment. That was the case of the Nahum family, originally from Izmir, who arrived in 1931, bringing with them an ancient Torah scroll known as *Sefer Torah*. The head of the family, Itzhak Nahum, who later acted as makeshift rabbi and *hazzan* (cantor) of the *ad hoc* Jewish community, had the permission to slaughter poultry (but not meat) for his own household consumption. His family, as others, had to wait for the arrival in 1933 of Mr. Gabbay, a qualified rabbi from Istanbul, who had the necessary papers and certification to provide *kosher* meat to the community. Only then did bovine meat become part of the menu for those who kept *kashrut*.[18] Photographs and testimonies of other Jewish migrants and refugees arriving to Barcelona, even among those coming from Germany in 1933, kept alimentary restrictions as far as cattle meat was concerned.[19] By then, the *kosher* slaughter ritual was performed by an Ashkenazi Rabbi, Manuel Kimstlinger, and by the Sephardi one, Jacob Toledo Córdoba, who used to go to the public slaughterhouse, where cattle were set aside to supply the Jewish demand. Oral testimonies maintained that an occasional *kosher* butchery survived underground functioning until 1947–48.[20]

Contrary to Madrid and Barcelona, the Spanish enclaves of Ceuta and Melilla have maintained a continuous Jewish presence since the fifteenth century, and the observance of *kashrut* dietary laws constituted a marker of identity of their ancient communities. In 1903, the Melilla census pointed to 1,225 Jews in its territory, by far outnumbering the Jewish presence of Madrid and Barcelona, which hardly mounted a few hundred at the time.[21] WWI and the 1921 Rif War further attracted the Jewish population, which by 1918 numbered 3,290.[22] By the mid-1930s, Melilla boasted no less than eleven synagogues, with a Jewish community that in 1936 consisted of 4,000 to 6,000 souls, almost 6 percent of the enclave's inhabitants.[23] Likewise, the presence of Sephardic and Arab Jews in the Spanish Protectorate dating from the early modern period was also significant.[24] In the city of Tetouan, known for its Jewish population and traditional community networks, *kashrut* laws were thoroughly respected even though the Jewish community administration institutionalized *kosher* regulations in the early twentieth century. J. Israel Garzón's testimony about Jewish households in Tetouan reveals that when *kosher* meat was difficult or expensive to obtain: "There were always people who had *teudaht shjitat ofot* (Jewish slaughtering license for poultry), which was even given to women for family use. I know that a great-aunt of mine, who lived in Tetouan, had it."

He recalls that most families made their own *matzah* at home to comply with the commandment of not eating yeast during the Passover.[25] *Kosher* wine, a major component of Jewish ritual in general, and of the Passover feast in particular, was also homemade: "the *kashrut* in our family was limited to meat, wine and *Pesach* products. By taking fish, [that is becoming pescatarian] and not eating meat; by bringing Passover wine and other products from Bayonne or Gibraltar, the issue was easily solved."

His testimony reinforces the idea that, in Tetouan, *kashrut* issues were circumscribed to the Jewish community's internal demand and consumption and these centered on meat, wine, and Passover products. The presence of Spain as a new colonial power since 1912 did not interfere with the internal organization, rites, and customs of the Jewish community under its control, which was able to keep its *kashrut* dietary tradition.

Together with some few *kosher* products that could be sporadically imported from Bayonne or Paris, the Jewish communities of Ceuta and Melilla (together with Seville) had *schochatim* (slaughterers in Hebrew), those individuals officially certified as competent to kill cattle and poultry as prescribed by Jewish law. This continuity during the Spanish Protectorate was to differ significantly from the situation in the Iberian Peninsula, where *kashrut* practices had to be established and institutionalized from scratch.

As it could have not been otherwise, the outbreak of the Spanish Civil War in July 1936, and the war conditions it imposed, deeply affected the Jewish communities, especially in Madrid and Barcelona, leading to the debilitation of *kashrut* observance, which, by then, was not backed up by a solid infrastructure. These vicissitudes are exemplified in the life trajectory of Menachem Coriat (b. Cueta, 1888–1968), a well-known member of the Madrid Jewish community. His famous portrait celebrating a Jewish wedding at the *Midrás Abarbanel* synagogue on the front page of the *ABC* in June 1931 tells of his links with the new Spanish democracy. This became an omen as the war advanced, forcing him to escape from different cities until he arrived in Barcelona in 1938. In 1939, he was authorized to represent Spain at the Jewish World Congress in Paris. Coriat shared the destiny of thousands of Spanish Republicans who found refuge in México years later, but he was unable to return to Spain until 1958, at the age of seventy.[26]

As his story reveals, the war brought the dismembering of the Jewish communities in Madrid and Barcelona. Among those who remained, some converted to Catholicism.[27] The establishment of the Francoist regime in 1939, with its clear anti-Semitic bent, led to the outlawing of the last possible remnants of Jewish communities and synagogues. By then, it was common to arrest Jews for their presumed republicanism or for their association with Freemasonry and to limit their access to work (a punishment that also applied to other religious minorities).[28] Such a menacing atmosphere exerted further pressure on Jews who had to live at the margins of society or else convert to Catholicism, with *kashrut* concerns been either ignored or carried out secretly. According to the testimony of Yehuda Saportas, a Thessalonian Jew and one of the 342 Sephardim who were brought from Bergen Belsen as a child to Barcelona in a convoy organized by S. Romero Radigales, the Spanish Consul in Athens, in 1944, it was the Joint Distribution Committee, with its base in New York, that took care of the well-being and food needs of the refugees in Spain during WWII. Under such delicate circumstances, survival rather than *kashrut* observance was probably their first priority.[29]

Toward the end of WWII, the Francoist regime's tense relationship with the Jews in continental Spain became more "amenable" as the dictator carefully orchestrated the myth of "Franco as savior of Jews."[30] This political strategy did not change the fact that the few real Jews still living in continental Spain remained behind the scenes, living at the limits of what was allowed by the strict and discriminatory Francoist laws, on the one hand, and secrecy, on the other.[31] Indeed, their almost clandestine existence and liminal situation did not allow for community records, even less for overall community decisions. Their passive resistance to the Francoist state apparatus and silent struggle toward autonomy were expressed in small private initiatives, as much as by actions and decisions taken by individual community leaders determined to re-establish roots in a devastated post-civil war Spain. During 1946–1947, there were timid attempts to restore Jewish life, and the Jews present in Madrid and Barcelona were allowed to celebrate their religious services in private gatherings. Synagogues were discretely opened in 1949.[32] Madrid, with around a thousand people, mostly from Germany, Poland, France, and Hungary, was then able to count on a synagogue and a graveyard (albeit with no permanent rabbi). Even when the regime tolerated the celebration of major festivities, such as *Rosh HaShanah* (the Jewish New Year) and *Yom Kippur* (the Day of Attornment), it was made clear to all that their functioning depended, first and foremost, on the goodwill of the Francoist authorities.[33]

Meanwhile, Barcelona also opened its synagogue on Roma Avenue in 1949 and a Community Center on Porvenir Street in 1954, which catered to two synagogues, one following the Sephardic rite and the other the Ashkenazi rite. The division reflected the heterogeneous Jewish population of Barcelona at the time, composed of Poles, Greeks, Germans, French, Bulgarians, Swiss, and Portuguese, and amounting to 2,500 individuals.[34] At this stage, the few *kosher* products available were imported from Bayonne or Paris. If the organization of the religious life of the Jewish communities in Spain still remained quite rudimentary until the mid-1950s, the observance of *kashrut*, probably kept in a very cautious manner, was restricted to the household's demand, which probably drew on poultry, home-made *matzah* for the Passover, and the like.[35]

The tough Francoist policies that characterized continental Spain somehow contrasted with the more moderate attitudes toward Jews in North Africa. In Ceuta and Melilla, the Spanish Protectorate and the International Zone of Tangier, which Spain occupied until the end of WWII, some thirty thousand Jews were allowed to continue with their communal life and creed. The religious liberty granted to Jewish communities not only made it possible to run their own schools and cemeteries but also to provide *shochatim* (slaughterers with a rabbinical license), allowing them to enjoy full Jewish life and *kashrut* observance, even when economic penalties were common.[36]

The testimony of Baruch "Benito" Sarfatti Garzón (b. 1937, Tetouan), the first Rabbi of the Balmes Synagogue in Madrid (1968–1978), helps to reconstruct the local as well as transnational *kosher* practices of the community of Tetouan in the 1940s and early 1950s:

> During the Passover, we used to make a special biscuit known as *pan leve* baked in a public *kosher* oven specially organized for this feast. We also had industrialized *matzah* and cheese, which were sent by the Jewish community in the Netherlands. Other *kosher* products were provided by the extended families living in major European cities. . . . A very rudimentary wine that resembled grape juice was used for the *Kiddush*, out of which a special supply was kept for the Passover. . . . It turned out that *we*, the Jews, were the only producers of wine in Tetouan, given that the Muslim population were not supposed to consume alcohol.[37]

With the independence of Morocco in 1956, the availability and acquisition of *kosher* food in Tetouan was facilitated by free access and commercial exchanges with the city of Casablanca, which produced a variety of products. However, it should be noted that the end of the Spanish Protectorate and of the Tangier International Zone led to a drastic reduction of the Jewish presence in these areas. These changes soon reverted the numerical imbalance between the larger Jewish communities in North Africa and the Peninsula, leading to tectonic transformations in the profile of the Jewish communities in Spain in general, and in Madrid in particular. Thus, the Jewish population of Madrid, which amounted to 1,000 individuals in 1959, reached 2,500 members by the end of 1960s.[38]

The massive arrival of Sephardic Jews from Spanish North Africa soon transformed them into a clear majority among the Jewish population of continental Spain.[39] However, the demographic change did not mean that the newcomers could easily replicate their mores and habits in a capital still under the influence of ultra-nationalist Catholic discourse. It is no wonder that semi-clandestine gatherings celebrating Jewish rites and calendar, informal religious schooling, in-group recreational activities, and kitchen practices and traditional cooking styles remained a distinctive feature of the silent and pacific forms of defiance and resistance, even if they were not originally conceived as such.[40] The already mentioned testimony of Rabbi Sarfatti Garzón, who had come to Madrid as a university student in 1965, is a case in point. By then, he recalls, "there was only one *kosher* eatery, always crowed, where Jewish students could have their meals if they had the patience to wait to be served." As for himself, he could have his *kosher* meals in the premises of an informal Jewish school where he worked as a community teacher. At that time, the supply of *kosher* food to the community was under the tutelage of the Moroccan Rabbi of Madrid, Salomon Ben-Sabat, who was responsible for providing *kosher* meat upon request. "Benito," together with the *Shammash*—the caretaker of the informal school and synagogue—personally delivered the meat (which was kept in the community refrigerator) to those who could not come. Such an act of service and personalized attention is considered a *zehut*, that is, a virtuous act highly appreciated in Judaism.

According to Rabbi Sarfatti Garzón, it was Rabbi Yehuda Banasuly, originally from Alcazarquivir and later the rabbi of the Jewish community of Madrid (1978–2000), who had initially worked as a *shochet* in Madrid in those years. The fact that, in the capital during the late 1960s, there was a *shochet* for meat and another for poultry (Mr. Isaac Ben Simon) speaks to the significant increase in demand for *kosher* meat. This development made possible the opening of the first *kosher* butchery in the capital.

While these testimonies still reveal the limited scope of the *kosher* infrastructure in Madrid, it is important to emphasize that the early 1960s witnessed various initiatives intended to strengthen the links between Spain and the Sephardic culture. However, such initiatives, mostly circumscribed to cultural, economic, and political diplomacy abroad, had *no* significant impact on the real Jewish communities living in Spain.[41] It was only in 1965, with the Declaration of Religious Freedom promoted by the Second Vatican Council, which stated that religious freedom "must be recognized as a civil right in the legal system," that the Jewish communities in Spain were officially recognized. The Declaration led to the modification of article six of the *Fuero de los Españoles*.[42] Later on, the 1967 Religious Freedom Law recognized minority religious denominations and provided the appropriate climate for the inauguration of the *Comunidad Israelita de Madrid* in 1968. Baruch "Benito" Sarfatti Garzón officiated as the first rabbi of the newly born Beth Yaacov Synagogue, which opened its doors that same year.[43] Soon, a *kosher* eatery began to function in the basement. The chef, Marcos Benveniste, originally from the city of Tangier, had been specially brought to prepare traditional North African Jewish meals there. Its success led to the opening of the first *kosher* restaurant in Madrid next to the synagogue.[44]

With the increasing demand for *kosher* products, the traditional toast during the celebration of the *Kiddush*, which had previously been made with grape juice, could now be made with real *kosher* wine from the Israeli winery Carmel. Soon, *kosher* wines from the American line Manischewitz were also available. A major step forward came with the Spanish production of the first *kosher* wines at the Valdepeñas winery. By then, there were already two *kosher* butcheries, one near the synagogue and the other at the Argüelles market, in the zone of Chamberí.[45]

In the meantime, the Madrid community kept on growing, as the 1973 Yom Kippur War brought to the capital a new wave of Hispano-Moroccan Jews who had remained in North Africa. This growth was accompanied by an expansion of the premises and services for Jews, including a working synagogue, an active school, a cemetery, and a social recreation farm. It should be noted that religious services, the observance and provision of *kosher* food, and the *Ezra* voluntary organizations that emerged, all followed the Hispano-Moroccan community rites of North Morocco. Their traditionalist Sephardic ethos, rituals, and style, and their willingness to observe *kashrut*, certainly in official community events and ceremonies, helped to explain the subsequent difficulties these Hispano-Moroccan Jews had in "absorbing" later migrant waves of Latin American Jews who came to the Peninsula. As opposed to the former, these newcomers were modern and secular, politically left-wing and mostly of Ashkenazi origin. That was the case of the political exiles from the Southern Cone, especially from Argentina, who arrived in the early 1970s and after the 1976 military coup. Unsurprisingly, they openly rejected the religious bent fostered by the more observant Hispano-Moroccan communal networks, and they did not care about *kashrut* observance or the acquisition of *kosher* food products. The resulting tensions and rivalries between the dominant traditionalist and neo-orthodox approach championed by North African Jews, for whom *Kium mitzvoth* (the observance of Jewish laws and commandments) is the most basic characteristic of Judaism, versus the new assimilationist liberalism championed by the Latin American Jews, made clear that the debate about the different ways of being a Jew and of understanding Judaism—so characteristic of the identity politics among established communities worldwide—was now taking place in Spain. Be that as it may, by the late 1970s, the Jewish community in Madrid housed nearly 7,000 Jews, surpassing the Jewish presence in Barcelona.[46]

At the same time, Spain was painstakingly initiating its second transition to democracy, which was to have an enormous effect on the visibility of the Jewish communities at home. The Constitution of 1978, and the Organic Law of Religious Freedom of 1980, which provided a new legal framework for religious minorities, led to the establishment of the Federation of Israelite Communities of Spain in 1982, in accordance with the Law of Religious Freedom 7/1980 of July 5, and the Royal Decree of January 9, 1981.[47] Later on, the 1992 Agreements, beyond officially establishing the role and position of ministers of worship, registration of community premises, exemption from certain taxes, and the like, made clear that Spain gave the Federation the power to decide on *kashrut* matters. In other words, the Agreements transformed the entity into the only institution entitled to provide *kosher* certificates in Spain. By giving complete liberty of action on *kosher* procedures (slaughtering, in particular), so long as they did not interfere with Spanish sanitary laws, the 1992 Agreements proved to be crucial in the years to come.

Moreover, the legitimacy of the Agreements awarded to *kashrut* practices made room for a more effective division of labor. The city of Córdoba, well-connected by an efficient railway network and easily accessible from any of the Jewish community centers in Spain, turned the Andalusian capital into the elected place for establishing a *kosher* slaughterhouse, even though Córdoba has no Jewish population. *Shochatim* from Madrid and Barcelona and the other northern regions would come to the city, which overnight became the *kosher* meat supplier for the rest of the communities, including Málaga and even Ceuta and Melilla in North Africa. These rapid developments in continental Spain were not only responses to the major transformations of Spanish society as a whole (democratization, modernization, orientation toward Europe), but also to the role played by an active cadre of Jewish community leaders originally from the Spanish Protectorate, who struggled to institutionalize Jewish life in democratic Spain.[48]

Certainly, the strengthening of the Jewish communities in continental Spain came at the expense of what was initially a vibrant Jewish presence in Ceuta and Melilla. The enclaves, which had enjoyed prosperity in the early sixties, suffered a significant economic decline in the 1970s.[49] This decline spurred various paths of migration within the Jewish communities, whose members emigrated to Israel, South America, and to the largest Spanish cities. The testimony of David Jiménez Benhamou, a former member of the Jewish community of Melilla, who now works at the Spanish Embassy trade office in Tel Aviv, Israel, sheds light on the processes that took place in the North African Spanish territories in the last decades. According to Benhamou, the 1990s coincided with his childhood and adolescence: "life in Melilla was quite satisfying and the Jewish community nurtured an easy-going Jewish lifestyle that was compatible with its non-Jewish surroundings [. . .] there was no problem whatsoever to get *kosher* meat and products because despite the relatively small size of the community, there were between four and five working butcheries."[50]

His mother, a traditionalist Jew and observant of the *kashrut* laws, had different kitchen sets and basins—one for dairy, another for meat, and a third one for Passover. She worked at the local hospital and felt perfectly at home with her Muslim neighbors. David's mother explained that the policy at the hospital refectory, which was a landmark of interfaith respect, did not transgress food taboos and no pork was included in the menu. Thus, she could always attend the canteen and eat vegetarian dishes whenever she did not take her own lunch to work. David's somewhat idyllic portrait of the 1990s does not correspond to the situation nowadays.[51] In his opinion, the deterioration of the economic situation in Melilla spurred Jewish emigration, while the remaining members underwent a process of religious revitalization.[52] David complained that "Melilla students attending Ultraorthodox Sephardic Yeshivot in Jerusalem and Benei Brak, Israel, who returned to the city on their summer holidays, brought to the city a stricter pathos of *kashrut* observance, to the point of campaigning for the consumption of unheard products as *kosher* Coca-Cola, *kosher* snacks, and even *kosher* ready-made food, attitudes that radically differed from the more tolerant outlooks that had characterized our community."

In this respect, it is important to point out that the changes affecting the Spanish Jewish communities nationwide began to transform the discrete and monolithic image attributed to them as they increasingly constituted a plural and polyphonic reality (most prominently in Madrid and Barcelona). They enjoyed a certain visibility in the public space, mainly since 1992. Certainly, the celebrations of the Fifth Centenary of 1492 gave rise to several cultural and political initiatives that officially reconnected Spain with its Jewish past and the Jewish world. At the diplomatic and symbolic level, the "recovery of the memory of *Sefarad*" resulted in a plethora of events and activities that reached a climax with the detailed coverage of King Juan Carlos's visit and landmark speech at the Beth Yaacov synagogue in Madrid in 1992. Quite significantly, these events ran parallel to the echoes of the 1991 Madrid Peace Conference, which had placed Spanish diplomacy in the spotlight of international politics.

As Spain rapidly normalized cultural and diplomatic relations with Israel (1986) and the Sephardic world Jewry, cultural state policies embraced Jewish heritage as flagship. A promising engine for the development of an economically sustainable tourism industry nationwide, the Red de Juderías, co-sponsored by the Spanish Ministry of Industry, Commerce and Tourism, turned their "supply" into specialized touristic products. The official promotion of and the popular and academic interest in the Judeo-Spanish past, music, and literature gave rise to romanticized publications about Sephardic cuisine.[53] A different case in point is *La cocina judía. Leyes, costumbres y algunas recetas sefardíes* (Jewish Cookery: Rules, Customs and some Sephardic Recipes), published by the Red de Juderías (Jewish Network) in 2003. Rather than a culinary text on Jewish cuisine, as its title and the official introduction written by then-President of the Red de Juderías and mayor of Cáceres suggest, the book's contents, written by a prestigious member of the Jewish community of Madrid, Uriel Macías Kapón, is a pretext to explain the basics of the Jewish calendar, rites, and complex *kashrut* laws to a Spanish, non-Jewish audience.[54]

In turn, the Red de Juderías published a ninety-page guide of Spanish *kosher* wineries, in Spanish, English, and Hebrew. *Viñedos de Sefarad* was endorsed by the president of the FCJE, Isaac Querub Caro. The guide offers "a heavenly journey through the vineyards of Sefarad" to both national and international publics. Targeted to transcend the tiny Jewish communities at home, the booklet, which ponders the virtues as well as difficulties involved in producing *kosher* wine in Spain, reveals the great varieties of wineries available and their different *kosher* certifications. Given that estimates of the Jewish presence in Spain oscillate between 20,000 and 40,000, a small population when compared to estimates of Jewish communities in other European countries or other non-Catholic religious groups within Spanish society, the production of *kosher* wine in Spain has become a strategic asset.[55] In other words, despite the increasing legitimacy and visibility that the Jewish communities enjoy nowadays, there remains a limited albeit much better structured internal demand, supply, and consumption of *kashrut* products nationwide, wine included. As major producers of top-quality wines, many Spanish wineries (together with other leading Spanish entrepreneurs in search of the diversification of agri-food exports) have opted for the international *kosher* niche market as a new, highly attractive venue for investment and growth. The following section addresses the processes that the specialization and internationalization of Spanish *kosher* products have prompted.

Kashrut as Opportunity: Spanish Exports in the New Millennium

Spanish food producers and exporters have understood that the specificities of *kashrut* offer a major strategy for market differentiation, one that perfectly adapts to global food trends sponsoring healthy eating, quality meat, and an absence of saturated fat. The same can be said of *kashrut*'s strict prohibition on mixing meat and dairy, which attracts, for reasons that have nothing to do with creed, both vegans and those who are lactose intolerant.[56] The economic potential of *kosher* food products has led Spanish producers to consider the demands of the Israeli market. Indeed, the capitalist and consumerist trends prevalent in Israeli society have turned its *kosher* market, albeit limited in relation to the American one, into a promising venue, even when the Israeli *kosher* market presents difficult religious and bureaucratic obstacles. In this respect, there are conditions *sine qua non* that Spanish producers are obliged to meet to qualify for selling *kosher* products in Israel. Yet, it is worth the effort because meeting the Israeli *kosher* standards opens the door to other much bigger *kosher* markets, especially in the USA, France, Belgium, and Latin America.

The trade office at the Spanish Embassy in Tel Aviv provides comprehensive knowledge, counselling, and personalized advice to Spanish producers interested in the Israeli and other *kosher* markets.[57] Video conferences organized by the Spanish economic *attaché* bring to the fore the embassy's role in assisting Spanish enterprises in getting acquainted with the *kashrut* laws and accessing attractive markets.[58] Most importantly, the Spanish Embassy provides Spanish-Israeli consultants, the majority being religious Jews well-versed in *both* Spanish and Israeli laws, ways, and customs, as well as in the intricate character of the world of *kashrut*. Their mediatory services are crucial, as not all Spanish enterprises and producers interested in exporting food products to Israel understand the complex *kashrut* restrictions, as this anecdote illustrates:

> Spanish producer: I want to export ham [jamón] to Israel.
> Embassy trade advisor: You cannot because it is not *kosher!*
> Spanish producer: Ok. Then, what do I have to do to make ham *kosher*?[59]

Notwithstanding the possible cultural gaps, the embassy insists that *kosher* exports to Israel should not be seen as an incommensurable obstacle but as a target to be reached. By belittling the *via-dolorosa* required to obtain *kosher* certification, the economic *attaché* spurs Spanish producers and companies to pick up the gauntlet:

> Make a virtue out of necessity and grab the business opportunity in the export of *kosher* products! It must be a strategic decision for companies to try and make the most of this golden set of circumstances . . . The *kosher* certificate is, without a doubt, an added value to your products and it will allow you to reach new markets not only in Israel . . . You have to see the *kosher* certificate as an engine of new opportunities.[60]

Boasting that the FCJE registered more than 500 Spanish enterprises that already have their *kosher* certificate, the *attaché'*s insistence that "selling *kosher* products is a highly profitable business" is confirmed by the dimensions of the Israeli *kosher* market. The Spanish export index to Israel reveals that they earned 68 million euros in 2012. By 2016, it rose to 105 million—an increase of 40 percent in four years. That reached 110 million by 2017.[61] These rising numbers are also confirmed by various reports showing that businesses with *kosher* certificates doubled their sales.[62] The increasing, exponential climb is explained by the quality and cleanliness generally attributed to *kosher* products. As for the Israeli market, *kosher* products, in this case from Spain, are equally attractive to Muslim citizens, both in Israel and in the Palestinian Authority.[63]

Spanish companies wishing to have access to *kosher* markets must obtain the *kosher* seal before exporting their products. In Spain, this certificate is first issued by the Federation of Jewish Communities of Spain—not only the sole entity that authorizes *kosher* domestic consumption and exports but also the one in charge of registering trademarks in the Spanish Industrial Property Registry for *kosher* food and *parve* (vegan) products. A higher quality control certificate can be obtained from the Orthodox Union (OU), which controls nearly 70 percent of *kosher* food production worldwide. Given that the degree of acceptance and recognition of the *kosher* seal depends on the standing of the rabbis, agencies, and authorities involved, the more prestigious, the more expensive the certification is. Even though there are many global agencies that issue the *kosher* certificate, very few enjoy unanimous recognition and acceptance.[64] Be that as it may, the resulting *kosher* seal or certificate functions as a food quality control system that confirms that the *kosher* product has been successfully subject to rabbinical inspection and can be safely commercialized. This is called *hechsher*, and it is identified by symbols that differ according to the institution conducting the inspection.[65]

The *hechsher* or *kosher* permit for wine offers a peeping hole into the complexities that Spanish producers must overcome to obtain the *kosher* seal for their product. Notwithstanding the high quality of Spanish wines, to provide for a foundation of Spanish exports to Israel and to the Jewish world at large, *kosher* wine requires *kosher* ingredients, which means that, from crushing grapes to bottling wine, only Shabbat-observant Jews can be involved in making it.[66] To overcome such requirements, Spanish producers turn to cooked or pasteurized wine—known as *mevushal*—as stipulated by the *Shulhan Arukh*, the most widely accepted compilation of Jewish law.[67]

Kosher cooked wine can be prepared by non-Jews, although part of its flavor is lost and is therefore considered of lesser quality. Historically, the intention behind such religious Jewish law (*Halakha*) was that the drinking of wine and or the use of wine in religious rituals were not to be associated with ancient pagan practices or idolatry. Another requirement includes that *kosher* wine for Passover needs to be free of yeasts, a forbidden ingredient in the one-week celebration commemorating the freedom of the Israelites from Egypt and the exodus to Canaan. One of the major Spanish wineries producing *kosher* wine is the Catalan Capçanes Winery in Tarragona, which makes five different *kosher* blends. One of them, *Peraj Ha'abib*, was the winner of numerous awards, such as the EUROKOSHER distinction in 2001, as well as many other recognitions. Undoubtedly, obtaining the *kosher* certificate has internationalized Spanish *kosher* wines, which nowadays count the United States, Israel, France, and the United Kingdom as their main customers.[68] As a global player in the competitive *kosher* markets, Spain has wisely added prestige to the *Marca España* (Spanish Brand), a soft-power state policy intended to promote the image of Spain both inside and beyond its borders.[69] Designed by the Spanish authorities, *Marca España* is a crucial pillar to frame and advertise the nation as equally competitive, talented, and innovative. By the same token, services, hotels, and resorts specially adapted to those among the diverse groups of tourists coming to Spain who are observant of *kashrut* laws can now catch the attention and pockets of Jews worldwide, helping to attract foreign investment and foster the internationalization of Spanish companies and expand cultural tourism and exchange.

Final Observations

The present overview of the viability and evolution of *kashrut* dietary in Spain and its North African territories from the early twentieth century to the present has revealed not only major regional differences, affected by socio-political, economic, and historical developments. It has also highlighted the transition of the world of *kashrut* from an issue that pertained to religious community needs and practices *vis-à-vis* Spain's tolerance, to a new entrepreneurial platform. Equally significant, the legitimacy and visibility that the Jewish communities so far acquired in democratic Spain, which *did* have an impact on the institutionalization and regularization of *kashrut*, has not necessarily brought a massive increase in the demand of *kashrut* products at the community level. This may respond to the fact that, for secular as opposed to Orthodox and Ultra-Orthodox Jews, in Spain as elsewhere, *kashrut* observance can be seen as an "aggregate" that may or may not be indulged rather than a condition *sine qua non*. No wonder then that the Gordian knot nowadays lies in the give and take between the commercial interest of the Spanish food and winery industries and producers, on the one hand, and the FCJE on the other, as the latter is the first and only entity that can grant them *kosher* certification at home.

At the same time, *kosher* meat, which is the most strictly regulated of *kosher* foods, is under increasing scrutiny, as *kosher* slaughterhouses, which kill animals without first stunning them, has unleashed a harsh debate in Europe between religious freedom and the wellbeing of animals.

In May 2018, the Court of Justice of the European Union ruled on the legality of this type of slaughtering, asserting in its resolution that religious slaughter must be considered among the acts of worship that are part of the right to religious freedom. However, pressure by activist groups in Belgium, forsaking the welfare of animals, reopened the debate about the rules surrounding the religious slaughter of the Jewish tradition and the Muslim *halal* in the old continent.[70] In Spain, the 1992 Agreements signed by the FCJE and the CIE (Islamic Commission of Spain) require that the sacrifice of animals according to Jewish laws or according to Islamic regulations should be respectful of current state health regulations in the statute of animal and food safety, food hygiene, and the labeling of products intended for human consumption. Thus, while both the FCJE and the CIE have the authority to apply and verify the slaughter conditions and the ability of the slaughterers to carry out the sacrifice in accordance with Jewish and Islamic laws, it is the state administration and the autonomous communities that determine the sanitary requirements of the technical-sanitary regulations of food, services, or products directly or indirectly related to human use and consumption. So far, the heated debates in various European countries, which have been echoed in public and academic forums in the Peninsula, have no clear path to revising the Spanish law and its unique arrangements with the creeds of Judaism and Islam. Whether the debate on religious slaughter in various European countries will affect not only the legitimacy of the religious observation of *kashrut* in Spain but also the 1992 State Agreements for the production of *kosher* (and of *halal*) meat, both for internal demand and for export (considering that Spain's Muslim population, as opposed to its Jewish population, amounts to two million people), only time will tell.

NOTES

1. Ethnonational cuisine refers to the unique foodways of a specific group of people that distinguishes them from their neighbors and sees emblematic dishes as representatives of specific cuisines. The definition essentializes ways of cooking, ignoring spatial and social variations. On Jewish cuisine diversity, see Barbara Kirshenblatt-Gimblett, "Kitchen Judaism," in *Getting Comfortable in New York: The Jewish Home, 1880–1950*, eds. Susan L. Braunstein and Joselit Jenna Weissman (New York: Jewish Museum, 1990), 75–105.
2. The laws of *kashrut* encompass moral and ritual aspects enumerated within the Torah, the Talmud, and later rabbinic writings. Their implementation is concerned with the relationship between God and humanity and between the existing world and its inhabitants. These aspects are not mutually exclusive. Rather, they constitute two of the major theological axes of debate that dominate religious discourse on *kashrut*.
3. The *Pentateuch* offers many passages that command: "of such food you shall not eat" or "you shall not cook this with that." See *Genesis* 9:4; *Exodus* 21:22; *Deuteronomy* 12:16, 23, 25; *Leviticus* 7: 23–27; *Leviticus* 17:12.
4. On taboo foods and kashrut laws, see Ella Stiniguță Laslo, "Purity and Impurity in Judaism: Taboo Foods and the Kashrut Laws," *Studia Judaica* 22, no. 1 (2017): 137–57.
5. S. Guzmen-Carmeli, "Eating the Bubbe: Culinary Encounters Between Secular and Haredi Jews in Bnei Brak," *Food and Foodways* 28, no. 2 (2020): 69–90; David Kraemer, *Jewish Eating and Identity through the Ages* (New York: Routledge, 2008).
6. Rabbi Nina H. Mandel, "Why Do They Care? Understanding the Need to Explain the Kosher Laws," in *Odysseys of Plates and Palates: Food, Society and Sociality*, eds. Simeon S. Magliveras and Catherine Gallin, (Boston, MA: Brill, 2014), 31–41.
7. Silvina Schammah Gesser and Teresa Pinheiro, "Guest Editors' Introduction to the Special Issue, 'Jewish (In)Visibility in Iberia: A View from the Margins,'" *Contemporary Jewry* 40 (2020): 503–17.
8. Martine Berthelot, *Cien años de la presencia judía en la España contemporánea* (Barcelona: KFM, 1995), 44–62.
9. Taking normative Judaism from the more to the less religious, the main current trends in Spain are "Ultra-Orthodox" and Chabad Lubavitch; "Orthodox" Sephardic, referred to "neo" or "modern orthodox"; and "Reformed" Judaism, also called "progressive," which has two strands: "traditionalist" Judaism, also called Masoreti, and

"liberal," "secular," or "humanist" Judaism that presents itself as non-religious. Each has its own way of understanding "Jewishness" and positioning vis-à-vis the world of *kashrut*. See Martine Berthelot *Memorias judías: Barcelona, 1914–1954: Historia oral de la Comunidad Israelita de Barcelona* (Barcelona: Fundación Baruch Spinoza-Riopiedras, 2001); Oscar Camargo Crespo, "Una aproximación sociológica a la población judía madrileña," *Raíces. Revista Judía de Cultura* 42 (2000): 17–32; Florencia Heitzmann, *Las fronteras y sus ambigüedades: el sistema de alimentación kosher en Barcelona*, MA thesis (Universidad de Barcelona, 2015); Julia Martínez Ariño, "Jewish spatial practices in Barcelona as claims for recognition," *Social Inclusion* 8, no. 3 (2020): 240–50; Analia Sznajderowski, Head of the *Masortí Aviv* Community of Valencia, interview with Silvina Gesser, April 16, 2019.

10. Nir Avieli, *Food and Power: A Culinary Ethnography of Israel* (Berkeley: University of California Press, 2018).
11. Jacobo Israel Garzón, *Los judíos en España (1789–1902)* (Madrid: Ediciones Hebraica, 2019).
12. Jacobo Israel Garzón, *Los judíos de España (1918–2007)* (Madrid: Ediciones Hebraica, 2007).
13. Jacobo Israel Garzón and Uriel Macías Kapón, *La comunidad judía de Madrid. Textos e imágenes para una historia, 1917–2001* (Madrid: Comunidad Judía de Madrid, 2001).
14. Synagogues and cemeteries are basic social and public Jewish institutions, whereas *kashrut* habits and practices concern the private sphere of observant (religious) and traditionalist families and individuals.
15. Jacobo Israel Garzón, recorded interview and video conference with the authors, October 4, 2020.
16. Berthelot, *Memorias judías*. Jewish newcomers who were determined to strictly keep the *kashrut* dietary were recommended to move to Portugal. Lisbon's Jewish community in the 1920s had a working synagogue, a school, a cemetery, and infrastructure that provided *kosher* food. These were strengthened with the first Portuguese Republic in 1911, which declared freedom of religion in the country. See also Schammah Gesser and Pinheiro, "Introduction."
17. Maite Ojeda-Mata, "The Turkish Sephardim of San Antonio Market, Barcelona, 1900–1945," *Journal of Modern Jewish Studies* 14, no. 3 (2015): 465–81.
18. Yom Tov Assis, Meritxell Blasco Orellana, and José Roberto Magdalena Nom de Déu, *De Esmirna a Barcelona (Avatares y aventuras de una familia sefardí: los Naḥum)* (Barcelona: Riopiedras Ediciones, 2015), 39–45.
19. Josep Calvet, Cristina García, Rosa Serra Rotés, Víctor Sörenssen, and Manu Valentín, *Barcelona, refugi de jueus (1933–1958)* (Barcelona: Angle Editorial, 2015), 22. See also Javier Sánchez-Ocaña, "Barcelona, paraíso de los jugadores de ajedrez. Cuarenta clubs; veinte mil aficionados," *Estampa*, no. 371 (1935), 11–14.
20. Berthelot, *Memorias judías*, 296–97.
21. José Antonio Lisbona Martín, *Retorno a Sefarad. La política de España hacia sus judíos en el siglo XX* (Barcelona: Riopiedras, 1993).

22. *Imágenes de Melilla y su judaísmo* (Jerusalem: Casa de Melilla en Jerusalén, Mesilot Hatorá, 1997), 37–43.
23. Léon Levy, "La colectividad judía en Melilla," *Aldaba: revista del Centro Asociado de la UNED de Melilla* 5 (1985): 200; Rafael Briones Gómez, Sol Tarrés, and Oscar Salguero Montaño, *Encuentros. Diversidad religiosa en Ceuta y en Melilla* (Barcelona: Icaria Editorial, 2013), 269–71.
24. Maite Ojeda-Mata, *Modern Spain and the Sephardim: Legitimizing Identities* (Lanham, MD: Lexington, 2018), 40–47.
25. At private households, families prepared homemade *Matzot* out of a dough that was punched with a weeping willow stick specially kept since *Sukkot*, the Jewish religious festival of the *Tabernacles*.
26. Jacobo Israel Garzón, *Los judíos en España (1903–1956). Escritores, Ilustrados y Artistas* (Madrid: Ediciones Hebraica, 2021), 107–16.
27. Assis, Orellana, and Magdalena Nom de Déu, *De Esmirna a Barcelona*, 41.
28. Jacobo Israel Garzón, "Spain and the Jews During the Holocaust," in *Spain, the Second World War, and the Holocaust: History and Representation*, eds. Sara J. Brenneis and Gina Herrmann (Toronto: University of Toronto Press, 2020), 83–99; Gonzalo Álvarez Chillida, "Antisemitism and Philosephardism in Spain, 1880–1945," in *Spain, the Second World War, and the Holocaust: History and Representation*, eds. Sara J. Brenneis and Gina Herrmann (Toronto: University of Toronto Press, 2020), 65–80.
29. Yehuda Saportas, interview with the authors, March 4, 2021.
30. Bernd Rother, "Myth and Fact: Spain and the Holocaust," in *The Holocaust in the Spanish Memory: Historical Perceptions and Cultural Discourse*, eds. López Quiñones and Susanne Zepp (Leipzig, Germany: Simon Dubnow Institut, Universitat Leipzig, 2010), 51–64.
31. Lisbona Martín, *Retorno a Sefarad*; Danielle Rozenberg, *La España contemporánea y la cuestión judía: Retejiendo los hilos de la memoria y de la historia* (Madrid: Marcial Pons—Casa Sefarad-Israel, 2010).
32. Garzón and Macías Kapón, *La comunidad judía*.
33. Rozenberg, *La España contemporánea*.
34. Ibid.
35. There were ten *kosher* butcheries in the city but not enough cattle for slaughter. Given the scarcity of meat, pregnant women and sick people had priority.
36. Jacobo Israel Garzón, recorded interview.
37. Rabbi Baruch "Benito" Garzón, recorded interview and video conference with the authors, October 19, 2020.
38. Garzón and Macías Kapón, *La comunidad judía*, 44–46.
39. Ibid., 47.
40. Lara Anderson, *Control and Resistance: Food Discourse in Franco Spain* (Toronto: University of Toronto Press, 2020), 13–18.
41. Cases in point were the organization of exhibitions and conferences, the First Symposium of Sephardic Studies, the creation of a Sephardic Museum in Toledo, a new

approach toward Judeo-Christian dialogue in Spain, and the like. See Aliberti.
42. Law 44/1967, of June 28, regulates freedom in religious matters as a civil right. See BOE no. 156, de 1 de julio de 1967: 9191.
43. Following the event, Jewish communities in Málaga, Alicante, Valencia, Palma de Mallorca, Tenerife, Las Palmas, Torremolinos, and Marbella emerged.
44. Rabbi Garzón remembers Queen Sophia's visit to the synagogue in 1976, where her Majesty, who is a vegetarian, was delighted to taste typical Jewish food.
45. Jacobo Israel Garzón, recorded interview.
46. Garzón and Macías Kapón, *La comunidad judía*, 50. According to Rozenberg, *La España contemporánea*, 10,000 Jews were living in Spain in the years following Franco's death. Only 40 percent had Spanish nationality.
47. In 2004, the entity changed its name to Federation of Jewish Communities of Spain, FCJE.
48. Moisés Benbunán, "Sobre el renacimiento de la comunidad judía de Madrid," *Raíces. Revista Judía de Cultura* (1997): 33–61.
49. The *Barrio Hebreo* neighborhood in Melilla was transformed and Christians and Muslims occupied the houses left by former Jewish inhabitants. See Levy, "La colectividad judía," 199–203.
50. David Benhamou, recorded interview and video conference with the authors, October 7, 2020.
51. Briones, Tarrés, and Salguero Montaño, *Encuentros*, 117–19.
52. On religious revitalization see M. H. Danzger, *Returning to Tradition: The Contemporary Revival of Orthodox Judaism* (New Haven, CT: Yale University Press, 1989); Neri Horowitz, *Chazará Bi'teshuvá Be'Israel: Itkarvut le'dat ba'chevrá Ha'Israelit* (Ramat Gan, Israel: Am Chofshi Publishing House, 1998; in Hebrew).
53. Alfredo Juderías, *Viaje por la cocina hispano-judía* (Madrid: Seteco, 1990); L. Benavides-Barajas, *Al-Andalus: La cocina y su historia. Los reinos de taifas, norte de África. Judíos, mudéjares y moriscos* (Motril, Spain: Dulcinea, 1996); Mimí Abecasis de Castiel, *Mis recetas de cocina sefardí* (Málaga, Spain: Ayuntamiento de Málaga, 2002); and L. Jacinto García Gómez and Rosa Tovar, *Un banquete por Sefarad. Cocina y costumbres de los judíos españoles* (Gijón, Spain: Trea, 2007).
54. The booklet offers food related medieval ballads and a dozen of North African Sephardic recipes as appendix. See Uriel Macías Kapón, *La cocina judía: Leyes, costumbres y algunas recetas sefardíes* (Girona, Spain: Ediciones Alfonso Martínez, 2003).
55. Rozenberg, *La España contemporánea*, 214–16.
56. Seafood is not *kosher*, and the certification reassures those who are allergic to crustaceans. Also some fruit and vegetable consumers are willing to pay more for *kosher* products because they associate them with greater control, while Muslims who are unable to find Halal food prefer to buy *kosher* products, which resemble the Muslim diet and ways of sacrifice. See Antonio Pita, "'Halal' y 'kosher'. Palabras que abren mercados," *El País*, August 29, 2016.
57. The Spanish Embassy in New York uses a similar strategy. See Marina Gisbert Climent, "El mercado de alimentos *Kosher* en Estados Unidos, Octubre 2016," *Estudio de Mercado. Resumen Ejecutivo*.

58. The authors had access to two video conferences of thirty minutes each, recorded at the Spanish Embassy in Tel Aviv. One was delivered by an Israeli food importer and exporter entrepreneur, and the other by the embassy's trade *attaché*. The latter insists on the "real" dimensions of the Israeli market that would reach more than 12 million by 2025, with 75 percent of its population being Jewish, 18 percent Muslim, and the rest Christian or other, with the consumption of *kosher* products being above 65 percent.
59. Benhamou, recorded interview.
60. Spanish Embassy, video I.
61. Spanish Embassy, video II. Different export branches include: sugar, candies, pastries, and other desserts, 20 million; biscuits, 20 million; olive oil, 14 million; sunflower oil, over 6 million; fresh and frozen meat, 6 million; fruits, 5 million. Also wine, canned products, and eggs. Israel is the greatest egg importer after the EU, which makes Spain its most important exporter.
62. Eduardo Estrada Alonso, Celina González Mieres, Juan A. Trespalacios Gutiérrez, Rodolfo Vázquez Casielles, *Omnichannel marketing: las nuevas reglas de la distribución y el consumo en un mundo omnicanal* (Oviedo, Spain: Universidad de Oviedo, 2019), 224.
63. Secular Israelis do not care about *kosher* certificates. Their interest lies on the product price and quality.
64. Estrada Alonso, González Mieres, Trespalacios Gutiérrez, and Vázquez Casielles, *Omnichannel marketing*, 211.
65. The *Hechsher* is a rabbinical product certification, qualifying items (usually foods) that conform to the requirements of *Halakha*, the Jewish laws. It also includes non-food products, such as clothing, cosmetics, or even hotels. To obtain the *kosher* certificate, Spanish food industrialists have to contact a company issuing the certificate, which requests logistical information on producers, the production plant, and all products it manufactures. A rabbi and an accounting specialist carry out the inspection. The recognition of the seal depends on the standing of the rabbi, agency, or authority involved. The most accepted certificates worldwide are issued by the Orthodox Union, known as OU *Kosher*. The latter is a 1923 *kosher* certification agency founded in New York, the largest of the "Big Five" major certification agencies providing the *kosher* seal for over 400.000 products in approximately 8,500 plants worldwide. Estrada Alonso, González Mieres, Trespalacios Gutiérrez, and Vázquez Casielles, *Omnichannel marketing*, 211–13.
66. The strict rules about only Jews dates back to ancient times, when wine was associated with polytheism and pagan rituals and was used in offerings to idol gods. By prescribing that only observant Jews could produce wine, the rules for *kosher* wine disassociate it from any kind of idolatrous offering.
67. The *Shulchan Aruch*, the most widely consulted of the various legal codes in Judaism, was authored in Safed (Israel) by Joseph Karo in 1563 and published in Venice two years later. Together with its commentaries, it is the most complete legal code

ever written. See Iker Morán, "Kosher, el vino judío también se elabora en España," *La vanguardia*, April 3, 2018. Notice that *kashrut* laws on wine also vary depending on whether the wine comes from Israeli wineries or not. In the Holy Land, regulations on wine are stricter because the Jewish law regulates the resting of the earth (*Shmitah*) where the vineyards grow.
68. The FCJE has a web site on *kosher* food and services throughout Spain, https://www.fcje.org/establecimientos-kasher-en-espana/. Here, all new restaurants and stores with *kosher* products in the capital are marketed by the culinary guide of Madrid.
69. See Real Decreto 49/2018, de 1 de febrero.
70. On *shechita* and Muslim *Halal* slaughter in Europe, with special focus on Belgium and Holland, see M. Miele, "'Killing Animals for Food': How Science, Religion and Technologies Affect the Public Debate about Religious Slaughter," *Food Ethics* 1 (2016): 47–60; Gerhard van der Schyff, "Ritual Slaughter and Religious Freedom in a Multilevel Europe: The Wider Importance of the Dutch Case," *Oxford Journal of Law and Religion* 3, no. 1 (2014): 76–102; P. S. Pozzi and Trevor Waner, "*Shechita* (Kosher Slaughtering) and European Legislation," *Veterinaria Italiana* 53, no. 1 (2017): 5–19. See also Rafael Valencia Candalija, "Sacrificio ritual y alimentación *kosher*: Referencia especial a las novedades legislativas sobre la *shechita* en Bélgica," *Anuario de Derecho Eclesiástico del Estado* 35 (2019): 377–414.

WORKS CITED

Abecasis de Castiel, Mimí. *Mis recetas de cocina sefardí*. Málaga, Spain: Ayuntamiento de Málaga, 2002.

Aliberti, Davide. *Sefarad: Una Comunidad Imaginada (1924-2015)*. Madrid: Marcial Pons Ediciones de Historia, 2018.

Álvarez Chillida, Gonzalo. "Antisemitism and Philosephardism in Spain, 1880–1945." In *Spain, the Second World War, and the Holocaust: History and Representation*, edited by Sara J. Brenneis and Gina Herrmann, 65–80. Toronto: University of Toronto Press, 2020.

Anderson, Lara. *Control and Resistance: Food Discourse in Franco Spain*. Toronto: University of Toronto Press, 2020.

Assis, Yom Tov, Meritxell Blasco Orellana, and José Roberto Magdalena Nom de Déu. *De Esmirna a Barcelona (Avatares y aventuras de una familia sefardí: los Naḥum)*. Barcelona: Riopiedras Ediciones, 2015.

Avieli, Nir. *Food and Power: A Culinary Ethnography of Israel*. Berkeley: University of California Press, 2018.

Benavides-Barajas, L. *Al-Andalus: La cocina y su historia. Los reinos de taifas, norte de África. Judíos, mudéjares y moriscos*. Motril, Spain: Dulcinea, 1996.

Benbunán, Moisés. "Sobre el renacimiento de la comunidad judía de Madrid." *Raíces. Revista Judía de Cultura* (1997): 33.
Benhamou, David. Recorded interview and video conference with the authors. October 7, 2020.
Berthelot, Martine. *Cien años de la presencia judía en la España contemporánea*. Barcelona: KFM, 1995.
———. *Memorias judías: Barcelona, 1914–1954: Historia oral de la Comunidad Israelita de Barcelona*. Barcelona: Fundación Baruch Spinoza-Riopiedras, 2001.
Briones, Rafael Gómez, Sol Tarrés, and Oscar Salguero Montaño. *Encuentros. Diversidad religiosa en Ceuta y en Melilla*. Barcelona: Icaria Editorial, 2013.
Calvet, Josep, Cristina García, Rosa Serra Rotés, Víctor Sörenssen, and Manu Valentín. *Barcelona, refugi de jueus (1933–1958)*. Barcelona: Angle Editorial, 2015.
Camargo Crespo, Oscar. "Una aproximación sociológica a la población judía madrileña." *Raíces. Revista Judía de Cultura* 42 (2000): 17–32.
Danzger, M. H. *Returning to Tradition: The Contemporary Revival of Orthodox Judaism*. New Haven, CT: Yale University Press, 1989.
Estrada Alonso, Eduardo, Celina González Mieres, Juan A. Trespalacios Gutiérrez, and Rodolfo Vázquez Casielles. *Omnichannel marketing: las nuevas reglas de la distribución y el consumo en un mundo omnicanal*. Oviedo, Spain: Universidad de Oviedo, 2019.
García Gómez, L. Jacinto, and Rosa Tovar. *Un banquete por Sefarad. Cocina y costumbres de los judíos españoles*. Gijón, Spain: Trea, 2007.
Garzón, Rabbi Baruch "Benito." Recorded interview and video conference with the authors. October 19, 2020.
Garzón, Jacobo Israel. *Los judíos en España (1789–1902)*. Madrid: Ediciones Hebraica, 2019.
———. *Los judíos de España (1918–2007)*. Madrid: Ediciones Hebraica, 2007.
———. *Los judíos en España (1903–1956). Escritores, Ilustrados y Artistas*. Madrid: Ediciones Hebraica, 2021.
———. Recorded interview and video conference with the authors. October 4, 2020.
———. "Spain and the Jews During the Holocaust." In *Spain, the Second World War, and the Holocaust: History and Representation*, edited by Sara J. Brenneis and Gina Herrmann, 83–99. Toronto: University of Toronto Press, 2020.
Garzón, Jacobo Israel, and Uriel Macías Kapón. *La comunidad judía de Madrid. Textos e imágenes para una historia, 1917–2001*. Madrid: Comunidad Judía de Madrid, 2001.
Gisbert Climent, Marina. "El mercado de alimentos *Kosher* en Estados Unidos, Octubre 2016." *Estudio de Mercado. Resumen Ejecutivo*.
Guzmen-Carmeli, S. "Eating the Bubbe: Culinary Encounters Between Secular and Haredi Jews in Bnei Brak." *Food and Foodways* 28, no. 2 (2020): 69–90.
Heitzmann, Florencia. *Las fronteras y sus ambigüedades: el isions de alimentación kosher en Barcelona*. MA thesis. Universidad de Barcelona, 2015.
Horowitz, Neri. *Chazará Bi'teshuvá Be'Israel: Itkarvut le'dat ba'chevrá Ha'Israelit*. Ramat Gan, Israel: Am Chofshi Publishing House, 1998 (in Hebrew).

Imágenes de Melilla y su judaísmo. Jerusalem: Casa de Melilla en Jerusalén, Mesilot Hatorá, 1997.
Juderías, Alfredo. *Viaje por la cocina hispano-judía*. Madrid: Seteco, 1990.
Kirshenblatt-Gimblett, Barbara. "Kitchen Judaism." In *Getting Comfortable in New York: The Jewish Home, 1880–1950*, edited by Susan L. Braunstein and Joselit Jenna Weissman, 75–105. New York: Jewish Museum, 1990.
Kraemer, David. *Jewish Eating and Identity through the Ages*. New York: Routledge, 2008.
Levy, Léon. "La colectividad judía en Melilla." *Aldaba: revista del Centro Asociado de la UNED de Melilla* 5 (1985): 199–203.
Lisbona Martín, José Antonio. *Retorno a Sefarad. La política de España hacia sus judíos en el siglo XX*. Barcelona: Riopiedras, 1993.
Macías Kapón, Uriel. *La cocina judía: Leyes, costumbres y algunas recetas sefardíes*. Girona, Spain: Ediciones Alfonso Martínez, 2003.
Mandel, Rabbi Nina H. "Why Do They Care? Understanding the Need to Explain the Kosher Laws." In *Odysseys of Plates and Palates: Food, Society and Sociality*, edited by Simeon S. Magliveras and Catherine Gallin, 31–41. Boston, MA: Brill, 2014.
Martínez Ariño, Julia. "Jewish spatial practices in Barcelona as claims for recognition." *Social Inclusion* 8, no. 3 (2020): 240–50.
Miele, M. "'Killing Animals for Food': How Science, Religion and Technologies Affect the Public Debate about Religious Slaughter." *Food Ethics* 1 (2016): 47–60.
Morán, Iker. "Kosher, el vino judío también se elabora en España." *La vanguardia*, April 3, 2018.
Ojeda-Mata, Maite. *Modern Spain and the Sephardim: Legitimizing Identities*. Lanham, MD: Lexington, 2018.
———. "The Turkish Sephardim of San Antonio Market, Barcelona, 1900–1945." *Journal of Modern Jewish Studies* 14, no. 3 (2015): 465–81.
Pita, Antonio. "'Halal' y 'kosher'. Palabras que abren mercados." *El País*, August 29, 2016.
Pozzi, P. S., and Trevor Waner. "*Shechita* (Kosher Slaughtering) and European Legislation." *Veterinaria Italiana* 53, no. 1 (2017): 5–19.
Rother, Bernd. "Myth and Fact: Spain and the Holocaust." In *The Holocaust in the Spanish Memory: Historical Perceptions and Cultural Discourse*, edited by Antonio Gómez López Quiñones and Susanne Zepp, 51–64. Leipzig, Germany: Simon Dubnow Institut, Universitat Leipzig, 2010.
Rozenberg, Danielle. *La España contemporánea y la cuestión judía: Retejiendo los hilos de la memoria y de la historia*. Madrid: Marcial Pons—Casa Sefarad-Israel, 2010.
Sánchez-Ocaña, Javier. "Barcelona, paraíso de los jugadores de ajedrez. Cuarenta clubs; veinte mil aficionados." *Estampa*, no. 371 (1935), 11–14
Saportas, Yehuda. Interview with the authors, March 4, 2021.
Schammah Gesser, Silvina, and Teresa Pinheiro. "Guest Editors' Introduction to the Special Issue, 'Jewish (In)Visibility in Iberia: A View from the Margins.'" *Contemporary Jewry* 40 (2020): 503–17.

Stiniguță Laslo, Ella. "Purity and Impurity in Judaism. Taboo Foods and the Kashrut Laws." *Studia Judaica* (2017): 137–57.
Sznajderowski, Analia. Head of the Masortí Aviv Community of Valencia. Interview with Silvina Gesser, April 16, 2019.
Valencia Candalija, Rafael. "Sacrificio ritual y alimentación *kosher*: Referencia especial a las novedades legislativas sobre la *shechita* en Bélgica." *Anuario de Derecho Eclesiástico del Estado* 35 (2019): 377–414.
van der Schyff, Gerhard. "Ritual Slaughter and Religious Freedom in a Multilevel Europe: The Wider Importance of the Dutch Case." *Oxford Journal of Law and Religion* 3, no. 1 (2014): 76–102.

◆ CHAPTER 6

Culinary Conflict or *Convivencia*?
Halal Food Practices, Perceptions, and Promotion in Spain

Jessica R. Boll

The *halal* food sector is one of the fastest growing food sectors in the world, with the global *halal* food market reaching a value of US$1.9 trillion in 2020.[1] Meaning "permissible" in Arabic, *halal* refers to products and behaviors that are sanctioned by Islamic law.[2] The term encompasses a wide range of activities that are considered ethical, beneficial, and healthy for human life, including food, fashion, hygiene, and health practices. In terms of gastronomy, *halal* designates food items that are strictly prepared according to Islamic dietary guidelines.[3] Among those items declared *haram* (forbidden or harmful) are pork, carnivorous animals, animals that were dead without slaughtering or slaughtered without pronouncing the name of Allah, and intoxicants.[4] In addition to avoiding *haram* items, *halal* practices also emphasize food safety, environmentally friendly production, substance purity, and the consumption of products closest to their natural state.[5]

Even in Spain, where the consumption of pork is a pronounced expression of national identity, there has been a marked increase in the availability of *halal* food products and production in recent years. The number of slaughterhouses throughout Spain that received *halal* certification quadrupled between 2008 and 2018, and in 2019, Barcelona's wholesalers' market Mercabarna reported that most of its lamb and beef came from animals slaughtered according to Islamic law.[6] Correspondingly, one of the five food trends featured in a 2022 trade show in Barcelona was *halal* food.[7] This recent evolution of Spain's foodscape reflects both the nation's contemporary Muslim community—a community of approximately two million inhabitants, comprised of immigrants and Spanish converts alike—and the influx of Muslim tourists that are drawn to Spain's Islamic history.[8]

Riesz notes Muslims' dependence on the kebab industry to maintain *halal* eating practices in Spain, and fast-food restaurants such as McDoner and Donor Kebab are becoming more and more popular throughout the country.[9] Yet some high-end restaurants have added *halal* foods to their menus as well, and Spain's *halal* food scene has become increasingly recognized as a result. One of Spain's top ten rural restaurants of 2017 was, in fact, a *halal* establishment, an eatery that received much press for being multicultural in terms of both offerings and ambiance.[10] Elsewhere in Spain there even exists a *halal* version of the country's famous *jamón* (ham), a combination of lamb and beef that allows those who abstain from pork to experience a quintessential taste of Iberia.[11]

While the *halal jamón* (*halal* ham) may ostensibly epitomize a harmonious coexistence between Muslims and non-Muslims, one must question whether the presence of *halal* food in Spain is truly a sign of contemporary *convivencia* (peaceful coexistence) or whether it is instead a continuation of historic conflict. For Muslim immigrants to Spain, eating *halal* serves to underscore cultural disparities, as *halal* establishments effectively isolate Muslim diners and relegate them to a separate gastronomic sphere. At the same time, there are promising efforts to incentivize and develop the *halal* industry as a means to integrate both the cuisine and its consumers into mainstream Spanish society. This chapter will thus examine scholarship, societal and governmental responses, and specific establishments to expose the dynamics of Spain's emerging *halal* food scene and how this foodway both antagonizes and integrates two seemingly antithetical foodscapes.

Related Scholarship: Role, Reception, and Representation

Although there is limited scholarship that specifically examines *halal* food in Spain, there are a few studies worthy of note.[12] Among those that approach the topic from the Muslim perspective are Abu-Shams's investigation of the role of food for Moroccan Muslim immigrants in Zaragoza and Riesz's analysis of Muslims' engagement with Spanish food culture through her research on Moroccan restaurateurs in Seville and Almería.[13] The work of both Abu-Shams and Riesz reveals the mutual influence of Moroccan and Spanish foodways and potential avenues of culinary reconciliation, to be discussed subsequently. Yet Riesz's study likewise indicates a reluctance of Muslim customers to trust that meat is truly *halal* in Spain, akin to the concerns noted by Wilkins et al. regarding cross-contamination.[14]

Regarding the attitudes of non-Muslims toward *halal* food in Spain, there is again minimal scholarship.[15] Significant, though, is a qualitative study conducted by Wilkins et al. of 1,100 non-Muslims in Spain, Canada, and the UK. They concluded that consumer cosmopolitanism and religious identity were positively related to *halal* product judgment, while consumer ethnocentrism and national identification were negatively related. Their results also revealed that non-Muslims possess very little knowledge of the notion of *halal* and of the implications of *halal* practices in the context of the food industry, and that many consumers regard *halal* products as foreign regardless of their actual origin.[16]

In broader terms, Anderson, Benbow, and Manzin note the fluctuating attraction/revulsion to "ethnic" cuisine in Germany, Italy, and Spain—contexts of increasing gastronationalism.[17] While much of their discussion of culinary xenophobia in Spain centers upon the media's portrayal of Chinese immigrants and their cuisine, the same ambivalence can be seen with regard to *halal* food. The authors highlight ingestion as a form of identification, both individually and collectively, and the perception of food choice as potential threat. This threat is particularly acute when migrants are a conspicuous part of the process: "Dishes such as curry or the *döner* find broad acceptance as food for the general public, but similar food prepared by and for migrants themselves still has the capacity to arouse intercultural acrimony."[18] Xenophobic reactions to immigrant cuisine include distrust, as indicated by the studies cited above, stereotyping, commodification, and trivialization.[19] Although food multiculturalism is often touted as proof of communal tolerance, policies, practices, and the public's reaction confirm that this is not always the case.

Anderson's individual study of the representation of immigrant culinary culture in official discourse and cultural texts in Spain reinforces this idea, exposing the tensions between a model that homogenizes food multiculturalism and one that features immigrants as protagonists. While the former emphasizes the integration of migrant communities through gastronomic assimilation, the latter underscores the centrality of immigrant cuisine in Spain. Although there are signs of progress toward the latter, a homogenized vision of Spanish cuisine continues to prevail. Ironically, as Anderson indicates, the "success" of a multicultural society is often measured by the degree to which minority cultures—and their cuisines—evanesce: "[La excesiva homogeneidad] presenta una gastronomía uniforme como señal del éxito del multiculturalismo en España" ([Excessive homogeneity] presents uniform gastronomy as a sign of the success of multiculturalism in Spain).[20] The discernable presence of *halal* food in Spain thus jeopardizes the established paradigm of societal success.

In a comparable analysis of the representations of Spain's changing foodways, Bou notes the potential of food to act as an instrument of physical and social control.[21] The presentation of ethnic food in media and cultural texts evinces such control. Bou's research and that of Anderson et al. call attention to the lack of migrants' perspectives with regard to their own cuisine, resulting in a problematic consumption of the ethnic other that further subordinates migrant populations. Anderson indicates the need for increased focus on production rather than consumption—thereby featuring immigrants as protagonists—as a means of preventing culinary encounter from becoming a new form of colonial encounter: "Cuando una serie de televisión o documental sobre comida étnica solo enfatiza el placer o la subjetividad del consumidor (del grupo dominante) es bastante alto el riesgo de que tenga implícito de alguna manera una dinámica o relación colonial" (When a television series or documentary about ethnic food only emphasizes the pleasure or subjectivity of the consumer [of the dominant group] the risk that it implies a colonial dynamic or relationship in some way is quite high).[22] Food often serves as a marker of cultural difference in both television and film, and the familiar motif of a majority host sampling minority food underscores the hierarchical relationship between the two populations.

Despite increased attention to both food and immigration in Spanish cultural productions in recent years, there have been limited references or representations specific to *halal* food.[23] Guardiola offers a comparative analysis of select Spanish television programs that have centered upon immigrants/immigration, among which the Catalan programs *Karakia* and *Nyam Nyam* dealt explicitly with food and included episodes on *halal* cuisine.[24] The studies of Anderson and Anderson et al. both point to *Karakia* as a series that successfully promoted intercultural relations through the lens of production via immigrant protagonists, part of overall efforts to foster (food) multiculturalism in Catalonia. The Andalusian program *Andalucía sin fronteras* (Andalucia without Borders) likewise included a segment titled *Cocina sin fronteras* (Cooking without Borders) that included recipes from immigrants' home countries. Moroccan-born Ahmed Sefiani served as one of the primary presenters.

In film, Fernando Colomo's *El próximo Oriente* (The Near East, 2006) is worth mentioning. Food—*halal* food in particular—is essential to the storyline, as is Islam. Much of the dialogue centers upon both dietary prohibitions and the tenets of Islam, as the director educates the Spanish public of the fundamentals of the religion along with the protagonist, Caín. Caín converts to Islam to marry Aisha, the mistress of his brother, Abel, after she discovers she is pregnant. Aisha's family is Bangladeshi and owns a failing *halal* restaurant at the start of the film.[25]

Bou and Zarco examine the role of food in the film, in which cuisine and alimentary traditions function as agents through which contemporary Spanish culture is transformed. The opening scene alone provides a snapshot of such change:

among the storefronts shown are Alimentación Bangla Town, Kurdistan Döner Kepab, and Tangier Islamic Butchery, whose presence attest to the physical transformation of the Madrid cityscape from massive waves of immigration and the accompanying expansion of culinary—in this case, *halal*—offerings. In fact, *halal* food in particular serves as an agent of change not only for the film's setting, but for the characters as well. As Zarco affirms, "la comida establece los límites que Caín debe superar para lograr la armonía, tanto familiar como personal" (food establishes the limits that Caín must overcome to achieve both familial and personal harmony).[26] Indeed, Caín's happy ending results from his conversion to Islam and his integration into his new Muslim family, just as the neighborhood butcher shop ultimately thrives because of the owner's decision to begin selling *halal* meat. Nonetheless, it is important to note that the primary backdrop of the film—Aisha's family's restaurant—succeeds due to its conversion from a *halal* establishment to a music venue that sells alcohol, permits smoking, and features the women of the family as sensual singer/performers—a space entirely discordant with Islamic law.

While *Karakia* and *El próximo Oriente* feature immigrants as producers of both their foods and their futures, Bou underscores the overall anonymity of immigrants in food production in Spain.[27] The lack of any official recognition of the contributions of immigrant producers is evidenced by recent governmental efforts to endorse Spanish cuisine. In 2019, the Ministry of Agriculture, Fisheries and Food of Spain launched a campaign to promote the Spanish brand "by valuing the work of the farmers, ranchers and fishmongers as essential creators of Spanish food."[28] That same Ministry, partnering with the Ministry of Industry, Trade and Tourism, implemented an international campaign in 2020 that sought to strengthen the overseas image of the Spanish agri-food section.[29] Immigrants do not figure in these or other such governmental campaigns, despite their critical role, as official discourse continues to center upon a homogenized version of both Spanish food and those that produce it.[30]

Dietary Discord

The culinary conflicts exposed by much of the scholarship cited above reflect historical tensions related to the *halal/jamón* divide. In "Food and Meaning: Christian Understandings of Muslim Food and Food Ways in Spain: 1250–1550," Constable examines pork as an emerging symbol of Christianity during a period of increasing anti-Muslim sentiment and the adherence to *halal* practices as a sign of Muslim identity. As Constable explains, "[s]hifting Christian Spanish attitudes toward Muslim food and food ways mirrored broader changes in thinking about Islam, and reflected growing intolerance in the period from the fourteenth to the sixteenth centuries."[31]

In the sixteenth century specifically, *moriscos*' consumption of pork and wine became a means to prove their authentic conversion to Christianity in order to escape the Inquisition. As Root notes, it was determined that "a 'true' Christian must and will enjoy pork."[32] Eating pork thus became tantamount to being Spanish and those who abstained were decidedly non-Spanish. In this way, food disparities became evidence of the fundamental incompatibility between Christians and Muslims and part of the justification for the 1609 *morisco* expulsion from Spain.[33]

Today, despite the promising economic, environmental, and health benefits of *halal* offerings, there has been resistance to such products due to rising Islamophobic attitudes worldwide. Dr. Barbara Ruiz-Bejarano, Director of International Relations at the Córdoba-based Halal Institute, has observed a notable surge in Islamophobic and xenophobic discourses in Spain and France in recent months.[34] Islamophobic discourse often portrays Muslims as violent terrorists that threaten the very foundation of Western society, and fears are especially acute in Spain due to the nation's Islamic past.[35] Far-right politicians and anti-Islam activists invoke history to warn of a Muslim *reconquista* of the peninsula, and the pervasive hostility toward Islam has had spill-over effects on the *halal* food scene.[36]

Various groups have directly opposed the growing presence of *halal* food in non-Muslim countries. When KFC introduced *halal* products in France, for example, global protests quickly ensued.[37] Social media has become an especially common avenue through which to express dissent, and the KFC decision incited an online crusade calling for a worldwide ban on *halal* KFC; one user responded by posting, "the muslims [sic] are taking over our nations."[38] Wilkins et al. likewise note the global presence of anti-*halal* Facebook groups.[39] The "Boycott Halal" campaign has spread worldwide to spur movements that are both country-specific and that appeal to a broader audience, such as "Boycott Halal in Europe."[40] One June 2017 post from the "Boycott Halal" page states, in majuscule, "HALAL FUNDS TERRORISTS," and one group member explicitly commented, "Buy pork. It's about the only safe meat left."[41]

In her analysis of the impact of Islamophobia on the *halal* market, Ruiz-Bejarano cites two tweets specific to Spain.[42] One user wrote, "Cada euro que gastas en los restaurantes halal de los invasores musulmantes, contribuyes a la ruina de España. ¡No comas como un moro!" (With each euro you spend in the *halal* restaurants of the Muslim invaders, you contribute to the ruin of Spain. Do not eat like a Moor!). Another user tweeted, "Si eres español ¿por qué comes como un moro en restaurantes de comida *halal*?" (If you are Spanish, why do you eat like a Moor in *halal* restaurants?). In these tweets, the conflation of the historic and contemporary Muslim presence in Spain is explicit, as modern immigrants and Spanish converts become invading Moors of al-Andalus and food choice is expressly linked to identity.

Claims against *halal* products and practices have even surfaced in the European Parliament, where consumer death, food unhealthiness, and animal cruelty have been suggested.[43] Spanish politicians have likewise challenged the *halal* sector directly. The conservative Popular Party (PP) aimed to prevent the expansion of the *halal* kebab industry, for instance, an approach also seen elsewhere in Europe.[44] PP political slogans during the 2015 election campaigns in Barcelona called for the end of the proliferation of kebab restaurants, and that same year a zoning law proposed in Tarragona attempted to limit the number and concentration of kebab shops and other Muslim-owned businesses in the region to prevent the formation of immigrant "ghettos."[45] Although the law ultimately did not pass, PP leader Alejandro Fernandez claimed such shops threatened "authentic and superior" Spanish eateries and thus reinforced the notion of *halal* establishments as decidedly non-Spanish.[46]

Indeed, in Spain there appears to be a reluctance to advertise as *halal*. As noted by Wilkins et al., the vast majority of *halal* food served in cafés, restaurants, and fast-food outlets is not clearly labelled as such.[47] While intended to help Muslims identify acceptable food sources, *halal* certification serves as a visible marker of difference and has become both an easily identifiable symbol and a concrete target for those denouncing Islam. As Riesz affirms in her study of kebab restauranteurs and customers in Andalucía, "[i]n several European nations and recently in Spain, halal food establishments and the concept of eating halal have come to represent the unwanted presence of Muslim immigrants, both construed as threats to national cohesion."[48] Even in those restaurants lauded for their *halal* cuisine, the term *halal* is seemingly avoided and replaced instead by more benign branding.

Halal Eateries

An example of one such establishment is Restaurante-Tetería Baraka, located in the Alpujarran capital of Órgiva. Qasim Barrio, a Spaniard who converted to Islam in the early 2000s, opened Baraka in 2003. From the Arabic word for "blessing," Baraka serves as a gathering space for locals and international tourists alike and was named one of Spain's top ten rural restaurants of 2017 by the British periodical *The Guardian*. Described as a "culinary echo of [Spain's] Moorish past," the article emphasizes the uniqueness of both the dishes and atmosphere of the popular eatery.⁴⁹

Worthy of note, though, is the fact that most of the restaurant's marketing and press lacks reference to the fact that the food offered and the environment in which it is served are *halal*. Linked from the restaurant's Web site are various articles and videos that feature the establishment, all of which underscore the fact that no alcohol or pork are served but without explicit use of the word *halal*. While most of the media sources note that Qasim is a Sufi Muslim and connections to the region's Islamic past are used to market the space, the word *halal* is systematically avoided—even by Qasim himself. In an interview with BBC, for instance, Qasim mentions *halal* tourism, but neither the proprietor nor the article mentions that his restaurant is *halal*.⁵⁰ The same is true of a segment of *Andalucía Directo* that first aired on Spain's Canal Sur on September 25, 2017.⁵¹ The narrator touts the restaurant as "un lugar de encuentro" (a place of encounter) that serves "la interculturalidad" (interculturality) and "el sabor de nuestra historia" (the taste of our history). The video describes the food as "ecológico" (organic), "vegetariano" (vegetarian), "auténtico" (authentic), and even "árabe" (Arab), and explains that the restaurant is run by "un vasco convertido al islam" (a Basque converted to Islam), but never is the word *halal* mentioned. Even on the restaurant's Web site the term *halal* only appears in small letters on the café's logo and at the bottom of the site in a link to the Islam Órgiva Halal resource center but nowhere in the text of the various Web pages or on the menu itself. Instead, the food is described as "arab" [sic] and "international" on the site ("Tetería").

While Baraka is an affordable, alternative food space whose entire menu is *halal*, on the other end of the culinary spectrum renowned chef Paco Morales offers a *halal* selection at his high-end restaurant, Noor, in Córdoba. Meaning "light" in Arabic, Noor opened in 2016 and has since been awarded two Michelin stars and named among the world's fifty best restaurants and bars.⁵²

As is the case with Baraka, the promotion of Noor is noteworthy. Although the section of Spain's official Web site dedicated to *halal* tourism lists Noor as "the first to specialise in halal haute cuisine," there is no mention of *halal* on the eatery's Web site itself.⁵³ Instead, the food is described as "contemporary 'Andalusi' cuisine," a "recovery" of "[t]he culinary legacy of Al-Andalus." While the many articles written on the restaurant recount the *cocina andalusi*, (Andalusian cooking), along with the "sensual" décor and "voluptuous" architecture inspired by the ruins of a Muslim medieval palace nearby—stereotypical descriptors of Orientalist presentment—none mention *halal* offerings specifically.⁵⁴ While overwhelmingly positive, the discourse constructed by the media emphasizes both Baraka's and

Noor's offerings and ambiance as exotic, unfamiliar, bohemian, eccentric, and thus implicitly not "Spanish."⁵⁵

The other two restaurants named on the primary page of Spain's *halal* tourism Web site are El Faro in Marbella and Los Almendros in Córdoba. Although they are listed expressly for their *halal* certification, they likewise obscure their *halal* offerings on advertising and promotional materials and overtly cater to non-Muslim clientele. El Faro's Facebook page promotes the site as a place to enjoy cocktails and barbecued pork and celebrate christenings, for example, while their Web site offers a special baptismal and communion menu and a dedicated page promoting the space for communion celebrations.⁵⁶ Regarding Los Almendros, a news segment aired by Canal Sur Córdoba in 2017 when the restaurant was first *halal* certificated details food preparation, discusses Muslim customers, and shows the dedicated Muslim prayer space within, but their current Facebook cover photo is of a roasted pig and recent pictures feature bacon ice cream.⁵⁷ Ironically, no mention is made of *halal* certification on the current online menus, Web sites, or social media pages of either of these two eateries that are highlighted as exemplars of such credentials by the National Tourist Office.

In terms of public reception, Baraka and Noor have received very favorable reviews on sites such as Yelp, TripAdvisor, and Foursquare, yet there is—again—little to no recognition or reference to their *halal* offerings. Baraka's food is most often described as Moroccan, Arabic, and Middle Eastern, for instance, with much commentary on the unique clientele and decor. Los Almendros received generally favorable reviews as well (in this case, on TripAdvisor and Facebook), but El Faro received critical reviews overall (specifically on TripAdvisor and Google). Los Almendros was the only one of the four eateries with repeated mention of *halal* food, perhaps due to the proximity of the restaurant to the remains of the tenth-century palace-city Madinat al-Zahra. This proximity was referenced multiple times in the comments, as well as the fact that Los Almendros has a Muslim chef. Los Almendros was also reviewed on the travel Web site halaltrip, where the absence of the others is noteworthy.⁵⁸

Halal Tourism

As indicated, the restaurants described above are promoted on Spain's official site dedicated to *halal* tourism. *Halal* tourism refers to recreational travel undertaken by Muslims who seek to adhere to Islamic values and practices. It is the fastest-growing segment of the travel industry—Muslim spending on travel was US$194 billion in 2019 and, notwithstanding the COVID-19 pandemic, it is expected to reach US$208 billion by 2024.⁵⁹ Spain is naturally positioned to attract *halal* tourism due to both its geographic proximity to the Muslim world and its historical connection to Islam.⁶⁰ By drawing upon Spain's Islamic past to attract Muslim visitors, *halal* tourism campaigns are consistent with broader marketing schemes that promote the nation's diversity and multicultural heritage as a means of distinguishing Spain from other holiday destinations.⁶¹

Numerous studies indicate that *halal* food is a primary concern of Muslim travelers and that the availability of *halal* food is a major destination determinant.⁶² The availability of *halal* food likewise has been shown to impact travelers' intentions of revisiting a destination and their length of stay.⁶³ Accordingly, a study conducted of academic and professional experts in tourism (30 percent of which were Spanish) specified the availability of *halal* food/restaurants as the top priority in terms of what characteristics a destination should have to successfully position itself in the *halal* tourism segment, and the majority of those polled suggested Spain should strive to be a *halal* tourism destination.⁶⁴ Yet the same study indicated barriers of ignorance and a scarcity of necessary infrastructure, including a lack of availability of certified *halal* food, and noted difficulties due to the rise of Islamophobia and resistance to such tourism on the part of the resident population. An article published in *The National* in 2019 also indicated the most problematic aspect of travel for Muslim tourists in Spain is a lack of *halal* food options, and northern Spain was noted to be especially challenging.⁶⁵

As Culinary Confluence

Despite efforts to undermine or obscure *halal* businesses and the identified shortage of *halal* eateries in Spain, there are nonetheless promising initiatives to develop this sector. Pradana et al. have indicated that Spain is one of the few countries that have planned and developed *halal* concepts seriously, along with New Zealand, Australia, South Korea, and Japan.⁶⁶ As indicated above, the National Tourist Office (Turespaña) has created a dedicated *halal* tourism Web site that currently lists approximately two dozen *halal* restaurants across eight cities, located primarily in southern Spain, and Wilkins et al.'s research indicates that there is much less negative bias toward *halal* products than suggested by the media.⁶⁷

In 2019, the travel company Ilimtour published an article titled "9 Reasons Why Spain Is Your Next Halal Travel Destination," explicitly citing gastronomy as the second reason to visit the nation.⁶⁸ That same year, Spain's Halal Institute created a certification program to indicate Muslim-friendly restaurants, hotels, and activities, and to help businesses adapt their services to accommodate the needs of Muslim travelers.[69] In 2015, the Halal International Tourism initiative was established to promote and expand *halal* tourism in Spain, and a European project called "Halal Markets" has similarly focused on fostering *halal* tourism in Andalucía and Portugal.[70]

Although food has no doubt been used historically to divide Christians and Muslims, the past also offers examples of alimentary concord. Before the *Reconquista*, Spanish Christians occasionally accepted food from Muslims and adopted Muslim eating practices such as sitting on the floor during meals. Charters, chronicles, cookbooks, recipe collections, and literary sources also confirm that it was not uncommon for Christians to enjoy food items that were associated with Muslim cuisine, such as figs, raisins, butter, milk, and honey. Accommodations such as separate butchers, ovens, cookware, and tables allowed Muslims to maintain *halal* practices as well.[71]

Riesz argues that these solutions to what she calls the *halal*/pork binary exist as historical examples of what is possible moving forward in terms of culinary coexistence in Spain. She offers insight into the experiences and identity negotiations of Muslim immigrants through her investigation of foodways and restaurant spaces in southern Spain and suggests the application of Islamic dietary code to Spanish dishes—a phenomenon she calls *halalization*—may serve as potential resolutions to the culinary, cultural, and religious tensions of Spain's *halal* food scene. While many scholars challenge the notion of historic *convivencia*, and the conflation of contemporary Spanish Muslims and those of al-Andalus is certainly problematic, Riesz suggests that by invoking Islamic Spain and the narrative of peaceful coexistence, Muslims restauranteurs may establish themselves in present-day Spanish society and create a sense of belonging.[72] One of the Moroccan restauranteurs she interviewed, in fact, explicitly positioned *halal* food within Spain's culinary tradition—rather than opposed to it—by emphasizing the commonalities of the two foodways.[73]

Abu-Shams likewise affirms that the daily contact between Moroccan and Spanish cultures has resulted in culinary exchanges and the expansion of food repertoires. Like Riesz, Abu-Shams notes new food practices on the part of Moroccan immigrants, like eating *tapas* and cured meats made from beef instead of pork, while Spaniards have begun incorporating dishes like couscous and tagine into their diets.[74] This, too, was seen historically, as early modern cookbooks showed evidence of Spanish Christians preparing Muslim recipes but adapting them by substituting their own ingredients.[75] Abu-Shams notes that sharing dishes, products, and preparation methods is a means of constructing new pathways of intercultural dialogue, even while food serves as a distinguishing marker of identity for immigrant minorities.[76]

Conclusion

As Spain's Muslim presence continues to increase and the nation's food scene further evolves, the question remains regarding the extent to which *halal* food will become integrated into the Spanish foodscape. Whether the *halal* certificate will serve as a seal of difference or as a sign of culinary *convivencia* moving forward is yet to be determined, but there are promising indications of the latter. Efforts are underway to develop the *halal* food industry and *halal* tourism alike, and Spain is well positioned to benefit from both. There is edible evidence of reciprocity and reconciliation as well, from *halal jamón* to Moroccan tapas. For Muslim immigrants, such dishes can provide both a connection to Spain's past and a sense of belonging moving forward.

The Cooperation Agreement of 1992 between the Spanish state and the Islamic Commission of Spain specifies the right for Muslims to have access to *halal* food in public institutions, such as schools and the military.[77] Yet, as this chapter illustrates, the availability of *halal* food now far exceeds these basic parameters. This trend is indicative of Spain's changing demographics and tourist population and may have far-reaching implications for Spanish society. Abu-Shams notes, "[c]omer no es un acto meramente biológico, sino que supone una actividad social y cultural" (eating is not merely a biological act, but rather a social and cultural activity).[78] As such, *halal* fare in Spain has the potential to bring together historically opposed peoples and practices. In a nation hitherto ambivalent to its Islamic history and against a global din of Islamophobia, this is certainly food for thought.

NOTES

1. Research and Markets, "$1.9 Trillion Halal Food Market: Global Industry Trends, Share, Size, Growth, Opportunity and Forecast to 2026," *Business Wire*, April 20, 2021.
2. Barbara Ruiz-Bejarano, "Islamophobia as a Deterrent to Halal Global Trade," *Islamophobia Studies Journal* 4, no. 1 (2017): 132.
3. See Marcus L. Stephenson, "Deciphering 'Islamic Hospitality': Developments, Challenges and Opportunities," *Tourism Management* 40 (2014): 155–64. For dining facilities to be classified as compliant with Islamic law, they should also not serve alcohol, display art that depicts human or animal form, or play music that expresses seductive messages (157). However, many eateries in non-Muslim countries that advertise *halal* offerings do not meet these requirements.
4. Maryam Taha Mannaa, "Halal Food in the Tourist Destination and its Importance for Muslim Travellers," *Current Issues in Tourism* 23, no. 17 (2020): 2199; Stephenson, "Deciphering," 159.

5. Elif Izberk-Bilgin and Cheryl C. Nakata, "A New Look at Faith-Based Marketing: The Global Halal Market," *Business Horizons* 59, no. 3 (2016): 287; Stephen Wilkins, Muhammad Mohsin Butt, Farshid Shams, and Andrea Pérez, "The Acceptance of Halal Food in Non-Muslim Countries: Effects of Religious Identity, National Identification, Consumer Ethnocentrism and Consumer Cosmopolitanism," *Journal of Islamic Marketing* 10, no. 4 (2019): 1311.
6. "Provacuno Announces an Increase in the Number of Spanish Halal Slaughterhouses," *Euromeat News*, July 11, 2018; Jenny Eagle, "Spain Sees a Rise in Halal Meat for Muslim and Non-Muslim Consumers," *FoodNavigator*, December 17, 2019.
7. Alimentaria is a leading food and beverage trade show in Spain, whose 2022 event featured *halal* food as a top trend for the industry. Alimentaria Exhibitions is a subsidiary of Fira de Barcelona, a consortium made up of Barcelona City Council, the Catalan Government, and the Chamber of Commerce of Barcelona. For a discussion of efforts to portray Catalonia as a community open to other cultures, see Lara Anderson, Heather Benbow, and Gregoria Manzin, "Europe on a Plate: Food, Identity and Cultural Diversity in Contemporary Europe," *Australian and New Zealand Journal of European Studies* 8, no. 1 (2016): 2–15.
8. According to the 2020 report published by the Unión de Comunidades Islámicas de España, there were approximately 2.1 million Muslims living in Spain at the end of 2019, approximately 4 percent of the total population (7, 14). Forty-two percent of Spain's Muslim population is of Spanish nationality, while 58 percent are immigrants; of the immigrant Muslim population, 66 percent are Moroccan (14). Unión de Comunidades Islámicas de España, "Estudio demográfico de la población musulmana de España," *Observatorio Andalusí*, 2020.
9. Leela Riesz, "The Challenge of the Halal/Pork Binary for Muslim Immigrants in Spain," *The Routledge Handbook of Halal Hospitality and Islamic Tourism*, eds. C. M. Hall, and G. Prayag (New York: Routledge, 2019), 296.
10. The British periodical *The Guardian* named Restaurante-Tetería Baraka among Spain's top ten rural restaurants of 2017. "10 of the Best Restaurants in Rural Spain: Readers' Travel Tips," *The Guardian*, July 20, 2017. See also the section of this chapter on *halal* eateries for a detailed discussion of this restaurant.
11. Lauren Frayer, "At Last, Muslims Can Savor A Halal Spin On Spain's Famous Jamón," *NPR*, December 16, 2014.
12. For an examination of the production, marketing, certification, and significance of *halal* food for Muslims living in European countries other than Spain, see Nur Aini Fitriya Ardiani Aniqoh and Metta Renatie Hanastiana, "Halal Food Industry: Challenges and Opportunities in Europe," *Journal of Digital Marketing and Halal Industry* 2, no. 1 (2020): 43–54; Karijn Bonne, Iris Vermeir, Florence Bergeaud-Blackler, and Wim Verbek, "Determinants of Halal Meat Consumption in France," *British Food Journal* 109, no. 5 (2007): 367–86; Karijn Bonne and Win Verbeke, "Muslim Consumer Trust in Halal Meat Status and Control in Belgium," *Meat Science* 79, no. 1 (2008): 113–23; Fedora Gasparetti, "Eating *Tie Bou Jenn* in Turin: Negotiating Differences and

Building Community among Senegalese Migrants in Italy," *Food and Foodways* 20, nos. 3–4 (2012): 257–78; Michelle Johnson, "'Nothing is sweet in my mouth': Food, Identity, and Religion in African Lisbon," *Food and Foodways* 24, nos. 3–4 (2016): 234–56; Laura Kurth and Pieter Glasbergen, "Serving a Heterogeneous Muslim Identity? Private Governance Arrangements of Halal Food in the Netherlands," *Agriculture and Human Values* 34 (2017): 103–18; Mehkar Sherwani, Afzaal Ali, Adnan Ali, and Sikander Hussain, "Determinants of Halal Meat Consumption in Germany," *Journal of Islamic Marketing* 9, no. 4 (2018): 863–83; Wynne Wright and Alexis Annes, "Halal on the Menu?: Contested Food Politics and French Identity in Fast-Food," *Journal of Rural Studies* 32 (2013): 388–99.

13. Leila Abu-Shams, "La alimentación como signo de identidad cultural entre los inmigrantes marroquíes," *Zainak* 30 (2008): 177–93; Reisz, "The Challenge."

14. Reisz, "The Challenge," 297; Wilkins et al., "The Acceptance of Halal Food," 1312.

15. Not specific to Spain, researchers have found that consuming *halal* products may be interpreted as a form of Islamic worship, that non-Muslim consumers' perceptions of religious labels on food packaging are influenced by their opinions of the religion itself, and that higher levels of animosity toward Muslim endorsements decreases non-Muslims' willingness to buy *halal* products. See A. J. Wilson and Jonathan Liu, "Shaping the Halal into a Brand?" *Journal of Islamic Marketing* 1, no. 2 (2010): 107–23; Philipp A. Rauschnabel, Marc Herz, Bodo B. Schlegelmilch, and Bjoern S. Ivens, "Brands and Religious Labels: A Spillover Perspective," *Journal of Marketing Management* 31, nos. 11–12 (2015): 1285–1309; Bodo B. Schlegelmilch, Mubbsher Munawar Khan, and Joe F. Hair, "Halal Endorsements: Stirring Controversy or Gaining New Customers?" *International Marketing Review* 33, no. 1 (2016): 156–74.

16. Wilkins et al., "The Acceptance of Halal Food," 1318, 1316. They found that 47.5 percent of their sample reported having no *halal* knowledge, and 44.2 percent had only some knowledge (1317). An unrelated questionnaire administered to tourism experts and professionals in Spain showed that health and ecological benefits of consuming *halal* food are not typically recognized either, despite rising concerns worldwide regarding the use of pesticides, preservatives, antibiotics, and genetically modified products and the insistence in *halal* on food purity. Alfonso Vargas-Sánchez and María Moral-Moral, "Halal Tourism, Where Are We? Particular Attention to the Situation in Spain," in *Handbook of Research on Socio-Economic Impacts of Religious Tourism and Pilgrimage*, eds. J. Álvarez-García, M. de la Cruz del Río Rama, M. Gómez-Ullate García de León (Hershey, PA: Business Science Reference, 2019), 219.

17. Anderson et al. draw from Michaela DeSoucey's concept of "gastronationalism," the idea that food and food practices have cultural capital and are central to the construction of national identity. While diverse culinary cultures coexist throughout Europe, Germany, Italy, and Spain are notable for the number of food products protected by label restrictions. Such a measure is indicative of the tendency toward gastronationalism. See Anderson et al., "Europe on a Plate."

18. Ibid., 8.

19. Lara Anderson, "El multiculturalismo culinario en España: De la asimilación a la diversidad," in *Fronteras y migraciones en ámbito mediterráneo*, eds. E. Bou and J. Zarco (Venice: Edizioni Ca'Foscari, 2017), 31.
20. Ibid., 33.
21. Enric Bou, "Food and the Everyday in Spain: Immigration and Culinary Renovation," *Bulletin of Spanish Studies* 97, no. 4 (2020): 681–700.
22. Anderson, "El multiculturalismo culinario," 39.
23. Zarco notes that six titles featuring immigrants debuted in 1996 alone, and the trend has since continued. Julieta Zarco, "Dime qué comes y te dire quién eres. Vida cotidiana, comidas e inmigración en el cine español," *Revista Taller de Letras* 59 (2016): 61–74. Bou points to the role of food in the revival of *Marca España* and the proliferation of cultural texts about Spanish cuisine in the 1990s and early 2000s. Bou, "Food and the Everyday," 682.
24. Ingrid Guardiola, "Invitations to Reconciliation: Immigration Via Local and Autonomous Community Informative Programmes," *Quaderns del CAC* 23–24 (2006): 131–39.
25. Fernando Colomo, dir., *El próximo Oriente* (Colomo Producciones, 2006).
26. Zarco, "Dime qué," 71.
27. Bou, "Food and the Everyday."
28. "New campaign to promote Spanish food launches," *Specialty Food*, May 23, 2019.
29. "Government of Spain invests four million euros in overseas promotion of Spanish foods," *La Moncloa*, September 9, 2020.
30. Anderson's study highlights two prior studies conducted by the Ministry of Agriculture, Fisheries and Food, realized in 2004 and 2007, that affirmed the integration of Spain's immigrant population in terms of dietary habits and preferences, thereby ignoring the nation's cultural and culinary diversity. Anderson, "El multiculturalismo culinario," 33.
31. Olivia Remie Constable, "Food and Meaning: Christian Understandings of Muslim Food and Food Ways in Spain, 1250–1550," *Viator* 44, no. 3 (2013): 229.
32. Deborah Root, "Speaking Christian: Orthodoxy and Difference in Sixteenth-Century Spain," *Representations* 23 (1988): 129.
33. Constable, "Food and Meaning," 229.
34. Heba Hashem, "Spain Must Be 'Genuinely' Welcoming to Attract More Muslim Tourists Amid Recent Rise in Islamophobia, Say Experts," *Salaam Gateway*, April 9, 2021.
35. Spain's Interior Ministry reported a 120 percent increase in instances of Islamophobia between 2017 and 2019. Inigo Alexander, "Muslims and Migrants in Spain: How Fake News is Keeping Minorities Sidelined," *Middle East Eye*, February 7, 2021. For details regarding the various forms of discrimination and hate incidents directed toward Muslims in Spain, see Aurora Ali, "Anti-Muslim Hatred and Discrimination in Spain 2020," *Asociación Musulmana por los Derechos Humanos*, November 25, 2020; Enes Bayrakli and Farid Hafez, eds., *European Islamophobia Report 2019* (Istanbul: SETA, 2020).
36. Vox, a far-right party formed in 2013 that has become increasingly popular in Andalucía, is a prime example of Islamophobic politics in Spain. At the start of 2021, Vox's

Twitter account was blocked specifically for "inciting hate" against Muslims through the online campaign #StopIslamization. See Miguel González, "Twitter bloquea la cuenta de Vox por 'incitar al odio' contra los musulmanes," *El País*, January 28, 2021. For an overview of other policies and practices that have targeted Islam in Spain, see Jessica Boll, "Uncommon Denominators? Christian-Muslim Relations and the Legacy of al-Andalus in Contemporary Spain," in *On Migrants Routes in the Mediterranean: Political and Juridical Strategies*, eds. G. Truda and J. Spurk (ICSR Mediterranean Knowledge, 2018), 97–112. For statistics regarding anti-Muslim sentiment throughout Europe, see Richard Wike, Jacob Poushter, Laura Silver, Kat Devlin, Janell Fetterolf, Alexandra Castillo, and Christine Huang, "Views on Minority Groups Across Europe," *Pew Research Center*, October 14, 2019.

37. Verena Gruber, "Case Study: KFC in France," in *Diversity in European Marketing: Text and Cases*, eds. T. Rudolph, B. B. Schlegelmilch, J. Franch, A. Bauer, and J. N. Meise (Wiesbaden, Germany: Springer Gabler, 2012), 51.
38. Ibid., 50.
39. Wilkins et al., "The Acceptance of Halal Food," 1309.
40. For more on the Boycott Halal movement worldwide, see Elizabeth C. Hirshman and Mourad Touzani, "Contesting Religious Identity in the Marketplace: Consumption Ideology and the Boycott Halal Movement," *Journal of Islamic Studies and Culture* 4, no. 1 (2016): 19–29.
41. Ruiz-Bejarano, "Islamaphobia as a Deterrent," 139.
42. Ibid., 138.
43. Ibid., 133.
44. For vilification of the kebab industry and/or *halal* food in general in Italy, France, Norway, and Poland, for instance, see Alberto Mucci, "Italian Mayor's Anti-Kebab Law," *Politico*, October 14, 2016; Feargus O'Sullivan, "France's Kebab Crackdown," *Bloomberg*, July 10, 2017; Paul Thomas and Amina Selimovic, "Sharia on a Plate? A Critical Discourse Analysis of Halal Food in Two Norwegian Newspapers," *Journal of Islamic Marketing* 6, no. 3 (2015): 331–53; Lukasz Woznicki, "Kebab Violence and Blatant Racism in Poland," *World Crunch*, January 9, 2017; Wright and Annes, "Halal on the Menu?"
45. Lauren Frayer, "In Spain, Proposed 'Kebab Law' Angers Muslim Business Owners," *LA Times*, May 5, 2015; Frayer, "Spain's Muslim Business Owners Feel Squeezed by New Zoning Proposals," *NPR*, March 1, 2015.
46. Frayer, "Spain's Muslim Business Owners."
47. Wilkins et al., "The Acceptance of Halal Food," 1310.
48. Riesz, "The Challenge," 299.
49. "10 of the Best Restaurants."
50. Inka Piesga-Quischotte, "The Europeans Who Chose Mystical Islam," *BBC*, September 29, 2016. See the section of this chapter on *halal* tourism for a detailed discussion of the industry.
51. Restaurante Baraka Orgiva, "Baraka Orgiva 'Andalucia Directo,'" *YouTube*, September 26, 2017.

52. See the Web site "Noor," *50 Best Discovery*.
53. Turespaña, "Halal Tourism," *Spain Info*, 2021.
54. Leslie Styles, "Noor: Haute Al-Andalus Cuisine of Chef Paco Morales," *Scrumpdillyicious*, May 1, 2018.
55. See, for example, the blog posts: Annie Bennett, "Noor – Paco Morales Opens His New Restaurant in Cordoba," *Mooching Around Spain*, March 15, 2016; Fiona Dunlop, "Noor – Cordoba's Top Restaurant Revisits Al-Andalus," *Fiona Dunlop Food and Travel*, June 27, 2019; Styles, "Noor."
56. Chiringuito La Pesquera del Faro, *Facebook*; *La Pesquera*.
57. Los Almendros Restaurante Córdoba, "Restaurante Los Almendros Halal Córdoba," *Facebook*, May 21, 2017.
58. When consulted for this chapter in October 2021, Noor was rated 5/5 based on 434 reviews on TripAdvisor and was ranked #1 of 2060 restaurants in Córdoba by Restaurant Guru. TripAdvisor rated Baraka as the #1 restaurant in Orgiva, with a rating of 4.5/5 from 455 reviews. El Faro was rated 3/5 on both TripAdvisor and Google and listed as #746 of 919 restaurants in Marbella. Los Almendros was rated 3.5/5 on TripAdvisor and ranked #285 of 941 restaurants in the area.
59. Dinar Standard, *State of the Global Islamic Economy Report 2020/21* (2020), 3, 15.
60. According to the National Tourist Office of Spain, most Muslim travelers to Spain hail from Algeria, Morocco, and Turkey. An estimated two million Muslim tourists visited Spain from outside the EU in 2018, whereas approximately five million Muslims visit from within the EU each year. See Kira Walker, "'Muslim Spain' Vies for Moment in the Sun as Halal Tourism Takes off," *The National*, April 3, 2019. For an early study on *halal* tourism in Spain, see María del Carmen de la Orden de la Cruz, Pilar Sánchez González, and Paloma Bernal Turnes, *Turismo Halal en España* (Madrid: OMM Editorial, 2014).
61. Unveiled in May of 2021, Spain's newest campaign—"You Deserve Spain"—continues to market beyond the classic pitch of sun and sand to highlight cultural, urban, rural, and nature tourism. For a thorough examination of the evolution of Spain's tourism campaigns and the power dynamics thereof, see Eugenia Afinoguénova and Jaume Martí-Olivella, eds., *Spain Is (Still) Different: Tourism and Discourse in Spanish Identity* (Lanham, MD: Lexington Books, 2008). For a discussion of the ways in which Spain's Islamic history is promoted to both Muslim and non-Muslim tourists, see Jessica Boll, "Selling Spain: Tourism, Tensions, and Islam in Iberia," *Journal of Intercultural Communication* 53 (2020): 42–55.
62. Mohamed Battour, Mohd Nazari Ismail, and Moustafa Battor, "The Impact of Destination Attributes on Muslim Tourist's Choice," *International Journal of Tourism Research* 13, no. 6 (2010): 535; Joan C. Henderson, "Halal Food, Certification and Halal Tourism: Insights from Malaysia and Singapore," *Tourism Management Perspectives* 19 (2016): 160; Asad Mohsin, Noriah Ramli, and Bader Abdulaziz Alkhulayfi, "Halal Tourism: Emerging Opportunities," *Tourism Management Perspectives* 19 (2016): 140.
63. Mannaa, "Halal Food," 2204.
64. Vargas-Sánchez and Moral-Moral, "Halal Tourism," 217.

65. Walker, "'Muslim Spain.'" Mohamed Tawfik, director of Spain Baraka Tours, noted the difficulty of finding *halal* food in northern Spain. Spain Baraka Tours is a *halal* tour company based out of Barcelona and is one of many such tour companies that aim to capitalize on the legacy of Islamic Spain to distinguish the nation from other destinations.
66. Mahir Pradana, Rubén Huertas-García, and Frederic Marimon, "Muslim Tourists' Purchase Intention of Halal Food in Spain," *Current Issues in Tourism* 24, no. 13 (2021): 1814.
67. Wilkins et al., "The Acceptance of Halal Food," 1321.
68. Yasin Maymir, "9 Reasons Why Spain is Your Next Halal Travel Destination," *Ilimtour*, March 21, 2019.
69. The Halal Institute is a dependent of the Islamic Board of Spain, a non-profit organization founded in 1989. The Islamic Board is composed mainly of Spanish converts to Islam and has consistently been one of the most active and vocal Islamic organizations in Europe.
70. Vargas-Sánchez and Moral-Moral, "Halal Tourism," 223; Hashem, "Spain Must Be."
71. Constable, "Food and Meaning," 201, 209, 210.
72. For more on the notion and problematization of historic *convivencia*, see Darío Fernández-Morera, *The Myth of the Andalusian Paradise: Muslims, Christians, and Jews under Islamic Rule in Medieval Spain* (Wilmington, DE: ISI Books, 2016); Maya Soifer, "Beyond *Convivencia*: Critical Reflections on the Historiography of Interfaith Relations in Christian Spain," *Journal of Medieval Iberian Studies* 1, no. 1 (2009): 19–35; Kenneth Baxter Wolf, "*Convivencia* in Medieval Spain: A Brief History of an Idea," *Religion Compass* 3, no. 1 (2009): 72–85. On the continuing legacy of al-Andalus in contemporary Spain, see Boll, "Uncommon"; Christina Civantos, *The Afterlife of Al-Andalus: Muslim Iberia in Contemporary Arab and Hispanic Narratives* (Albany: State University of New York Press, 2017); Mariano Delgado, "From Acceptance to Religious Freedom: Considerations for Convivencia in Medieval Spain and Multireligious Coexistence Today," in *Contested Spaces, Common Ground*, eds. U. Winkler, L. Rodríguez Fernández, and O. Leirvik (Leiden, Netherlands: Brill, 2016), 225–40; Nicola Gilmour, "Transforming Legacies: The Denial and Rediscovery of Spain's Islamic Past," *Journal of Iberian and Latin American Research* 23, no. 3 (2017): 219–34; Mikaela Rogozen-Soltar, "Managing Muslim Visibility: Conversion, Immigration, and Spanish Imaginaries of Islam," *American Anthropologist* 114, no. 4 (2012): 611–23.
73. Leela Riesz, "*Convivencia*: A Solution to the Halal/Pork Tension in Spain?" *Journal of Business Management* 58, no. 3 (2018): 223, 226.
74. Abu-Shams, "La alimentación," 188–89.
75. Constable, "Food and Meaning," 215.
76. Abu-Shams, "La alimentación," 189.
77. Charles Hirschkind, "The Contemporary Afterlife of Moorish Spain," in *Islam and Public Controversy in Europe*, ed. N. Göle (Surrey, England: Ashgate, 2013), 238.
78. Abu-Shams, "La alimentación," 186.

WORKS CITED

"10 of the Best Restaurants in Rural Spain: Readers' Travel Tips." *The Guardian*, July 20, 2017.
Abu-Shams, Leila. "La alimentación como signo de identidad cultural entre los inmigrantes marroquíes." *Zainak* 30 (2008): 177-93.
Afinoguénova, Eugenia, and Jaume Martí-Olivella, eds. *Spain Is (Still) Different: Tourism and Discourse in Spanish Identity*. Lanham, MD: Lexington Books, 2008.
Alexander, Inigo. "Muslims and Migrants in Spain: How Fake News is Keeping Minorities Sidelined." *Middle East Eye*, February 7, 2021.
Ali, Aurora. "Anti-Muslim Hatred and Discrimination in Spain 2020." *Asociación Musulmana por los Derechos Humanos*, November 25, 2020.
Almendros Restaurante Córdoba, Los. "Restaurante Los Almendros Halal Córdoba." *Facebook*, May 21, 2017.
Anderson, Lara. "El multiculturalismo culinario en España: De la asimilación a la diversidad." In *Fronteras y migraciones en ámbito mediterráneo*, edited by E. Bou and J. Zarco, 29-42. Venice: Edizioni Ca'Foscari, 2017.
Anderson, Lara, Heather Benbow, and Gregoria Manzin. "Europe on a Plate: Food, Identity and Cultural Diversity in Contemporary Europe." *Australian and New Zealand Journal of European Studies* 8, no. 1 (2016): 2-15.
Ardiani Aniqoh, Nur Aini Fitriya, and Metta Renatie Hanastiana. "Halal Food Industry: Challenges and Opportunities in Europe." *Journal of Digital Marketing and Halal Industry* 2, no. 1 (2020): 43-54.
Battour, Mohamed, Mohd Nazari Ismail, and Moustafa Battor. "The Impact of Destination Attributes on Muslim Tourist's Choice." *International Journal of Tourism Research* 13, no. 6 (2010): 527-40.
Bayrakli, Enes, and Farid Hafez, eds. *European Islamophobia Report 2019*. Istanbul: SETA, 2020.
Bennett, Annie. "Noor - Paco Morales Opens His New Restaurant in Cordoba." *Mooching Around Spain*, March 15, 2016.
Boll, Jessica. "Selling Spain: Tourism, Tensions, and Islam in Iberia." *Journal of Intercultural Communication* 53 (2020): 42-55.
———. "Uncommon Denominators? Christian-Muslim Relations and the Legacy of al-Andalus in Contemporary Spain." In *On Migrants Routes in the Mediterranean: Political and Juridical Strategies*, edited by G. Truda and J. Spurk, 97-112. ICSR Mediterranean Knowledge, 2018.
Bonne, Karijn, Iris Vermeir, Florence Bergeaud-Blackler, and Wim Verbeke. "Determinants of Halal Meat Consumption in France." *British Food Journal* 109, no. 5 (2007): 367-86.
Bonne, Karijn, and Win Verbeke. "Muslim Consumer Trust in Halal Meat Status and Control in Belgium." *Meat Science* 79, no. 1 (2008): 113-23.
Bou, Enric. "Food and the Everyday in Spain: Immigration and Culinary Renovation." *Bulletin of Spanish Studies* 97, no. 4 (2020): 681-700.
Chiringuito La Pesquera del Faro. *Facebook*.

Civantos, Christina. *The Afterlife of Al-Andalus: Muslim Iberia in Contemporary Arab and Hispanic Narratives.* Albany: State University of New York Press, 2017.
Colomo, Fernando, dir. *El próximo Oriente.* Colomo Producciones, 2006.
Constable, Olivia Remie. "Food and Meaning: Christian Understandings of Muslim Food and Food Ways in Spain, 1250–1550." *Viator* 44, no. 3 (2013): 199–235.
de la Orden de la Cruz, María del Carmen, Pilar Sánchez González, and Paloma Bernal Turnes. *Turismo Halal en España.* Madrid: OMM Editorial, 2014.
Delgado, Mariano. "From Acceptance to Religious Freedom: Considerations for Convivencia in Medieval Spain and Multireligious Coexistence Today." In *Contested Spaces, Common Ground*, edited by U. Winkler, L. Rodríguez Fernández, and O. Leirvik, 225–40. Leiden, Netherlands: Brill, 2016.
Dinar Standard. *State of the Global Islamic Economy Report 2020/21.* 2020.
Dunlop, Fiona. "Noor – Cordoba's Top Restaurant Revisits Al-Andalus." *Fiona Dunlop Food and Travel*, June 27, 2019.
Eagle, Jenny. "Spain Sees a Rise in Halal Meat for Muslim and Non-Muslim Consumers." *FoodNavigator*, December 17, 2019.
Fernández-Morera, Darío. *The Myth of the Andalusian Paradise: Muslims, Christians, and Jews under Islamic Rule in Medieval Spain.* Wilmington, DE: ISI Books, 2016.
Frayer, Lauren. "At Last, Muslims Can Savor a Halal Spin On Spain's Famous Jamón." *NPR*, December 16, 2014.
———. "In Spain, Proposed 'Kebab Law' Angers Muslim Business Owners." *LA Times*, May 5, 2015.
———. "Spain's Muslim Business Owners Feel Squeezed by New Zoning Proposals." *NPR*, March 1, 2015.
Gasparetti, Fedora. "Eating *Tie Bou Jenn* in Turin: Negotiating Differences and Building Community among Senegalese Migrants in Italy." *Food and Foodways* 20, nos. 3–4 (2012): 257–78.
Gilmour, Nicola. "Transforming Legacies: The Denial and Rediscovery of Spain's Islamic Past." *Journal of Iberian and Latin American Research* 23, no. 3 (2017): 219–34.
González, Miguel. "Twitter bloquea la cuenta de Vox por 'incitar al odio' contra los musulmantes." *El País*, January 28, 2021.
"Government of Spain invests four million euros in overseas promotion of Spanish foods." *La Moncloa*, September 9, 2020.
Gruber, Verena. "Case Study: KFC in France." In *Diversity in European Marketing: Text and Cases*, edited by T. Rudolph, B. B. Schlegelmilch, J. Franch, A. Bauer, and J. N. Meise, 41–55. Wiesbaden, Germany: Springer Gabler, 2012.
Guardiola, Ingrid. "Invitations to Reconciliation: Immigration Via Local and Autonomous Community Informative Programmes." *Quaderns del CAC* 23–24 (2006): 131–39.
Hashem, Heba. "Spain Must Be 'Genuinely' Welcoming to Attract More Muslim Tourists Amid Recent Rise in Islamophobia, Say Experts." *Salaam Gateway*, April 9, 2021.
Henderson, Joan C. "Halal Food, Certification and Halal Tourism: Insights from Malaysia and Singapore." *Tourism Management Perspectives* 19 (2016): 160–64.

Hirschkind, Charles. "The Contemporary Afterlife of Moorish Spain." In *Islam and Public Controversy in Europe*, edited by N. Göle, 227–40. Surrey, England: Ashgate, 2013.
Hirshman, Elizabeth C., and Mourad Touzani. "Contesting Religious Identity in the Marketplace: Consumption Ideology and the Boycott Halal Movement." *Journal of Islamic Studies and Culture* 4, no. 1 (2016): 19–29.
Izberk-Bilgin, Elif, and Cheryl C. Nakata. "A New Look at Faith-Based Marketing: The Global Halal Market." *Business Horizons* 59, no. 3 (2016): 285–92.
Johnson, Michelle. "'Nothing is sweet in my mouth': Food, Identity, and Religion in African Lisbon." *Food and Foodways* 24, nos. 3–4 (2016): 234–56.
Kurth, Laura, and Pieter Glasbergen. "Serving a Heterogeneous Muslim Identity? Private Governance Arrangements of Halal Food in the Netherlands." *Agriculture and Human Values* 34 (2017): 103–18.
Mannaa, Maryam Taha. "Halal Food in the Tourist Destination and its Importance for Muslim Travellers." *Current Issues in Tourism* 23, no. 17 (2020): 2195–206.
Maymir, Yasin. "9 Reasons Why Spain is Your Next Halal Travel Destination." *Ilimtour*, March 21, 2019.
Mohsin, Asad, Noriah Ramli, and Bader Abdulaziz Alkhulayfi. "Halal Tourism: Emerging Opportunities." *Tourism Management Perspectives* 19 (2016): 137–43.
Mucci, Alberto. "Italian Mayor's Anti-Kebab Law." *Politico*, October 14, 2016.
"New campaign to promote Spanish food launches." *Specialty Food*, May 23, 2019.
O'Sullivan, Feargus. "France's Kebab Crackdown." *Bloomberg*, July 10, 2017.
Piesga-Quischotte, Inka. "The Europeans Who Chose Mystical Islam." *BBC*, September 29, 2016.
Pradana, Mahir, Rubén Huertas-García, and Frederic Marimon. "Muslim Tourists' Purchase Intention of Halal Food in Spain." *Current Issues in Tourism* 24, no. 13 (2021): 1814–18.
"Provacuno Announces an Increase in the Number of Spanish Halal Slaughterhouses." *Euromeat News*, July 11, 2018.
Rauschnabel, Philipp A., Marc Herz, Bodo B. Schlegelmilch, and Bjoern S. Ivens. "Brands and Religious Labels: A Spillover Perspective." *Journal of Marketing Management* 31, nos. 11-12 (2015): 1285–1309.
Research and Markets. "$1.9 Trillion Halal Food Market: Global Industry Trends, Share, Size, Growth, Opportunity and Forecast to 2026." *Business Wire*, April 20, 2021.
Restaurante Baraka Orgiva. "Baraka Orgiva 'Andalucia Directo.'" *YouTube*, September 26, 2017.
Riesz, Leela. "The Challenge of the Halal/Pork Binary for Muslim Immigrants in Spain." *The Routledge Handbook of Halal Hospitality and Islamic Tourism*, edited by C. M. Hall, and G. Prayag, 293–302. New York: Routledge, 2019.
———. "*Convivencia*: A Solution to the Halal/Pork Tension in Spain?" *Journal of Business Management* 58, no. 3 (2018): 222–32.
Rogozen-Soltar, Mikaela. "Managing Muslim Visibility: Conversion, Immigration, and Spanish Imaginaries of Islam." *American Anthropologist* 114, no. 4 (2012): 611–23.
Root, Deborah. "Speaking Christian: Orthodoxy and Difference in Sixteenth-Century Spain." *Representations* 23 (1988): 118–34.

Ruiz-Bejarano, Barbara. "Islamophobia as a Deterrent to Halal Global Trade." *Islamophobia Studies Journal* 4, no. 1 (2017): 129–45.

Schlegelmilch, Bodo B., Mubbsher Munawar Khan, and Joe F. Hair. "Halal Endorsements: Stirring Controversy or Gaining New Customers?" *International Marketing Review* 33, no. 1 (2016): 156–74.

Sherwani, Mehkar, Afzaal Ali, Adnan Ali, and Sikander Hussain. "Determinants of Halal Meat Consumption in Germany." *Journal of Islamic Marketing* 9, no. 4 (2018): 863–83.

Soifer, Maya. "Beyond *Convivencia*: Critical Reflections on the Historiography of Interfaith Relations in Christian Spain." *Journal of Medieval Iberian Studies* 1, no. 1 (2009): 19–35.

Stephenson, Marcus L. "Deciphering 'Islamic Hospitality': Developments, Challenges and Opportunities." *Tourism Management* 40 (2014): 155–64.

Styles, Leslie. "Noor: Haute Al-Andalus Cuisine of Chef Paco Morales." *Scrumpdillyicious*, May 1, 2018.

Thomas, Paul, and Amina Selimovic. "Sharia on a Plate? A Critical Discourse Analysis of Halal Food in Two Norwegian Newspapers." *Journal of Islamic Marketing* 6, no. 3 (2015): 331–53.

Turespaña. "Halal Tourism." *Spain Info*, 2021.

Unión de Comunidades Islámicas de España. "Estudio demográfico de la población musulmana de España." *Observatorio Andalusí*, 2020.

Vargas-Sánchez, Alfonso, and María Moral-Moral. "Halal Tourism, Where Are We? Particular Attention to the Situation in Spain." In *Handbook of Research on Socio-Economic Impacts of Religious Tourism and Pilgrimage*, edited by J. Álvarez-García, M. de la Cruz del Río Rama, M. Gómez-Ullate García de León, 211–33. Hershey, PA: Business Science Reference, 2019.

Walker, Kira. "'Muslim Spain' Vies for Moment in the Sun as Halal Tourism Takes off." *The National*, April 3, 2019.

Wike, Richard, Jacob Poushter, Laura Silver, Kat Devlin, Janell Fetterolf, Alexandra Castillo, and Christine Huang. "Views on Minority Groups Across Europe." *Pew Research Center*, October 14, 2019.

Wilkins, Stephen, Muhammad Mohsin Butt, Farshid Shams, and Andrea Pérez. "The Acceptance of Halal Food in Non-Muslim Countries: Effects of Religious Identity, National Identification, Consumer Ethnocentrism and Consumer Cosmopolitanism." *Journal of Islamic Marketing* 10, no. 4 (2019): 1308–31.

Wilson, Jonathan A. J., and Jonathan Liu. "Shaping the Halal into a Brand?" *Journal of Islamic Marketing* 1, no. 2 (2010): 107–23.

Wolf, Kenneth Baxter. "*Convivencia* in Medieval Spain: A Brief History of an Idea." *Religion Compass* 3, no. 1 (2009): 72–85.

Woznicki, Lukasz. "Kebab Violence and Blatant Racism in Poland." *World Crunch*, January 9, 2017.

Wright, Wynne, and Alexis Annes. "Halal on the Menu?: Contested Food Politics and French Identity in Fast-Food." *Journal of Rural Studies* 32 (2013): 388–99.

Zarco, Julieta. "Dime qué comes y te diré quién eres. Vida cotidiana, comidas e inmigración en el cine español." *Revista Taller de Letras* 59 (2016): 61–74.

Part III: Gastrocratic Institutions

◆ CHAPTER 7

The Institutionalization of the Asturian *Espicha* during the Franco Regime

Luis Benito García Álvarez

Still a traditional product in Asturias today, cider used to be the main drink of its people and an important alternative to scarce, expensive wine. In the early modern times, a complex ritual known as the *espicha*—the pricking of a barrel—developed in spaces such as the apple press and the cider house, becoming an essential element of other rituals like patron-saint celebrations (the *romerías*), gatherings around the stringing of corn (the *esfoyaces*), the spinning of yarn (the *filandones*), or the roasting of chestnuts (the *amagüestos*). These traditional customs, however, changed in the middle of the nineteenth century due to industrial development in the region. This was also the time when the cider sector itself experienced a dramatic growth and became an industry with a high degree of decentralization of its production cycle and a transatlantic distribution capacity, also serving the Asturian expat communities in the Americas.

Importantly, *espicha* remained a quintessential cider consumption event. Since the beginning of the twentieth century, this traditional practice of agrarian communitarianism (when opening the barrel was a way of thanking the neighbors for their help) became commercialized. And paying to enjoy the celebration increased the effects of sociability and tavern commensality. Literary and visual testimonies of the time, as well as the reports published in the press or carried out internally by business owners, public officials, and religious authorities offered insights concerning the activities related to the *espicha*, as well as the social groups that practiced this ritual in rural and urban areas. These sources point to significant changes in the ritualization of cider consumption at that time. The *espicha* became a backdrop for games, music, and food sampling that were considered an important part of Asturian identity. At the same time, this commercialized ritual became a focal point for behavior associated with virility. Such modern reframing of the *espicha* increased its attractiveness amongst male consumers and its commercial value to business-owners.[1]

In rural areas, the protocol of the *espicha* presented strong features of solidarity and redistribution of community resources, including, for example, the rule for the owner of an apple press with a significant volume of business to invite neighbors who had helped in the elaboration of cider destined for sale or self-consumption before being corked. That way, the producer (always male) offered to his closest friends the foretaste of a barrel and "lo que da la casa" (whatever the house provided)—eggs, omelets, sausages, or, in the coastal areas, sardines—to snack on.[2] Over time, as the levels of popular consumption increased, in different parts of Asturias the owners began to include empanadas, cheese, ham, and, finally, shellfish.[3]

Meanwhile, in urban areas the *espichas* became a very profitable business and the opening of a barrel in a public place attracted a large and varied clientele. On some occasions, the presence of bourgeois and middle-class groups in the city brought in music and the types of food that were very different from those of the popular classes. The change was especially noticeable in seafaring areas, where it was easy to find shellfish whose price generally relegated its consumption to the middle or upper social strata. The growth of the urban middle classes, the consolidation of the bourgeoisie, and the greater visibility of the local working classes stimulated continuous changes in the social base of cider consumption in both urban and rural areas throughout the 1930s.[4]

These activities, which over the previous decades had elevated the *espicha* to the status of a cultural industry, were deeply affected by Franco's dictatorship. The dictatorship limited severely and hastily the rights of assembly, demonstration, and association, thereby greatly restricting social interactions, both everyday and festive. Because playful celebrations were viewed negatively by the authorities, *espichas* were subject to control and restriction.[5] Describing the noise of rockets and loudspeakers at full blast that disturbed neighbors until the early hours of the morning, the officials classified these celebrations as similar to the popular nightly gatherings known as the "verbenas" (open air parties), as opposed to "romerías" (pilgrimages), which were also dedicated to patron saints, yet happened in daylight and were, therefore, considered much less suspicious. The regime's hegemonic groups eager to have everything managed and well under control regarded cider-related gatherings as dangerous.

By the end of the 1950s, traditional *espichas* that had been commercialized entered a new phase of decline. Although, judging by the advertisements, they were still often held in the cider regions, they lost part of their originality and appeal. Some people, who still remembered the famous *espichas* of thirty years before, suggested that back then the cider was also better.[6] Witnesses suggested, for instance, that in the municipality of Carreño cider had gone into decline because it refused to "get sold"—meaning, lose its identity—preferring to stay "honest" without transforming itself into a "sidrina" (soft cider) according to the new tastes. Other witnesses observed that more *pipas* (smaller capacity vessels) than barrels were pricked and complained by claiming that the barrels had much more style and produced better cider. In addition, after the war the celebrations related to the openings of the barrels occurred on one single day, thereby becoming more modest in comparison with the previous tradition of gathering for three days in a row: Saturday, Sunday, and Monday.[7]

Continuities and Transformations in the Celebration of the *Espicha*

The social interactions associated with cider also suffered because of the Civil War. While scarcity and austerity had an impact on all leisure and consumer habits, in the case of the *espicha*, the decline was even more noticeable. Press advertisements for these events disappeared until well into the 1940s. Even when some recreational activities such as the *romerías* (pilgrimages), which had coevolved with the *espicha* before the war, began to reemerge in the 1950s, mass consumption grew so slowly that commercialized celebrations were still falling behind the pre-war levels.[8] The traditions related to the *espicha*, however, endured and their essential ingredients were preserved. At present, the *espicha* constitutes a tradition, a leisure activity, and a well-established social act that is quickly rising in popularity beyond Asturias. How exactly these traditions were preserved, and when the *espicha* became a pastime and a celebration of food, rather than just a drink, is a story that can be inferred from newspaper ads.

The ads suggest that, shortly after the war, venues such as the Ideal Rosales, which had been leading the organization of the *espicha* before the war, tried to host much more limited yet similar gatherings. Instead of large announcements in the press of provincial capitals, the ads morphed into mere summaries announcing the opening of a barrel. Still, it was also pointed out that the best orchestra would be present and the best dance floor would be awaiting guests. Praising the venue's capacity and fast service, the ads also promised an opportunity of enjoying a succulent snack at a good price and, of course, accompanied by good cider. It was, however, a much more modest program than what the clientele of commercialized *espichas* were used to, and in a few years, the Ideal Rosales stopped pricking barrels.[9]

The Gran Parque Venecia, another renowned establishment, offered wonderful cider made by the local manufacturer José Evaristo and, like in the best times of the business, arranged special trains for its customers—a practice that required a major investment and that would eventually disappear. Over the years, many of these places that at the time were main promoters of *espichas*, ended up becoming simple summer inns, such as the Gran Parque de Verano Continental, which appeared in the media as a splendid country picnic area. Another relevant case would be the prestigious Jai-Alai, a legendary hotel in the cider-centered leisure network that would just announce such events as a festival with an orchestra or focus its advertising strategy on informing that it had cider from the town of Breceña.[10] The commercials in regional newspapers became as discreet as they used to be in the nineteenth century, at the dawn of the daily press in Asturias. Only the opening of a barrel or *pipa* (a container of smaller capacity) would be announced, which usually denoted a much more limited gathering with fewer snacks—a gathering that no longer supported the growth of the venue that hosted it.

Still, hotel entrepreneurs such as the Viuda de Rosales from Gijón never stopped advertising the cider accompanied by "all kinds of snacks" and, by the mid-1940s, spider crabs and "taquinos"—skewers with small pieces of bread, sausages, and other meat products were mentioned as snacks to accompany cider.[11] Even more importantly, the ads of the openings of the barrel began to mention the *fabada* (bean stew) seasoned with good *compangu* (smoked meats and sausage). Prior to the war, *fabada* had changed how the *espichas* were celebrated. Because the stew was not "finger food," prior to the war, the *espichas* were events at which people had to sit down and use spoons. Now that the *fabada* was served again, one can assume that those who gathered at the opening of the barrel would be seated as they were sampling the drink. These activities were also accompanied by music. In Prendes, for instance, the opening of a monumental barrel was celebrated with a "new and wonderful" Phillips jukebox.[12]

Though most of these advertisements were brief and hardly referenced anything beyond the availability of cider, more elaborate ads would appear on some occasions, following the custom born in the early years of the century. These involved facile but mostly funny verses. Such is the case of the following ad from 1944:

No ye corriente beber / sidra de primera, hoy día, / a excepción de cuando rompen / un tonel los de la Guía. / En casa los fíos de Alfonso, / los días Domingo y Lunes, / Váis a tener a discrepción / sidra, taquinos, gaiteru / y centollos un camión, / a cien metros del Rosales / frente al campo de balón.

It is uncommon to drink / first-class cider today, / except when people from the Guía / open a barrel. / At the house of Alfonso's kids, / on Sundays and Mondays, / you'll have larger amounts / of cider, taquinos, a bagpiper / and a truck load of spider crabs, / a hundred meters from Rosales / in front of the soccer field.[13]

As another outstanding example of the survival of the *espicha* tradition, its gastronomic and musical accompaniments, and the opportunity for men and women to mingle, one advertisement reads as follows:

El mejor tonel / A dos pasos del pedreru / y con vistas al Musel / espicha SENÉN EL PERI / un riquísimo tonel. / Como les xarres son grandes / y les va a vender barates / ya vemos pasar la gente / el puente Piles a gates. / De comida y de mariscos / cosa buena y abundante / y la sidra ye de AMARO / ye del todo espampanante. / Ya lo sabéis mujeres / ir con ellos al tonel / que para que no falte de nada / habrá gramola también. / Sábado, domingo y lunes en el MIRADOR DEL PILES.

The best barrel / Just steps away from the stony field (pedreru) / and overlooking the Musel / espicha SENÉN EL PERI / a delicious barrel. / Since the jars (xarres) are big / and will be sold cheap / we can already see people go by / the Piles bridge on all fours. / Of food and seafood / lots and good / and the cider is from AMARO / and quite amazing. / Women should bear in mind / to go with men to the barrel / so that nothing is missing / there will be a jukebox too. / Saturday, Sunday and Monday at the MIRADOR DEL PILES.[14]

In addition to referencing the usual features such as the quality of cider and delicacies, or the typical consumption in traditional jugs (unlike the specific glass of Asturian cider already established), the text insists that women should accompany their husbands (although the women could also be girlfriends or companions) to dance to the sound of the jukebox. This appeal isn't at all gratuitous. Apparently, women, who since the second decade of the century had a pretty important role in these playful acts turning into authentic festivals, were now failing to attend these leisurely samplings of cider. It was, most likely, due to the return to strong Catholic morality imposed by the new authorities.

Still, an *espicha* appeared to be a good plan to pass time on a Sunday. The well-known Sunday gatherings organized by the Ideal Rosales were advertised as having "all the attractions," including diverse types of food and seafood or cider from the prestigious manufacturer Manolo de Ángel, besides bagpipes and drum music. The fact that the ads mention both the jukeboxes and musical instruments suggests that modern media were combined with traditional music. There were also sponsors who hired the Gijón music band for a show. Other attractions were usually added to the jukebox, such as the recording of the most recent hits. In the mid-1940s, songs like "Recuérdame" (Remind me) and "Viviendo en mi casita de papel" (Living in my paper house) were widely enjoyed by the Asturian public.[15]

Even at a time when multi-day events were all but banned, Hijos de Alfonso, an inn located in the Gijón parish of La Guía, held numerous *espichas* that usually lasted from Saturday to Monday.[16] Conversely, another original tradition related to the *espicha*—the peculiar practice of baptizing a pricked barrel with the name of a politician—seemed lost at this time or very rare due to the regime's repression of political speech. On the very few occasions in which a "titled" barrel was advertised, current events were mentioned as a source for naming the barrels. The barrels' names now referenced the quality of the drink or the effects of cider on the body. The vessel opened in the old Casa Demetrio (in the municipality of Carreño) in 1944 had been baptized with an adjective as bland as "Champion."[17]

In any case, there were always more ambitious initiatives, and some entrepreneurs would try to bestow the aura of the great leisure industry that it had previously enjoyed on their *espicha*. In 1945, Casa Marcelo (Marcelo House) included in its Saturday, Sunday, and Monday *espichas* parties and *romerías* (pilgrimages) in an apple orchard, without specifying the food or entertainment offered. The following month, however, it only announced one *espicha*, with *taquinos* and snacks enlivened by a "powerful jukebox." This seems to indicate a little more than the discreet success of the previous events. At about the same time, Casa Marcelo also advertised a great "sacramental" party in which, once again, gatherings and *romerías* would take place in a "grandiose orchard."[18]

Against this backdrop of commercial strategies deployed to maximize profits with hosting larger *espichas*, the one carried out by El Rancho Grande de Gijón stands out. At the opening of the season in July of 1948, the owners gave their customers and patrons no less than a barrel of cider as a free sample. There were some prestigious bars that would organize *espichas* on the occasion of a commemoration. Casa Justo, for example, offered cider from Nava and *fabada* to celebrate the festivities of Santiago held in the new neighborhoods of Ceares.[19] Some *espichas* were also presented as picnics with diverse attractions, and even religious services. Such a religious connection was coherent within the character of rigorous Catholic observance of the period. Places like El Descanso in Gijón followed the trend, organizing in October of 1946 a picnic with a large bowling contest, a great dance after the mass, and fireworks.[20]

The Institutionalization of the *Espicha*

The return of *espichas* by the 1950s demonstrates the growing interest on the part of Francoist officials to use these leisurely gatherings for the goals of achieving the long-desired legitimacy and consensus necessary for the reproduction of the social order.[21] This was the origin of the institutionalization of the *espicha* as an event held under the aegis of civic associations or government institutions rather than private business owners. At the same time, one needs to remember that other, less adaptable celebrations were prohibited and eventually disappeared. The *espicha*, which could have followed the same path to extinction, took new form and shape and survived as a leisure activity no matter the identity of its promoter. The authorities simply gained full control of this celebration as time went by. Crucially, *espichas* were not subject to significant changes or limitations that the institutionalization process usually implied. It may be said, in this sense, that the obvious popularity of the *espicha* became a decisive factor in its survival and preservation.[22]

The first steps in this institutional overtaking of the initiative from business owners can be traced back as early as 1948, when the Club Hispania of the popular Gijón neighborhood of El Llano held three festivals with pricking of barrels in honor of its members using a local school's soccer field. The celebration thus moved from its traditional space to a new location that was a state facility unconnected to the usual place of celebration.[23] Not long after, a day was devoted entirely to the province of Asturias at the 1950 Madrid Field Fair, and among other events, the Official Chamber of the Agrarian Union of Oviedo organized an *espicha*. It was promoted as a "classical" celebration, with a large cider barrel moved to the fairgrounds, accompanied by displays of the most "authentic" Asturian folklore. The Civil Governor of Oviedo and numerous national and provincial authorities were invited, and the gathering was enlivened by the performance of the Co-ed Choirs of Education and Leisure dressed in their traditional costumes. This time, they were accompanied by the Llanes dance group, which specialized in El Pericote.[24]

The 1953 edition, celebrated on "Asturias Day," began with the performance of the Choir and Dance groups of the Women's Section of the Falange and the Turón Mining Choir. Those entertainments served as a prelude to an *espicha* held in what was advertised as a "traditional apple press" installed in the Fair's Asturias pavilion. The institutional power was thus asserted through typifying and recreating the popular consumer premises that had always been a space of freedom out of reach of the ruling classes. The act was enlivened by the most famous Asturian pipers, and the evening ended with theatrical performances, including dance groups from Oviedo and Gijón, Son de Arriba and Vaqueiros de Alzada, alongside other choral groups. The program ended with the crowd singing the regional anthem "Asturias patria querida" (Asturias dear homeland) and a prima dance—a dance channeling the community's strength. As always happened on these institutional occasions, neither the song nor the dance followed their original meaning.

Later in the 1950s, the consumption of cider became an indispensable staple of the Asturias Pavilion at the Fair, with the *espichas* following the earlier protocols with very few variations.[25] It was frequently remarked that this pavilion was always bursting with people, mostly as a result of the *espicha* of the cider barrels.[26] In 1958, the First World Congress of Asturian Societies was organized by the Office of Relations with Residents in America to get in touch with all Asturian organizations throughout the world with the goal of strengthening ties of friendship and arranging improvements for the Asturian community. The most relevant events in the program included a solemn mass in Covadonga in front of the main provincial authorities and an espicha hosted in the town of Siero.[27]

Nothing in these shows and entertainments loaded with folklore was gratuitous, as they responded to the needs of a state eagerly seeking international recognition. The set-up clearly reflected the image of a moderate, anti-communist, Catholic, and neutral regime that the dictatorship wanted to project in order to emerge from the quagmire of autarky and isolationism and join the European Economic Community. The redefined regional dances and costumes were used to show the diverse and rich historical past and the popular cultures of Spain. Initially, it was the Women's Section of the Falange that tried to take control over these demonstrations. Alongside its duties of assistance and education of women, this organization had been entrusted with safeguarding the authenticity of a vast national folklore. Eventually, it was replaced by the Choirs and Dances of Education and Leisure, dependent on the regime's official Vertical Union.

Showcasing and energizing local cultures, the Choirs and Dances became the ambassadors of the image that Spain, which was now positioning itself as an international tourist destination, wanted to project. It goes without saying that, due to both the ideological conditioning of the moment and the lack of means, the Choirs' re-enactments suffered from a good dose of adulteration. In this new context, the institutionalized *espicha* could play a prominent role in bringing dancing and singing back to something that was at least reminiscent of their local contexts. Paradoxically, in this renewed format, the *espichas* would once again resemble the original gatherings more than their fully commercialized sequels.[28]

Only starting in the early 1960s did the institutionalized *espichas* become omnipresent, but they were used for many purposes unrelated to the openings of the cider barrels. Multi-functional competitions such as the Villaviciosa Apple Festival used *espichas* as their closing events. Large institutionalized *espichas* become common in the municipalities of Gijón, Oviedo, Siero, Nava, or Villaviciosa.[29] This new scope of cider sociability could be extended to educational settings. Thus, in August 1964, the City Council of Castrillón held an *espicha* in honor of the students of the summer course at the University of Oviedo. The Nava cider cooperative had already held another for them a few days earlier.[30]

The corporate sector began displaying the same dynamics. During the summer of 1965, Gifesa (a partnership for celebrations conducted by retailers from Gijón and unrelated to the city council) offered an *espicha* for its members at Ideal Rosales, with the performance of the folk group Los Xustos, winners of the Hispanic-American Song Contest held in Cáceres that year, and also a pourer contest for the occasion. The celebration spanned a second day during which the Turón Mining Choir sang. To cite another case, in 1974, the departure of José María Guerra Zunzunegui from the post of the director of HUNOSA (a public coal company created in 1967 by the State to take over a struggling sector) was celebrated by an *espicha* in which prestigious regional artists performed alongside traditional bagpipes and drum musicians.[31]

Different organizations would host an *espicha* as a corporate relationship-building activity *avant la lettre*. Thus, in September 1965, the Tennis Club Gijón from the Somió neighborhood held on the grounds of a local apple orchard a great Asturian *romería* (pilgrimage) with traditional music, wonderful cider, taquinos, pies, and an orchestra performance. The event coincided with the festivities of San José in March, when the season of *espichas* traditionally begins in Asturias. The students of the summer course of the Seven Villages tourist office from Bordeaux were invited as special guests.[32]

By the mid-1960s, the practices related to the *espicha* extended to all types of institutions. Thus, in 1964, the COFEMI (Mieres Festivities Commission) opened two thousand liters of cider to celebrate the arrival of spring and gave gifts to its more than 1,700 members. The event featured several Asturian solo singers. The newspaper *Voluntad* stated that, apart from their originality, the rituals of the *espicha*, previously vilified by the authorities and condemned by the press, undoubtedly responded to the tastes, demands, and idiosyncrasies of the Asturian people.[33] Coming from a Francoist newspaper, such rhetoric legitimated and even redeemed for the regime the image of a celebration that just a few years earlier had undeniably worried the higher officials.

An *espicha* could now be used to celebrate some corporate meetings, such as the Brotherhood (the name given to the agrarian unions during Franco's dictatorship) meals that took place during the festivities of San Isidro Labrador or the ones arranged by sports clubs.[34] There were even events that could be described as samples of what Peter Burke calls "cultural hybridity." The spread of North American lifestyles through the mass media could lead, for instance, to hosting barbecues—a kind of celebration that one author admitted having experienced in Ibiza—combined with the traditional consumption of cider by way of an *espicha* or picnic.[35]

Another relevant aspect to be analyzed when assessing the evolution of the *espicha* during the final decades of the dictatorship is the touristic lure of the Asturian coasts. Manuel Fraga, who became the head of the Ministry of Information and Tourism in 1962, and his cadre in the Institute of Tourism Studies (a true governmental think-tank created for this purpose) acted wisely regarding the profits that could be accrued from combining the two parts of the Ministry's name—information and tourism. By the 1960s, tourism was already seen as a factor of modernization, visibility, counter-propaganda, and international peace. In the last stage of the dictatorship, the political evolution was accompanied by the development of a consumer society ending the hardships of the previous decades. This led to a change in values and access to levels of consumption that were presented as a kind of substitute to democracy, while promoting what could be considered a middle-class culture. The hegemony of the middle classes contributed to dissolving the worker identity, which was an undeniable reality in the Asturian case. Festivities and traditional songs and dances were distorted and introduced artificial traditional types for commercial purposes.

This was also the time when *espichas* began to be marketed as a product that brought together the "esencias de la Asturianía" (essences of Asturiania), as Victor Labrada described it. The expanding tourism sector led to the opening of numerous cider houses. The pouring ritual—when cider is poured into the glass by a server holding both the bottle and the glass behind their back—became a tourist attraction that increased the popularity of cider on the coastal strip, where, aside from the summer period, consumption had always been lower.[36] Sometimes, the ritual was carried out by linking tourist activities with sporting events, such as the International Descent of the Sella or the festivity of *les piragües* (canoes), attended by participants from all over Europe and accompanied by an increasingly large crowd and a growing recreational pageantry. For some years, the celebration began with an *espicha* and Asturian cheese sampling enlivened by bagpipe

Figure 7.1. The official poster of the Third Apple Festival in Villaviciosa (1963)

music. Over time, the event grew in scale and fame, and would also incorporate a Folklore Fair with attractions such as a river train or festive parade floats representing different municipalities. The float of the municipality of Nava, for example, looked like a barrel of cider surrounded by bagpipers and drummers. Nava sponsored an *espicha* in the town of Llovio, located on the way to the competition. The program included dances or shows of *gigantes y cabezudos* (giants and figures with oversized heads, popular characters of the street celebrations in Northern Spain), followed by numerous musical performances. Many attendees wore regional costumes.[37]

The first weddings held in an apple press facility date back to the 1960s, and today they are a well-established option. More and more apple presses are acquiring the equipment to host these large celebrations, along with first communions, bachelor parties, and all kinds of banquets and mass gatherings.[38] Another new tradition that is still enjoying popularity is the organization of *espichas* in conjunction with the apple and cider festivals that began to be held in Asturias in the 1960s. Their main purpose was to stimulate the pomological and manufacturing sectors that were experiencing difficulties because of the competitiveness of new ways of drinking.

Such was the case of the Villaviciosa Apple Blossom Festival, inspired by the Apple Blossom Festival in Yakima (Washington, USA), which was first celebrated in 1960. In a clever move, the event was made to coincide with the popular patron saint festivities of the Virgen del Portal, celebrated at the time the first apple of the season is harvested. This pioneering festival was born with a series of goals in mind, such as making the Asturian apples known in different national markets, improving cultivation systems, promoting the foundation of new apple orchards, and boosting tourism. The slogan "Spanish Apple Capital" was soon coined for Villaviciosa and was registered in the Industrial Property Registry of the Ministry of Industry.[39]

To a large extent, organizing a festival promised to become an inexpensive propaganda formula to open national markets and minds to the Asturian apple and its derivatives. The systematic and organized advertising in the written press, radio, and on television was intended to confront the powerful commercial network of select fruit producers from outside of Asturias. In a region lacking these advertising capacities, the use of the mass media acquired great importance.[40] The closing of the festival was marked by an *espicha* that became the largest ever held in Asturias.[41]

Another Cider Festival, held in Nava, was led and promoted by the mayor of this municipality and cider-press owner José María Caso Mayor. This festival grew from an *espicha* organized by a group of friends in the Peñamayor apple press. In June 1969, the *espicha* became a festival and a first-rate informative event for a sector that was experiencing difficulties. As such, the town's thirty apple presses opened their doors to celebrate, with an estimated consumption of 5,000 liters of cider, which refreshed the throats of those who never stopped singing the best repertoire of traditional Asturian songs. The first National Pouring Competition emerged during the festival's 1970 edition.[42]

After Franco's death in 1975, cider consumption gatherings began to be added to any political or cultural event, be it a conference, exhibition, contest, assembly, or rite of passage.[43] Note, for instance, the famous *espicha* held in honor of the socialist leader Felipe González in a Tiraña apple press in the Laviana council in 1976.[44] Not only was the spread of the *espicha* a likely consequence of its institutionalization over the previous decade, but it also inserted itself into a different gastronomic tradition. If earlier *espichas* included certain types of food—of uneven quality and, in some case, high prices—more elaborate dishes became a mark of its success in the 1970s. The consumption of fish and seafood that were not merely boiled or deep fried became a new trend taking hold alongside the

Figure 7.2. Local authorities and "ladies" representing different municipalities of Asturias posing in front of the sculpture of *An Apple Harvester* by Mariano Benlliure. Apple Festival, 1960s

characteristic forms of cider consumption, which remained unchanged. The *espicha* thus reached the phase of the increasing "dignification" of popular cultural practices, when communal and individual forms of consumption are combined with practices deemed relevant for financially sustainable local, regional, and national identity-making. Except in cases of excessive formality that require guests to be seated around a table, the tasting is carried out standing, so the snacks must be suitable for eating by hand, thus challenging the practice of charging per person that began in the eighteenth century.[45]

Conclusion

As we have seen, between the 1930s and the 1960s, the rituals surrounding cider had to adapt to the habits of modern consumer society without losing their essential identity. If between the Restoration and the Civil War (1875–1936), peasant customs had been repurposed many times for commercial interests, this new stage bore witness to an evolution toward institutionalizing traditional types of consumption. The growing popularity of such events as the pourer contests—present since the early 1950s—or the apple festivals, occasions that combined leisure with business, were part and parcel of this process. This new reality also transformed the most outstanding event of cider consumption—the *espicha*—which, in an institutionalized form, spread and extended to legitimize not only the structure of Franco's society, but also the most important rites of life after the dictator's death. Cider is the result of knowledge and a complex technology that, as a cultural product, moves between tradition and innovation. We bear witness to a process of increasing dignification, or "enrichment," of a product whose humble origins did not prevent it from rising to become a part of a modernized gastronomic and symbolic system.[46] This process also transformed cider into a commercially viable drink that can hold its own with the competition.

With few exceptions, historical studies on alcoholic drinks produced in Spain use a limited set of sources that focus on economic and institutional development of the drink itself, leaving out its shifting social significance, forms of consumption, or role in everyday life.[47] Eating and drinking are, first and foremost, social activities through which the individuals build their identity. Vital spaces and forms of sociability have been developed around drinking activities in the daily experience of some social groups, and the production and consumption of these substances have generated a rich and varied material culture as well as various trade cultures. All of this can be seen in the case of the cultural forms related to consumption, but also in the production of Asturian cider. The study of this type of small reality often reveals unexpected surprises.

NOTES

1. Luis Benito García Álvarez, "Comensalidad, sociabilidad solidaridad en el ciclo festivo asturiano (1850–1936)," *Historia Contemporánea* 48 (2014): 185–214; Jorge Uría, "Ocio, espacios de sociabilidad y estrategias de control social: La taberna en Asturias en el primer tercio del siglo XX," in *Sindicalismo y movimientos sociales (siglos XIX–XX)*, ed. M. Redero (Madrid: UGT-Centro de Estudios Históricos, 1994), 73–98.
2. Luis Benito García Álvarez, *Sidra y manzana en Asturias. Sociabilidad, producción y consumo (1875–1936)* (Oviedo, Spain: KRK, 2013).
3. Regarding the foods in rural *espichas*, see Gustavo Bueno, ed., *El libro de la sidra* (Oviedo, Spain: Pentalfa, 1992); and Sergio Álvarez Requejo, ed., *La manzana y la sidra en Asturias* (Gijón, Spain: Bankunión, 1982). Nevertheless, the food repertoire

described in the espichas usually shows a strong tendency to timelessness, presenting as tradition something that has a chronology yet to be accurately defined.

4. Regarding the evolution of the forms of consumption in Asturias and their increasing presence in the middle class during this time, see Gracia Suárez Botas, *Hoteles de viajeros en Asturias* (Oviedo, Spain: KRK, 2006).

5. Regarding the control over festivities during the Franco regime see Javier Escalera Reyes, "El franquismo y la fiesta. Régimen político, transformaciones sociales y sociabilidad festiva en la España de Franco," in *La cultura popular en la España contemporánea: doce estudios*, ed. Jorge Uría (Madrid: Biblioteca Nueva, 2003), 253–62; Mirta Núñez Díaz-Balart, *Los años del terror. La estrategia de dominio y terror del general Franco* (Madrid: La Esfera de los Libros, 2004).

6. Luis Benito García Álvarez, "La sociabilidad sidrera durante el franquismo," *Historia Social* 92 (2018): 47–62.

7. Ibid.

8. Regarding *romerías* during the Franco Regime, see García Álvarez, "La sociabilidad"; and Enrique Antuña Gancedo, "La fiesta como fenómeno sociocultural. Asturias, 1937–1996," PhD diss. (University of Oviedo, 2019).

9. García Álvarez, "Comensalidad."

10. *Voluntad*, 23/V/1940, 30/V/1943, and 20/V/1945; García Álvarez, "La sociabilidad." *Voluntad* has been key to carry out this investigation. Published between 1937 and 1975 in Gijón, it was owned by the FET and the JONS, the only official party under the Franco regime. It allowed advertising in Asturian, even when the regime repressed languages other than Castilian. Issues of *Voluntad* are archived in the Hemeroteca de Gijón.

11. *Voluntad*, 21/IV/1939, 21/VI/1939, 2/XII/1941, 1/III/1942, 5/VI/1944, 25/XI/1944, 19/IV/1945, 5/V/1945, 13/V/1945, 18/VII/1947, 12/IV/1953, 5/II/1954, 9/VI/1956. Some ads would even offer cider and "everything else," *Voluntad*, 28/II/1956. Regarding meals that go with the *espicha*, see García Álvarez, "Comensalidad."

12. *Voluntad*, 14/IV/1944, 2/VI/1944, 13/V/1945. See García Álvarez, *Sidra*.

13. This example follows the original text. The magnifying epithets become more frequent, for example, when taquinos able to "strengthen the dead" were offered. See *Voluntad*, 20/V/1944. The original text in Asturian.

14. *Voluntad*, 27/V/1945. The original text in Asturian.

15. *Voluntad*, 2/VI/1944, 8/VII/1944, 14/VII/1944, 22/VII/1944, 30/IX/1944, 31/III/1945, 5/IV/1945, 20/V/1945, 7/VII/1945, 23/III/1946, 20/IV/1946. García Álvarez, "La sociabilidad."

16. *Voluntad*, 13/V/1945.

17. This espicha was held on June 8 to celebrate the festivity of Corpus Christi, and requests of *fabada* or the desired menu were taken, along with offerings of *taquinos* and seafood. Also, in the venue of classic references, the cider was said to have the typical color of the one from Nava and the body of the one from Carreño. *Voluntad*, 4/VI/1944.

18. *Voluntad*, 2/VI/1945, 7/VII/1945, and 18/VII/1945.
19. *Voluntad*, 4/VIII/1945, 19/VIII/1945, 12/IX/1945, 3/VIII/1948, 19/VIII/1945, and 23/IX/1947.
20. *Voluntad*, 27/X/1946.
21. Apart from the works cited by Escalera Reyes and Antuña Galcedo, see the following publications on the festivities during the Franco Regime: Claudio Hernández Burgos and César Rina Simon, eds., *El franquismo se fue de fiesta. Ritos festivos y cultura popular durante la dictadura* (Valencia, Spain: Universidad de Valencia, 2022); Gil Manuel Hernández i Marti, *La fiesta reinventada: calendari, política i ideología en la Valencia franquista* (Valencia, Spain: Universidad de Valencia, 2022); Alberto Ramos Santana, "El control de las fiestas en el franquismo," in *El poder de la historia. Huella y legado de Javier María Donézar*, eds. Pilar Díaz Sánchez, Pedro Antonio Martínez Lillo, and Álvaro Soto Carmona (Madrid: Universidad Autónoma de Madrid, 2014), 380–406; Pilar Díaz Sánchez, Pedro Antonio Martínez Lillo, and Álvaro Soto Carmona, *El poder de la historia. Huella y legado de Javier María Donézar* (Madrid: Universidad Autónoma de Madrid, 2014).
22. *Voluntad*, 23/III/1946; Escalera Reyes, "El franquismo y la fiesta."
23. *Voluntad*, 7/VIII/1948.
24. *Voluntad*, 9/VI/1950; Denis Smyth, "Franco y los aliados en la Segunda Guerra Mundial," in *España y las grandes potencias en el siglo XX*, eds. Sebastián Balfour and Paul Preston (Barcelona: Crítica, 2002), 142–61; Boris N. Liedtke, "España y EEUU, 1945–1957," in *España y las grandes potencias en el siglo XX*, eds. Sebastián Balfour and Paul Preston (Barcelona: Crítica, 2002), 179–83.
25. *El Eco de Luarca*, 17/VIII/1958, and 14/VIII/1953.
26. *Voluntad*, 29/V/1953; *El Eco de Luarca*, 7/VI/1959.
27. *Voluntad*, 19/IX/1958.
28. Fe Santoveña, "En la encrucijada. Traje tradicional asturiano, identidad y transformaciones sociales en los inicios del siglo XXI," *Periferia* 25, no. 1 (2020): 144–69; Yolanda Cerra Bada, "Baile y danza. La tradición y el presente," in *Los asturianos: raices culturales y sociales de una entidad*, ed. Javier Rodríguez Muñoz (Oviedo, Spain, 2004), 657–72; Luis Benito García Álvarez, "Las representaciones de la filiatelia franquista," *Historia Contemporánea* 40, (2009): 217–45.
29. Esteban Díaz Campillo and Miguel Palacios Valderrama, *La manzana y la sidra en Asturias* (Oviedo, Spain: Bankunión, 1982).
30. *Voluntad*, 25/VIII/1964.
31. *Voluntad*, 27/VII/1965; *El Comercio*, 17/XI/2009; and *Hulla* 42, May 1974.
32. *Voluntad*, 27/XII/1962 and 7/IX/1965.
33. *Voluntad*, 19/IV/1964.
34. *Voluntad*, 16/VI/1962; Valles Asenjo, "Una 'barbacoa' en la cuenca del Nalón (Sardinas, culetes y . . . sidra)," *Hulla*, no. 36 (September–October 1973): 40.
35. Valles Asenjo, "Una 'barbacoa.'"
36. Juaco López and Manuel Cabriffosse, "El vino y la sidra: entre la industria y la artesanía," in *Los asturianos: raices culturales y sociales de una entidad*, ed. Javier Rodríguez

Muñoz (Oviedo, Spain, 2004), 469–70; Arturo Álvarez Pinilla, "El consumo de sidra natural." In *Sidra y manzana de Asturias*, ed. José Antonio Fidalgo (Oviedo, Spain: Prensa Ibérica, 1994), 421–36; García Álvarez, *Sidra*. Information contained in a survey conducted for the Principality of Asturias to support the candidacy of the cider culture for the UNESCO certification as the intangible world heritage. Pouring, the most visible part of the cider rituals, has evolved from the traditional way of transferring cider from old wood vessels to pottery jugs. The modern way of pouring (holding the bottle with the extended arm up high and the glass thigh-height) dates back to the emergence of drinking glasses in the nineteenth century. Regarding tourism during the Franco regime, see Sasha D. Pack, *La invasión pacífica. Los turistas y la España de Franco* (Madrid: Turner, 2009); Jordi Gracia and Miguel Ángel Ruiz Carnicer, *La España franquista. Cultura y vida cotidiana* (Madrid: Sínteis, 2001); Fernando de Terán, *Historia del urbanismo en España III. Siglos XIX y XX* (Madrid: Cátedra, 1999).

37. *Voluntad*, 5/VIII/1959 and 7/VIII/1960. The Descent of the Sella began in 1929 with a failed attempt and was already consolidated in the early 1930s. The competition was suspended during the Civil War and resumed in 1944. In 1951, other Europeans registered for the first time, and in 1955, participants from another continent—a Cuban team—took part in the competition. For more information, see García Álvarez, *Sidra*.
38. Enrique García García, "El chigre y la espicha," in *Sidra y manzana de Asturias*, ed. José Antonio Fidalgo (Oviedo, Spain: Prensa Ibérica, 1994), 129–44.
39. Sergio Álvarez Requejo, "El Festival de la Manzana," in *El libro del siglo XX en Villaviciosa*, ed. Rubén García Pérez (Villaviciosa, Spain: Cubera-La Oliva, 2002), 209–12; *Voluntad*, 8/IX/1960; Modesto González Cobas, "Sidra y turismo," in *Sidra y manzana de Asturias*, ed. José Antonio Fidalgo (Oviedo, Spain: Prensa Ibérica, 1994), 309–24.
40. AHA (Historical Archive of Asturias), Fondo de la Diputación Provincial, SIG 1796, Exp. "Informe sobre el Festival de la Manzana celebrado en Villaviciosa durante los días 11 al 14 de septiembre de 1960."
41. "Con gran brillantez se celebró en Villaviciosa el VII festival de la Manzana y la Exposición Provincial de Manzana Selecta de Asturias," *Campo Astur* 384 (October 1971).
42. García Álvarez, *Sidra*.
43. Álvarez Requejo, "El Festival"; Viltro Godoy, "La sidra asturiana no morirá nunca," *La Nueva España*, 9/V/1982.
44. García Álvarez, *Sidra*.
45. Jean-François Revel, *Un festín en palabras. Historia literaria de la sensibilidad gastronómica de la antigüedad a nuestros días* (Barcelona: Tusquets Editores, 1980); Jorge Uría and Luis Benito García Álvarez, "Alimentación y comensalidad en la época contemporánea," *Historia Contemporánea*, no. 48 (2014): 11–32.
46. Luis Benito García Álvarez, *Introducción a la historia de la sidra en Asturias* (Oviedo, Spain: Universidad de Oviedo-Cátedra de la Sidra de Asturias. 2020).
47. See a detailed discussion of this problem in Luis Benito García Álvarez, *Beber y saber. Una historia cultural de las bebidas* (Madrid: Alianza Editorial, 2005).

WORKS CITED

AHA (Historical Archive of Asturias). Fondo de la Diputación Provincial. SIG 1796. Exp. "Informe sobre el Festival de la Manzana celebrado en Villaviciosa durante los días 11 al 14 de septiembre de 1960."

Álvarez Pinilla, Arturo. "El consumo de sidra natural." In *Sidra y manzana de Asturias*, edited by José Antonio Fidalgo, 421–36. Oviedo, Spain: Prensa Ibérica, 1994.

Álvarez Requejo, Sergio. "El Festival de la Manzana." In *El libro del siglo XX en Villaviciosa*, edited by Rubén García Pérez, 209–12. Villaviciosa, Spain: Cubera-La Oliva, 2002.

———, ed. *La manzana y la sidra en Asturias*. Gijón, Spain: Bankunión, 1982.

Antuña Gancedo, Enrique. *La fiesta como fenómeno sociocultural. Asturias, 1937–1996*. PhD diss. University of Oviedo, 2019.

Bueno, Gustavo, ed. *El libro de la sidra*. Oviedo, Spain: Pentalfa, 1992.

Burke, Peter. *Hibridismo cultural*. Madrid: Akal, 2010.

Cerra Bada, Yolanda. "Baile y danza. La tradición y el presente." In *Los asturianos: Raices culturales y sociales de una entidad*, edited by Javier Rodríguez Muñoz, 657–72. Oviedo, Spain, 2004.

El Comercio. Hemeroteca. Access date 11 December 2023. elcomercio.ed/hemeroteca

"Con gran brillantez se celebró en Villaviciosa el VII festival de la Manzana y la Exposición Provincial de Manzana Selecta de Asturias." *Campo Astur* 384, October 1971.

Díaz Campillo, Esteban, and Miguel Palacios Valderrama. *La manzana y la sidra en Asturias*. Oviedo, Spain: Bankunión, 1982.

Escalera Reyes, Javier. "El franquismo y la fiesta. Régimen político, transformaciones sociales y sociabilidad festiva en la España de Franco." In *La cultura popular en la España contemporánea: Doce estudios*, edited by Jorge Uría, 253–62. Madrid: Biblioteca Nueva, 2003.

Fidalgo, José Antonio. *Sidra y manzana en Asturias*. Oviedo, Spain: Prensa Ibérica, 1994.

García Álvarez, Luis Benito. *Beber y saber. Una historia cultural de las bebidas*. Madrid: Alianza Editorial, 2005.

———. "Comensalidad, sociabilidad solidaridad en el ciclo festivo asturiano (1850–1936)." *Historia Contemporánea* 48 (2014): 185–214.

———. *Introducción a la historia de la sidra en Asturias*. Oviedo, Spain: Universidad de Oviedo-Cátedra de la Sidra de Asturias, 2020.

———. "Las representaciones de la filiatelia franquista." *Historia Contemporánea* 40 (2009): 217–45.

———. *Sidra y manzana en Asturias. Sociabilidad, producción y consumo (1875–1936)*. Oviedo, Spain: KRK, 2013.

———. "La sociabilidad sidrera durante el franquismo." *Historia Social* 92 (2018): 47–62.

García García, Enrique. "El chigre y la espicha." In *Sidra y manzana de Asturias*, edited by José Antonio Fidalgo, 129–44. Oviedo, Spain: Prensa Ibérica, 1994.

Godoy, Viltro. "La sidra asturiana no morirá nunca." *La Nueva España*, 9/V/1982.

González Cobas, Modesto. "Sidra y turismo." In *Sidra y manzana de Asturias*, edited by José Antonio Fidalgo, 309–24. Oviedo, Spain: Prensa Ibérica, 1994.

Gracia, Jordi, and Miguel Ángel Ruiz Carnicer. *La España franquista. Cultura y vida cotidiana*. Madrid: Sínteis, 2001.

Hernández Burgos, Claudio, and César Rina Simon, eds. *El franquismo se fue de fiesta. Ritos festivos y cultura popular durante la dictadura*. Valencia, Spain: Universidad de Valencia, 2022.

Hernández i Marti, Gil Manuel. *La fiesta reinventada: Calendari, política i ideología en la Valencia franquista*. Valencia, Spain: Universidad de Valencia, 2022.

Liedtke, Boris N. "España y EEUU, 1945–1957." In *España y las grandes potencias en el siglo XX*, edited by Sebastián Balfour and Paul Preston, 179–83. Barcelona: Crítica, 2002.

López, Juaco, and Manuel Cabriffosse. "El vino y la sidra: entre la industria y la artesanía." In *Los asturianos: Raices culturales y sociales de una entidad*, edited by Javier Rodríguez Muñoz, 469–70. Oviedo, Spain, 2004.

Núñez Diaz-Balart, Mirta. *Los años del terror. La estrategia de dominio y terror del general Franco*. Madrid: La Esfera de los Libros, 2004.

Pack, Sasha D. *La invasión pacífica. Los turistas y la España de Franco*. Madrid: Turner, 2009.

Ramos Santana, Alberto. "El control de las fiestas en el franquismo." In *El poder de la historia. Huella y legado de Javier María Donézar*, edited by Pilar Díaz Sánchez, Pedro Antonio Martínez Lillo, and Álvaro Soto Carmona, 380–406. Madrid: Universidad Autónoma de Madrid, 2014.

Revel, Jean-François. *Un festín en palabras. Historia literaria de la sensibilidad gastronómica de la antigüedad a nuestros días*. Barcelona: Tusquets Editores, 1980.

Santoveña, Fe. "En la encrucijada. Traje tradicional asturiano, identidad y transformaciones sociales en los inicios del siglo XXI." *Periferia* 25, no. 1 (2020): 144–69.

Smyth, Denis. "Franco y los aliados en la Segunda Guerra Mundial." In *España y las grandes potencias en el siglo XX*, edited by Sebastián Balfour and Paul Preston, 142–61. Barcelona: Crítica, 2002.

Suárez Botas, Gracia. *Hoteles de viajeros en Asturias*. Oviedo, Spain: KRK, 2006.

Terán, Fernando de. *Historia del urbanismo en España III. Siglos XIX y XX*. Madrid: Cátedra, 1999.

Uría, Jorge. "Ocio, espacios de sociabilidad y estrategias de control social: La taberna en Asturias en el primer tercio del siglo XX." In *Sindicalismo y movimientos sociales (siglos XIX–XX)*, edited by M. Redero, 73–98. Madrid: UGT-Centro de Estudios Históricos, 1994.

Uría, Jorge, and Luis Benito García Álvarez. "Alimentación y comensalidad en la época contemporánea." *Historia Contemporánea*, no. 48 (2014): 11–32.

Valles Asenjo. "Una 'barbacoa' en la cuenca del Nalón (Sardinas, culetes y ... sidra)." *Hulla*, no. 36 (September-October 1973): 40.

Voluntad. Hemeroteca del Ayuntamiento de Gijón. Access date 11 December 2023. Hemeroteca.gijon.es

CHAPTER 8
Cava's Place

Bob Davidson

While Catalan cava may be the most popular sparkling wine in Spain, in the first decades of the twenty-first century, it has become a controversial product.[1] From campaigns protesting Catalonia's push for increased sovereignty to internal divisions within its regulatory Denomination of Origin system, the very meaning of "cava"—what it is, where it is from, and what is denoted by drinking it—has become contested. In this essay, I build on existing work on Catalan *terroir*—and the surprising fact that cava is *not* restricted to a geographic area, as we typically understand *terroir* to be—to propose that the symbolic charge of "cava" has become unstable. I argue that exposure to ideological fights in the form of politically motivated boycotts and the breaking away from the DO by a splinter group both raise the same questions: what and where is cava's place? The answer, I propose, is that cava is a "moveable" drink and that this deterritorialized indeterminacy opens the door for a resignification of what it means and where its metaphoric and literal place(s) might be located. That the story of cava highlights how territorial identities continue to clash, both within nation-states and at the supranational level of the European Union, is a further reminder of the importance of studying foodways and culinaria.

Like its still counterpart, sparkling wine is symbolic. Synonymous with celebration since its adoption by French royalty in the seventeenth century, sparkling wine, and champagne especially, has become a marker of joy and luxury. Its liquid effervescence denotes gaiety and effusiveness, and in the wake of the Benedictine monks' discovery of how to regulate the beneficial effects of secondary fermentation in bottle, sparkling wine production took hold in growing regions throughout Europe.[2] With the word "champagne" legally restricted to bubbly produced in the eponymous region, imitators eventually took on different names while employing the same style or variations of it.[3] Thus, today, the "méthode champenoise," "traditional method," and "*charmat*" sparkling wine market includes *crémant*,[4] some versions of prosecco, and the subject of this present study: cava.[4]

Cava and Catalan Modernity

Cava may share a production method with champagne, but it is not a drink that is—or has been—restricted to the elite. Firmly middle-class, it is more accessible than champagne and occupies a wider role in local foodways than its French counterpart.[5] That sparkling wine made in this manner is so labor intensive is key to how it and its markets developed. Its production method creates a demand for economies of scale that other wines simply do not require, and when this fact is tied to the challenges of mobility that the product's inherent instability poses, one sees how industrial modernity and sparkling wine go hand in hand.[6] It is not surprising then, that the cava industry is dominated by three large companies—Freixenet, Codorníu, and García Carrión—who make up between 80–90 percent of its output. While their dedication to a relatively low price point through lax sourcing of fruit has contributed to popular appeal at home and driven export markets abroad, the product's abundance, unorthodox lack of official geographic specificity, as well as a reputation for being "cheap" have contributed to dissent amongst the ranks of smaller producers. This dissatisfaction in turn helped lead to the aforementioned fissure within the DO. But price notwithstanding, cava is still created in the same painstaking manner as champagne, even though modern technology has greatly aided its "traditional method" fabrication. Critically, the history of *xampany*, as cava was originally known in Catalan, tracks both Catalonia's industrial modernity and its concomitant cultural revival. Thus, before examining in detail the contemporary conflicts surrounding cava and the questions of place that they elicit, it is necessary to better understand these origins, how the drink is produced, how it slips from one modern movement to the next, as well as how it is regulated.

While viticulture in Catalonia grew and consolidated during the Middle Ages and Renaissance, grapes had long been a principal crop in the region, thus giving credence to the claim that wine is part of "Catalanness."[7] Likewise, vineyards have played an important economic role in Catalan life, with land use being adapted to match changing market demands. As Badia-Miró et al. observe:

> The first areas where vineyards were established to make and export brandies during the 17th and 18th centuries were located along the coastline, near the towns of Mataró and Tarragona-Reus. But later on, most of these early specialized locations abandoned viticulture in favor of other more profitable crops or economic activities, except grape-growing areas that had developed a high-quality brand. Catalan vineyards moved location towards the pre-littoral corridor while table wines replaced brandy as the main export product during the 19th century.[8]

By the time cava was born in the 1870s, the province of Barcelona was the largest producer of wine in Spain alongside Zaragoza and Valencia.[9] While Spain's nineteenth century was tumultuous on many land-related fronts, Catalonia's specific tradition of the *hereu* (the heir in a primogeniture system) provided stability for elites through land integrity.[10] This system had a domino effect for those who worked the land according to the *rabassa morta* scheme, which was a contractual arrangement that had figured prominently in the expansion of commercial viticulture in the region from the late seventeenth century until the late nineteenth century and saw the sharecropper essentially own the vines that he managed for the life of the vineyard, that is, indefinitely.[11] The growth and development of viticulture and other agricultural practices during the region's industrialization also benefited from the organization of collectives and the establishment of the Institut Agrícola Català Sant Isidre, one of Europe's oldest farming associations, which facilitated the exchange of information amongst farmers and technical innovation.

The sparkling wine industry that would emerge during this period has its roots in transnational trade, specifically, the international sales tours made by its founder, Josep Raventós, in the 1860s. As Karen MacNeil points out, after visiting the Champagne region in France, Raventós returned to Catalonia determined to use the same methods with the local grapes that were the base of his still wine production.[12] That said, creating champagne-style sparkling wine was and is complicated. The wine must acquire its carbonation as a result of a process of secondary fermentation in each individual bottle and not in bulk in a vat, as is the case with prosecco.[13] Once this secondary fermentation has taken place, it is then necessary to slowly coax the lees into the neck of the bottle by gradually turning and tilting them upside down in a process called "riddling" or "remouage." This particularly labor-intensive activity would be made considerably easier in the 1970s when Freixenet developed a mechanized "gyropalette" capable of riddling hundreds of bottles at a time and thus eliminating the need to turn each by hand.¹⁴ In order to remove the accumulated lees, the necks of the bottles are then chilled, disgorgement occurs, and the bottle is topped up with a wine and sugar mix before being sealed once more.

Here then, one sees how the need to commit to a specialized industrial process sets cava apart from its low-market competitor, prosecco, and draws it alongside champagne in terms of its complexity of manufacture—even as the differences in grapes and soil make it a different product. And while industrialization is often thought of in urban terms, Martín rightly underlines the rural aspect of the innovations that took place during this period in Catalonia: Catalan sparkling wine was "un producto industrial (muy industrial: necesita una producción secuenciada) que nacería en el campo, no en la urbe, y que fue hijo de un sistema económico que, aun modernizado, hundía sus profundas raíces en la estructura agraria" (an industrial product (very industrial: it required a sequenced production process) that would be born in the countryside, not in the city, and that was the child of an economic system that while modernizing, plunged its deep roots into the agrarian structure).¹⁵

By 1872, Raventós had produced his first sparkling wine according to the "traditional method," and through his efforts and those of other growers and agronomists in the Penedès region's main town, Sant Sadurni d'Anoia, the cava business in Catalonia was born. Its timing was propitious, for not only had the area recently been connected to Barcelona and Tarragona via the railway, thus ensuring the product's mobility, but the trade's growth would soon coincide with the arrival of the phylloxera louse, which was first seen in the region's vineyards in the 1880s. Initially sparking fierce debates as to how to try to stop it, phylloxera's advance wrought wholesale changes in the sector.¹⁶ Fortunately, as was the case for devastated producers in other parts of Europe, the splicing of phylloxera-resistant American rootstock with indigenous vines eventually saved the local industry.¹⁷ Wineries that had been mainly producing red took advantage of this major disruption to reorient their businesses by uprooting and replacing vines with autochthonous varieties that could be used for the new "traditional method" sparkling. These grapes, which would become the foundation of cava production going forward, included the floral Macabeo (also known as Viura in Rioja), Parellada, which marks a middle ground in terms of sugars and acidity, and Xarel·lo, a grape that bestows both aging potential and an added textural quality.¹⁸

The radical transformation of the vineyards in Catalonia, combined with the process adopted by Raventós and those who followed him, ensured the industry's survival. That both literal and metaphoric grafting were at the heart of this success is highly suggestive. On the one hand, organic splicing provided the crucial botanical resistance needed, while on the other, the figurative "grafting" of French techniques helped created a modern product alternative with a deep connection to Europe at the very moment that Catalonia's cultural renaissance was looking to express itself beyond its borders, as well.[19] And while that product would bear the transculturated name of *xampany* or *champán* for decades, it *was* a novel creation that, in addition to symbolically complementing Catalan modern processes, also pointed to how a rural technology such as the "traditional method" could contribute to and become implicated in developing metropolitan taste.

Ramon Casas's famous *modernista* advertisements for Codorníu speak at once to the penetration of local sparkling wine into Catalan society and how the drink easily slipped from one modern moment to another—from the initial entrepreneurial impetus of the *Renaixença* to *Modernisme*'s stimulating urbanity (Figs. 8.1 and 8.2). Both posters display a compelling tension between the countryside and metropolis. In the first (Fig. 8.1), the classic, lounging woman extends her glass for it to be filled by a faceless, tuxedoed man, while her other hand lingers in the flowers off to the side. In the second (Fig. 8.2), a smiling woman is again situated between urbanity—symbolized by the white linen tablecloth and champagne bucket—and the wooden cases of cava on her left, which are redolent of the space of production outside the city. Further to this last point, the choice of Josep Puig i Cadafalch as the architect for the winery's new cellars in 1902 (Fig. 8.3) would bring *Modernisme*'s architectural expression to the very edge of the

Figure 8.3. *Caves Codorniu (Sant Sadurní d'Anoia)*. Photo credit: Angela Llop

vineyards that were filling the growing middle classes' *copes*. And, while a few years later, *Noucentisme*, the institutional movement of cultural Catalanism, would idealize the "civilizing" concept of "Catalunya Ciutat," it is salutary to remember that, on the ground, transfer can and did go both ways.[20] *Xampany*'s allure and success would not only lead it to cross social strata in Catalonia but to traverse the rural/urban divide in a meaningful way.[21]

It is this deep-seated identification with Catalonia that would bring cava into the line of fire over a hundred years later. Not only would its existing metonymic association with Catalan culture make the sparkling wine a prime target for Spanish consumer boycotts in the wake of pushes for increased Catalan sovereignty at the start of the twenty-first century, but ironically, it would also lead to several important producers abandoning the DO Cava to establish their own brand on the grounds that it was not place-based *enough*.

One of the most intriguing and problematic aspects regarding modern cava lies in how it is defined in geographic terms by its Regulatory Council. Whereas French champagne carries the name of a specific *place*, Spanish sparkling wine refers to the generic *space* where it is aged: the cava or cellar where bottles rest and are periodically turned during secondary fermentation.[22] No doubt, cava's borrowing of the term "champagne" helped its profile over the years, but this was unsustainable. Even though champagne producers had long protested the use of the name by others and had received an appellation law in 1906, it was not until 1941 that "champagne" would start to be actively protected by the Comité Interprofessionnel du Vin de Champagne.[23] While the cava moniker was officially approved by Spain's own newly created Sparkling Wine Regulatory Council in 1972, the wine continued to be marketed and known colloquially as *xampany* and/or *champán*, much to French consternation. The situation eventually changed with Spain's entry into the European Economic Community in 1986, when the "Designated Cava Region" was legally established. Then, five years later, cava's Denomination of Origin was proclaimed by ministerial order along with its Regulatory Council.

Now, by bestowing the name of a subterranean space to the wine that develops there, one would think that the drink's claim to a specific rootedness, or *terroir*, might be well served. After all, the still base wines that will become the bubbly are literally surrounded by the earth where it is being elaborated. However, this is not the case; the *caves* are for cool, stable temperatures—and in the DO system, they are not connected at all to the land or soil where the grapes may or may not have been grown. Thus, while cava was developed in the Penedès area of Catalonia and much of its production still comes from there, it is not restricted officially to that geographic place. Producers in other parts of the Spanish state—outside the wine's symbolic home—were granted the right to label their product as "DO Cava" based on their existing sparkling production when the official name was

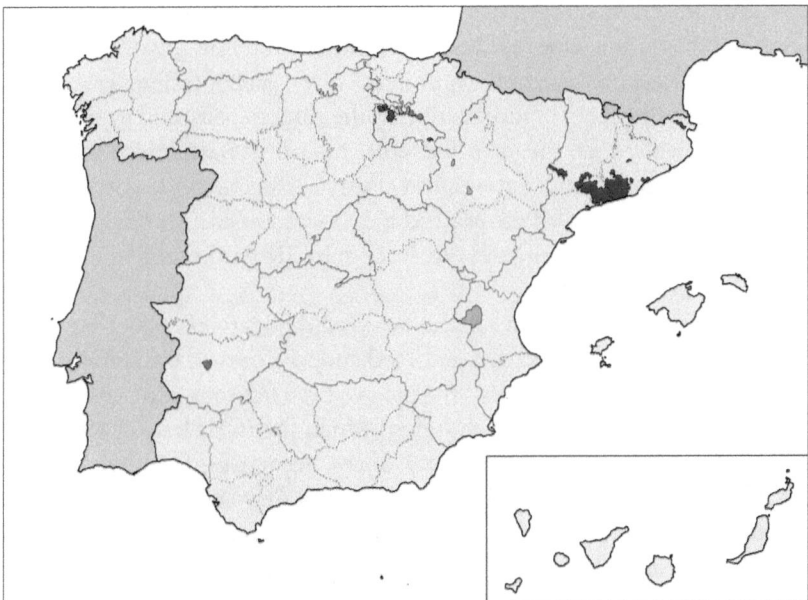

Figure 8.4. DO cava locater map. Image credit: dieghernan

created. This is why one finds wines marketed as such from Valencia, Rioja, the Basque Country, and even as far away as Extremadura.

These regions have deeply varied climates and sport extremely different soil compositions, exactly the qualities that one would imagine a DO would mean to limit.[24] The result of this flexibility in the attribution of the name is that it changes consideration of cava's general *terroir* by radically privileging winemaking and process over the specificity of the soil and growing conditions.[25] This is why I consider cava to be a "moveable" drink. The DO Cava's unorthodox approach may have accommodated sparkling wine producers who happened to be outside Catalonia when it was created, but in eschewing more conventional *terroir*-based guidelines, the council unwittingly prepared the ground for the destabilization to come.

Boycotts

In November 2004, the International Roller Sports Federation, which earlier in the year had provisionally approved the membership of the Catalan hockey team, withdrew their support. Esquerra Republicana de Catalunya (ERC) leader Josep

Lluís Carod Rovira suspected that Spanish state officials had intervened, and he proclaimed in an interview that he "didn't understand how anyone in Catalonia could support Madrid's Olympic aspirations" given such interference.[26] His comments ignited a firestorm of indignation in the rest of Spain, and even though he had not specifically used the term "boycott," his words were interpreted as a call for such. Although he would attempt to clarify his statement and eventually did come to express support for the Madrid bid, it was too late; a popular boycott of Catalan products had begun, and one item in particular became the focal point of Spanish anger: cava.

The backlash against Carod Rovira's words did not appear out of nowhere. As the cause of Catalan nationalism gathered support during the last years of the twentieth century and early part of the twenty-first, tensions had been rising. The fraught subject of Catalan nationhood, of which the roller hockey kerfuffle was just a small example in a long list of grievances, became especially acute after the death of Francisco Franco in 1975. When Spain's new constitution of 1978 heralded the transition to democracy, its second article recognized Catalonia rather ambiguously as a "historical nationality." The following year, the region received its own Statute of Autonomy—its first since 1932—which outlined the nature of its self-rule in terms of the organization of government, its powers, and its relationship to the Spanish state. In the decades that followed, various political groups within Catalonia pressed for even more sovereignty, if not outright independence. Carod Rovira's comments and the backlash against Catalan products coincided with the period of nationalist "Tri-partit" rule in Catalonia and the drafting of a new statute that pointedly replaced the term "nationality" with "nation." This latest law was approved by a popular referendum in Catalonia in June 2006, but fiercely criticized by Spanish parties, and especially so by the conservative, Spanish nationalist Partido Popular (PP), who filed a constitutional appeal against it. After a lengthy process, in 2010, the Constitutional Court of Spain struck down fourteen of its two hundred articles.[27] Although turnout for the referendum had been under 50 percent, almost 73 percent of those who had gone to the polls voted in favor. The rejection of key provisions of the law, including the "nation" designation, was very poorly received in Catalonia and sparked a massive demonstration of over one million people.[28]

I suggest that the boycotts, especially the first one, not only sought to punish Catalan business but, in the case of the region's most symbolic product, to both reject it and claim it through a parallel championing of non-Catalan cava, thus taking advantage or even "weaponizing" the DO's disregard of place. Regardless of the eventual financial consequences, the boycott's focus on the Catalanness of cava served to bring its accrued meaning into question at the same time as the

Figure 8.5. Alcampo supermarket sign. Credit: Avui

development of the Catalan cava industry was, itself, raising questions in the minds of its own producers.

The first wave of boycotts against Catalan products by citizens in the rest of Spain began with an anonymous SMS that went viral in December 2004, which was forwarded thousands of times. The text read: "Si Carod quiere boicot, tendrá boicot. Ni una gota de cava catalán en esta Navidad. ¡Pásalo!" (If Carod wants a boycott, he'll get a boycott. Not one drop of Catalan cava this Christmas. Pass it on!).[29] At the time, the response by Catalan officials was varied. Convergència i Unió (CiU) member of parliament Joan Raventós blamed Carod Rovira for having provoked a "real boycott" that had quickly resulted in the cancellation of an order for 80,000 bottles of cava; in an added viticultural flourish, he proclaimed that the ERC leader had been "as destructive as hail that harms the harvest."[30] Not surprisingly, on the other side of the political spectrum, Republicans such as Josep Huguet and Josep Bargalló played down the possible existence of a boycott, with the former pointing out that, given the majority of cava produced in Catalonia is exported, there would not be any "special suffering" were Catalan sparkling wine to be boycotted in cities like Madrid.[31]

This initial posturing soon gave way to concern as it became clear that even though overall production of cava was up in 2004, consumption over the Christmas period in Madrid and the Mediterranean coast for one of the largest and most symbolic producers, Codorniu, was down.[32] Over the course of 2005, the boycott stayed in the news, with fears for a repeat of the previous Christmas on the minds of producers. At the end of October of that year, Mariano Rajoy, the leader of Spain's opposition Partido Popular, traveled to Sant Sadurní d'Anoia to cool talk of a boycott and allay fears; this, even as his own party had invested half a million euros for an internet-based campaign against the proposed Catalan Statute of Autonomy.[33] Rajoy visited Freixenet, a company that has always presented itself as Spanish overseas and does not share the Catalanism of other large firms.[34] His comments are notable in two ways. First, he connects the boycott and the Statute: "Batallaré tanto contra el Estatut de Cataluña como contra la gente que realice boicot al cava" (I will fight as hard against the Catalan Statute as against the people who boycott cava), and then he maintains that cava, along with other Catalan goods, are "just as Spanish" as wine from Rioja or turron from Alicante.[35] Of course, the question here becomes one not only of provenance but of the superseding power of the adjective "Spanish" to function as a unifier in political terms. Rajoy's statement and the poor reaction to it in Catalan nationalist circles makes clear that, in addition to the economic battle emanating from the boycott or even the potential for a boycott, the symbolic was also clearly in play.[36]

Rajoy's trip to the heartland of cava did not stem the tide of the boycott. And while his words would generate controversy, the symbolic power of the growing campaign would materialize in a much more mundane way: in the aisles of Alcampo grocery stores throughout Spain during the run up to the 2005 holiday season.[37] In December of that year, multiple news outlets reported both the presence of signs pointing clients toward "non-Catalan" cava and the fact that the images of them were circulating online.

The matter-of-fact inclusion of "cavas no catalanes" (non-Catalan cavas) amongst the holiday items, and the fact that it was included on a sign, suggests that either the announcement was responding to client inquiries or a managerial will to differentiate. What is more, boycotts can be both explicit and implicit, with visibility in a market setting an important point to consider.[38] Here, one sees an early instance of the place of Catalan cava being brought into question in a retail sense—where it is literally positioned for the gaze of the consumer. And while overall sales of Catalan bubbly remained strong, a 6.6 percent drop in national sales shows that the boycott did have an effect.[39]

Where exactly did those sales go? Clearly, in the first instance, a lot of them went to other producers, the non-Catalan ones within the DO, who had a record year.[40] This is indicative of exactly how the irony of the lax geographic regulations comes into play. At the time, DO Cava did not privilege provenance in any way (this has since changed slightly for certain types of products) but ideologically driven consumers certainly did. In this way, we can see how cava's symbolic charge as a specifically Catalan product begins to be chipped away at from the inside thanks to its own regulations. The label "non-Catalan cava" allows the consumer to still purchase "cava" but to do so in a way that not only permits them to be true to their political preferences but also to actively punish Catalan producers for their government's actions as part of a "surrogate" boycott action.[41] The DO Cava may have long had this geographic anomaly, but thanks to the boycott, it became activated in a political way. This, I would argue, is perhaps the most symbolic effect of the campaigns against the product's Catalanness. That the increased demand for non-Catalan cava would subsequently lead some producers to have allegedly purchased bottles from Catalan wineries and labeled them as their own, is both further indication of this hedonic product's figurative power and supremely ironic.[42]

A lesser-known consequence of the boycott was the immediate shift of some consumers not just to non-Catalan cava, but to French champagne. For context, consider that in 2004, champagne sales in Spain posted a healthy but relatively modest 6 percent rise. The following year, with the cava boycott underway, they exploded for a 36 percent increase in growth.[43] One can speculate about the different factors at play here: that holidays inspire splurging, especially during boomtimes like the one that Spain was experiencing pre-2008; that the long association of cava and the word *xampany* made the switch symbolically easy, as well as the prestige factor involved in purchasing something foreign. Regardless, those sales represented money that would not go to Spanish producers.[44]

The cava boycott, which began at the end of 2004, lasted through 2006 and then became less relevant after the first part of 2007.[45] Cuadras-Morató and Raya conclude:

> the boycott had little impact in the aggregate Spanish market, but that this was the result of different behavior of consumers in different regional submarkets. Thus, Catalan consumers counteracted the boycott calls and, relative to a long-term time trend of diminishing consumption, increased their purchases of Catalan cava during the boycott years. Consumers from some regions in Spain, particularly in the South and the East coast and also Madrid in the case of our main empirical specification, decreased their purchases of Catalan cava during the period. Finally, we do not observe a clear negative impact of the boycott in the consumption choices of residents in the rest of [the] regions in Spain.[46]

Nevertheless, even with exports and a local "buycott"—or counter-boycott—cushioning the drop in national sales during these years, the fact remains that the image of cava had been affected. As the former head of Mont-Ferrant explains: "El retroceso del cava no es sólo numérico . . . ha perdido peso en la Navidad; ni publicitariamente es tan importante como hace unos años cuando copaba la televisión, ni tiene ya un peso específico en los regalos de empresa" (Cava's regression is not just numerical . . . it has lost importance during Christmastime; it's not as important from an advertising perspective as it was a few years ago when it dominated television, nor does it still have its specific importance as a business present).[47] And although hardly surprising given the entity, another symbolic gesture came a few years later when, in September 2010, the Spanish national football team *la Roja* announced that their "official cava" would be one produced in Extremadura.[48]

There were renewed calls for boycotts around the 2017 referendum on Catalan independence and even some apps created to help consumers identify Catalan products.[49] This time, though, there seemed to be a greater awareness of the interconnectedness of production and supply chains. As Colman Andrews points out regarding cava having become a target once again: "The two major cava producers, Freixenet and Codorníu, bottle their wares using glass from Aragón and León, cork from Extremadura, capsules from La Rioja Alavesa, and labels from Murcia, and are shipped in boxes made in the Valencian Community—so decreased sales of their wines means lost income all over Spain."[50] Business leader Francisco Javier Peinado from Extremadura also warned against this so-called "boomerang effect": "Cada vez que boicoteamos un producto catalán, nos pegamos un tiro en el pie" (Every time that we boycott a Catalan product, we shoot ourselves in the foot).[51] Still, while one poll did find that 23 percent of those surveyed in Spain outside Catalonia in November 2017 said that they were already boycotting Catalan products in general, the DO Cava closed the year with record numbers.[52] And while the cava sector would see a 3.2 percent production decline in 2018 due to protests around the independence bid, it "bounced back to an overall 2 percent rise [in 2019] despite a slim fall in exports."[53] The effects of Covid-19 remain to be seen, but from an economic perspective, Catalan cava producers seem to have withstood the boycotts mainly through increased exports and solid sales at home. Nevertheless, the attacks on cava's Catalanness, along with the greater realization of the existence of non-Catalan cava, raised important questions as to its status, as well as its physical and symbolic place.

Corpinnat

Politically motivated boycotts from outside Catalonia have not been the only actions to both materially threaten the Catalan sparkling wine industry and figuratively bring into question what "cava" is and represents. The ideological differences that became increasingly patent within the DO also put the industry under pressure and eventually lead to the breaking away of a splinter group. It is important to keep in mind the utter domination of the market by the "big three": Freixenet, Codorníu, and García Carrión. Through mass production practices, buying in base wine, the use of non-traditional grapes, and arrangements to produce private label wines for chains such as the UK's Tesco, they have succeeded in increasing volume and market share at home and abroad while keeping prices low. These companies have made cava the standard bearer for cheap, bottom-shelf bubbly. In this way, one sees how the ostensible "success" of deterritorialized cava, along with the mixing of "Spanish" symbolisms, such as Freixenet's use of flamenco in its advertising abroad, as well as with a DO that eschews geographic specificity, would become untenable for frustrated smaller producers interested in making high-quality cava. The first warning of real trouble for the DO came in 2012, when iconic winery Raventós i Blanc quit the classification. Then, the creation of "Clàssic Penedès" within the DO Penedès offered another potential avenue for producers to leave the DO Cava but still remain within a recognized denomination.[54] Still, nothing changed, and tensions continued to build.

In 2015, the DO finally reacted to internal pressure to create space for higher-quality, small-parcel wines by creating an elite category called "Cava de Paraje Calificado" (Qualified Single-Estate Cava), which would "recognize the excellence of exceptional vineyards" with the first vintages appearing in 2017.[55] Nevertheless, it was too little too late; a small group of quality-driven cava producers were already working on a separate, even stricter set of guidelines than the CPC category, which would act as a rigid framework for producing high-quality cava. Formed in 2015, ratified by the European Union at the end of 2017, and officially announced in April 2018, the Association of Wine Producers and Growers Corpinnat was established.[56] The DO immediately declared that it would study the extent to which Corpinnat and DO Cava might mesh but, over the next nine months, decided that not only was the word "Corpinnat" *not* allowed on official labels, but that any promotion of the venture would have to cease by January 31, 2019.[57] On January 30, the original six wineries, along with recently-joined Can Feixes, Júlia Bernet, and Mas Candí, collectively left DO Cava.[58]

So why, exactly, did the Corpinnat group want to leave? In a word: *terroir*. With the big houses commanding such a striking amount of the DO's output and its presidency changing hands from giant Freixenet to equally massive Codorníu, the direction of the DO and its overall attitude toward the value of place stayed the same: mass production with no real limits. The producers of the new Corpinnat brand have espoused a completely different ideology when it comes to wine and place making. They favor returning to the specificity of cava's heartland and bringing organic methods to the fore to show that high-quality cava from the Penedès can command both more respect and higher prices. To try to capture this terroir-oriented approach and mindset, they combined two concepts to create their name: "COR, the cradle where, more than 130 years ago, the very first sparkling wines in Spain were made and PINNAT which stems from the etymological root Pinnae which refers to the origin of the word Penedés, documented in the 10th Century as Penetense. This Latin adjective is derived from pinna, which means crag or rock and which applied to the Penedés is equivalent to rocky soil."[59]

One of the important ways the Corpinnat brand differentiates itself from the DO—and its new CPC designation—is that the association takes the entire production of a winemaker into account rather than just those used for individual wines. Producers must use at least 90 percent "historic" varietals, which the association defines as the original three: Xarel·lo, Macabeu, Parellada, along with Malvasia for whites, and Garnacha, Monastrell, Sumoll, and Xarel·lo Vermell for reds.[60] What is more, the grapes must be handpicked from sustainable vineyards and then entirely vinified on their winery premises before being aged for a minimum of 18 months, and up to as long as 60 months in some cases. Of course, given their strictness, these regulations effectively rule out the largest cava producers from participating in the association and labeling their wines "Corpinnat."[61]

With the break having occurred, what will be the next step for the Corpinnat brand? In May 2020, there was talk of the group and the producers of Clàssic Penedès forming a new DO. Miquel Hudin, who has followed the Corpinnat saga closely, observes: "Corpinnat is a trademarked name and a regulated brand under EU law. It is not a DO within Spain, so its functions are limited. Clàssic Penedès is a sub-classification under the DO Penedès regulations, so it too is not a DO, but is served by one."[62] This path would require a lot of ironing out of issues regarding both geography and the varieties of grapes permitted because Corpinnat is much more stringent than Clàssic Penedès.[63] It remains to be seen how this new alliance, which would bolster both groups of high-end sparkling wine producers, will develop. One thing is certain though: the exodus of a cohort of highly respected, quality winemakers can only hurt the DO Cava's reputation and aspirations to be more than just a producer of bargain sparkling wine.

Conclusion

Having considered cava's history and timing in Catalan modernity, how it has been named, regulated, boycotted, and then contested from within, let us return to the question of what is cava's place? Is cava merely a cellar, a space to age wine made according to a method imported or "grafted" from France long ago? Or does the sparkling wine known as cava actually pertain to a place—to the soil and climate of the Penedès, where Macabeu, Parellada, and Xarel·lo suffer drastic swings in diurnal temperatures but are also protected from the humidity of the sea by a small mountain range?[64] If cava's *terroir* is insisted upon, does it cease to officially *be* cava because cava can technically come from elsewhere in Spain? What does it mean that the "new" Corpinnat wines, which are made by producers wholly dedicated to the traditional geographic place of Catalan sparkling wine, now exist outside the DO Cava? Their bottles are not even permitted to bear the word "cava" on their labels. They are "quality sparkling wine," or just simply "Corpinnat," an awkward-sounding portmanteau. This slipperiness of "cava," an invented term that stuck and became part of a culture's vernacular, compels us to think about the intersection of foodways and politics, both of which aspire to express the local in terms of culture and taste.

Of course, cava has been associated with Catalonia, but as I have shown, this connection has been tested.[65] This was especially true during the initial boycott around the *Estatut*, the moment when the unrestricted scope of the DO Cava allowed for its Catalanness to be contested. The bureaucratic angle was essentially weaponized in a campaign to punish producers for what the regional government was itself doing regarding citizens' pertinence and identity. I would argue that those two and half years, from the end of 2004 through 2006, were cava's initial destabilization period as a specifically Catalan signifier. After that, "cava" became open to modification and the potential to be combined and coopted as a new sign: a sparkling wine that no longer carries the Catalan charge. Ideology interfered with cava's ostensible, accrued meaning. But that said, who drinks it— and when—is important. Is cava only for Catalan nationalists? Clearly not if the head of Freixenet and the leader of the PP can proudly drink it. It is a drink for celebrations, baptisms, and inaugurations of all sorts, and it is an insider's secret for study-abroad students, who quickly realize that their money goes a lot further when one orders "*una copeta de cava*" instead of more trendy drinks.

So, I would venture that the place of cava resides in one's position to Catalan culture. It is a moveable drink, an accessible experience, one that, on account of its wide range of prices, is open to whomever wishes to drink it in any setting at any time. Here, we see experience and taste reach beyond labels. Whether it is *xampany*, cava, Corpinnat, *escumòs de qualititat*, or even "non-Catalan cava," this sparkling wine, a modern beverage made according to the traditional method, serves as both a path and a vehicle. Its very instability has become a marker of its importance.

NOTES

1. 95 percent of the cava produced in Spain comes from Catalan vineyards, mainly around the town of Sant Sadurní d'Anoia. Jancis Robinson and Julia Harding, *The Oxford Companion to Wine*, 4th ed. (Corby, UK: Cambridge University Press, 2015).
2. For a concise history of the wines of Äy, from which the champagne as we know it today emerged, see Maguelonne Toussaint-Samat, *History of Food*, trans. Anthea Bell (Chichester, UK: Blackwell, 2001), 285.
3. The Champagne region permits the use of Arbane, Petit Meslier, and "Pinot" grapes, with this latter category including the main three: Pinot Noir, Pinot Meunier, and Chardonnay. Robinson and Harding, *Oxford Companion to Wine*.
4. Variations include: crémant de Limoux, Bourgogne, and Alsace. Franciacorta DOCG and Trentino DOC in Italy use traditional method.
5. For a compelling history of the marketing of champagne as an aspirational beverage, see chapter two, "Consuming the Nation: Champagne Marketing and Bourgeois Ritual, 1789–1914" in Kolleen M. Guy, *When Champagne Became French: Wine and the Making of a National Identity* (Baltimore, MD: Johns Hopkins University Press, 2003).
6. I thank Daniel Bender for this observation.
7. Joan C. Martín, *El cava: Un vino feliz y mediterráneo* (Barcelona: Los libros del lince, 2017).
8. Marc Badia-Miró, Enric Tello, Francesc Valls, and Ramón Garrabou, "The Grape Phylloxera Plague as a Natural Experiment: The Upkeep of Vineyards in Catalonia (Spain), 1858–1935," *Australian Economic History Review* 50, no. 1 (March 2010): 54.
9. Martín, *Un vino feliz*.
10. For more on the *hereu*, see Llorenç Ferrer l'Alos, "Sistema hereditario y reproducción social en Cataluña," *Mélanges de l'École française de Rome. Italie et Méditerranée* 110, no. 1 (1998): 53–57.
11. Juan Carmona and James Simpson, "The 'Rabassa Morta' in Catalan Viticulture: The Rise and Decline of a Long-Term Sharecropping Contract, 1670s–1920s," *The Journal of Economic History* 59, no. 2 (June 1999): 291. As Carmona and Simpson further point out, "For several centuries this institution was sufficiently flexible to adapt to changing factor markets and the wider changes taking place within society. From the late 19th century, however, the increasingly capital-intensive nature of viticulture and the divergence of wages and wine prices significantly raised the possibilities of postcontractual opportunistic behavior on the part of the sharecropper, and eroded the trust, or social capital, that had developed over the previous centuries. Although sharecropping continued to be used, the conflicts that developed between the principal and agent in their attempts to adjust to the new situation raised transaction costs and therefore reduced significantly the efficiency of the *rabassa morta* contract" (291).
12. Karen MacNeil, *The Wine Bible*, 2nd ed. (New York: Workman Publishing Company, 2015), 476.
13. The first attempts to imitate champagne involved the gasification of still wine using compressor technology that had been developed in Russia for the creation of *Seltz*.

Martín, *El cava*, chap. 1.
14. MacNeil, *The Wine Bible*, 477.
15. Martín, *El cava*.
16. Andreas Oestreicher, "La Crisis Filoxérica En España," *Hispania* 56 (1996): 593.
17. Barcelona and Tarragona area producers fared better than those in Lleida and Girona, as they were better equipped to deal with the disruption and weather the shock of declining prices from the late 1880s, just as phylloxera began to devastate Catalonia's own vines. Carmona and Simpson, "Rabassa Morta," 303. As Carmona and Simpson further point out: "In Catalonia, three problems had now to be overcome simultaneously: the replanting of the dead or dying vines; the need to adapt to lower wine prices; and, peculiar to this region, the need for landowners to decide whether to renegotiate contracts with their sharecroppers as phylloxera, which had destroyed the vines, automatically brought thousands of *rabassa morta* contracts to an end" (303).
18. "Macabeo - Parellada Xarel·lo Wine," *Wine-Searcher*.
19. Catalonia's modern predisposition toward greater connection to Europe was manifest especially in its hosting of the 1888 World's Fair and would also feed a desire for a greater say in the region's political matters.
20. Knowledge transfer also occurred between workers as Codorníu became a "school" where new employees learned the complex techniques of sparkling wine production. Francesc Valls-Junyent, "The International Competitiveness of Cava: Success of a Particular Firm or the District?" *Working Papers in Economics* 224, Universitat de Barcelona, Espai de Recerca en Economia (2009): 29. For more on Catalunya-Ciutat, see Joan Ramon Resina, "'Barcelona ciutat' en la estética de Eugeni d'Ors," *Revista hispánica moderna* 43, no. 2 (1990): 167–78.
21. Among the ways that the middle classes adopted cava is the practice of Saturday picnics in Sant Sadurní d'Anoia, where cava bodegas sell locally raised lamb and rent out grills. MacNeil, *The Wine Bible*, 476.
22. The name "cava" appears for the first time in 1959 in a document that would become Spain's first legislation regarding sparkling wines. "Boletín," *Boe.es*, August 4, 1959.
23. "Terroir and Appelation," *Champagne.fr*.
24. Tim McKirdy, "Almost One Year In, Corpinnat Strains to Make Its Case as Higher-Quality Cava," *VinePair*, December 2, 2019. The slick website of the DO Cava mentions "zones" outside Catalonia as "Valle del Ebro," "Viñedos de Almendralejo," and "Levante" instead of using place names such as Aragon, Castilla y León, Extremadura, La Rioja, Navarra, and Valencia. As of 2020, subzones have also been approved that further specify the exact provenance of grapes for higher quality cavas within the DO.
25. For more on the subject of *terroir* in the Catalan context, see Robert Davidson, "The Priorat and the Landscaping of Catalan *Terroir*," in *The New Ruralism: An Epistemology of Transformed Space*, eds. Joan Ramon Resina and William Viestenz (Orlando, FL: Iberoamericana Vervuert, 2012), 93–103, and "*Terroir* and Catalonia," *Journal of Catalan Studies* 10 (2007): 58–72.
26. Daniel Lifona, "ERC pide que Cataluña no apoye a Madrid 2012 por el caso del patinaje," *El Mundo*, November 26, 2004.

27. "El TC rebaja las aspiraciones de Catalunya en lengua, justicia y tributos catalanes," *La Vanguardia*, June 28, 2010.
28. Eva Belmonte, "Masiva manifestación en Barcelona en apoyo al Estatut y contra el Constitucional," *El Mundo*, July 10, 2010.
29. "CiU culpa a las palabras de Carod sobre Madrid 2012 del supuesto boicot al cava catalán en Navidades," *El Mundo*, December 15, 2004.
30. Ibid.
31. Ibid. The first call for a boycott of cava during this period was actually not related to the question of Catalan nationhood but rather the refusal of the Catalan government to allow the transfer of water from the Ebro to southeastern Spain, a decision that prompted hoteliers and restaurant owners in Bendiorm to stop buying Catalan cava. E. Pinter and B. Deltell, "Hotels i restaurants de Benidorm fan boicot al cava català per Nadal," *Avui*, December 4, 2004, 25.
32. "Les vendes de cava a l'Estat van augmentar un 2,3% l'any 2004," *Avui*, March 3, 2005; "Codorníu va notar el boicot," *Avui*, February 27, 2005.
33. "Cuando el PP abonó el boicot a los productos catalanes ante la reforma del Estatut de 2006," *Público*, December 13, 2017.
34. Michael Eiuade, *Catalonia: A Cultural History* (Oxford, UK: Oxford University Press, 2008). One website became especially notorious during this period: stopelnacionalismo.com. Housed on servers in Asturias, the page called for a blanket boycott of Catalan companies such as Caixa Catalana, Grupo Planeta, and, ironically, the same non-Catalan nationalist Freixenet cava house that had welcomed Rajoy.
35. "Mariano Rajoy: 'Batallaré contra la gente que haga boicot al cava tanto como contra el Estatut,'" *El Mundo*, October 27, 2005.
36. Enric Sòria, "Com el jabugo," *Avui*, October 29, 2005.
37. Ferran Casas, "Alcampo ajuda a no consumer cava català," *Avui*, December 15, 2005.
38. Ibid.
39. "Las ventas de cava cayeron un 6,6% en 2005 por el boicot," *ABC*, February 2, 2006.
40. Jordi Sacristán, "El boicot al cava catalán 'vuelve a casa' por Navidad," *El economista*, December 21, 2007.
41. Xavier Cuadras-Morató and Josep Maria Raya, "Boycott or Buycott?: Internal Politics and Consumer Choices," *IDEAS Working Paper Series from RePEc*, 2014, 6.
42. Lluís Martínez, "Espoli," *Avui*, July 3, 2010.
43. "Las ventas de cava."
44. Substitutions of high-value cava by champagne were most pronounced in the metropolitan area of Madrid during the boycott. Cuadras-Morató and Raya, "Boycott or Buycott," 22.
45. Ibid., 4.
46. Ibid., 24.
47. Sacristán, "El boicot al cava catalán."
48. "España beberá cava extremeño," *Marca.com*, September 27, 2010.
49. Colman Andrews, "Boycotts of Catalan wine and food products are affecting other parts of Spain," *Los Angeles Times*, November 14, 2017.

50. Ibid.
51. Patricia Blanco, "Los extremeños alertan del efecto bumerán de boicotear los productos catalanes," *El País*, October 24, 2017.
52. "El 23% de los españoles reconoce hacer boicot a los productos catalanes," *Cotizalia*, November 8, 2017; C. Morell, "El cava supera el boicot amb un nou rècord de vendes," *El Punt Avui*, April 5, 2018.
53. Joan Faus, "Coronavirus reduces sparkle in Spain's cava industry," *Financial Post*, May 28, 2020.
54. Miquel Hudin, "Corpinnat and the Death of Fine Cava?" Hudin.com, February 1, 2019.
55. "Cava de Paraje Calificado," *D. O. Cava*.
56. McKirdy, "Almost One Year In."
57. Hudin, "Corpinnat and the Death."
58. Ibid. Those original six producers were Gramona, Llopart, Nadal, Recaredo, Sabaté i Coca, and Torelló. Corpinnat, "Who We Are," Corpinnat.com.
59. Corpinnat, "The Brand," Corpinnat.com.
60. McKirdy, "Almost One Year In."
61. Amanda Barnes, "Corpinnat—an Emerging Category of Spanish Sparkling Wine," *SevenFifty Daily*, March 1, 2019.
62. Miquel Hudin, "Corpinnat and Clàssic Penedès have been in discussions to form new sparkling DO," Hudin.com, May 7, 2020.
63. Miquel Hudin, "Corpinnat: Going forward," Hudin.com, December 11, 2019.
64. Hudin, "Corpinnat and the Death."
65. In 2018, the two biggest producers stopped being family run. That year, Germany's Oetker Group took a majority stake at Freixenet, and American private equity Carlyle Group assumed the nearly five-century-old Codorníu brand. Faus, "Coronavirus."

WORKS CITED

"23% de los españoles reconoce hacer boicot a los productos catalanes, El." *Cotizalia*, November 8, 2017.
Andrews, Colman. "Boycotts of Catalan wine and food products are affecting other parts of Spain." *Los Angeles Times*, November 14, 2017.
Badia-Miró, Marc, Enric Tello, Francesc Valls, and Ramón Garrabou. "The Grape Phylloxera Plague as a Natural Experiment: The Upkeep of Vineyards in Catalonia (Spain), 1858–1935." *Australian Economic History Review* 50, no. 1 (March 2010): 39–61.
Barnes, Amanda. "Corpinnat—an Emerging Category of Spanish Sparkling Wine." *SevenFifty Daily*, March 1, 2019.
Belmonte, Eva. "Masiva manifestación en Barcelona en apoyo al Estatut y contra el Constitucional." *El Mundo*, July 10, 2010.
Blanco, Patricia. "Los extremeños alertan del efecto bumerán de boicotear los productos catalanes." *El País*, October 24, 2017.

"Boletín." *Boe.es.* August 4, 1959.
Carmona, Juan, and James Simpson. "The 'Rabassa Morta' in Catalan Viticulture: The Rise and Decline of a Long-Term Sharecropping Contract, 1670s–1920s." *The Journal of Economic History* 59, no. 2 (June 1999): 290–315.
Casas, Ferran. "Alcampo ajuda a no consumer cava català." *Avui*, December 15, 2005.
"Cava de Paraje Calificado." *D. O. Cava.*
"CiU culpa a las palabras de Carod sobre Madrid 2012 del supuesto boicot al cava catalán en Navidades." *El Mundo*, December 15, 2004.
"Codorníu va notar el boicot." *Avui*, February 27, 2005.
Corpinnat. "The Brand." Corpinnat.com
———. "Who We Are." Corpinnat.com.
Cuadras-Morató, Xavier, and Josep Maria Raya. "Boycott or Buycott?: Internal Politics and Consumer Choices." *IDEAS Working Paper Series from RePEc*, 2014.
"Cuando el PP abonó el boicot a los productos catalanes ante la reforma del Estatut de 2006." *Publico*, December 13, 2017.
Davidson, Robert. "The Priorat and the Landscaping of Catalan *Terroir*." In *The New Ruralism: An Epistemology of Transformed Space*, edited by Joan Ramon Resina and William Viestenz, 93–103. Orlando, FL: Iberoamericana Vervuert, 2012.
———. "*Terroir* and Catalonia." *Journal of Catalan Studies* 10 (2007): 58–72.
Eiuade, Michael. *Catalonia: A Cultural History*. Oxford, UK: Oxford University Press, 2008.
"España beberá cava extremeño." *Marca.com*, September 27, 2010.
Faus, Joan. "Coronavirus reduces sparkle in Spain's cava industry." *Financial Post*, May 28, 2020.
Ferrer l'Alos, Llorenç. "Sistema hereditario y reproducción social en Cataluña." *Mélanges de l'École française de Rome. Italie et Méditerranée* 110, no. 1 (1998): 53–57.
Guy, Kolleen M. *When Champagne Became French: Wine and the Making of a National Identity*. Baltimore, MD: Johns Hopkins University Press, 2003.
Hudin, Miquel. "Corpinnat and Clàssic Penedès have been in discussions to form new sparkling DO." Hudin.com, May 7, 2020.
———. "Corpinnat and the Death of Fine Cava?" Hudin.com, February 1, 2019.
———. "Corpinnat: Going forward." Hudin.com, December 11, 2019.
Lifona, Daniel. "ERC pide que Cataluña no apoye a Madrid 2012 por el caso del patinaje." *El Mundo*, November 26, 2004.
"Macabeo - Parellada Xarel·lo Wine." *Wine-Searcher.*
MacNeil, Karen. *The Wine Bible*. 2nd edition. New York: Workman Publishing Company, 2015.
"Mariano Rajoy: 'Batallaré contra la gente que haga boicot al cava tanto como contra el Estatut.'" *El Mundo*, October 27, 2005.
Martín, Joan C. *El cava: Un vino feliz y mediterráneo*. Barcelona: Los libros del lince, 2017.
Martínez, Lluís. "Espoli." *Avui*, July 3, 2010.
McKirdy, Tim. "Almost One Year In, Corpinnat Strains to Make Its Case as Higher-Quality Cava." *VinePair*, December 2, 2019.
Morell, C. "El cava supera el boicot amb un nou rècord de vendes." *El Punt Avui*, April 5, 2018.
Oestreicher, Andreas. "La Crisis Filoxérica En España." *Hispania* 56 (1996): 587–622.

Pinter, E., and B. Deltell. "Hotels i restaurants de Benidorm fan boicot al cava català per Nadal." *Avui*, December 4, 2004.
Resina, Joan Ramon. "'Barcelona ciutat' en la estética de Eugeni d'Ors." *Revista hispánica moderna* 43, no. 2 (1990): 167–78.
Robinson, Jancis, and Julia Harding. *The Oxford Companion to Wine*. 4th edition. Corby, UK: Cambridge University Press, 2015.
Sacristán, Jordi. "El boicot al cava catalán 'vuelve a casa' por Navidad." *El economista*, December 21, 2007.
Sòria, Enric. "Com el jabugo." *Avui*, October 29, 2005.
"TC rebaja las aspiraciones de Catalunya en lengua, justicia y tributos catalanes, El." *La Vanguardia*, June 28, 2010.
"Terroir and Appelation." *Champagne.fr*.
Toussaint-Samat, Maguelonne. *History of Food*. Translated by Anthea Bell. Chichester, UK: Blackwell, 2001.
"Las ventas de cava cayeron un 6,6% en 2005 por el boicot." *ABC*, February 2, 2006.
"Les vendes de cava a l'Estat van augmentar un 2,3% l'any 2004." *Avui*, March 3, 2005.
Valls-Junyent, Francesc. "The International Competitiveness of Cava: Success of a Particular Firm or the District?" *Working Papers in Economics* 224, Universitat de Barcelona. Espai de Recerca en Economia, 2009.

◆ CHAPTER 9

Food, Heritage, and Tourism
On the Uses of Food Heritage and Its Relations with Culture, Politics, and Socioeconomic Development

F. Xavier Medina

A few years ago, I penned an article published in Spanish, in which I sought to reflect upon food-related intangible cultural heritage and its social and socioeconomic usages.[1] This chapter will follow the path of that previous publication, placing the focus on the complex and often conflicting context of food's relationship with heritage, a relationship that often ends up creating unequal power relationships affecting the ability of different social agents to act—government and public institutions and/or authorities; local, regional, or national NGOs; representatives of local people; private foundations, partnerships, or alliances; small/medium enterprises, artisans, academia, and so on—particularly those arising from civil society.

As it was pointed out more than a decade ago by Laurajane Smith, the organs of state power (especially those of the Western hemisphere) have fostered a discourse still firmly rooted today in the immutable and inherent nature of the value and meaning of heritage within the practices associated with its conservation, preservation, and management.[2] Although said practices may well arise in association with, and are mainly related to, tangible heritage, at times they have also been transposed to intangible cultural heritage. Recognized only more recently, the category of cultural heritage may be regarded as still being at the establishment—if not even the "under construction"—stage. Its relation to power, principally public, but also private, and with society in general, is yet to be developed.

Regarding Heritage

At the risk of falling into the trap of making simplistic definitions, it can be said that cultural heritage is a social contract between different social agents, between institutions and individuals, between the public sphere and civil society, and so on. This contract regulates those aspects of a culture that we, firstly, consider to be representative of our production (that represent us and that therefore form part of our collective identity) and that are, for this very reason, worth conserving and handing down to future generations. Regarded as a nexus between the past and the present, and even as an indispensable part of building the future, as well as an element or part of tradition, heritage is commonly associated with collective identities, in the sense that it forms part of the production and the passage of time that gives sense and originality to a society as such.

Additionally, it must be said that heritage is, as often noted, changeable (because culture is, too). Furthermore, it is possessed of a degree of arbitrariness: it is built upon the basis of selections of specific, recognizable things, collectively regarded as forming part of a certain culture, but not of others.[3] Nevertheless, one important aspect to bear in mind is that, even when forming part of a social contract, it must be "felt" by the majority of the population involved as "theirs"; it is often power structures that propose (or receive proposals from civil society), convey, and/or recognize heritage. Lastly, said structures are also usually those most directly responsible for preserving it. We can therefore see that heritage, far from being disinterested, often serves specific interests.

According to Smith, heritage intersects with a range of social and cultural debates about the legitimacy of a range of values and identities and subsequently plays a part in their validation, negotiation, and regulation. So, by recognizing that the management of heritage has consequences beyond the preservation of historic fabric, it will be possible to explore the social uses of heritage in the fields of politics, economics, or religion. Smith speaks of the "preservation of historic fabric."[4] She introduces here an important factor worth bearing in mind: heritage is something that must be preserved. And normally (although not always), the responsibility for said preservation rests with the public authorities. Nevertheless, it should also not be forgotten that heritage, although it comes in some shape or form (more remotely or more recently) from the past, is always part of the present and must still be in use. Something that no longer exists cannot be heritage but rather a historical memory. Lastly, we should consider economic development as closely tied to tourism. Nowadays, cultural heritage is regarded as a tourism resource with great potential, and in this same sense, heritagization projects occur more and more within the framework of tourism and its associated discourse of local development. This has been the case of food culture: it is deeply intertwined with landscapes, produce, dishes, wines and drinks, infrastructure, routes, industries, etc.

Hence, the purpose of this article is to reflect upon the intersections between food culture, heritage, and socioeconomic development/tourism from both a practical and a critical standpoint, noting different applications and, at the same time, discussing them.

Heritage under Construction: Time, Tradition, and Identities

Nearly all our originality comes from the stamp that time impresses upon our sensibility.
    CHARLES BAUDELAIRE, *Écrits sur l'art* (1863)

Heritage has to do (among many other things) with something inherited from a more or less distant past that is regarded as being worth conserving. "Heritagize," for its part, means to turn into heritage or to construct heritage based on certain pre-existing things, chosen from amongst others that are not included in this process.[5] Heritage is thus socially and culturally constructed and applied.

The objects and events making up heritage allow one to refer to tradition, to construct a certain relationship with history—more or less real or mythical and more or less recent, but in one or another way adopted—and the territory in question, with time and space, and with local memory: "The time evoked by tradition is lost beyond memory, beyond what is socially possible to recall and affirm, and even beyond the limits of mythical imagination. It is, however, a time commonly accepted as belonging to and even initiating collective memory. In this way, it is projected from the past to legitimize and justify the present."[6]

Additionally, by means of the distinction between tangible and intangible heritage, objects (or assets or procedures, in the broadest sense) that are heritagizable escape from the bounds of physical vestiges, written testimonies, and classical artistic production and spread to encompass more everyday items, such as everything associated with food: cuisines, cookbooks, food production and crafts, consumption habits, table manners, and more.[7]

It should nevertheless be noted that intangible cultural heritage, as a living culture, even if it has a markedly historical origin, must always belong to the present and must remain in use. Something that no longer exists cannot be a living heritage. To give just one example, an old recipe book can be regarded as heritage, a testimony to times past that has survived down to our times (and therefore the present), but not all its recipes will necessarily remain part of the food heritage of the society that produced it. Many of them, now fallen out of favor, will form part of history, and only those still used will be part of its heritage, from a contemporary perspective.

At the same time, we are used to "venerating" heritage. We normally associate heritage as something immovable, which has come down to us from the past in a "pure" state and which must be preserved as such. From this perspective, observing any food product solely would mean abstracting said production from any holistic perspective and lead one to think that said productions, before acquiring any tourism-related functionalities or meanings, were "authentic" in an abstract and/or primordial way. In other words, they were isolated in a determined time and space in which they had not been affected by social and cultural (or political, economic, or even religious) influences and, far from evolving, had remained unchanged until the arrival of tourism. From our standpoint, tourism is just one further aspect in the processes of cultural evolution within a much broader framework of globalization and, under no circumstances, is an isolated factor that can be regarded as solely responsible for any process. There are no "pure" trajectories, either in society or in culture.

So, tourism is based on and uses heritage and local resources as a culture-based attraction, whilst also acting directly with regard to their uses and social transformations. The interrelation is thus constant but far from unequivocal. Additionally, as with any other social aspect, the interrelations, usages and negotiations between the different powers, be they public or private, are constant and far from disinterested.

A Living, Shifting Heritage

Regarding food production, the notion of heritage raises undoubtedly complex issues, as heritage is living, shifting, and constantly evolving, with all the problems this implies for its management and maintenance. Sometimes, far from being inherent to a specific territory, these products or dishes may be the result of borrowings, interchanges, and adaptations that interpret the culinary preferences of contemporary society, whether or not they are associated with any identitary dimension.[8] Additionally, the interests of contemporary societies have an impact upon heritage products, upon production and consumption contexts, and upon their forms of expression, which may have changed considerably and even become divorced from local traditions (or the wishes of local authorities) or have transformed how they are communicated or disseminated toward less orthodox or hitherto unexplored methods.

All this places us on an unstable, still-forming, and constantly evolving footing, in which the dictates of cultural evolution and social change itself call for flexibility and an ability to adapt, which, to date at least, have tended to lag behind the requirements created by everyday practices.

Heritage, Food, and Sociocultural Identities

Heritage also has a significant identificatory aspect to it, often fed by a feeling of belonging to a group with its own identity. As Prats remarks, one of the core features of heritage is its symbolic nature, its ability to represent, through a system of symbols, a particular identity.[9] The process of heritagization is therefore a feature of modern societies, which have a need to install sociocultural and identity benchmarks regarding their own conceptions of time and space.[10]

Local (and not so local) societies have been able to identify themselves and even, today, define themselves in terms of heritage through the foods and dishes they select, cook, and eat. As Igor de Garine pointed out more than forty years ago, it is no coincidence that gastronomy is at the foreground of the panoply of regional demands.[11] However, if we focus our gaze upon a society's food culture, we can see that it is only recently that it has become worth "heritagizing." As the scope of heritage (regarded as a construction) has been expanding, aspects of intangible culture that were previously difficult to identify have joined the ranks of things "heritagizable," and everyday aspects such as those associated with food, which previously formed an intrinsic part of everyday life but not of Culture (with a capital "C"), have been deemed worthy of becoming a heritage and, therefore, of being officially recognized as prompting a sense of belonging and identity. The products of the land and local cuisines share both their uniqueness and complexity because they simultaneously refer to living practices and techniques, on the one hand, and to specific identities, affective links, and taste preferences, on the other. All this plays a role within a context of increasingly generalized heritagization.

The Institutionalization of Food Heritage: Officialness and the Powers that Be

Heritage is a social contract regarding specific aspects of culture that societies regard as being representative of our production and, for this very reason, as being worth conserving and handing down to future generations. Because not everything is heritagizable, this contract implies selecting what is heritage based on certain criteria, which, even if they have some points in common, may vary from one society to another and even, with a degree of arbitrariness, within the same society. The selection and formulation of these criteria tend to take place within a sector that we could describe as "expert," usually stemming from academe (involving definition, delimitation, etc.) and often associated with "the authorities." This expert sector and, at a subsequent stage, the official one are to be found at different territorial levels, from the local to the supranational, and embracing all possible intermediary spaces, which need not be the same in all contexts. In this way, heritage—food heritage in this case—exists at different levels and is pursuant to different criteria and interests in every given case.

However, in any case, as Llorenç Prats states, it should be remarked that heritage does not exist unless activated by specific official bodies with the prerogative to do so.[12] Without them, recognition of heritage does not exist as such, as least officially or in a socially recognized form. The initiative for heritage activation may come from official circles or arise directly from civil society. Nevertheless, even in the latter case, it must enjoy the (more or less explicit) support of powers or counter-powers. Without power, there is no heritage activation and thus no heritage. Accordingly, how heritage objects are selected, put together, and written or spoken about have political effects.[13] Associations with power are also implicit.

Furthermore, as Smith writes, "there is a hegemonic 'authorized heritage discourse,' which is reliant on the power/knowledge claims of technical and aesthetic experts and institutionalized in state cultural agencies."[14] This has meant that the most recent heritagization movements have been shaped more in line with the procedures associated with established or predefined trajectories than with those associated with the specific needs of new heritages. In this regard, when preparing inventories of gastronomic heritage, one should avoid paying more attention to products or dishes than to other equally important and defining aspects of gastronomy, such as culinary techniques or forms of consumption.

The relationships between political and economic powers are as clear as they are close: "del Patrimonio cultural, hoy, se espera una rentabilidad económica, y se inserta por distintas vías y con distintas formas en todos los discursos sobre desarrollo local, sostenible, territorial" (Today, cultural heritage is expected to provide an economic return, and is inserted in different ways and forms into all discourses on local, sustainable, territorial development).[15] As pointed out, for their part, by Bessière, Poulain, and Tibère, the exploitation of local food heritages is an economic driving force for the agricultural production of a territory, offering new options for development and building new forms of territorial appeal.[16] The promotion of products (through designations of origin, geographic indications, etc.), food crafts, recipe books, and local cuisines provides territories with socially constructed—and often consensual—singularities that articulate their uniqueness and that, at the same time, are a socioeconomic catalyst (with tourism playing no small part in this regard) that can help boost social cohesion and bolster identities. In such cases, heritage represents a considerable added value to be taken into account.

Food Heritage and Socioeconomic Development: Gastronomy as a Tourism Resource

The role of gastronomy in the definition and differentiation of tourism destinations is increasingly important at an international level. However, I believe that the concept should be as broad as possible, covering the entire agri-food chain, from production and productive landscapes to forms of preparation, consumption, dishes, restaurants, and even the use of resources. Sometimes, the definition of gastronomy covers, or attempts to cover, all or a significant part of this spectrum.[17] However, it is often the case that "gastronomy" has been focused on the final links of the food chain, giving priority to the selection, preparation, consumption, and appreciation of foods and dishes. Santich writes, for example, that gastronomy refers to the rules or norms regarding food and drink and can be expanded to include advice and guidance on what, where, when, and how to eat and drink, and in what combinations.[18] Similarly, in Scarpato's words, gastronomy in a tourism destination refers to "the reflective cooking, preparation, presentation and eating of food in general."[19] This is why, from our perspective, we refer principally to food in tourism, aiming to cover the entire aforementioned spectrum, and, when we speak of gastronomy, we shall also try to give it this conceptual breadth, which it has been denied so often.

Avoiding reductionist essentialisms and great modernizing policies that do not always fulfil their mandates, Gascón asserts that food-based tourism

> en tanto que propuesta turística post-fordista, valora la especificidad de la experiencia alimentaria. Y esta especificidad se basa en las variedades agrícolas locales producidas por campesinos y en la producción artesanal de alimentos elaborados. Productos peculiares, arraigados al territorio, y de producción limitada. Por tanto, huye de usos gastronómicos cosmopolitas y de la producción homogeneizadora que comporta la agricultura moderna y tecnificada.[20]

> *as a post-Fordist tourism proposal, attaches value to the specificity of the food experience. And this specificity is based upon local agricultural varieties produced by peasants and the artisanal making of food. [Food-based tourism] is about peculiar products rooted in the territory, and whose production is limited. Therefore, it avoids*

cosmopolitan gastronomies and homogenizing production that comes with modern technically enhanced agriculture.

It is obvious that no kind of tourist activity, certainly no kind of activity dedicated to food and gastronomy, can ignore specific requirements, such as effective food security and food safety. Nor can it avoid paying special attention to key aspects, such as the destinations' load capacity; the agreement, collaboration, and active participation of those involved; the collective rather than solely individual socioeconomic benefit; or the unnecessary adaptation of specific recipes to an alleged tourist taste. Nevertheless, food-based tourism appears, for the moment, to show a healthier balance in all the above aspects than other types of tourism (sun and beach or travels for attending festivals and conferences). So, if care is taken and unnecessary tensions around them avoided, this type of tourism may end up giving rise to relatively positive symbioses. According to Medina, Gómez Patiño, Puyuelo, and Tomás,

> El turismo enogastronómico aparece como una posibilidad aún por explorar, y que reúne distintos aspectos que son considerados como muy favorables por parte de los especialistas; a saber: menor presión turística y mayor sostenibilidad; mayor integración territorial y mayor incidencia de los beneficios en el territorio; mejor reparto social de los beneficios en los territorios locales; relación íntima con determinados productos (alimentos, vinos...) y platos que forman parte de la cultura local, estableciendo sin prejuicios el turismo enogastronómico dentro del marco del turismo cultural; relación en red entre las empresas turísticas y agroalimentarias; turismo de mejor calidad y mayor gasto por turista y día.[21]

> *Food and wine tourism is an unexplored possibility that boasts a range of features regarded as highly favourable by specialists, to wit: less tourist pressure and greater sustainability; greater territorial integration and a greater impact on benefits in the territory; better social allocation of the benefits in local territories; a close relationship with certain products (foods, wines, etc.) and dishes that form part of the local culture, placing food and wine tourism squarely within the framework of cultural tourism; the networked relationship between tourism and agro-food companies; better-quality tourism with a higher spend per tourist and per day.*

Espeitx remarks that "Los productos y los platos, la cocina de un territorio, cuando son *patrimonializados* con éxito, se convierten en auténticos recursos turísticos, perfectamente equiparables a otros elementos del patrimonio cultural" (products and dishes, a territory's cuisine, become, when successfully heritagized, real tourism resources, perfectly comparable with other elements of cultural heritage).[22] So it is that the heritagization that has been built from food culture is increasingly occurring within the framework of tourism and the local development discourse surrounding it. In addition to this, heritage is one of the main assets and attractions of tourism, especially that which is based around culture, as food/gastronomic tourism unquestionably is.[23] As a very significant and growing economic activity, tourism finds in gastronomic heritage a valuable resource for attracting visitors, one that is also highly adaptable to market demands, creating business in different sectors (production, restaurants, hotels, retail, etc.) and appearing to be able to weather the hardships of socioeconomic crises better than other tourism sectors.[24] Throughout 2020, for example, we could see how, having recently visited different territories, denominations of origin, food companies or shops, producers, and wineries as gastronomic tourists, people continued to order the same products and brands online during the Covid-19 pandemic. Gastronomic tourism brings visitors closer to the culture of a place through its local food. But it also facilitates the development of knowledge, as well as loyalty, to certain products or brands that can later be searched for and acquired at home. In this regard, the products purchased can evoke the good times spent during travels and allow producers to continue selling later, even in difficult times.

Food heritage also fully integrates into the economic and heritage-related field in another way: representative of a territory, its products can be given a boost by categories such as designations of origin, geographical indications, and other "quality" labeling that stimulates and preserves local production and also provides a tourist appeal that is closely linked to the territory.[25] As Tresserras, Medina, and Matamala argue, political and tourism policies have helped bolster the role of food products as heritage and a symbol of identity, although, in some cases, the authenticity of food heritage and its place in the collective imaginary is the subject of some dispute.[26] So, today, gastronomic tourism is defined as an activity created by agents (producers, processors, restaurateurs, etc.) whose chief goal is to provide tourists with an experience that may be enjoyed through food. In this regard, it is important to consider that, as these same authors explain, gastronomy is a decisive factor in planning the journeys and carrying them out.[27] Food is one of tourists' main expenditure items (in the form of local consumption, souvenirs, etc.). Additionally, gastronomic tourism possesses its own market, boosted by the development of the tourism sector and its need for diversification, without losing sight of the fact that tourism provides an exceptional platform for promoting food products and brands. In this regard, and in light of the above, we can see that heritage (the awareness of heritage and everything this implies with regard to the sense of cultural union between a product and a territory) holds a highly significant place within this context.

All these factors link concepts that, in our view, are of significant value: territory, gastronomy (agriculture-product-dish or production-sale-consumption), culture and heritage, and local development. Equally important are the relations with public, private, and civic power centers, as well as the political and economic players that are fostered by gastronomic heritage. The effects of heritagization on products, cuisines, or even forms of consumption are, therefore, many and varied. The selection and preservation of heritage is also a productive activity, creating economic value above and beyond any demands related to its belonging to what is symbolic and constitutive of memory, to territoriality, and to identity. All these discourses can be used by all power levels, of whatever type.

This differentiating ability of heritagized food culture can be—and often is—an effective tool for developing tourism in any territory. Indeed, food culture appears in all the leaflets, guides, brochures, and television advertisements promoting a given location's tourist appeal. There are many examples of the food-focused heritage initiatives, and these days, no proposal for any tourism initiative can fail to include, on a more or less central or more or less complementary basis, local produce and dishes.[28] According to Gascón, from the perspective of local rural communities, the heritagization and conservation of food as a tourism attraction can help to enhance the value of the farming production supplying its raw materials. This is a model characterized by the production of quality foods and sustainable agricultural production, as well as the creation of benefits for the ecosystem, which, unlike agroindustry, is mostly unsustainable and homogenizes landscapes and foods. From this standpoint, the intentional creation of gastronomic heritage appears, for Gascón, to be apposite and fitting.[29] The words of this author, who is usually highly critical of some forms of tourism and their impact, would appear to point toward a situation that, despite its obvious limitations (and risks), may end up becoming a factor for cultural heritage-based territorial development that involves local communities in both its construction and implementation, as well as in the enjoyment of its benefits.

Clearly, any tourism strategy associated with heritage and culture runs the obvious risk of banalization, commercialization, or even commodification or loss of authenticity.[30] Food heritage may lead to "translation," in the sense of the processes by which food becomes a tourist attraction, but also in the sense of how local cuisines are selected, modified, and translated so that they may be consumed by visitors (with the hypothetical loss of authenticity that this may entail). The debate is a long and complex one, and it does not seem that it will be resolved in the near future.

Conclusions

Over the course of this chapter, we have reviewed the intersections between food culture, heritage, and tourism from both a critical and a practical standpoint. It is based on cultural heritage being a social contract that is evolving and shifting (as is culture itself) and is built upon selections of some things over others. In this selection process, both experts and different types of powers play key roles in the activation and officialization of gastronomic heritage, and in all cases, they need to play a significant part in its management, conservation, and administration as a resource. Additionally, we argued that food products and practices are benchmarks in self-representation and the building of identities, meaning that the vocabulary of heritage has become strongly associated with them in recent decades. Nevertheless, this is a relatively recent heritage for officialdom, which has been forced to include aspects of intangible culture once difficult to identify but now included amongst the ranks of what is "heritagizable." Lastly, there is the final factor: tourism. The fact is food heritage is regarded as a tourism resource with great potential has become a core part of the management of culture and tourism, with the promotion of local products and culinary recipes forming part of the strategy for boosting local and regional economies.

To date, without ignoring possible limitations, like cultural tourism, gastronomic tourism has been held as a form of leisure that fits within the local productive structure without subordinating it (for the moment, at least) to the tourist industry. Similarly, it is a form of tourism that tends to involve the local community more integrally with what tourism offers and its benefits. Normally, it does not entail mass tourism and therefore does not exert excessive pressure on the territory. Proper monitoring of this point is, however, important, especially in urban destinations, some of which are already overcrowded. Differing experiences in the urban context, such as the huge number of tourist visits to some markets (like the Rialto in Venice and the Boqueria in Barcelona), call these claims into question and show the need for significant qualifications and specific studies.

There is no doubt that much is yet to be done. Firstly, given its economic importance and the role that food plays in building different local, regional, or national identities, the link between tourism and gastronomy continues to broadly require greater analytical and academic attention, from both gastronomic and tourism perspectives. Although it is growing in both prestige and business volume, gastronomic tourism, and the intersections of food, heritage, and tourism, has still not given rise to much analysis from an academic standpoint, whilst, from a technical and on-the-ground perspective, and despite its limited implementation, the actions and results have been rather more productive.

Secondly, we believe that food heritage is a unique form of heritage. Fungible and consumable, it must constantly be recreated within the cultural frameworks that are still being shaped and undergoing continuous evolution, calling for both flexibility and adaptability. These qualities, to date at least, have lagged behind the needs of everyday practices and, when they come into contact with tourism, need much more attention than they are currently receiving. The recognition of food-related heritage needs to be constantly redefined and honed, ensuring more specific analysis of how heritagization affects—both positively and negatively—different assets, what its practical relations with the powers that be are, how it is to be managed and preserved, how access and use are guaranteed, and how and in what way these assets become tourism resources. At the same time, on-the-ground analysis must be as critical as possible, detecting any points of friction and fostering practical debates and proper, speedy solutions to problems.

NOTES

1. F. X. Medina, "Reflexiones sobre el patrimonio y la alimentación desde las perspectivas cultural y turística," *Anales de Antropología* 51, no. 2 (2017): 106–13.
2. L. Smith, *Uses of Heritage* (New York: Routledge, 2006).
3. See A. Santana, "Patrimonio culturales y turistas: Unos leen lo que otros miran." *PASOS. Revista de Turismo y Patrimonio Cultural* 1, no. 1 (2003): 1–12.
4. Smith, *Uses of Heritage*, 6.
5. Santana, "Patrimonio culturales."
6. F. X. Medina, "Mediterranean diet: The Return of Tradition," *Rivista di Antropologia* 76, suppl. (1998): 344.
7. See J. Contreras, "El patrimonio alimentario en el área mediterránea," in *Patrimonio gastronómico y turismo cultural en el Mediterráneo*, eds. J. Tresserras and F. X. Medina (Barcelona: Universitat de Barcelona-Ibertur, 2007), 17–37; G. Laborde and F. X. Medina, "De los recetarios nacionales a los expedientes patrimoniales: cocinas, identidades y políticas estatales entre América y Europa," in *Alimentos, cocinas e inteercambios culinarios. Confrontaciones culturales, identidades, resignificaciones*, eds. R. Ávila, M. Álvarez, and F. X. Medina (Guadalajara: Estudios del Hombre/Universidad de Guadalajara, 2015), 89–104; F. X. Medina, "Mediterranean diet, culture and heritage: Challenges for a new conception," *Public Health Nutrition* 12, no. 9A (2009):

1618–1620; J.-P. Poulain, "Los patrimonios gastronómicos y sus valorizaciones turísticas," in *Patrimonio gastronómico y turismo cultural en el Mediterráneo*, eds. J. Tresserras and F. X. Medina (Barcelona: Universitat de Barcelona-Ibertur, 2007), 39–71.
8. Contreras, "El patrimonio alimentario," 21.
9. L. Prats, *Antropología y patrimonio* (Madrid: Ariel, 1997), 294.
10. Contreras, "El patrimonio alimentario."
11. I. de Garine, "Culture et nutrition," *Communications* 31 (1979): 82.
12. Prats, *Antropología*, 295.
13. C. Kelly, "Heritage tourism politics in Ireland," in *Cultural Tourism in a Changing World. Politics, Participation and (Re)presentation*, eds. M. K. Smith and M. Robinson (Clevedon, UK: Channel View Publications, 2006), 36.
14. Smith, *Uses of History*, 11.
15. E. Espeitx, "Patrimonio alimentario y turismo: una relación singular," *PASOS, Revista de turismo y patrimonio cultural* 2, no. 2 (2004): 195.
16. J. Bessière, J.-P. Poulain, and L. Tibère, "L'alimentation au coeur du voyage. Le rôle du tourisme dans la valorisation des patrimoines alimentaires locaux." in *Tourisme et recherche*, eds. J. Bessière, J.-P. Poulain, and S. Rayssac (Paris: Éditions Espaces, Tourismes Loisir, 2013), 76.
17. A.-M. Hjalager, "A typology of gastronomy tourism," in *Tourism and Gastronomy*, eds. A.-M. Hjalager and G. Richards (New York: Routledge, 2002), 21–36.
18. B. Santich, "The study of gastronomy and its relevance to hospitality education and training," *International Journal of Hospitality Management* 23 (2004): 15–24.
19. R. Scarpato, "Sustainable gastronomy as a tourist product," in *Tourism and Gastronomy*, eds. A.-M. Hjalager and G. Richards (New York: Routledge, 2002), 139.
20. J. Gascón, "Turismo, agricultura y alimentación. De la Teoría del Enlace a la patrimonialización de la gastronomía," in *Gastronomía y turismo en Iberoamérica*, eds. F. X. Medina and P. Leal Londoño (Gijón, Spain: Trea, 2018), 28.
21. F. X. Medina, M. Gómez Patiño, J. M. Puyuelo, and C. Tomás, "Turismo enogastronómico en España: cultura, patrimonio, economía y capacidad de reacción ante la crisis socioeconómica," in *Gastronomía y turismo en Iberoamérica*, eds. F. X. Medina and P. Leal Londoño (Gijón, Spain: Trea, 2018), 219.
22. Espeitx, "Patrimonio alimentario," 210.
23. J. Tresserras and F. X. Medina, eds., *Patrimonio gastronómico y turismo cultural en el Mediterráneo* (Barcelona: Universitat de Barcelona-Ibertur, 2007).
24. See Medina, Gómez Patiño, Puyuelo, and Tomás, "Turismo enogastronómico."
25. Espeitx, "Patrimonio alimentario."
26. J. Tresserras, F. X. Medina, and J. C. Matamala. "El patrimonio gastronómico como recurso en las políticas culturales y turísticas en España: el caso de Catalunya," in *Patrimonio gastronómico y turismo cultural en el Mediterráneo*, eds. J. Tresserras and F. X. Medina (Barcelona: Universitat de Barcelona-Ibertur, 2007), 236.
27. Ibid. 218.
28. Espeitx, "Patrimonio alimentario," 200.

29. Gascón, "Turismo," 28–29.
30. N. Macleod, "Cultural tourism: aspects on authenticity and commodification," in *Cultural Tourism in a Changing World. Politics, Participation and (Re)presentation*, eds. M. K. Smith and M. Robinson (Clevedon, UK: Channel View Publications, 2006), 177.

WORKS CITED

Bessière, J., J.-P. Poulain, and L. Tibère. "L'alimentation au coeur du voyage. Le rôle du tourisme dans la valorisation des patrimoines alimentaires locaux." In *Tourisme et recherche*, edited by J. Bessière, J.-P. Poulain, and S. Rayssac, 71–82. Paris: Éditions Espaces, Tourismes Loisir, 2013.
Contreras, J. "El patrimonio alimentario en el área mediterránea." In *Patrimonio gastronómico y turismo cultural en el Mediterráneo*, edited by J. Tresserras and F. X. Medina, 17–37. Barcelona: Universitat de Barcelona-Ibertur, 2007.
Espeitx, E. "Patrimonio alimentario y turismo: una relación singular." *PASOS, Revista de turismo y patrimonio cultural* 2, no. 2 (2004): 193–213.
Garine, I. de. "Culture et nutrition." *Communications* 31 (1979): 70–92.
Gascón, J. "Turismo, agricultura y alimentación. De la Teoría del Enlace a la patrimonialización de la gastronomía." In *Gastronomía y turismo en Iberoamérica*, edited by F. X. Medina and P. Leal Londoño, 15–32. Gijón, Spain: Trea, 2018.
Hjalager, A.-M. "A typology of gastronomy tourism." In *Tourism and Gastronomy*, edited by A.-M. Hjalager and G. Richards, 21–36. New York: Routledge, 2002.
Kelly, C. "Heritage tourism politics in Ireland." In *Cultural Tourism in a Changing World. Politics, Participation and (Re)presentation*, edited by M. K. Smith and M. Robinson, 36–55. Clevedon, UK: Channel View Publications, 2006.
Laborde, G., and F. X. Medina. "De los recetarios nacionales a los expedientes patrimoniales: cocinas, identidades y políticas estatales entre América y Europa." In *Alimentos, cocinas e inteercambios culinarios. Confrontaciones culturales, identidades, resignificaciones*, edited by R. Ávila, M. Álvarez, and F. X. Medina, 89–104 (Guadalajara: Estudios del Hombre/Universidad de Guadalajara, 2015).
Macleod, N. "Cultural tourism: aspects on authenticity and commodification." In *Cultural Tourism in a Changing World. Politics, Participation and (Re)presentation*, edited by M. K. Smith and M. Robinson, 177–90. Clevedon, UK: Channel View Publications, 2006.
Medina, F. X. "Mediterranean diet: The Return of Tradition." *Rivista di Antropologia* 76, suppl. (1998): 343–51.
———. "Mediterranean diet, culture and heritage: Challenges for a new conception." *Public Health Nutrition* 12, no. 9A (2009): 1618–1620.
———. "Reflexiones sobre el patrimonio y la alimentación desde las perspectivas cultural y turística." *Anales de Antropología* 51, no. 2 (2017): 106–13.
Medina, F. X., M. Gómez Patiño, J. M. Puyuelo, and C. Tomás. "Turismo enogastronómico en España: cultura, patrimonio, economía y capacidad de reacción ante la crisis

socioeconómica." In *Gastronomía y turismo en Iberoamérica*, edited by F. X. Medina and P. Leal Londoño, 201–23. Gijón, Spain: Trea, 2018.

Poulain, J.-P. "Los patrimonios gastronómicos y sus valorizaciones turísticas." In *Patrimonio gastronómico y turismo cultural en el Mediterráneo*, edited by J. Tresserras and F. X. Medina, 39–71. Barcelona: Universitat de Barcelona-Ibertur, 2007.

Prats, L. *Antropología y patrimonio*. Madrid: Ariel, 1997.

Santana, A. "Patrimonio culturales y turistas: Unos leen lo que otros miran." *PASOS. Revista de Turismo y Patrimonio Cultural* 1, no. 1 (2003): 1–12.

Santich, B. "The study of gastronomy and its relevance to hospitality education and training." *International Journal of Hospitality Management* 23 (2004): 15–24.

Scarpato, R. "Sustainable gastronomy as a tourist product." In *Tourism and Gastronomy*, edited by A.-M. Hjalager and G. Richards, 132–52. New York: Routledge, 2002.

Smith, L. *Uses of Heritage*. New York: Routledge, 2006.

Tresserras, J., and F. X. Medina, eds. *Patrimonio gastronómico y turismo cultural en el Mediterráneo*. Barcelona: Universitat de Barcelona-Ibertur, 2007.

Tresserras, J., F. X. Medina, and J. C. Matamala. "El patrimonio gastronómico como recurso en las políticas culturales y turísticas en España: el caso de Catalunya." In *Patrimonio gastronómico y turismo cultural en el Mediterráneo*, edited by J. Tresserras and F. X. Medina, 217–42. Barcelona: Universitat de Barcelona-Ibertur, 2007.

Part IV: Hard to Swallow

CHAPTER 10

Ideology "à la Carte"

Food Politics in Franco's Spain

Suzanne Dunai

The victory of the Nationalist Front that ended the Spanish Civil War (1936–1939) led to the consolidation of power and authoritarian dictatorship of Francisco Franco (1939–1975). The regime ushered in sweeping policies that attempted to dismantle the political, economic, and social structure of Spain's Second Republic in favor of a "New State" built on conservative ideology.[1] Whereas the nation was torn politically during the civil war, Franco's concept of a "New State" was consolidated under one political party, the F.E.T y de las J.O.N.S., and one leader, the Caudillo Franco, intent on uniting Spain under a singular culture of conservative values and a manufactured social peace based on repression. The edification of the New State through repressive and coercive policies transformed Spanish culture and how Spaniards experienced their everyday lives, including how they cooked a dish or ate a meal at home. The coalition that fueled the Nationalist front in the Spanish Civil War was propelled by ultra-nationalism, strict gender norms that highlighted social division, and religious conservatism. These values were written into the policies of the New State, including the legislation of the food supply. This chapter illustrates how the Franco regime attempted to embed political ideologies into the policies that shaped the physical production, distribution, and consumption of food, also known as a "foodway," as well as the divergence and refraction of messaging that occurred as food traveled from the public sphere to the private sphere. The ideologically driven nature of the dictatorship also monitored and censored the cultural meaning and symbolism of food in public discourse, but the internalization of food remained autonomous at the private, individual level. Ideology fueled food policy, policy created food culture, and food culture shaped everyday food habits, creating a "cultural foodway" as food discourse traveled from ideology to politics to the public sphere, finding its way into the private life of the home.

The objective of this chapter is twofold. First, it examines the mechanisms employed by the Franco regime to control food and by extension the Spanish population. Second, it identifies and disentangles the significance of individual acts within the practice of everyday life from the larger political environment of the time. How Spaniards bought food, the quantities that they were allowed to purchase, and the prices set by the state were all determined according to the food ideologies of the regime. At the same time, Franco's control of food weakened as food passed from the market to the family table, limiting the ability of the regime to enact nationalism, patriarchy, and Catholicism in the Spanish home. Because of this limitation, the Franco regime, while able to influence and shape consumer habits within public spaces, lacked totalitarian control over private life, and was ultimately unable to transform Spain's society into the desired New State.

The first section of this chapter explains how food ideologies were developed and enacted into policy in the aftermath of the Spanish Civil War. The "victors" of the civil war sought to instill conversative values into the conquered population, and food was a convenient mechanism to embed with Francoist ideology in that all Spaniards needed to eat. The subsequent sections demonstrate how policy became embedded with meaning and how the meaning was transformed as food discourse and food as a commodity traveled along its foodway. The practice of eating became a performance of nationalism, gendered views of a healthy body, and religious devotion for some Spaniards, but the fluctuations in food supply and the practice of everyday cooking and eating opened up forms of resistance, nonconformity, and acquiescence to the policies and culture of Franco's New State. Taken together, despite the attempt of the political and cultural apparatuses of the New State to create a singular, uniform culture that included how Spaniards cooked and ate their daily meals, individual Spaniards maintained agency within the Spanish food culture, thwarting the totalitarian goals of Franco and his regime.

Francoism as Food Policy

Within the Nationalist camp, the arms of the Franco regime—the military, the FET-JONS party, and the Catholic Church—took steps to infuse ideology and values within the practice of eating. The intent of the regime was to transform how Spaniards practiced their everyday lives, and through the daily action of eating, Spaniards would actively participate in the creation of Francoist culture. Recent scholarship by Lara Anderson has shown that food discourse during the Franco regime was "a potent biopolitical tool" by which individuals were submitted to rigid guidelines that "promoted a stoic, patriotic, ultra-nationalist, gendered, and healthy body."[2] The regime aimed to control Spaniards' characters by controlling how food was internalized and consumed within daily eating practices.

However, food—both discursively and physically—was a two-way street of power negotiation between the state and the individual. Food meaning continued to fracture and become reinterpreted as food discourse traveled from elite discussions to form state policy to daily, intimate conversations around a family table. While the meaning of food was manipulated by the regime from ideology into policy, food took on new meaning when it traveled from the public sphere of food markets and eateries into the private sphere of the home and the kitchen. Food scholars Kathleen LeBesco and Peter Naccarato identify food as a vehicle for both repressive and productive power by the state and the individual.[3] In other words, political power pushed into the home by way of policy, but individual power pushed back into the streets by way of consumer habits. For a Spanish example, the Franco regime restricted meat consumption to Tuesdays, Wednesdays, and Saturdays by limiting the days that meat could be sold to the public.[4] While this is a form of food power exercised by the state, the individual could always choose not to eat meat on the designated day. In other words, the Franco regime could not implement a uniform food ideology because individual variation would occur within each home and with every meal. While the state tried to coerce Spaniards into certain eating habits, this article elucidates how Spanish individuals maintained some of their autonomy in food practices.

Restrictions were placed on food at the aggregate level—dictating how food was grown, distributed, and priced for consumption throughout Spain—but in the private sphere, food served a very different role. Spanish families, particularly housewives, valued food not for its political significance or its export value, but for its role in a favorite recipe or dish. Within the home, food was viewed as an ingredient in a dish instead of a nationally controlled commodity. Regulations placed on the availability of food or its price were how the Nationalists sought to inscribe food with meaning. Wide distribution of a commodity communicated that the food was abundant or a staple product for a nationalized Spanish diet, while high prices and limited availability communicated that the item was a luxury or valuable good. But this top-down messaging mattered little when Spanish women bought the ingredient in amounts necessary for a recipe or because it was their favorite food. For this reason, the Franco regime sought to prescribe women's habits so that the food would be internalized within the home with the correct meaning. It was not enough to incentivize or restrict certain foods through availability or price regulation; they had to encourage Spanish women to shop according to the government's incentives and prohibitions as well.

In practice, the injection of social value into food was not as hegemonic or uniform as the Francoist state would have liked. There were three main factors that limited the creation of a monolithic state food culture. First, internal ideological divisions within the regime inhibited the uniformity of values encoded into Spanish foods. For example, the Madrid-based beer distributor Mahou benefitted greatly from its political connections with Franco's government through economic incentives and corporate favoritism, but its business of selling alcohol conflicted with the state's campaign for austerity and sobriety.[5] While it was not the intent of the regime to promote alcohol consumption, Mahou used its government favoritism to incentivize Spaniards to drink their beer as a patriotic act. Likewise, state-managed dining halls run through the *Auxilio Social* program provided much-needed food to impoverished families during the 1940s, but state-served meals stymied family-style meals within the home that were prepared by a Spanish housewife.[6] While much of the food culture of the 1940s was a direct consequence of state ideology, many of the ultra-conservative values supported the regime were incompatible at the level of food policy.

Second, when purchasing power allowed for it, individuals varied their diets according to personal taste and preferences. Regardless of food shortages, many Spaniards retained the ability to decide how much salt or spice to add to a dish or whether to use boiling or roasting as a cooking method for an ingredient. While the acute consumer shortages in the aftermath of the civil war greatly limited food availability for many families, Spaniards slowly regained some of their food choice during the 1940s. The growth in consumer power and opportunity to pursue consumer preference varied greatly by class and political affiliation, with wealthier Spaniards having greater access to a diverse array of luxury goods. Still, while the publications of the FET-JONS instructed Spanish women to prepare a recipe following specific instructions, housewives maintained their autonomy to add less salt, substitute one type of fish for another, or add extra sauce to a dish according to their individual tastes. Thus, despite explicit instructions on what to cook and how to cook, Spanish housewives maintained the ability to adapt or ignore these recipes within their homes.

Third, food sub-cultures persisted among certain demographics of the population, especially those with dietary restrictions or in specific regions. As Josep Roselló analyzed in the case of the Naturalist movement, much of naturalist culture was repressed by Franco due to its ties with anarchism during the Second Republic.[7] However, their tenet of vegetarianism fit well with the meat shortages suffered in Spanish cities during the 1940s and coincided with the Catholic doctrine of meatless days during Lent. Similarly, most cookbooks published during the Franco regime were written in Castilian Spanish, but a few cookbooks in the Basque and Catalan regional languages represented those regional cultures within their cooking publications.[8] The bulk of culinary cultural production occurred in Castilian Spanish during this time, but food subcultures within different regional languages of Spain persisted. Likewise, fish and seafood remained abundant and available along Spain's coastal cities, where seafood was an integral part of the diet.[9] Seafood rarely traveled to the interior of Spain, leaving the people of Madrid with very little fish as part of their diet or cuisine. Thus, regional and philosophical subcultures of food consumption remained despite the regime's control of the country's food supply. While these are just a few examples, there is sufficient evidence to indicate that small cracks in the Francoist food culture existed. Although there was little food, Spaniards retained some of their individuality and agency in their daily meals.

Food discourse broke down or was re-signified at every injunction from policy to print, cooking to eating. The Franco regime was a coalition of multiple influences that broadly agreed on conservative values, but disparities existed in the ideological details. Conservatives recognized the value in culturally embedding meaning within the practice of eating and assigning meaning to the commodities of food, but what constituted conservative consumption was more ambiguous and a subject of contention between government technocrats, party leaders, military officials, and church clergy. Using meat as an example, military officials considered meat an important source of protein and necessary for strong soldiers and Spanish men. But meat was also expensive to produce and conflicted with meatless days within the Catholic religious calendar, leading government technocrats and religious leaders to consider meat more of a luxury item than an essential food. Because of discrepancies in the vision for specific foodstuffs in Spanish society, the food ideology of Francoism never fully congealed into a singular set of values, and the regime failed to implement a hegemonic, totalitarian culture on Spanish society. Policy was inconsistently enforced on a daily basis, leading to ignorance or resistance to its implementation. Nationalist culture was limited by countercultures that blocked aspects of the original message from being transmitted and internalized. By the time food reached the Spanish household, much of the original ideological intent was lost. Thus, far from creating a totalitarian culture or repression, Spanish food culture became a site for the practice of multiple subcultures.

Nationalizing Cuisine in Franco's New State

Spanish nationalism was one of the fundamental values that the Franco regime attempted to infuse into daily eating habits. Ultra-nationalist ideology and policy informed Spain's food policies during the 1940s and specifically targeted women's activities in the home and their relation to food via cooking and serving meals to their families. Within the New State, Spanish patriotism was expressed through glorifying the total victory of the Francoist army during the Spanish Civil War, so the regime promoted a nationalized Spanish diet to celebrate and reinforce their victory. While there were no set ingredients that were uniformly eaten across Spain, a nationalized diet was established through a system of repression and coercion that controlled the availability of certain goods. The Franco regime subsidized certain foods, which incentivized their consumption across the country. While these subsidized foods would change periodically, they were widely available across the country. Other foods were repressed through high prices or were only available illegally through the black market.[10] While some Spaniards were able to quickly adopt patriotic eating habits compatible to Franco's New State, others failed to conform to the nationalist diet due to lack of food availability.

The regime's food policies prioritized national identity above regional or local identities, asserted the importance of celebrating Spain's imperial past, and glorified rural life over urban society. To promote Spanish nationalism, the regime implemented an economic system of autarky, or self-sufficiency, which, when applied to food policy, promoted a Spanish diet of traditional ingredients as well as regulated consumer habits.[11] One of the premises of autarky was that Spaniards were to only consume what was produced in Spain and to sacrifice the consumption of foreign goods as a sign of devotion to the nation.[12] As historian Carlos Barciela laments, Franco considered himself knowledgeable enough in economics to create his own policy, ignoring actual economic expertise to guide the creation of policy.[13] His inner circle also lacked economic knowledge, so policy was largely based on ideology. Blaming the economic hardship of the 1940s on the "anti-economics" of the Second Republic, the regime claimed that all economic decisions made by Franco were in the service of the country.[14] The policy of autarky was based on ideology rather than economic reality, exacerbating the dismal living conditions in the aftermath of the civil war.

In theory, autarky implied that Spaniards only consumed products produced in Spain by Spanish farmers or processed in Spanish factories. Bananas came from the Canary Islands, grapes from Almeria, milk from Asturias, and fish from both the Mediterranean and the Atlantic, so the Spanish population could enjoy a diversified yet traditional Spanish diet.[15] Yet in practice, many Spaniards went hungry—especially those living in cities—because rural areas retained their harvests to feed themselves, choosing the monotony of their own harvests over trust in the Francoist system to properly redistribute Spain's food supply. This distrust was compounded by the destruction of many of the roads and trains used to transport food across regions during the war. Individual diets were influenced heavily by the local availability of goods and by the limited infrastructure that survived the war. This prioritized local power dynamics over the official national food ideology and the intended message of Francoism. Many regional farmers and community leaders distrusted the plan to send away their harvests with the hope that other regions would satisfy their food needs, so they hoarded more of their own food supply instead of distributing food throughout Spain.[16] For rural Spaniards, a monotonous diet was preferable to an inadequate one, so few goods produced in Spain made it into national circulation, and Spaniards who lived in cities experienced hunger. Some farmers provided Spanish cities with luxury goods to maximize their profits, but for most Spaniards, the most affordable food was what was available locally. Franco's desire for a nationalized diet was impossible because Spaniards no longer trusted each other to exchange commodities on the national market nor did they trust the Francoist government to manage the distribution of the food supply from farm to market.

Nonetheless, with food policies in place that affirmed Francoist nationalist identity, the act of eating could be considered a patriotic act as long as Spanish cooks followed the prescribed recipe laid out through food policies. Spaniards could perform their patriotism with the consumption of every autarkic meal. When women bought and prepared food for their families in the home, state ideology was either affirmed or ignored through eating a meal in the private sphere. When Spanish women cooked using state-promoted ingredients such as oranges or rice, the meal itself could be considered a form of devotion and service to Franco's New State project.[17] Thus, cooking practices were considered women's contribution to Spain, and the preparation of family meals were communicated to women to be their patriotic duty.

State-sponsored publications led the way in instructing Spaniards in the contours of national cuisine in Franco's New State. For example, publications by the FET-JONS party included magazines such as *Alimentación Nacional*, *Medina*, and *Y: Revista para la mujer*, as well as the newspaper *Arriba*, all of which praised and promoted Franco's food policy within Spain's tightly controlled public sphere. Supporters of the Francoist government followed suit by publishing material that praised Francoist food policies and promoted the food ideologies of the regime. The technocrat Antonio Barroso Rodríguez published the study *Pan Para España* in 1949 that argued that the import of foreign goods threatened the country's security and power. It also criticized the consumption of processed foods, advocating that fresh foods from the countryside were superior to industrial foods.[18] This argument achieved several objectives. First, it affirmed the glorification of Spain's natural, rural bounty. Second, it obscured the shortcomings of the Spanish government to adequately develop the country's food processing industries, which were woefully underdeveloped compared to other European countries at the time. During the early twentieth century, many of Spain's processed foods, such as canned meat or packaged biscuits, were imported from Britain, so the consumption of British foods subverted the ultra-nationalist objectives of autarky. Rather than reporting the limitations of the ideologically driven policy—that Spain lacked the infrastructure to distribute and store industrialized foods—state technocrats perpetuated Francoist extreme nationalism by adhering and supporting state food policy of eating nationally grown foods and abstaining from foreign ingredients. State-vetted print culture ranging from the newspaper *Alimentación Nacional* to the women's magazine *Medina* affirmed Francoist policy, which further propped up the nationalist ideology embedded in food habits.

Following the lead of state-sponsored publications, Juan Ortiz Such (using the pen name Alberto León) published the cookbook *La Cocina clásica española* in 1941 with the intent of glorifying the nutritional benefits and diversity of Spanish cuisine. The cookbook highlighted the seasonality of Spanish foods and the nutritional benefit of Spanish food for the Spanish race. He declares in the prologue: "Este es precisamente nuestro pensamiento: dar preferencia a las viejas normas culinarias españolas sobre las demás reglas extranjeras, que ni se acomodan a nuestros paladares, ni están en consonancia con nuestro clima ni con nuestras circunstancias geográficas" (This is our thought on the matter: [we] need to prioritize the old Spanish style of cooking over those of foreign nations. Those foods do not suit our tastes, and their products are not conducive to be grown in our climate or geography).[19] The book, in accordance with the ideology celebrated in Franco's New State, affirmed national ideology by claiming the superiority of Spanish goods and the exceptionalism of Spanish products as superior to foreign foods.

Ortiz Such clarifies this point in a critical way. While he claims that Spanish cooking was best for the country, he praises the merits of foreign styles of cooking, just not for the Spanish people. He writes: "Cada nacional tiene el deber de conservar lo que la diferencia, lo que forma parte de su modo peculiar. Bien está que sepamos guisar a la francesca, a la italiana y hasta a la rusa y a la china, pero la base de nuestra mesa, por ley natural, tiene que reincidir en lo español" (Every nation should preserve their own style of cooking that distinguishes them from other countries and makes them unique. It is good that we know how to cook in the French style or the Italian style, even Russian and Chinese, but the foundation of our dishes, determined by natural law, should be the Spanish style).[20] In essence, the cookbook claims that the Spanish way is best for Spain, not the best in the world as Franco's nationalism would suggest. Similar to the Social Service program that taught Spanish women how to cook in a specified "Spanish" manner, *La cocina clásica española* promotes a singular style of cooking that is considered "Spanish style," and it was the duty of Spanish women to cook according to the nationalized cooking methods.[21] Abiding by the precedent set by state publications, the rhetoric adopted in this exemplary cookbook promotes Francoist food culture and ideology.

In practice, Franco's food policies lacked pragmatism and engagement with Spain's post-civil war social reality, leading to mismanagement of already scarce resources with poor implementation and enforcement.[22] The disparities between the motivation behind a policy and the actual application of the law created an uneven food culture. On the one hand, ideology and policy glorified the richness and bounty of Spain's countryside, but many markets suffered from empty shelves and Spaniards from hungry bellies.[23] Spaniards were encouraged to eat a standardized diet that was carefully curated through rationing and price-setting, but in practice, Spaniards ate whatever foods they could find during the shortages of the 1940s. Reports of eating banana peels or shrimp shells indicate that Spaniards satisfied their hunger through shifting social definitions of edibility in order to survive.[24] The country's foodscape incorporated some aspects of Francoist ideology, while other ideological points were obscured by Spaniards' impulse for survival and their abysmal social reality. A cultural spectrum ranging from affirmation to resistance developed in response to Franco's food policy, far from the uniformity of national identity desired by the regime.

Even so, additional incongruities existed within the realm of national ideology. One critical caveat to the glorification of Spanish cuisine was that it included foods from former imperial lands in the Americas, such as black beans with cheese and Salvadorean empanadas.[25] Cooking recipes and eating dishes that celebrated Spain's colonial past was one way that Spaniards could affirm Francoist food nationalism. The Franco regime glorified the export of Spanish traditions to the Americas through centuries of conquest and colonization, and food was one way that Spaniards could glorify the Catholic monarchs. The introduction to the special edition of the women's magazine drew parallels between the conquest of diverse lands by the Catholic monarchs and their unification under one flag and one faith to the civil war led by Franco and the nationalists.[26] By incorporating diverse foods from the former empire, Spaniards symbolically ate Franco's conquest and conversion of Spain in the New State.

Thus, despite Franco's ideology of Spanish isolation and the policy of autarky, an exception was made for the United States and Latin America and the movement of peoples and goods from across the Atlantic continued during the 1940s, especially through Catholic networks. With a national discourse of racial superiority and conquest adapted for Francoism, only some foods from Latin America were accepted. The regime prioritized European culture over mestizo, indigenous, or enslaved cultures, despite their fundamentality to the region's cultural heritage. The Americas, both real and in popular imagination, were very much part of Spain's empire-building and proved vital to Franco's nation-building project after the civil war. The connections forged between Spain and its former colonies crossed diplomatic, religious, literary, economic, and political ties, but the cultural exchanges and integration took on new meaning with the cooption of *Hispanidad* by the Franco regime.[27]

The glorification of Spain's imperial conquests was written into the recipes that were printed in women's magazines. The October 1940 issue of the women's magazine *Menaje* guided women in how to celebrate Spain's past empire with flavorful dishes that "tienen mucho de parecido con nuestra propia cocina, conservándose en general con robustez de contenido y exentos de exotismo" (are very similar to our own [Spanish] cooking, generally maintaining the richness of the dish and lacking exoticism).[28] The racialization of the Americas was clear from the cover of the magazine. It bore a dark-complexioned woman carrying fruit on her head and braided hair. The background contains Spanish galleons with the Christian cross on their sails clearly visible. The magazine contains forty-one recipes to represent a country or region of Latin America or the southwestern United States. The descriptions did not contain additional cultural information for the readers, such as the significance or origin of the dish. And next to, but very much separated from the Hispanic-American recipes, were many recipes considered quintessentially Spanish, such as "fideos cazadores" (hunter's noodles) and "remo hervido en salsa divina" (wing boiled in divine sauce).[29]

Spain's connection to the Hispanic world was not only imported in the form of culinary discourse through exoticized recipes meant to reminisce upon the former glories of conquest and empire, but also by Franco Spain's heavy reliance upon aid in the form of donated foodstuffs from its former colonies. The United States (considered by the regime as part of Spain's former empire), Argentina, and Uruguay all sent relief aid to Spain during and after the Spanish Civil War.[30] In the case of Uruguay, the country supplied aide through the networks of the Catholic Church, sending as many Bibles and religious texts as cans of preserved meat.[31] Although Spaniards greatly needed foodstuffs due to the food shortages caused by civil war and autarky, the regime skewed the delivery of humanitarian aid to promote Franco's ambition for soft empire in the Americas.

IDEOLOGY "À LA CARTE"   249

Figure 10.1. *Menaje para la mujer,* año X, núm 18. October, 1940.
With thanks to the Biblioteca Francesca Bonnemaison, Fonds Cuina

In sum, despite the ideological efforts of the Franco regime to create a uniformed national identity, Spain's food culture consisted of a diversity of local, regional, and international ingredients and cooking techniques. Ultra-nationalism fueled the adoption of the economic policy of autarky, which stated that Spaniards would only consume Spanish products and that rural life was preferable to that in cities. The mismanagement of agricultural resources and inconsistent bans on imports led to chronic food shortages and the inconsistent arrival of foreign aid. Government publications failed to accurately report the food situation in Spain's major cities, choosing instead to affirm ideological objectives rather than solving the food crisis. As a consequence, some Spaniards affirmed their loyalty to Spain by eating Spanish products prepared in a prescribed "Spanish" way, but others consumed Latin American food prepared according to regional or local customs. The Spanish foodscape continued to consist of diverse ingredients and dishes, although scarcity of foodstuffs remained a persistent problem in Franco's New State.

Rationing Health: Nourishing the Gendered Body

Similar to how nationalism traveled from abstract ideology to the Spanish table, discourse on gender and the Spanish body was conceptualized as ideology, written into policy, and adapted into food habits to be consumed in the home. The Franco regime glorified the importance of health for the preservation and future of the Spanish collective body. Similar to other fascist parties in Italy and Germany, the FET-JONS also adopted sport and physical education as an important part of nation-building, and nutrition was an important aspect of health.[32] However, the desire for healthy Spaniards collided with the regime's gender ideal, so men and women were assigned separate expectations for healthy weights and dietary needs. Men were expected to consume nutrients and calorically dense foods according to their professions—intellectuals and soldiers requiring more calories than workers.[33] Women were discouraged from working outside the home, and their caloric consumption as housewives and mothers was discouraged for causing obesity.[34] In discourse, Spanish medical experts and intellectuals debated the proper levels of calories necessary for Spaniards according to their age, gender, and medical conditions. Many doctors retained patriarchal bias in their approach to science, using biological determinism to shape gender in society and what Spaniards should eat. With nutrition science firmly planted within a patriarchal discourse, the female aesthetic was contoured in magazines, newspapers, and radio announcements to control women's eating habits.

To control the distribution of food within the New State, the Franco regime adopted a rationing system that dictated the diet of Spaniards from 1939 until 1952. The system was family-based from 1939 until 1943, with ration coupons issued to male heads of household, followed by individual ration cards and the eventual phasing out of the program in 1952. The impetus of Spain's rationing system was to standardize food consumption among Spaniards and to unite the population into one collective national body through a common meal.[35] The implementation of a rationing system provided different quantities of food for men and women, young and old.[36] Once the standards were set through food provisioning, magazines reinforced these divisions by glorifying thin female bodies and muscular male bodies in articles and pictures. While the ideals of the masculine and feminine body in Spanish print culture were not new, the implementation of a patriarchal rationing system that divided access to food according to sex was unique to the war and post-civil war society. Cultural ideals for gendered body types were imposed on Spanish individuals—especially women—through Francoist policies.

Curiously, health professionals and the publishers of the time lamented the problem of obesity as much, if not more, than the issue of hunger. Anderson identifies the erasure of hunger during the early Franco dictatorship through censorship of reports on famine.[37] Yet weight-loss articles and advertisements for diet pills peppered the media of the 1940s. Dr. Carlos Blanco Soler, appointed as director of the Spanish Red Cross at the end of the civil war, claimed that obesity was such a major problem of the time that the only solution was to lower the food supply.[38] Concurrent with the food shortages and hunger suffered by many Spaniards during the 1940s, nutritionists and health enthusiasts launched a weight-loss campaign, directed mostly toward Spanish women, to consume less food.

Spanish medical experts expressed concern for the country's "obesity problem," and some of the medical knowledge trickled down to popular printing of the time. For example, the women's magazine *Menaje*, published in Barcelona in the 1940s, periodically ran advertisements for weight-loss pills from the companies such as Sabelin.[39] Diet ads played on the radio during women's programming and appeared in women's sections of mainstream newspapers, and moderation of and abstention from food fit well within the principles of autarky. The development and marketing for these diet products were supported by the obesity research conducted by Dr. Andrius Vander, Dr. Carlos Jimenez Diaz, Dr. Carlos Blanco Soler, and Dr. José Serret Tristany, all of whom concluded that obesity was a serious national problem that could lead to other illnesses such as gout or diabetes. A form of consensus formed between doctors and popular culture, one that advocated for an ideal Spanish figure and the other that displayed a thin national body as the feminine ideal. The coercion of the Spanish body to fit the Francoist ideal took form as policy. As with nationalism, these policies were specifically targeted to women because they were considered the principal consumers for a household and therefore the most in need of policing. Legislation dictated clothing designs, food rationing, and pharmaceutical products, while propaganda created a coercive aesthetic for women.

Despite the amount of academic scholarship on hunger during the early Franco dictatorship, few studies have focused on the significance of obesity literature within the larger social history of Spain in the 1940s. Historian Giraldez Lomba dismisses the ads as an expression of ambivalence and also the opulence of the Spanish elite, concluding that diet pills showed the great disparity between rich and poor.[40] Wealthy Spaniards were able to eat too much while poor Spaniards ate too little. But these diet ads did not exist within a political or cultural vacuum.

Women's magazines and weight loss books could be confined to wealthier women who had expendable wealth and were literate, but radio ads reached the popular classes as well. The concerns for Spanish subjects' expanding waistlines were reinforced by many medical experts and nutritionists of the time and echoed throughout popular culture that reached multiple classes of individuals. Thus, the phenomena of dieting during a famine correlates to the food culture and food policies of the era that restricted food available for women.

The condemnation of obesity was not directed toward all Spaniards but rather specifically toward Spanish housewives. Dr. Andrius Vander reported that ten out of every one hundred Spanish women over the age of 55 were obese, while only one out of every hundred Spanish men fell into that category.[41] His diet guide, with the hefty price of twenty-five pesetas, *La Obesidad: Su curación radical y definitive*, only features images of women, making his intended audience clear. Another physician, Dr. Carlos Jiménez Díaz, published that many women were prone to gain weight during motherhood due to their idleness during the day. He claimed, "Pero evidentemente no todo sujeto delgado lo es a permanencia; hay por el contrario muchas personas delgadas durante su juventud y adolescencia que a media que alcanzan la madurez van aumentando de peso para llegar a hacerse obesas; ocurre esto con especial frecuencia en mujeres después del matrimonio y haber tenido hijos" (There are many people who are thin during their youth and adolescence but then gain weight disproportionately as they mature to become obese. This occurs with special frequency in women after marriage and having children).[42] Medical discourse from the time targeted women to lose weight, and these ideas echoed through society's fashion and cuisine.

Diet fads fit well within the objective of the Francoist state to restrict and manipulate the Spanish body. A healthy Spanish body would best imply a healthy Spanish society. The application of the standardized rationing system for all Spaniards achieved the uniformity desired by the regime, but it did not accommodate for variation of nutritional needs and the special dietary requirements to treat obesity, anemia, malnutrition, lathyrism, gout, or diabetes. The imposition of a top-down food policy created a paradox—standardized food distribution created uniform eating practices but would not create uniform Spanish bodies because individual Spaniards required individual diets based on their metabolic needs.

Religious Eating: The Role of the Catholic Church in Cooking Practices

Food and religion were intertwined within Spanish culture long before the establishment of National-Catholicism under the Franco dictatorship.[43] Cooking often contained religious significance with feasts and fasts throughout the religious calendar, which provided Spaniards the opportunity to act in devotion or heresy. With the creation of Franco's New State and imposition of traditional Catholic beliefs in policy, cooking and eating practices could be interpreted as a form of adherence or acquiescence to Francoist culture. Church doctrine affirmed the familial aspects of Francoism that strictly prescribed men's and women's roles within the family and Christian society. Historian Ángela Cenarro termed the marriage between the Catholic Church and the Franco regime as "divine totalitarianism," or the implementation of Catholic coercive norms through the intervention of the Franco dictatorship.[44] Spain was a Catholic nation, so piety was considered an affirmation of the country's heritage and cultural identity. Furthermore, religion provided an inlet into the private life of Spaniards, and this included how and what Spaniards ate. Food became one of many ways that Spaniards performed their religious convictions, in both the home and in public life.

Initiatives such as the "plato único" (one plate) program contained many elements of the Catholic religion—austerity, sacrifice, devotion, weekly practice—that were reformatted from the faith to apply to secular food policy. The Nationalists began the "one plate" program during the Spanish Civil War to garner popular support for the war effort and to raise money for Nationalist war veterans. As historians Comín Comín and Martorell Linares have concluded, the "one plate" program was adopted so that the wealthy, who stayed safe behind the front lines, could still contribute to the war effort with only the inconvenience of reduced food options.[45] The one plate program was later expanded to include one day without dessert. On Mondays, Spaniards were to abstain from consuming desserts in restaurants, cafés, or bars, and the restaurant was to make a 10% charitable contribution to Nationalist veteran organizations.[46] Abstaining from luxuries such as dessert and sacrificing food choice at a restaurant was presented to Spanish consumers through policy written in a religious tone in an effort to evoke devotion to the needs of the state. Particularly focused on public eating, Francoist religiosity was on display for everyone to see, and programs such as "one plate" day and "day without dessert" were intended to redirect Spaniards' Catholic devotion to the needs of the New State, creating an austere and sacrificial public life.

Austerity was also practiced within the religious calendar's days of abstention and religious food prohibition. The abstention from certain foods followed the religious calendar and shaped Spain's foodscape during the Franco dictatorship. Whereas celebratory menus remained largely within the private domain of the individual or the family, Catholic fast days conveniently relieved some of the pressure on the regime to provision the population. For example, the Catholic

Church required the abstention of meat during Lent, and to further enforce this belief, the regime required restaurants to serve vegetarian foods during the meatless days.[47] The prohibitions and regulations established in the privacy of the home were mirrored in the public spaces of restaurants.

Despite the greater intervention of the state into regulating and enforcing religious fasts through food policies, there were ample ways for Spaniards to ignore and resist these requirements. Even though meat could not be sold on certain days, Spaniards could always eat preserved or leftover meat in their home. Likewise, abstention or consumption of certain foods did not necessarily carry the same religious significance for individuals. Spaniards could choose to eat a plant-based diet for health or ethical reasons and not because it was mandated by the Catholic Church. Vegetarians and vegans, while a minority of the Spanish population, had their dietary beliefs coincide with practicing Catholics on meatless days.[48] Although both groups enjoyed plant-based meals as a substitute for meat on certain days, it was not for the same religious beliefs or convictions as the regime wanted. Although Catholic doctrine aimed to instill religious piety among its practitioners in a way that became visible within the practice of everyday life, neither the Catholic Church nor the Franco regime could control the beliefs that motivated adherence to the religious calendar of feasting and fasting.

As food passed from ideology to policy, the cultural implications of religious eating were applied unevenly to Spanish society. Catholic charity was as prevalent in 1940s Spain as the need for humanitarian relief, and charitable programs incorporated religion into food service. Charitable dining halls required a prayer before each meal, and every dining area included a crucifix and a portrait of Franco.[49] For those who relied on meals from the state or the Church charity programs, prayer became entrenched in daily life because it was contingent on receiving a meal. Pictures of Christ and Franco overlooked hungry Spaniards as they consumed their meals, bringing a new significance to the watchful surveillance of the state. Nonetheless, despite the presence of charity workers to monitor the patrons and enforce the bowing of heads during the prayer prior to every meal, the state could not control the minds of Spaniards or force them to pray.

In general, the Church supported these initiatives for Franco's New State because it furthered the reach of the Church into daily life. Some religious intellectuals considered the Eucharist a full meal both spiritually and physically, and priests wrote sermons on food-provisioning miracles in the Bible and how Christ was bread and nourishment enough for his flock. The Pious Society of Saint Paul connected the food issues of the 1940s with scriptures well. They wrote: "Tan necesario como el estar bien convencido de que Jesús está realmente presente en la Sagrada Eucaristía, es el estar bien persuadido de esta otra verdad: de que en este divino

Sacramento ha querido darnos el Señor algo que sirva y sea para ser comido, es decir, un verdadero alimento" (Just as it is important to be convinced that Jesus is really present in the Sacred Eucharist, another truth is also just as important: that the divine Sacrament that is given to us by our Lord is a form of food. That is to say, a truly nourishing food).[50] The Church drew a connection between the physical and spiritual need of Spaniards to be fed. By utilizing Spaniards' physical hunger and desire to eat regular meals during the food shortages of the 1940s, the Church was able to further its mission to nourish the spiritual starvation that it perceived had occurred during the Second Republic and Spanish Civil War. Some Spaniards eagerly received communion for its spiritual nourishment while others sought its physical sustenance instead. Although the Church emphasized the spiritual aspect of communion, it could not control how Spaniards interpreted and internalized the meal.

At other times, religion clashed with the food policy enacted by the Franco regime or with the material consequences of Franco's food policies. For example, as noted previously, the "one plate" program was promoted in Spanish cities using religious terminology as a means to promote adherence and devotion to the initiative. By equating fewer consumer options with religiosity, Spaniards were able to affirm their status as good Catholics by participating in restaurant culture. But this program came under fire during days of Catholic fasting from meat. Practicing Catholics found that some restaurants and hotels only served meat dishes to adhere to the "one plate" rule, and restaurants chose to serve meat because it was more lucrative and valued by the public. To remedy this potential religious taboo, the state allowed for three meal options to be served on the designated "one plate" day: one meat, one fish, and one vegetarian.[51] By accommodating the needs of practicing Catholics, the purpose of having "one plate" expanded into three, providing consumers more food choices than those offered by the state or church.

Within the home, Catholic cooking involved celebrating religious holidays with family and abstaining from taboo foods during times of fasting. One article in the women's magazine *Medina*, "Stuffed Vegetables for Days without Meat," provided recipes for making stuffed eggplant, stuffed zucchini in omelet, fish-stuffed cucumbers, and vegetable-stuffed tomatoes. The introduction of the recipes is revealing. The article tells its readership, "Os quejáis algunas veces de que una comida sin carne no resulta sustanciosa; probar a servir esos días un plato de legumbres rellenas y veréis cómo os resulta más nutritivo y mucho más agradable al paladar. No os cansaréis de ella" (You've heard complaints at times that a meal without meat is not filling. Try and serve our stuffed legume dishes and you will see that the meals are more nutritious and more enjoyable to eat. You will never tire of them).[52] The article acknowledges the religious taboo of eating meat during Lent and other fast days, but it dismisses the inconvenience or blandness of meat-abstention for religious purposes. At no point does the article question or justify why Spanish women needed to cook without meat, but the article assumes that Spanish women would follow the instructions without question. The article provides housewives with solutions to live and cook during times of religious fasting, but its author also assumes that its readers would follow the ritual without hesitation or criticism.

Other cookbooks and women's magazines followed the lead of publications of the FET-JONS party in promoting special recipes to celebrate Christmas and Lent, stressing the importance of the meal by emphasizing the need for special foods and large portions. Barcelona home economist Gonzalo Bosch Bierge created a cookbook that included recipes for Holy Week. The author stressed the importance of sacrifice and somber attitudes during Lent while simultaneously promoting consumerism by juxtaposing advertisements for "Lavasol" laundry soap and "Bably" cough syrup along with the religious recipes.[53] For example, while providing a brief religious lesson on Holy Week and the Last Supper from the Bible, readers were treated to coupons for free "Potax" soup packets.[54] Another cookbook, *Comidas de vigilia: Las Mejores recetas para prepararlas* by Bernard de Ferrer presented 105 recipes that a resourceful Spanish housewife could prepare to celebrate fast days.[55] Unlike Bosch Bierge, Bernard de Ferrer did not include any advertisements or explanation for religious observance in her book. Instead, she offered meat-free recipes to keep meals interesting and the family satisfied. Her recipes consisted of artichokes, cod, cheeses, eggs, legumes, potatoes, and fish as the main ingredient. Because the book did not attach any religious meaning to the recipes through a prologue or description, many of the dishes resembled meals that could be eaten on any given day. Thus, although religious observance was an important part of Spanish life during the dictatorship, meals could be diluted of their religious significance in the practice of everyday life.

Christmas was another religious holiday that required special recipes to celebrate. The FET-JONS magazine *Medina* recommended that Spanish women prepare the most luxurious meal of the year to celebrate, publishing an article on how to choose the best turkey at the market.[56] Bosch Bierge also created a cookbook for Christmas cuisine as an alternative source of holiday recipes to the FET-JONS publication, but still his recipes and commentary on Christmas reinforced many of the party's values of family and gender stereotypes. Like *Medina*, the book included instructions on how to prepare a Christmas bird, but it also provided readers more leeway in the type of fowl a housewife could select for the Christmas Eve dinner. The author wrote, "De todas maneras, aunque no todos pueden llegar el orgulloso pavo, hay escalones descendentes hasta el vulgar pollo, con mayor o menor lujo de huesos, y rara es la familia que no goza en esos días del plato de pluma" (Nonetheless, although some families are not able to enjoy a prized turkey on Christmas, there are many degrees of fowl available in the markets, all the way to the humble chicken. Chicken has fewer bones and less richness than a turkey, but scarce is the family that doesn't take pride in a feathered dish on this special day).[57] Unlike his cookbook for Holy Week, Bosch Bierge's cookbook omitted mention of religious aspects, instead educating the reader only on cooking and shopping. If the cookbooks' instructions were followed as they were presented in the cookbook, Spanish women would learn how to cook a delicious meal for their family and not the spiritual significance of the holiday. The cookbook encouraged the enjoyment of Christmas but for different reasons than Catholic doctrine. Thus, the cookbook gave a nod to the religious culture of Franco's New State, but in other ways, it omits the intended significance behind the religious practices, demonstrating non-conformity to the ideology of the regime.

Conclusion

Every food commodity that circulated through Spain during the post-civil war period of rationing (1939–1952) was infused with aspects of Francoist ideology—patriotism, patriarchy, and Catholicism. But the social meaning embedded within food via state food policy was not enough to provide cultural and social cues to consumers to enact adherence to the ideals of Franco's New State. Quality and consistency of both food discourse and physical foodstuffs were needed for the policies to be successful, and both of these aspects were lacking in Spain's post-civil war society. Due to scarcity of resources caused by food shortages and the inconsistency of food policy implemented by the regime, much of the original ideology intended to be embedded within the legislation was lost or transformed by the time it reached Spanish tables. Francoist food policy lacked the ability to communicate all ideological aspects touted by the regime, and the uneven application and failure of many of the food policies only acted to further undermine the ideologies of Franco's New State.

Spanish dishes took on new identity in the aftermath of the Spanish Civil War because the consumption of food was viewed as a way to affirm Franco's victory and his creation of a New State. Yet, deviations persisted as Spaniards practiced other preparations that promoted local or regional belonging as opposed to nationalized uniformity. Health conditions, preference of taste, and access to food shaped an individual's diet so that no two Spanish bodies were alike, and very few bodies aligned with the Francoist ideal. Likewise, with the integration of religious meaning into food policies, the practice of religion became a political performance rather than an individual belief, and this led to the dilution of the motivations behind religious practices for some Spaniards.

As food traveled from ideological discourse to physical consumption in the home, it was embedded with social and cultural meaning that reflected elements of the ideology of Francoism and his New State. Food policy promoted a united national identity, physical health, and religious fervor that all wove together to create the social fabric of the New State. These tenets propelled the creation of policy that further imposed these ideologies on Spanish society. But some aspects of food ideology were lost when it became policy, and the message intended to be communicated to Spaniards through the legislation of the New State became more ambiguous as food traveled from discourse to the meal. When Spaniards ate their daily dishes in the comfort of their homes, despite the coercion and repression of Franco's authoritarian regime, Franco's New State could not control what Spaniards ate and what each individual meal meant to them.

NOTES

1. For more reading on the political and implications of the term, "New State" at the end of the Spanish Civil War, see: Carme Molinero y Pere Ysas, *La anatomía del franquismo: de la supervivencia a la agonía, 1945–1977* (Barcelona: Critica S. L., 2008); Jordi García García and Miguel Ángel Ruíz Carnicer, *La España de Franco (1939–1975): Cultura y vida cotidiana* (Madrid: Editorial Sintesis, 2001); Michael Richards, *A Time of Silence: Civil War and the Culture of Repression 1936–1944* (Cambridge, UK: Cambridge University Press, 1998); and Enrique Moradiellos, *La España de Franco, 1939–1957: Politica y sociedad* (Madrid: Editorial Sintesis, 2003).
2. Lara Anderson, *Control and Resistance: Food Discourse in Franco Spain* (Toronto: University of Toronto Press, 2020), 15.
3. Kathleen LeBesco and Peter Naccarato, "Introduction," in *Edible Ideologies: Representing Food and Meaning*, eds. Kathleen LeBesco and Peter Naccarato (Albany, NY: SUNY Press, 2008), 3.
4. Tomás Espuny Gómez, *Legislación de abastos. Exposición metódica de las principales disposiciones vigentes* (Tarragona, Spain: Imprenta de José Pijoán, 1942), 241.
5. "Correspondencia entre la Fábrica Mahou y la Asociación de Fabricantes de Cerveza Madrid, 1939," Fábrica de Cervezas Mahou, Secretaría, Correspondencia, 1939, Con otras entidades y Particulares, Asociaciones de Fabricantes de Cerveza, Archivo Regional de Madrid.

6. Suzanne Dunai, "Food Politics in Postwar Spain: Eating and Everyday Life during the Franco Dictatorship, 1939–1952," PhD diss. (University of California San Diego, 2019), 91.
7. Josep María Roselló, *Vuelta a la Naturaleza. El Pensamiento naturista hispano (1890-2000): naturismo libertario, trofología, vegetarismo naturista, vegetarismo social y librecultura* (Barcelona: Virsu Editorial, 2003), 235.
8. Dunai, "Food Politics," 159–60.
9. Antonio Giráldez Lomba, *Sobrevivir en los Años del hambre en Vigo* (Vigo, Spain: Instituto de Estudios Vigueses, 2002), 182.
10. Dunai, "Food Politics," 57–58, 63.
11. Anderson, *Control and Resistance*, 28.
12. Richards, *A Time of Silence*, 91.
13. Carlos Barciela, *La España de Franco (1939–1975) Economía* (Madrid: Editorial Síntesis, 2001), 28.
14. "Lo económico y lo antieconómico," *Alimentación Nacional* II, no. 5 (March 15, 1942): 1.
15. M. Pérez Urruti, *España en números. Síntesis de la producción, consumo y comercio nacionales, 1940–1941* (Madrid: M. Aguilar, 1942), 9.
16. Antonio Cazorla Sanchez, *Fear and Progress: Ordinary Lives in Franco's Spain, 1939–1975* (Chichester, UK: Wiley-Blackwell, 2010), 61.
17. Anderson, *Control and Resistance*, 28, 39; "Recetas con artículos que abundan en el mercado," *Alimentación Nacional* II, no. 4 (February 15, 1942): 24.
18. Antonio Barroso Rodríguez, *Pan para España. Estudio sobre el cultivo del trigo para normalizar el abastecimiento de pan, Año 1949* (Madrid: Nueva Imprenta Radio SA, 1949), 13.
19. Alberto León, *La Cocina clásica española* (Madrid: Editorial Estudio, 1941), 9.
20. Ibid., 8–9.
21. For more information on Social Service cooking classes for women, see: Suzanne Dunai, "Cooking for the Patria: The Sección Femenina and the Politics of Food and Women during the Franco Years," MA thesis (University of New Mexico, 2012).
22. Dunai, "Food Politics," 119.
23. "La Carne, su escasez y la prensa madrileña," *La Carne* II, no. 22 (January 15, 1946): 3–4.
24. Ángela Cenarro, *Los Niños del Auxilio Social* (Madrid: Espasa Calpe, 2009), 178; "Correspondence from JH Janney to Dr. Wilbur," Rockefeller Foundation, December 13, 1940, 3.
25. *Menaje para la mujer*, no. 18, October 1940, 4, 9.
26. Ibid., 1.
27. Zira Box, "Spanish Imperial Destiny: The Concept of Empire during Early Francoism," trans. Wendy Gosselin, *Contribution to the History of Concepts* 8, no. 1 (Summer 2013): 103.
28. *Menaje para la mujer*, no. 18, October 1940, 1.

29. Ibid., 19.
30. Eric R. Smith, *American Relief Aid and the Spanish Civil War* (Columbia, MO: University of Missouri Press, 2013), 3; Richards, *A Time of Silence*, 92.
31. Adolfo Capella, *Todo por España. La Obra y Memorias de un Cruz Roja* (Barcelona: Papirus, 1940), 41.
32. Teresa Gonzalez Aja, "Spanish Sports policy in Republican and Fascist Spain," in *Sport and International Politics: Impact of Facism and Communism on Sport*, eds. Pierre Arnaud and Jim Riordan (London: Taylor and Francis, 1999), 105.
33. José Serret Tristany, *Alimentación de Hombre*, 2nd ed. (Barcelona: Imprenta Borras, 1943), 306, 308.
34. Andrius Vander, *La Obesidad: Su curación radical y definitiva: Comer bien sin engordar*, 3rd ed. (Barcelona: Librería Sintes, 1949), 32.
35. Benito Cid de la Llave, *Consideraciones sobre el problema del abastecimiento Nacional, su origen y causas. Encauzamiento para su solución y fundamento racional y económico de las medidas adoptadas* (Madrid: Patronato de Huérfanos de oficiales de ejército, 1944), 31.
36. Giráldez Lomba, *Sobrevivir*, 95.
37. Anderson, *Control and Resistance*, 28.
38. Carlos Blanco Soler, *Las Enfermedades de la nutrición* (Madrid: Ediciones y Publicaciones Españolas (EPESA), 1948), 149.
39. "Advertisements," *Menaje para la mujer*, April 1940, 39; May 1940, 13.
40. Giráldez Lomba, *Sobrevivir*, 198.
41. Vander, *La Obesidad*, 13.
42. Carlos Jiménez Díaz, *Lecciones sobre las enfermedades de la nutrición*, 2nd ed., vol. 2 (Madrid: Editorial Científico Médico, 1941), 185.
43. F. Xavier Medina, *Food Culture in Spain* (Westport, CT: Greenwood Press, 2010), 126.
44. Ángela Cenarro, *La Sonrisa de Falange: Auxilio Social en la guerra civil y en la posguerra* (Barcelona: Crítica, 2006), 71.
45. Francisco Comín Comín and Miguel Martorell Linares, *La Hacienda pública en el franquismo. La guerra y la autarquía (1936–1959)* (Madrid: Ministerio de Hacienda y Administraciones públicas, 2013), 88.
46. Ibid., 57.
47. Medina, *Food Culture in Spain*, 131.
48. For more information on the history of vegetarianism in Spain, see: Roselló, *Vuelta a la Naturaleza*.
49. Cenarro, *La sonrisa*, 57.
50. Pia Sociedad de San Pablo, *Tomad y comed. La Eucaristía es comida, hechos y ejemplos* (Bilbao, Spain: Pía Sociedad de San Pablo, 1944), 35.
51. Manuel Mínguez de Rico, *Reglamento de trabajo para la industria de Hotelería, Cafés, Bares y similares: Disposiciones vigentes obligatorias saber "El Plato único", precios de hospedajes, sanciones y régimen de comidas en el Nuevo Estado* (Madrid: Editorial Ibérica, 1939), 58.
52. "Cocina. Legumbres rellenas para los días sin carne," *Medina*, no. 105 (March 21, 1943).

53. Gonzalo Bosch Bierge, *Cocina de vigilia* (Barcelona: Editorial Hogar, 1940), 43–46.
54. Ibid., 49, 58.
55. Genoveva Bernard de Ferrer, *Comidas de vigilia. Las Mejores recetas para prepararlas* (Barcelona: Editorial Molino, 1947).
56. "Hablamos del pavo," *Medina*, no. 145 (December 20, 1943): 13.
57. Gonzalo Bosch Bierge, *La Cocina en Navidad* (Barcelona: Editorial Hogar, 1939), 59.

WORKS CITED

Anderson, Lara. *Control and Resistance: Food Discourse in Franco Spain*. Toronto: University of Toronto Press, 2020.
Barciela, Carlos. La España de Franco (1939–1975) Economía. Madrid: Editorial Síntesis, 2001.
Barroso Rodríguez, Antonio. Pan para España. Estudio sobre el cultivo del trigo para normalizar el abastecimiento de pan, Año 1949. Madrid: Nueva Imprenta Radio SA, 1949.
Bernard de Ferrer, Genoveva. Comidas de vigilia. Las Mejores recetas para prepararlas. Barcelona: Editorial Molino, 1947.
Blanco Soler, Carlos. Las Enfermedades de la nutrición. Madrid: Ediciones y Publicaciones Españolas (EPESA), 1948.
Bosch Bierge, Gonzalo. La Cocina en Navidad. Barcelona: Editorial Hogar, 1939.
———. Cocina de vigilia. Barcelona: Editorial Hogar, 1940.
Box, Zira. "Spanish Imperial Destiny: The Concept of Empire during Early Francoism." Translated by Wendy Gosselin. Contribution to the History of Concepts 8, no. 1 (Summer 2013): 89–106.
Capella, Adolfo. Todo por España. La Obra y Memorias de un Cruz Roja. Barcelona: Papirus, 1940.
"La carne, su escasez y la prensa madrileña." La Carne II, no. 22 (January 15, 1946): 3–4.
Cazorla Sanchez, Antonio. Fear and Progress: Ordinary Lives in Franco's Spain, 1939–1975. Chichester, UK: Wiley-Blackwell, 2010.
Cenarro, Ángela. Los Niños del Auxilio Social. Madrid: Espasa Calpe, 2009.
———. La Sonrisa de Falange: Auxilio Social en la guerra civil y en la posguerra. Barcelona: Crítica, 2006.
Cid de la Llave, Benito. Consideraciones sobre el problema del abastecimiento Nacional, su origen y causas. Encauzamiento para su solución y fundamento racional y económico de las medidas adoptadas. Madrid: Patronato de Huérfanos de oficiales de ejército, 1944.
"Cocina. Legumbres rellenas para los días sin carne." Medina, no. 105 (March 21, 1943).
Comín Comín, Francisco, and Miguel Martorell Linares. La Hacienda pública en el franquismo. La guerra y la autarquía (1936–1959). Madrid: Ministerio de Hacienda y Administraciones públicas, 2013.
"Correspondence from JH Janney to Dr. Wilbur." Rockefeller Foundation. December 13, 1940.
"Correspondencia entre la Fábrica Mahou y la Asociación de Fabricantes de Cerveza Madrid, 1939." Fábrica de Cervezas Mahou. Secretaría, Correspondencia. 1939. Con otras

entidades y Particulares, Asociaciones de Fabricantes de Cerveza. Archivo Regional de Madrid.

Dunai, Suzanne. "Cooking for the Patria: The Sección Femenina and the Politics of Food and Women during the Franco Years." MA thesis. University of New Mexico, 2012.

———. "Food Politics in Postwar Spain: Eating and Everyday Life during the Franco Dictatorship, 1939–1952." PhD dissertation. University of California San Diego, 2019.

"Lo económico y lo antieconómico." Alimentación Nacional II, no. 5 (March 15, 1942): 1.

Espuny Gómez, Tomás. Legislación de abastos. Exposición metódica de las españolas disposiciones vigentes. Tarragona, Spain: Imprenta de José Pijoán, 1942.

García García, Jordi, and Miguel Angel Ruíz Carnicer. La España de Franco (1939-1975): Cultura y vida cotidiana. Madrid: Editorial Sintesis, 2001.

Giráldez Lomba, Antonio. Sobrevivir en los Años del hambre en Vigo. Vigo, Spain: Instituto de Estudios Vigueses, 2002.

Gonzalez Aja, Teresa. "Spanish Sports policy in Republican and Fascist Spain." In Sport and International Politics: Impact of Facism and Communism on Sport, edited by Pierre Arnaud and Jim Riordan, 97–113. London: Taylor and Francis, 1999.

"Hablamos del pavo." Medina, no. 145 (December 20, 1943): 13.

Jiménez Díaz, Carlos. Lecciones sobre las enfermedades de la nutrición. 2nd edition. Volume 2. Madrid: Editorial Científico Médico, 1941.

LeBesco, Kathleen, and Peter Naccarato. "Introduction." In Edible Ideologies: Representing Food and Meaning, edited by Kathleen LeBesco and Peter Naccarato, 1–11. Albany, NY: SUNY Press, 2008.

León, Alberto. La Cocina clásica española. Ciudad Lineal, Spain: Editorial Estudio, 1941.

Medina, F. Xavier. Food Culture in Spain. Westport, CT: Greenwood Press, 2010.

Mínguez de Rico, Manuel. Reglamento de trabajo para la industria de Hotelería, Cafés, Bares y similares: Disposiciones vigentes obligatorias saber "El Plato único", precios de hospedajes, sanciones y régimen de comidas en el Nuevo Estado. Madrid: Editorial Ibérica, 1939.

Molinero, Carme, and Pere Ysas. La anatomía del franquismo: de la supervivencia a la agonía, 1945–1977. Barcelona: Critica S. L., 2008.

Moradiellos, Enrique. La España de Franco, 1939–1975: Politíca y sociedad. Madrid: Editorial Sintesis, 2003.

Pérez Urruti, M. España en números. Síntesis de la producción, consumo y comercio nacionales, 1940–1941. Madrid: M. Aguilar, 1942.

Pia Sociedad de San Pablo. Tomad y comed. La Eucaristía es comida, hechos y ejemplos. Bilbao, Spain: Pía Sociedad de San Pablo, 1944.

"Recetas con artículos que abundan en el mercado." Alimentación Nacional II, no. 4 (February 15, 1942): 24.

Richards, Michael. A Time of Silence: Civil War and the Culture of Repression in Franco's Spain, 1936–1945. Cambridge, UK: Cambridge University Press, 1998.

Roselló, Josep María. Vuelta a la Naturaleza. El Pensamiento naturista hispano (1890-2000): naturismo libertario, trofología, vegetarismo naturista, vegetarismo social y librecultura. Barcelona: Virsu Editorial, 2003.

Serret Tristany, José. *Alimentación de Hombre*. 2nd edition. Barcelona: Imprenta Borras, 1943.
Smith, Eric R. *American Relief Aid and the Spanish Civil War*. Columbia, MO: University of Missouri Press, 2013.
Vander, Andrius. *La Obesidad: Su curación radical y definitiva: Comer bien sin engordar*. 3rd edition. Barcelona: Librería Sintes, 1949.

CHAPTER 11

Creating a "Land of Charcuterie"

Cured Meat Producers, Culinary Marketing, and the Construction of Gastronationalist Discourses in Twentieth-Century Catalonia

Alejandro J. Gómez del Moral

In 2010, the Generalitat de Catalunya, Catalonia's autonomous government, sponsored the publication of a richly illustrated cookbook and collection of historical and gastronomic essays devoted to the region's sausages or *embotits*. The title was unassuming and straightforward—*Els Embotits de Catalunya*—but some of its claims suggested that cultural and social meanings were at play that were far more consequential than simple culinary interest or promotion of a local product. Thus, in his introduction to the volume, Joan Estapé i Mir, president of the Catalan Federation of Butchers and Charcutiers, proclaimed that what this book was about was nothing less than "a product, a way of life, a tradition, a country."[1] One year later, the marketing copy for a second, new cookbook devoted to Catalan charcuterie by the popular historian Gerard Buxeda, *El Llibre dels Embotits*, declared in still bolder terms that Catalonia was a "land of embotits."[2]

Though bold, Buxeda's claim was hardly uncommon—to the contrary, by then, this perception that Catalan food (especially its cured pork) was a key marker of regional identity had filtered into popular culture. Since its founding in 2007, Catalunyam, a design company specializing in apparel that whimsically celebrates Catalan national identity as expressed through the region's foods, has echoed this link between Catalan nationhood and charcuterie.[3] One t-shirt design, for

Figure 11.1. "Noble Terra d'Embotits." Source: Catalunyam Facebook Page

instance, depicts the iconic Catalan *llonganissa* sausage with marks showing the rate at which pork-loving Catalans will consume a whole link during a single week. More explicitly, another depicts a warrior intentionally reminiscent of medieval Catalonia's feared *almogàver* mercenaries brandishing a *llonganissa* instead of a sword and accompanied by a banner that, echoing Buxeda, proclaimed Catalonia a "Noble Terra d'Embotits," or "Noble Land of Sausages."

How did this link between the production and consumption of cured pork and expressions of Catalan national identity come to be? How recent a development is this? And, perhaps most importantly, what actors—Catalan pork producers; officials in Catalonia's regional government, the Generalitat; as well as culinary authors and other voices in gastronomic circles—participated in its construction? This study explores the above questions by tracing the development of a cured-pork industry in late nineteenth and early twentieth century Catalonia, including the birth of leading makers of the region's most renowned sausages: *llonganissa/salchichón, botifarra/butifarra,* and *fuet*.[4] In addition, it examines how a diverse range of parties within the industry, gastronomic literary figures, and representatives of the Generalitat have promoted and discussed Catalan charcuterie. Finally, this research examines how ensuing discourses surrounding the larger social, cultural, and political meanings that are mapped onto these foods have emerged, particularly since the restoration of Catalan regional autonomy in the late 1970s and early 1980s, and traces the identitarian discursive uses to which these various parties have put these products.

The significance of these discourses, and of the cured pork products that have functioned as sites for their articulation, should not be underestimated. Scholars working in the emerging field that Hispanist Lara Anderson has termed "Spanish Food Studies" are increasingly highlighting how critical engagement with Iberian food cultures holds the potential for new insights into modern Spanish society and political life.[5] Such scholarship has shown how, during the nineteenth and twentieth centuries, diverse actors leveraged Spanish culinary successes and essentialized images of a unitary Spanish food culture—notwithstanding Spain's regional cultural diversity—to advance different and sometimes conflicting Spanish national identities. Scholars working on other nations' food cultures have similarly explored the complex interactions that have taken place between private businesses and agents; government officials; symbolically charged "national" foods such as French foie gras and Israeli falafel; and local notions about how to define the nation and national belonging.[6]

What has yet to garner similar scholarly attention is the role that Spain's famed pork charcuterie, its producers, and the myriad private and public actors that have promoted the country's prized *ibérico* pigs, have together played in disseminating narratives of Spanish national identity, as well as claims to national distinctiveness in regions like Catalonia. And yet, understanding how pork came to emblematize these Iberian identities is indispensable to any complete analysis of Spanish foodways and efforts to market them abroad. This is partly due to the pork industry's contemporary economic importance—by some estimates, it is the nation's fifth-largest sector. It also stems from the centuries-old centrality of pork to daily life in Spain, where this food has historically served both as a reliable caloric source in times of scarcity and as a means to display one's Christian faith when such belief was required for acceptance in Spanish society.[7]

More broadly, such research into pork as a vehicle for Iberian, and in this case specifically Catalan, national identities also represents an opportunity to contribute to an ongoing scholarly exploration into the nature and functioning of what sociologist Michaela de Soucey has termed *gastronationalism*—that is, use of foods and food cultures to reassert the cultural boundaries of collective national identities, often undertaken in response to the threat of cultural homogenization posed by globalization.[8] The case of Catalan cured pork adds to this conversation in several ways. Scholarship on culinary nationalisms has noted how these ideologies at times fuse culturally, deeply rooted food traditions with comparatively new narratives of national selfhood, or conversely leverage foods that only recently have become national symbols to advance preexisting nationalist claims.⁹ This study likewise explores how such instrumentalizing relationships develop. It reveals that, indeed, despite pork's longstanding importance in Catalonia's food culture, and charcuterie-making's seemingly timeless rootedness in the Catalan hinterland, sausage production only transitioned from an artisanal basis over to mass production in the late nineteenth and early twentieth century. It underlines that this took place at about the same time that ham production commercialized in the rest of Spain and was to a great extent the result of the industrialization then unfolding in Spain and particularly in Catalonia.

In a similar vein, analysis of pork's place in Catalan gastronationalism offers opportunities to build upon existing scholarship examining the various ways that specific foods become vehicles for claims about national identity and how industrial as well as cultural agents interact with government actors in bringing about this fusion. Thus, this study examines how, over the course of the twentieth century, and especially as the Spanish economy flourished from the 1960s onward, commentary on the region's charcuterie proliferated within the pork industry, in literary circles that included some of Spain's leading gastronomes, and, with the restoration of Catalan autonomy in the late 1970s, in the ranks of the Generalitat. Once again, this unfolded as part of a more general rise in attention paid to Iberian gastronomy. This manifested in the steady stream of new cookbooks, gastronomy magazines whose editors and authors again included some of Spain's most accomplished culinary voices, and promotional materials, including pamphlets and books, published both by Catalan and Spanish government agencies, as well as by some of Catalonia's leading charcuterie producers. This commentary, I conclude, steadily reproduced and reinforced the status of *embotits* as more than simply a food, but rather a symbol of a culturally distinct Catalan people. And notably, this is a symbol that has gained new potency in recent years, as local foods have increasingly functioned as vehicles for asserting an ever more frequently politicized Catalan national identity as separate from Spain's.

A Gastronationalist Approach to Culinary Narratives of Catalan Nationhood

As has been noted previously, this study's conclusions draw especially on the analytical category of gastronationalism as developed by Michaela de Soucey and expanded upon by other scholars, and so the ways that de Soucey's concept figures in this research merit a brief pause. By its nature, gastronationalism centers around how narratives develop and spread—specifically, narratives that employ foods as symbols by which to disseminate notions about national identity. Consequently, from its inception, this concept has also relied and built upon Michael Billig's category of banal nationalism, which describes the myriad ways that nations are ideologically reproduced in daily life.[10] Notwithstanding this concern for narrative, gastronationalism's significance extends beyond the strictly rhetorical—as de Soucey herself and other scholars have underlined, gastronationalisms have wide-ranging social, cultural, and political consequences. During the late 1990s and early 2000s, for instance, French authorities drew on the gastronationalist claim that consuming foie gras is central to France's cultural identity to successfully lobby the European Union to declare the food a geographically protected product, which thereafter shielded local producers from foreign competition.[11] Japanese defense of its whaling industry has similarly leveraged claims that eating whale meat is a primary marker of Japan's unique cultural heritage.[12]

The elite political character of these examples is, some scholars would argue, no coincidence. In a recent volume on food and nationalism, political scientists Atsuko Ichijo and Ronald Ranta have distinguished between top-down and bottom-up uses of food to articulate national identity, situating de Soucey's gastronationalism model firmly in the former category.[13] By such reckoning, when a French web content producer published an unorthodox recipe for *pasta alla carbonara* in 2016, and Italians who venerate the dish as a national symbol (with an inviolably sacred preparation method) reacted with such outrage that the incident is now known as "Carbonara-Gate," this might be considered a case of banal nationalism expressed in food discourse rather than gastronationalism in strictest terms.[14] And indeed, as it explores the role that pork has played as a vehicle for notions of Catalan national identity, this article does engage extensively with efforts by arguably elite parties—prominent cultural figures, policymakers, and pork industry professionals—to construct and deploy nationalist narratives.

However, it is not assumed here that this socio-political positionality necessarily vitiates the significance of such gastronationalist measures. Sociologist Melissa Aronczyk, for instance, has argued that construction of national brand identities—nation-branding—is a communications strategy by which nations can exercise a form of "soft power," advancing their interests more subtly than via traditional "hard" methods like military action or trade policy.[15] This is strongly evident in the case of Catalan gastronationalism. Targeted efforts to shape a national brand might, for example, bypass diplomatic channels and instead appeal to public opinion abroad to achieve a political result, such as tempering international criticism.[16] Similarly, during the past four decades, Catalan cultural outreach via promotion of the region's gastronomy, including its pork specialties, has served as a means to disseminate narratives that depict Catalonia as socially and culturally distinct from the rest of Spain. And, highlighting the potential significance of nation branding strategies in cases where political sovereignty is lacking, this outreach has remained steady even as the central government in Madrid nullified the Generalitat's decades-old initiatives to build diplomatic ties abroad, judging these to have infringed on the Spanish state's sovereignty.[17]

Moreover, even if gastronationalism is seen as a specifically top-down process of idea transmission, cases also abound in which popular discourse has figured centrally in how particular foods become national symbols and sites for banal expressions of nationalism. In some instances, material rather than ideological motives have been the primary drivers behind the measures and rhetoric that establish such ties between foods and national identities. For example, scholars, including Ichijo, Ranta, Aronczyk, as well as de Soucey and sociologist Arjun Appadurai, have all observed that, when symbolically charged foods serve as vehicles for nationalisms, oftentimes these ideologies are forced to reckon with the mundane interests of the businesses that make and market those foods.[18] In Scotland, for example, whisky distillers have in the past had little genuine interest in nationalist claims-making but have readily encouraged public perception of scotch as Scotland's national drink (and by extension, of the reality of a Scottish national identity) because of the marketing power afforded by the Scottish nation-brand.[19]

In this vein, the approach taken here has been to pair scrutiny of gastronationalist efforts by elite culture and policymakers with attention to instances where this work has encountered and contended with more common perspectives, or where ordinary Catalans have used food—in this case, charcuterie—to make claims about the nation and national identity. Thus, the Generalitat as well as prominent Catalan gastronomes and food periodicals have, on the one hand, often sought to position Catalan pork traditions as one more marker of the region's cultural difference from other Spanish territories. Yet, on the other hand, this study notes how working butchers as well as Barcelona's guild of butchers and charcutiers showed little interest in identitarian questions during the 1980s and early 1990s, and instead cared far more about leveraging a Catalan nation-brand to take fullest advantage of the opportunities for international exposure that Spain's rising global profile appeared to offer. However, it also takes seriously the significance of a venture like Catalunyam, whose designs rely upon appealing to a seemingly active popular belief that Catalan foodways (in this case, specifically its pork specialties) are distinct from other Spanish cuisine, and that this difference is a viable site for referencing larger claims about Catalonia's de facto status as a socially and culturally separate nation with aspirations to political independence as well.

Embotits in Catalonia: Deep Cultural Roots, Recent Commodification

As noted above, the pig has figured centrally in Spanish, and more specifically in Catalan, food culture for centuries. Culinary historian Jaume Fàbrega has argued that pork's place in Catalan foodways may be traced back as far as two millennia, citing the fact that the modern *llonganissa* derives its name from a Roman predecessor, as well as literary evidence of the esteem Romans held for the cured sausages of the Cerdanya valley in the Catalan Pyrenees. The importance of pork sausages and hams in the Catalan kitchen was better recorded from the medieval period on. While sausages figured sparsely in the earliest cookbooks—unsurprising, according to Fàbrega, because they formed a different culinary genre than the recipes these manuals contained—pork in general appeared frequently, and significant texts like the *Llibre del Sent Soví* (1324) referenced foods like *botifarra* and *cansalada* (salt-cured bacon). Works from several centuries later, such as the seminal cookbook *Llibre de l'art de quynar*[sic], which details how to chop pork finely for making *llonganissa*, likewise attest to these foods' presence and relevance in the Catalan kitchen.[20]

Meanwhile, in Spain more generally, as historian Jodi Campbell has recently observed, consumption of pork—especially as cured hams and sausages—figured significantly in everyday life following the genesis of the Holy Inquisition as a means of displaying the Christian faith mandated by the Spanish Crown and Church. Its popularity likewise stemmed from being one of the cheapest and most commonly available meats, and so more affordable than more patrician options like lamb.[21] Likewise, in Catalonia as in the rest of Spain, the annual *matanza* or pig-slaughter evolved into one of the principal unifying events that took place during the yearly calendar of community happenings, a role it retained sufficiently in some rural areas that the long-running national newsreel program *Noticias y Documentales* (1943–1981) documented this aspect of the *matanza* as recently as early 1981.[22] Indeed, in testament to the rural and perhaps even atavistic character that pork continues to occupy in modern notions of authentically Spanish and Catalan culture, it is telling that, when American chef Jeffrey Weiss penned a cookbook on Spanish charcuterie in 2014, he titled it *Charcutería: The Soul of Spain* (emphasis mine).

Yet, despite these cultural roots and pork's seemingly transhistorical place in Spanish life, the history of these products as commodities, and most especially of pork-curing as a commercialized industry, is relatively short. In Catalonia as in Spain more generally, ham and sausage production began to evolve into a cogent, commercialized, and—inasmuch as the term may be used at this early point in time—professionalized industry no earlier than the latter half of the nineteenth century and only truly started to come into its own after the turn of the century.

Most of Spain's best-recognized charcuterie producers began to appear only from the mid-nineteenth century onward, including industry heavyweights like ham producer Cinco Jotas Sánchez Romero. Though it is the oldest producer in the Andalusian town of Jabugo, Cinco Jotas launched in 1879.[23] Two other major figures in the export market, ham producer Fermín, whose hams were the first imported to the United States, and Chorizos Palacios, are as much as a century younger, launching in 1956 and 1983, respectively.[24] Likewise, many of Catalonia's notable *embotit* producers, most especially producers of the dry-cured *llonganissa* sausage for which the region of Osona and the regional capital of Vic are particularly known, launched during the late nineteenth and early twentieth century. One of Vic's oldest and most prestigious *llonganissa* makers, Riera Ordeix, opened its first facility in 1852; while two of the region's other established producers, Embotits Espina and Embotits Salgot, launched in 1911 and 1928.[25] Casa Tarradellas, which is undoubtedly Catalonia's most well-known mass producer of *fuets*, *llonganissa*'s thinner cousin, is a particular newcomer, as it was founded only in 1976, again in the general vicinity of Vic.[26]

There are several likely reasons for this timing. A published history of Casa Riera Ordeix that doubles as a history of Vic's famed *llonganissas* reckons the origin of sausage production in that city as the result of a felicitous moment of historical contingency—specifically, of company founder Pau Riera's commercial savoir-faire. By this telling, in the early 1850s, Riera, a Catalan traveling merchant known in the region as a canny businessman, recognized the commercial opportunity that Osona's peasant-made cured sausages represented. Believing the sausages would prove popular in Barcelona's markets, he also deduced that concentrating production in Vic, rather than relying on scattershot purchase from local farms, would let him take advantage of economies of scale.[27] At first glance this story seems suspiciously self-serving. However, there is reason to trust it, at least in part: the author was a respected journalist, not a company hack, and later Vic's official municipal historian, Josep Maria Solá i Sala, as well as Jaume Fàbrega, likewise acknowledged Riera's role in founding one of the city's oldest sausage factories—if perhaps not the very first.[28]

Whether or not Pau Riera pioneered the concentration of *llonganissa* production in Vic, this tale does suggest another reason for the emergence of commercial sausage production in late nineteenth-century Catalonia. As historian Montserrat Miller has noted, it was in the 1840s that construction began on Barcelona's now-extensive network of neighborhood market halls, a project driven especially by authorities who thereby sought to improve food distribution and nutrition throughout the Catalan capital.[29] And as Barcelona was Catalonia's largest potential market for these foods, the opening of its municipal market halls almost certainly served the interests of sausage-makers looking to recoup the initial expense of concentrating the production in Vic through sales in the Catalan capital. Naturally, this went hand in hand with the industrial growth, particularly in textiles, that Barcelona and its environs experienced during the late nineteenth century, as this brought both urbanization and improved transportation links that generated increased food demand, the latter only incentivizing centralized production as in Vic.[30] Finally, the choice of Vic specifically was due to the local climate: in an era predating refrigeration technology (and indeed, the need for more and better cold-storage for meats remained a topic of concern among Catalan sausage and ham producers as recently as the late 1970s), the cool mountain breezes and fog common in the Plana de Vic, a long geological depression in which much of central Catalonia's sausage-making has traditionally been located, are what made the dry-curing process possible.[31]

Pages of Pork: Growth in Writing on Catalan Cuisine in the Twentieth and Early Twenty-First Centuries

These enterprises were fortunate to begin developing at a moment of growing interest in the region's food culture. From the late nineteenth century onward, Catalan culture in general garnered a growing amount of popular and literary attention, both as part of a contemporaneous regional cultural renaissance known as the *Renaixença* and later in connection with a broader Spanish cultural regenerationism. Catalonia's culinary traditions were no exception to this. The first decades of the new century alone saw the publication of several seminal modern texts about Catalan cuisine, including Ignasi Domènech's *La Teca: La veritable cuina casolana de Catalunya* (1924) and Ferran Agulló's *El Llibre de la Cuina Catalana* (1928). Contemporaneously, several periodicals aimed at culinary professionals in Catalonia also appeared.[32]

Literary commentary on Catalan cuisine was rooted in a legacy of gastronomic critique stretching to the medieval period, and to a limited degree, this continued into the mid-century. Yet the impact of Generalissimo Francisco Franco's four-decade-long dictatorship (1936–1975) on Catalan culture and regional identity—including its foodways—should not be overlooked. The Franco regime's pursuit of cultural and social as well as political centralization is amply documented. Use of regional languages like Catalan was stigmatized when not banned outright.

And where expressions of regional cultural distinctiveness were countenanced, these were reduced to the status of cultural curios, otherwise decoupled from their territories of origin, or recast as evidence of Spanish cultural richness writ large. Such was the case with the inclusion of dances like the Aragonese *jota* in the repertoire of the *Coros y Danzas,* a traveling folkloric music-and-dance troupe organized by *Sección Femenina,* the official women's organization within the Francoist political system.[33]

It was no different in the culinary field. Historian Suzanne Dunai has argued that Franco-era cookbooks produced by *Sección Femenina* evinced a tension-laden effort to marry acknowledgment of the regional origins of dishes like Asturian bean stew (*Fabada a la Asturiana*) and Catalan-style omelette (*Tortilla Catalana*) with a narrative that continued to define them narrowly as part of a larger body of Spanish cuisine (and nearly always gave their names in Spanish rather than the relevant regional language). In other cases, Dunai has noted that these cookbooks papered over regional origins by titling a particular dish a la española (Spanish-style).[34] Lara Anderson has taken this argument a step further, contending that "[Franco-era] food writing upheld fascist or Francoist space through the production of a unified gastronomic space that reimagined the country's culinary borders. Functional culinary zones served to erase culinary regionalism, while Castilian cuisine was positioned not just at the center of Spain's gastronomic map, but also as the very essence of Spanish cuisine."[35]

Catalan sources dating from the regime's immediate wake as well as decades later show that some of Catalonia's foremost cultural figures believed that such culinary oppression had very much taken place there, too. Thus, in his formative 1977 culinary manifesto, pugnaciously titled *L'Art del Menjar a Catalunya: Crònica de la resistència dels senyals d'identitat gastronòmica catalana* (The Art of Eating in Catalonia: Chronicle of the Resistance [Posed by] Catalonia's Markers of Gastronomic Identity), renowned writer, journalist, political dissident, and cookbook author Manuel Vázquez Montalbán wrote that, in most of Catalonia, "gastronomic memory has been reduced to one or two dishes half-hidden in menus of ridiculous state character (I am referring to the Spanish State) or no less ridiculously international ones."[36] More recently, in a 2018 column for Catalan political and cultural weekly *El Temps,* Jaume Fàbrega has suggested that, by requiring restaurants to provide and prominently advertise inexpensive three-course *menús turísticos* (tourist's prix-fixe meals), which for example often featured dishes like *paella* that were quick to prepare and already familiar to the tourist masses, rather than local dishes with deeper cultural roots, Manuel Fraga Iribarne's Ministry of Information and Tourism (in office 1962–69) contributed significantly to Franco-era erasure of regional food cultures.[37]

As the Franco regime's demise unfolded during the 1970s, the situation for Catalan cuisine changed again. The years bracketing the collapse of the Franco regime, and most especially from the mid-1970s onward, saw a marked resurgence of literature celebrating Catalan culinary traditions, including its autochthonous charcuterie, which featured notable interventions by the region's most renowned gastronomes. Some of these were works by private individuals. These included Luján and Juan Perucho's sprawling *El Libro de la Cocina Española*, first published in 1970; Vázquez Montalbán's *L'art del menjar a Catalunya* (1977); and *La Cocina Moderna en Catalunya* (1985) by Néstor and Tin Luján. Private organizations and government agencies meanwhile produced other works. These included acclaimed journalist and gastronome Llorenç Torrado's 1985 work *Els Embotits a Catalunya: Una Tradició, Un Art, Una Indústria*, which was partially underwritten by the Catalan Meat Industries Federation (FECIM), and a follow-up 2010 edition, *Els Embotits de Catalunya,* sponsored by the Generalitat's own Department of Agriculture, Livestock, and Fishing. Torrado's volume was an exhaustive and pioneering survey of Catalonia's cured meats that explored the cultural and social history behind these foods and offered recipes for making staple sausages like *botifarra* and *llonganissa*, as well as using them in finished dishes. Its impact among Catalan charcuterie-producers and butchers was extensive. For months following its publication, the respected and by then decades-old professional journal for Barcelona's official Butchers' and Charcutiers' Guild, *La Indústria Tocinera* (relaunched after 1986 as *Gras i Magre*) ran regular ads for the book, and glowing reviews ran in both the former journal and Spain's preeminent gastronomy magazine since its launch in 1976, *Club de Gourmets*.[38]

The transition era more specifically witnessed a flood of new periodicals devoted to Spanish cuisine in general and Catalan cuisine in particular, which included content on charcuterie. *Club de Gourmets* pioneered this wave of publications, and though based in Madrid and published in Spanish, the magazine had clear ties to Catalonia, with a second office in Barcelona and Catalan culinary notables like Juan Perucho as well as journalist Luis Bettónica on staff.[39] Other titles followed over the next decade, and like *Club de Gourmets*, which launched as the Spanish transition to democracy began, they typically did so at key moments when international attention was focused on Spain, including the democratic transition of 1975–1982 and a turn as host nation for the FIFA World Cup (coinciding with the historic takeover of the reins of government by the once-banned Socialist Party) in 1982.[40] It bears note, too, that, even though these periodicals did typically devote more attention to other products like the region's wines, content on pork and charcuterie also appeared. In 1982, for instance, Llorenç Torrado contributed a column to the Catalan-language magazine *La Cuina* that explored the cultural significance of the *matança*, or pig slaughter, and the importance of pork products to Catalan society.⁴¹

Still more publications followed during the latter half of the 1980s. New titles meant to publicize Spanish (and Catalan) cuisine launched as Spain joined the European Economic Community in 1986—likely no coincidence. In 1985, the Spanish Institute for Foreign Trade (Instituto Español de Comercio Exterior, henceforth ICEX), launched *Spain Gourmetour*, an English-language monthly magazine that promoted Spanish foods and wines to foreign audiences, and circulated for free out of Spanish embassies abroad. More locally, the Catalan-language *Girona Gastronòmica*, which focused on publicizing northern Catalonia's local specialties, began to circulate the following year. This was also when the Barcelona butchery and charcutier guild's thirty-year-old journal *La Industria Tocinera* relaunched as *Gras i Magre* (Fat and Lean [cuts]), a rebranding effort prompted by a desire to stress the artisanal—and by implication, higher quality—rather than industrial character of the guild's craft and products.⁴² Notably, this impulse seems to have been at least partly fueled by a conviction that artisanal products were an important vehicle for the preservation of Catalan culture and also had significant export potential, particularly as Spain joined the EEC. Thus, in its last issue before the name change, *La Industria Tocinera* printed a review of Llorenç Torrado's book that cautioned:

> Careful not to lose sight of your roots, friends in the industrial sector!,[sic] lest Chicago-style superproduction of sausages ultimately cause us to become unmoored from [our cultural roots], as one Vic-based lover of *llonganissas* and the art of prose, has intuited [might happen]. Reading the book about charcuterie in Catalonia and taking to heart the desires of the consumer who wants the highest quality, we will move toward the future with pork products that are as modern as they are traditional and artisanal.⁴³

This article appeared just one month after the Generalitat established subsidies for the commercial promotion of local artisanal goods, the reasoning for which was—again tellingly—that "[artisanal production] has contributed in historic fashion to Catalonia's economic development . . . [and] at present, fostering artisanal activity is a dynamizing force for deepening the region's economic resources and wealth-creation."⁴⁴

Books and pamphlets devoted to Catalan gastronomy in general, and charcuterie in particular, likewise multiplied from the late 1980s on. In 1989, the Generalitat published both a cookbook with a foreword by Catalan president Jordi Pujol himself, as well as an English-language booklet titled *Gastronomy in Catalonia* that surveyed the region's culinary traditions for foreigners and has gone through various editions since.⁴⁵ During the latter half of the 1990s, Jaume Fàbrega penned a pair of prize-winning volumes on food culture in Catalonia and other Catalan-speaking regions, which included commentary on the region's pork products.⁴⁶ Catalan charcuterie drew an increasing amount of specific attention, too. *Gastronomy in Catalonia* made a point of stressing the quality and "great importance to [Catalan] cuisine" of sausages like *llonganissa*.⁴⁷ Several leading Catalan characuterie producers published company histories with chapters on the history and socio-cultural significance of the region's cured meats, the most extensive of these being Casa Riera Ordeix's *La Llonganissa de Vic: Del rebost del pagès a la taula del rei*, published 1992.⁴⁸ And between 2010 and 2016 alone, the Generalitat released its follow up to Torrado's 1985 oeuvre, Gerard Buxeda published *El Llibre dels Embotits* (2014), and Fàbrega penned *El Llibre de la Llonganissa* (2016).⁴⁹

Fuets to "Fer País": Construction of Cured Pork as Symbol of Catalan Identity

As the body of popular as well as academic writing on Catalan gastronomy and the region's cured meat products grew amid the Franco regime's late-1970s dissolution and in the decades that followed, several broad notions about the relationship between Catalonia, Catalan identity, and the region's cured meats took form, most especially gastronationalist arguments about the distinctiveness of Catalan food traditions and the social, cultural, and even political implications of this particularity. Several threads run clearly through these texts. One is a sustained link between discourses, on the one hand, about the region's charcuterie, particularly the history and traditions underlying production of these foods, and on the other, about Catalan identity as a distinct and separate social and cultural entity within Spain. Another—more practical but at points still profoundly identitarian—has centered around a longstanding concern over Catalonia's and its artisanal charcutiers' ability to maintain the region's cultural distinctiveness as Spain increasingly integrated into European and global markets, and also to respond effectively to the business opportunities and challenges this posed.

Often implicit, but frequently voiced explicitly as well, discussion about Catalan charcuterie as it related to regional identity has been especially pronounced within Catalan gastronomic literary circles, involving some of Spain's foremost thinkers on cuisine and culture, including Néstor Luján, Joan Perucho, Jaume Fàbrega, Josep Pla, and Manuel Vázquez Montalbán, perhaps Spain's most well-known cultural and political commentators. Vázquez Montalbán, for instance, devoted an entire section of his seminal 1977 *L'Art del Menjar* to the region's sausages. In line with his book's stated mission of recounting how a fundamental "symbol of Catalan identity"—the region's cuisine—had survived the culturally centralizing onslaught of the Franco dictatorship, the author writes:

> There is no county in Catalonia that has not had its own [variety of] botifarra ... and though they are all similar, none are the same. Even in one region, two sausage-making families could over the decades champion their own distinct methods, each with its own following and reputation. One might even support a statement [about Catalonia's regions] declaring, "by their *embotits* you shall know them," [a phrase] in the spirit of Brillat-Savarin's [own] sage maxim, "Nations' destinies are determined by how most of their people eat." So we see that the Spain of the central plain is a land of *chorizos*, while Catalonia is a land of mildly-spiced sausages, the greatest among these being the *llonganissa*, and the humblest being the mild egg-based *botifarra* typically eaten on Fat Tuesday. And, if we continue with this line [of thinking in terms of food and] national identity, we discover the problem that has arisen from a decline in [Catalan] sausage-making that has unfolded alongside a more generalized decline in Catalan gastronomy. At present, only a few places still make unusual and imaginative *embotits* ... one need only visit a rural or urban butcher shop to confirm that Catalan charcuterie's splendid past [diversity] has been reduced to just two or three varieties of *botifarras* and *llonganissa*.[50]

With this, Vázquez Montalbán established Catalan sausage making as a mark of cultural distinction from the rest of Spain and, importantly, a cultural signifier that had survived to the present but nevertheless was in critical danger. This was particularly so, he argued, because the distinguishing virtue of Catalan sausage making was its historical, but now increasingly dwindling, variety and subtlety of flavors, which contrasted sharply with what the author described monolithically as *chorizo*'s dominance in the Spanish interior.

This anticipated other claims, including some in the 2010 *Els Embotits de Catalunya*. As noted previously, Joan Estapé i Mir's introduction to the volume underscored that what this book was about was nothing less than "a product, a way of life, a tradition, a country."[51] And in the collection's first chapter, Jaume Fàbrega, who is an outspoken advocate of Catalan independence, also observed that in Catalan territory (Catalonia, Valencia, and the Balearics, as well as portions of Aragón and France), smoked paprika has historically only been used in sausages of foreign origin, however locally entrenched they might have become, as for instance in the case of Majorcan *sobrassada*.[52] Fàbrega, a radical but by no means fringe figure, as he is generally considered the most prolific author on Catalan cuisine ever with seventy-one books to his name, has since been still more pointed in the national-identitarian conclusions he has drawn from the study of Catalan gastronomy, and its *embotits* in particular. In his 2016 *El Llibre de la Llonganissa,* Fàbrega opened by declaring:

> Every country offers us a repertoire of tastes, products, and dishes. The Germans [offer] the[ir] famous smoked sausages, Spaniards *chorizo,* and the Italians genuine *mortadella*. Catalonia proffers the *llonganissa,* a magnificent dry-cured *embotit* that, among its genre of products, is without a doubt the #1 charcuterie product. A well-made *llonganissa,* made with choice cuts of pork, is unique, unforgettable . . . it is the art and the taste of a land, as indeed, Catalan *llonganissa* has a taste and bouquet entirely its own . . . because like the [Catalan] nation, this *embotit* possesses common, unifying qualities present everywhere [in Catalonia], but each county imparts its own particular characteristics and sometimes even a different name.[53]

Lest the reader presume that Fàbrega meant only to stress the uniqueness and excellence of *llonganissa,* in an interview that same year with leading pro-independence Catalan news organ *Vilaweb,* he declared, "Spain always wants to appropriate our [culinary] successes." Two decades before, in his 1995 prize-winning book on Catalan culinary tastes, he had directly linked an influx of Castilian Spanish foods into Catalan supermarkets, which displaced local counterparts, to a bastardization of the Catalan language's culinary vocabulary, as words like *recuit* (milk curds) and even *pernil* (ham) gave way respectively to *cuajada* and *jamón*. Independence, Fàbrega now concluded in his interview with *Vilaweb,* was the only sure way to guarantee linguistic survival.[54]

Meanwhile, Catalan pork producers and retailers themselves—butchers, charcutiers, and other professionals similarly involved in the making and handling of cured meat products—often seemed more concerned with practical, professional concerns, though, as hinted above, these did often enough refer back to matters related to the Catalan national question. Columns printed in several trade and professional gastronomy journals from the early and mid-1980s—the years leading up to and surrounding Spain's EEC entry—covered changes to the legal regime governing the butcher's and charcutier's trades, such as the Generalitat's 1985–86 reclassification of charcuterie production as an artisanal rather than industrial activity. They reported on local and international trade fairs and Catalan participation therein. They addressed the critical issue of the African swine fever virus' persistence in Spain's pig population, which limited the nation's pork exports. And crucially, Catalonia's butchers and charcutiers worried over their ability to remain competitive as Spain joined the EEC in 1985–86 and Spanish markets opened that much more to foreign competition—a concern unsurprisingly shared in the rest of Spain. Thus, the March–April 1986 issue of *La Industria Tocinera* reprinted an article from Madrid-based food distribution trade journal *Mercaconsumo*, which advised that small producers needed to specialize and professionalize in response to the rise in competition that Spain's entry into the EEC would soon bring.[55] The magazine *Gras i Magre* ran several articles in 1987 warning readers that "belonging to the Europe of the 12 [the EEC] is not a simple formality . . . [because] Europe favors the small business, but does so subject to a series of conditions that only underline [the need for] professionalism" and, similarly, that following entry into the European Common Market, either a focus on industrial-scale production or specialization was "the key to the future for all [Spanish commercial] enterprises . . . but in all cases true professionals would be indispensable." This was especially so, the magazine stressed, because the retail model of the shopping center filled primarily with specialized, high-prestige—and highly professionalized— boutiques was rapidly gaining ground across Europe.[56] In similar vein, the more locally minded *Girona Gastronòmica* noted while reporting on a March 1987 charcuterie trade fair that one of the event's primary subjects of discussion had been "the importance . . . of the private sector acting to respond to the challenge that EEC membership represents."[57]

Again, this unease over the dislocations that might follow from Spain's growing global integration at times bled over into concerns about preservation of Catalan regional identity. Hence, the review of Llorenç Torrado's book that ran in *La Industria Tocinera*'s last issue in mid-1986 closed with the warning, already detailed above, that Catalonia's sausage producers must not lose sight of their cultural roots as they adopted foreign methods of industrial production. And the following January, *Girona Gastronòmica* ran a column on pork's nutritional and cultural importance across the globe, in which author Jaume Fàbrega closed by praising the variety and quality that marked Catalonia's sausages—so significant, he argued, that this defined Catalonia much as cheese did France—but also, tellingly, by fretting, "let's hope that the EEC will let us keep it this way."[58]

These texts strongly imply that their authors and the journals that printed them believed that Catalonia's particular pork-curing traditions contributed significantly to defining and reproducing the region's cultural distinctiveness within Spain; this view has been similarly evident in the decades since. From the 1980s onward, and especially since Spanish producers became able to export beyond Europe in the 1990s, cured pork products like the famed *jamón ibérico* and *chorizo* have come to function internationally as talismans of Spanish identity—one need only consider the opening passage of the chapter covering pork in celebrity chef José Andrés' bestselling cookbook *Made in Spain*: "Only in Spain could you make a movie called *Jamón, jamón*, a romantic comedy in which ham is an expression of passion. Pork in all its forms—from smoky red *chorizo* sausage to translucent slices of cured ham—is a national obsession." Donald Harris, the founder of the preeminent North American Spanish foods importer LaTienda.com, has also described how he realized after sounding out whether Americans would be interested in imported Spanish hams: "it was clear that La Tienda had made contact with the Spanish soul."[59] Catalonia's sausages remain a similarly evocative regional symbol—so much so that in an April 2019 appearance on Catalunya Ràdio's popular daily talk-show *Estat de Gràcia*, Barcelona-based ham producer Enrique Tomás, whose chain of boutiques has locations across Spain, the United States, and Latin America, felt compelled to protest:

> Good ham is the nation's product . . . bread with tomato and ham, that's our identity. If we can all agree on something it's that ham is our product . . . how many times when I was with Jordi Pujol, when he was president [of the Generalitat] did he tell me, "but, Enrique, why don't you say it . . . people think that in Catalonia we only make *fuet* . . . ok? And the largest concentration of pigs is in Catalonia. It is where the most ham is made, where the most kilos of ham are made and really good ham is made . . . it's tremendous, but people don't know, *and it seems like here all we make is* butifarra.[60]

Most recently, this link between Catalonia's prized charcuterie and its sense of national selfhood has taken on a more pointedly identitarian dimension, as the gastronomically defined Catalan national identity has become part of the social and cultural lexicon that supporters of Catalan independence use to articulate claims that Catalonia is a well-defined nation in every sense but the political. Thus, if Jaume Fàbrega's decades-long body of work has consistently displayed a concern for preserving the distinctiveness and internal variety of Catalan charcuterie, recent interventions by the culinary historian, such as his 2017 interview with Vilaweb, have, in keeping with Catalonia's more radicalized recent political climate, stressed how this culinary particularity highlights the region's fundamental difference from the rest of Spain and the need for independence. Hence too the work of Catalan graphic designer Catalunyam referenced above: in 2012, the company launched a range of t-shirts based around the relationship between Catalonia's pork curing traditions and its regional identity. In addition to its shirt sporting a sausage-wielding *almogàver* presumably defending his "noble land of sausages," Catalunyam introduced another that draws attention to how the region's gastronomy intersects with its language—one of the area's fundamental identity markers—through depiction of a fuet in connection with the idiom, "penjat com un fuet" (Stuck all alone). It is telling too that in Barcelona seven stores stock these designs—among them pro-independence news agency Vilaweb's store, where Catalunyam's *almogàver* hangs among shirts bearing slogans like "Antifeixista Sempre" (Always Antifascist), "Hola República" (Hello, [Catalan] Republic), "Llibertat Presos Polítics" (Freedom for [Catalan] Political Prisoners), or simply "Independència."[61] As for the company's own intentions, it is telling that, when asked in correspondence about their pork-related designs, Catalunyam's public liaison Oriol Janer responded: "Design allows us to find new ways of expressing, of communicating aspects of our culture that have never been represented in an aesthetically up-to-date way. We're talking about design with a markedly local character. Our intended public is basically Catalan speakers, so we have a small market, but our products also have a powerful pedagogical value that cannot be ignored. They create culture. They build national sentiment [*fan país*]."[62]

Conclusions

In Catalonia as in the rest of Spain, cured pork is serious business—both in a literal sense, but also in cultural and political terms. Meat production and processing is now Spain's fifth-largest industry, as noted previously, and Spain has become the European Union's foremost pork exporter by volume, and fourth-biggest worldwide, with noted industrial ham and sausage producers Campofrío, El Pozo, Argal, and Casa Tarradellas—a Catalan company headquartered just outside of Vic—numbering among a short list of firms that monopolize nearly a third of the market by volume.[63] And in the years surrounding Spain's 1985–86 entry into the European Economic Community, Barcelona's butchers and charcutiers were to a great extent concerned with the practical implications this might have for their businesses. On the whole, however, Catalonia's *embotits* are far more than just a commodity to be sold or a delicacy to be enjoyed. Particularly over the course of the latter half of the twentieth century, and in sometimes unexpected ways, a diverse range of gastronomes, charcuterie professionals, and other interested parties have implicitly and explicitly invoked Catalonia's charcuterie traditions in ways that have reproduced conceptions of an imagined Catalan national community that have circulated continuously since at least the reinstatement of regional autonomy in the late 1970s. Put another way, over the last forty years, sausages have consistently figured as one more (and, by virtue of their ubiquity in Catalan pantries, a pervasive if at times also subtle) means to build a sense of Catalan national selfhood, or, as it is phrased locally, *fer país*.

NOTES

1. Josep Dolcet and Ignasi Pons I Argimon, eds., Ignasi Pons i Argimon, eds. *Els Embotits de Catalunya* (Barcelona: Edicions 62: Generalitat de Catalunya, Departament d'Agricultura, Alimentació i Acció Rural, 2010), 11.
2. Gerard Buxeda i Majoral, *El llibre dels embotits* (Girona, Spain: Sidillà, 2016); Edicions Sidillà, "El Llibre Dels Embotits," Edicions Sidillà.
3. Indeed, the firm's name itself playfully links the region's identity to a food-related cultural marker, as it is a portmanteau of the region's name—Catalunya—and "nyam," the Catalan onomatopoeia designating the experience of munching tasty food.
4. *Fuet* and *llonganissa* are in most respects nearly identical products. Both are pork sausages made with a casing, are dry-cured using the same methods, and are usually seasoned with little more than salt and pepper—and never with *pimentón*, the smoked red paprika that features heavily in other Iberian sausages like *chorizo*. Where they differ is in size: *fuets*, which originated as tasting samples for larger *llonganissa* batches, are much thinner at about 4 centimeters in diameter, while their thicker cousins can be as large as 10 centimeters and somewhat shorter in length. *Botifarra*, meanwhile, is an uncured raw pork sausage that can include additives such as egg or pig's blood, depending on the variety—but again, never *pimentón*—making it more akin to France's *saucisses* than an Italian salami.
5. See, for instance: Lara Anderson, "Cooking up the Past: Culinary Nostalgia and Gender Critique in Cuéntame Cómo Pasó," *Hispanic Research Journal* 17, no. 1 (2016): 34–48, "A Recipe for Spain: Un País Para Comérselo's Centralizing Promotion and Othering of Regional Cuisines," *Bulletin of Spanish Visual Studies* 1, no. 2 (2017): 287–302, and "Writing from and for the Periphery: Carving Out a Place for Spanish Food Studies," in *Repensar Los Estudios Ibéricos Desde La Periferia*, eds. José Colmeiro and Alfredo Martínez-Expósito (Venice: Edizioni Ca' Foscari, 2019), 103–14; as well as Lara Anderson and Rebecca Ingram, "Introduction. Transhispanic Food Cultural Studies: Defining the Subfield," *Bulletin of Spanish Studies* 97, no. 4 (April 2020): 471–83. For specific examples of scholarship in this field, see the above, as well as Eugenia Afinoguénova, "De la carta a la papeleta: el 'menú del día' entre la dictadura y la democracia en España, 1964–1981," *Bulletin of Spanish Studies* 97, no. 4 (April 2020): 515–38; Enric Bou, "Food and the Everyday in Spain: Immigration and Culinary Renovation," *Bulletin of Spanish Studies* 97, no. 4 (April 2020): 681–700; Leigh K. Mercer and H. Rosi Song, "*Catalanidad* in the Kitchen: Tourism, Gastronomy and Identity in Modern and Contemporary Barcelona," *Bulletin of Spanish Studies* 97, no. 4 (January 2020): 1–22; María Paz Moreno, "Discurso Ideológico e Idea de España En *El Cocinero Español* de 1898 y 1938," *Bulletin of Spanish Studies* 97, no. 4 (April 2020): 635–58. See also Venetia Congdon, "Narratives on an Independent Cuisine: Catalan Food as Identity in the Contemporary Independence Movement," in *Food, Social Change and Identity*, eds. Cynthia Chou and Susanne Kerner (Basingstoke, UK: Palgrave Macmillan, 2022), 91–120, and "Nourishing the Nation: Manifestations of Catalan Identity through Food," IV Congreso Internacional, "Otras maneras de comer" (Other ways of eating), University

of Barcelona, 2015; Francesc Fusté Forné, "Food Journalism: Building the Discourse on the Popularization of Gastronomy in the Twenty-First Century," PhD diss. (Universitat Ramon Llull, 2017); Montserrat Miller, *Feeding Barcelona, 1714–1975: Public Market Halls, Social Networks, and Consumer Culture* (Baton Rouge: Louisiana State University Press, 2015); Ainhoa Aguirregoitia Martínez and María Dolores Fernández Poyatos, "La Gastronomía En La Prensa Española Del Siglo XIX," *Estudios Sobre El Mensaje Periodístico* 21, no. 1 (July 21, 2015): 17–33; and Laura Solanilla and F. Xavier Medina, "Gastronomy and Social Networks: Heritage and Foodblogging in Catalonia," in *Food and the Internet: Proceedings of the 20th International Ethnological Food Research Conference, Department of Folklore and Ethnology, Institute of Ethnology and Cultural Anthropology, University of Lódz, Poland, 3.–6. September 2014,* eds. Violetta Krawczyk-Wasilewska and Patricia Lysaght (Frankfurt, Germany: Peter Lang, 2015).

6. Examples from just the last few years include Yael Raviv, *Falafel Nation: Cuisine and the Making of National Identity in Israel* (Lincoln: University of Nebraska Press, 2015); Thomas Parker, *Tasting French Terroir: The History of an Idea* (Berkeley: University of California Press, 2015); and, most recently, Roberta Sassatelli, ed., *Italians and Food* (Cham, Switzerland: Palgrave Macmillan, 2019).

7. Antonio Valencia García and José Ros Mayor, "ElPozo: Una Decisión Firme Por La Innovación y La Diferenciación. Plan de Marketing Para La Gama de Productos Bien-Star de ElPozo" (UCAM-Universidad Católica San Antonio, 2014), 8; Jaume Castell, *Per què mengem el que mengem* (Barcelona: Edi-Liber, 1999), 109–10; Jodi Campbell, *At the First Table: Food and Social Identity in Early Modern Spain* (Lincoln: University of Nebraska Press, 2017), 76–78.

8. Michaela DeSoucey, "Gastronationalism: Food Traditions and Authenticity Politics in the European Union," *American Sociological Review* 75, no. 3 (June 2010): 432–34.

9. For further exploration of regional cuisine as an increasingly prevalent vehicle for claims about Catalan national identity, see, for instance, Venetia Johannes, *Nourishing the Nation: Food as National Identity in Catalonia* (New York: Berghahn, 2020); H. Rosi Song and Anna Riera, *A Taste of Barcelona: The History of Catalan Cooking and Eating* (Lanham, MD: Rowman and Littlefield, 2019), esp. Chapter 1.

10. Michael Billig, *Banal Nationalism* (London: Sage, 1995). For a reevaluation of Billig's original thesis, see Michael Skey, "The National in Everyday Life: A Critical Engagement with Michael Billig's Thesis of *Banal Nationalism*," *The Sociological Review* 57, no. 2 (May 2009): 331–46.

11. DeSoucey, "Gastronationalism," 433–436, 442–444; Atsuko Ichijo, "Food and Nationalism: Gastronationalism Revisited," *Nationalities Papers* 48, no. 2 (March 2020): 215–23; and Atsuko Ichijo and Ronald Ranta, *Food, National Identity and Nationalism: From Everyday to Global Politics* (Cham, Switzerland: Palgrave Macmillan, 2016).

12. Ichijo and Ranta, *Food, National Identity and Nationalism*, 133–37.

13. Ibid., 5–13, 16–17.

14. Sebastiano Benasso and Luisa Stagi, "The Carbonara-Gate: Food Porn and Gastro-Nationalism," *Italians and Food*, eds. Roberta Sassatelli (Cham, Switzerland: Palgrave Macmillan, 2019), 237–67.

15. Melissa Aronczyk, "'Living the Brand': Nationality, Globality, and the Identity Strategies of Nation Branding Consultants," *International Journal of Communication* 2 (2008), 43–44.
16. Ibid., 44.
17. For closure of Catalan diplomatic efforts, see "Cierra el Diplocat en aplicación de las medidas del artículo 155," *La Vanguardia*, April 13, 2018. For the history of these efforts, see for instance, Diplocat, "Benvinguda," *Diplocat*; and Manuel Duran, *Mediterranean Paradiplomacies: The Dynamics of Diplomatic Reterritorialization* (Leiden, Netherlands: Brill Nijhof, 2015), Chapter 7. For an example of continued cultural outreach, see Catalan Tourist Board (Agència Catalana de Turisme), *Annual Report 2019* (Generalitat de Catalunya, Agència Catalan de Turisme, 2019).
18. Ichijo and Ranta, *Food, National Identity and Nationalism*; Melissa Aronczyk, "Living the Brand," 55–57; DeSoucey, "Gastronationalism," 442–44; and Arjun Appadurai, "How to Make a National Cuisine: Cookbooks in Contemporary India," *Comparative Studies in Society and History* 30, no. 1 (January 1988): 3–24.
19. Ichijo and Ranta, *Food, National Identity and Nationalism*, 72–79.
20. Jaume Fàbrega, *La cuina antiga: ibers, grecs i romans: els primers plats de la nostra memòria gustativa, per menjar avui* (Barcelona: Viena, 2017), 130, and *El llibre de la llonganissa: mítics embotits catalans: la seva història, la seva expansió i la seva cuina* (Girona, Spain: Curbet, 2016), 15–16, 21–22; as well as Llorenç Torrado, *Els Embotits a Catalunya: una tradició, un art, una indústria* (Barcelona: FECIC, Federació Catalana d'Indústries de la Carn: Generalitat de Catalunya, Departament d'Agricultura, Ramaderia i Pesca, 1985), 20–21.
21. Campbell, *At the First Table*, 76–78.
22. *Noticias y Documentales*, February 16, 1981.
23. "Jabugo, the Town That Knows Cinco Jotas," *Cinco Jotas Blog*, November 22, 2018.
24. "FERMÍN, a cut above – Fermin Iberico," *Embutidos Fermín*; Eurocarne, "Embutidos Fermín: Primer Matadero de Porcino Autorizado Para Exportar a Estados Unidos," *Eurocarne*, October 2011; Amanda Hesser, "Truly Spanish Chorizo, In America At Last," *The New York Times*, March 6, 2002; Chorizos Palacios, "Sobre Nosotros: Historia y evolución," *Chorizos Palacios*. ("FERMÍN, a cut above—Fermin Iberico"; Eurocarne; Hesser; Chorizos Palacios).
25. Néstor Luján, "Editorial," *La Cuina: revista mensual de gastronomia i vins* 1, no. 1 (1982); Joaquim Comella Riera, et al., eds., *Salchichón de Vic, Emociones En El Plato* (Vic, Spain: Casa Riera Ordeix, 2018); Santi Ponce i Vivet, *Embotits Espina: 1911-2011, Cent Anys* (Barcelona: Embotits Espina, 2011); and Pere Salgot, ed., *Embotits Salgot, 75 Anys d'història* (Barcelona: l'Empresa, 2003).
26. Alejandra Aramayo García and Anna Sabata Aliberch, "Casa Tarradellas: Tradició e Innovació," *Estratègia Competitiva a La Petita i Mitjana Empresa: Notes Pedagògiques* (Vic, Spain: Universitat de Vic, 2010), 23–36.
27. Néstor Luján, *La Llonganissa de Vic: del rebost del pagès a la taula del rei* (Vic, Spain: Casa Riera Ordeix, 1992), 16–17.
28. For Josep Maria Solá i Sala, see Pere Pratdesaba, "Vic nomena Josep M. Solà i Sala cronista oficial de la Ciutat," *Nació Digital*, May 7, 2012.

29. Miller, *Feeding Barcelona*.
30. Ponce i Vivet, *Embotits Espina*, 22–23; Fàbrega, *El llibre de la llonganissa*, 14, 53–54.
31. Comella Riera et al., *Salchichón*.
32. These included *Revista Culinaria: Órgano de la Asociación Profesional de Cocineros de Cataluña* (published from 1928 till at least 1936) and the Madrid-based but Ignasi Domènech-led *El Gorro Blanco: Revista Culinaria Mensual* (1906–1945). See Johannes, *Nourishing the Nation*, 49–53. See also Simón Palmer and María del Carmen, "Ignacio Doménech, Editor y Autor Culinario," *Cincinnati Romance Review*, no. 33 (2012): 4–26; and Song and Riera, *A Taste of Barcelona*, esp. Chapter 3.
33. See for instance Sandie Holguín, *Flamenco Nation: The Construction of Spanish National Identity* (Madison: University of Wisconsin Press, 2019), 187–203. For another instance of regional culture reduced to the status of curio, see Alejandro J. Gómez del Moral, *Buying into Change: Mass Consumption, Dictatorship, and Democratization in Franco's Spain, 1939–1982* (Lincoln: University of Nebraska Press, 2021), 192–93.
34. Suzanne Dunai, "Cooking for the Patria: The *Seccion Femenina* and the Politics of Food and Women during the Franco Years," MA thesis (University of New Mexico, 2012), 129, and "Food Politics in Postwar Spain: Eating and Everyday Life During the Early Franco Dictatorship, 1939–1952," PhD diss. (University of California, San Diego, 2019), 157–60.
35. Lara Anderson, *Control and Resistance: Food Discourse in Franco Spain* (Toronto: University of Toronto Press, 2020), 108.
36. Manuel Vázquez Montalbán, *L'Art del Menjar a Catalunya* (Barcelona: Edicions 62, S. A., 1977), 22. Here Vázquez Montalbán appears to be playing a bit with ambiguous language: the original Catalan "llistes de menjar ridículament estatal" could mean food menus that evidence a pronounced alignment with the State, as his subsequent parenthetical allusion to the Spanish State might suggest; food menus that aspire to somehow encompass the totality of the Spanish State's many different culinary traditions, as his later quip about "ridiculously international menus" seems to suggest; or some combination of the two meanings.
37. Jaume Fàbrega, "Existeix la cuina espanyola?" *El Temps*, April 23, 2018. See also Afinoguénova, "De la carta."
38. "Mesa Revuelta: estudio sobre embutidos catalanes," *Club de Gourmets* 116 (December 1985): 14–15; "Societat i Cultura - Els Embotits a Catalunya: Una Tradició, Un Art, Una Indústria," in *La Industria tocinera: órgano oficial del Gremio Provincial de Industriales Tocineros Detallistas de Barcelona: revista técnica - especializada al servicio de la industria chacinera*, edited by Gremi Provincial de Cansaladers-Xarcuters de Barcelona, Consell de Cent, 80, l'entitat (1960); "Un Llibre Recommanable: Els Embotits a Catalunya," *Gras i Magre* 38 (October-December, 1986): 23.
39. See for instance, Club de Gourmets, "Sumario," *Club de gourmets*, no. 1 (1976).
40. These included *Catalunya Gastronòmica*, which counted Bettónica and Nestor Luján among its editors, launched in Barcelona in 1976; the hospitality journal *Santa Marta Hostelera*, which included considerable content on cuisine and gastrotourism, founded in the western Catalan city of Lleida in 1977; and *La Cuina: Revista Mensual de Gastronomia i Vins*, on whose editorial board Nestor Luján also served along with Llorenç

Torrado, first circulated in 1982. See Catalunya Gastronómica, "Editorial: Nuestro saludo cordial e ilusionado," *Catalunya gastronómica* 1, no. 1 (March 1976); Enrique Ribera Gabande, "Editorial - Un nuevo formato," *Santa Marta hostelera* 3, no. 11 (1980); Luján, "Editorial."

41. Llorenç Torrado, "El Porc: Miscellània," *La Cuina: revista mensual de gastronomia i vins* 1, no. 3 (January 1983), 22.
42. Spain Gourmetour, "Editorial." *Spain Gourmetour: Food, Wine and Travels Magazine*, September 1985; Francesc Sabater i Mecre, "Editorial – Salutació," *Girona gastronòmica revista de turisme, viatges i gastronomia* 1, no. 0 (May 1986), 5; La Junta Directiva, "Editorial - Amb 'Gras i Magre,' Una Nova Etapa de La Revista Gremial," *Gras i Magre: Portaveu Del Gremi Provincial de Cansaladers i Xarcuters de Barcelona* 26, no. 37 (September 1986), 5.
43. "Societat i Cultura."
44. Generalitat de Catalunya, "Ordre de 10 d'aril de 1986, per la qual s'estableixen el proceidment i els criteris de concessió de subvencions a institucions sense finalitat de lucre per la realització d'accions de promoció comercial a l'artesania," *Diari Oficial de la Generalitat de Catalunya*, April, 10, 1986.
45. Montserrat Canals and Generalitat de Catalunya, *Joc de taula: 150 receptes culinàries de restaurants selleccionats al dian Avuib* (Barcelona: Generalitat de Catalunya, 1989); Marta Ribalta et al., *Gastronomy in Catalonia* (Barcelona: Generalitat de Catalunya, Departament de Comerç, Consum i Turisme, Servei d'Informació, Documentació i Publicacions, 1993).
46. Juame Fàbrega, *Nació i Deglució: Fílies i Fòbies de La Cultura Del Gust* (Lleida, Spain: Pagès, 1997), and *La Cultura Del Gust Als Països Catalans: Espais Geogràfics, Socials i Històrics Del Patrimoni Culinari Català* (Tarragona, Spain: Edicions El Mèdol, 2000).
47. Ribalta et al., *Gastronomy in Catalonia*, 6.
48. Luján, *La Llonganissa de Vic*; Salgot, *Embotits Salgot*; Ponce i Vivet, *Embotits Espina*; Comella Riera et al., *Salchichón de Vic*.
49. Dolcet et al., *Els Embotits de Catalunya*; Buxeda i Majoral, *El llibre dels embotits*; Fàbrega, *El llibre de la llonganissa*.
50. Vázquez Montalbán, *L'Art del Menjar*, 152.
51. Dolcet and Pons i Argimon, *Els Embotits de Catalunya*, 11.
52. Ibid., 22.
53. Ibid., 13.
54. Sebastià Bennasar, "Jaume Fàbrega: 'Espanya s'ha apropiat la nostra cuina i els nostres èxits,'" *VilaWeb*, September 29, 2017.
55. Mercaconsumo, "El Comercio Que Viene," *La Industria Tocinera* 35 (March–April 1985).
56. Nicolás Betancor Gómez, "Artesania Alimentaria – II," *Gras i Magre* 40 (March–April 1987): 12; "Profesionalidad, Hoy," *Gras i Magre* 38 (October–December 1986): 11.
57. "Editorial – Llotja de xarcuteria," *Girona Gastronòmica* 7 (March 1987): 5.
58. Jaume Fàbrega, "Productes del mes – El Porc: Plaer prohibit, plaer disfrutat," *Girona Gastronòmica* 5 (January 1987): 15.

59. José Andrés and Richard Wolffe, *Made in Spain: Spanish Dishes for the American Kitchen* (New York: Clarkson Potter/Publishers, 2008), 172; Donald B. Harris, *The Heart of Spain: Families and Food* (Williamsburg, VA: Duende Press, 2011), xxi–xxii).
60. Roger de Gràcia, "Enrique Tomás: 'Es creu que a Catalunya només fem fuet i botifarres, però és on més pernil es fa,'" *Estat de Gràcia*, Catalunya Ràdio, April 8, 2019, emphasis mine.
61. Catalunyam, "Penjat Com Un Fuet," Catalunyam. For an indication of the range of unisex t-shirts sold at the Vilaweb store, see "La botiga de Vilaweb - Samarretes unisex," *VilaWeb.cat*.
62. Oriol Janer, "Correspondence with Catalunyam Info," September 15, 2019.
63. Valencia García and Ros Mayor, "ElPozo," 8; Ismael Díaz Yubero, "Historia y futuro del jamón, un alimento excelente y emblemático," *Distribución y Consumo* 157, no. 2 (2019), 74; Asociación Nacional de Industrias de la Carne de España, "El Sector Cárnico Español," *Anice.es*.

WORKS CITED

Afinoguénova, Eugenia. "De la carta a la papeleta: el 'menú del día' entre la dictadura y la democracia en España, 1964–1981." *Bulletin of Spanish Studies* 97, no. 4 (April 2020): 515–38.
Aguirregoitia Martínez, Ainhoa, and María Dolores Fernández Poyatos. "La Gastronomía En La Prensa Española Del Siglo XIX." *Estudios Sobre El Mensaje Periodístico* 21, no. 1 (July 21, 2015): 17–33.
Agulló, Ferran. *Llibre de la cuina catalana*. Barcelona: Editorial Alta Fulla, 1999.
Anderson, Lara. "Cooking up the Past: Culinary Nostalgia and Gender Critique in *Cuéntame Cómo Pasó*." *Hispanic Research Journal* 17, no. 1 (2016): 34–48.
———. "A Recipe for Spain: *Un País Para Comérselo*'s Centralizing Promotion and Othering of Regional Cuisines." *Bulletin of Spanish Visual Studies* 1, no. 2 (2017): 287–302.
———. *Control and Resistance: Food Discourse in Franco Spain*. Toronto: University of Toronto Press, 2020.
———. "Writing from and for the Periphery: Carving Out a Place for Spanish Food Studies." In *Repensar Los Estudios Ibéricos Desde La Periferia*, edited by José Colmeiro and Alfredo Martínez-Expósito, 103–14. Venice: Edizioni Ca' Foscari, 2019.
Anderson, Lara, and Rebecca Ingram. "Introduction. Transhispanic Food Cultural Studies: Defining the Subfield." *Bulletin of Spanish Studies* 97, no. 4 (April 2020): 471–83.
Andrés, José, and Richard Wolffe. *Made in Spain: Spanish Dishes for the American Kitchen*. New York: Clarkson Potter/Publishers, 2008.
Appadurai, Arjun. "How to Make a National Cuisine: Cookbooks in Contemporary India." *Comparative Studies in Society and History* 30, no. 1 (January 1988): 3–24.
Aronczyk, Melissa. "'Living the Brand': Nationality, Globality, and the Identity Strategies of Nation Branding Consultants." *International Journal of Communication* 2 (2008), 41–65.

Asociación Nacional de Industrias de la Carne de España. "El Sector Cárnico Español." *Anice.es.*
Benasso, Sebastiano, and Luisa Stagi. "The Carbonara-Gate: Food Porn and Gastro-Nationalism." *Italians and Food*, edited by Roberta Sassatelli, 236–67. Cham, Switzerland: Palgrave Macmillan, 2019.
Benaul i Berenguer, Josep M. "Los orígenes de la empresa textil lanera en Sabadell y Terrassa en el siglo XVIII." *Revista de Historia Industrial* 1 (1992): 39–62.
Bennasar, Sebastià. "Jaume Fàbrega: 'Espanya s'ha apropiat la nostra cuina i els nostres èxits.'" *VilaWeb*, September 29, 2017.
Betancor Gómez, Nicolás. "Artesania Alimentaria – II." *Gras i Magre* 40 (March–April 1987).
Billig, Michael. *Banal Nationalism*. London: Sage, 1995.
"La botiga de Vilaweb - Samarretes unisex." *VilaWeb.cat*.
Bou, Enric. "Food and the Everyday in Spain: Immigration and Culinary Renovation." *Bulletin of Spanish Studies* 97, no. 4 (April 2020): 681–700.
Buxeda i Majoral, Gerard. *El llibre dels embotits*. Girona, Spain: Sidillà, 2016.
Campbell, Jodi. *At the First Table: Food and Social Identity in Early Modern Spain*. Lincoln: University of Nebraska Press, 2017.
Canals, Montserrat, and Generalitat de Catalunya. *Joc de taula: 150 receptes culinàries de restaurants selleccionats al dia d'Avui*. Barcelona: Generalitat de Catalunya, 1989.
Castell, Jaume. *Per què mengem el que mengem*. Barcelona: Edi-Liber, 1999.
Catalan Tourist Board (Agència Catalana de Turisme). *Annual Report 2019*. Generalitat de Catalunya, Agència Catalan de Turisme, 2019.
Catalunya Gastronómica. "Editorial: Nuestro saludo cordial e ilusionado." *Catalunya gastronómica* 1, no. 1 (March 1976).
Catalunyam. "Penjat Com Un Fuet."
Chorizos Palacios. "Sobre Nosotros: Historia y evolución." *Chorizos Palacios.*
"Cierra el Diplocat en aplicación de las medidas del artículo 155." *La Vanguardia*, April 13, 2018.
Club de Gourmets. "Sumario." *Club de gourmets*, no. 1 (1976).
Comella Riera, Joaquim, et al., eds. *Salchichón de Vic, Emociones En El Plato*. Vic, Spain: Casa Riera Ordeix, 2018.
Congdon, Venetia. "Narratives on an Independent Cuisine: Catalan Food as Identity in the Contemporary Independence Movement." In *Food, Social Change and Identity*, edited by Cynthia Chou and Susanne Kerner, 91–120. Basingstoke, UK: Palgrave Macmillan, 2022. See also Johannes, Venetia.
―――. "Nourishing the Nation: Manifestations of Catalan Identity through Food." IV Congreso Internacional, "Otras maneras de comer" (Other ways of eating), University of Barcelona, 2015. See also Johannes, Venetia.
de Gràcia, Roger. "Enrique Tomás: 'Es creu que a Catalunya només fem fuet i botifarres, però és on més pernil es fa.'" *Estat de Gràcia*, Catalunya Ràdio, April 8, 2019.
DeSoucey, Michaela. "Gastronationalism: Food Traditions and Authenticity Politics in the European Union." *American Sociological Review* 75, no. 3 (June 2010): 432–55.
Díaz Yubero, Ismael "Historia y futuro del jamón, un alimento excelente y emblemático." *Distribución y Consumo* 157, no. 2 (2019).

Diplocat. "Benvinguda." *Diplocat.*

Dolcet, Josep, and Ignasi Pons i Argimon, eds. *Els Embotits de Catalunya*. Barcelona: Edicions 62: Generalitat de Catalunya, Departament d'Agricultura, Alimentació i Acció Rural, 2010.

Domènech, Ignasi. *La Teca: la veritable cuina casolana de Catalunya*. Tipografia Bonet, 1924.

Dunai, Suzanne. "Cooking for the Patria: The *Seccion Femenina* and the Politics of Food and Women during the Franco Years." MA thesis. University of New Mexico, 2012.

———. "Food Politics in Postwar Spain: Eating and Everyday Life During the Early Franco Dictatorship, 1939–1952." PhD dissertation. University of California, San Diego, 2019.

Duran, Manuel. *Mediterranean Paradiplomacies: The Dynamics of Diplomatic Reterritorialization*. Leiden, Netherlands: Brill Nijhof, 2015.

Edicions Sidillà. "El Llibre Dels Embotits." Edicions Sidillà.

"Editorial – Llotja de xarcuteria." *Girona Gastronòmica* 7 (March 1987).

Eurocarne. "Embutidos Fermín: Primer Matadero de Porcino Autorizado Para Exportar a Estados Unidos." *Eurocarne*, October 2011.

Fàbrega, Jaume. *El llibre de la llonganissa: mítics embotits catalans: la seva història, la seva expansió i la seva cuina*. Girona, Spain: Curbet, 2016.

———. *La cuina antiga: ibers, grecs i romans: els primers plats de la nostra memòria gustativa, per menjar avui*. Barcelona: Viena, 2017.

———. *La Cultura Del Gust Als Països Catalans: Espais Geogràfics, Socials i Històrics Del Patrimoni Culinari Català*. Tarragona, Spain: Edicions El Mèdol, 2000.

———. "Existeix la cuina espanyola?" *El Temps*, April 23, 2018.

———. *Nació i Deglució: Fílies i Fòbies de La Cultura Del Gust*. Lleida, Spain: Pagès, 1997.

———. "Productes del mes – El Porc: Plaer prohibit, plaer disfrutat." *Girona Gastronòmica* 5 (January 1987).

"FERMÍN, a cut above – Fermin Iberico." Embutidos Fermín.

Fusté Forné, Francesc. "Food Journalism: Building the Discourse on the Popularization of Gastronomy in the Twenty-First Century." PhD dissertation. Universitat Ramon Llull, 2017.

García, Alejandra Aramayo, and Anna Sabata Aliberch. "Casa Tarradellas: Tradició e Innovació." *Estratègia Competitiva a La Petita i Mitjana Empresa: Notes Pedagògiques*, 23–36. Vic, Spain: Universitat de Vic, 2010.

Generalitat de Catalunya. "Ordre de 10 d'aril de 1986, per la qual s'estableixen el proceidment i els criteris de concessió de subvencions a institucions sense finalitat de lucre per la realització d'accions de promoció comercial a l'artesania." *Diari Oficial de la Generalitat de Catalunya*, April, 10, 1986.

Gómez del Moral, Alejandro J. *Buying into Change: Mass Consumption, Dictatorship, and Democratization in Franco's Spain, 1939–1982*. Lincoln: University of Nebraska Press, 2021.

Harris, Donald B. *The Heart of Spain: Families and Food*. Williamsburg, VA: Duende Press, 2011.

Hesser, Amanda. "Truly Spanish Chorizo, In America At Last." *The New York Times*, March 6, 2002.

Holguín, Sandie. *Flamenco Nation: The Construction of Spanish National Identity*. Madison: University of Wisconsin Press, 2019.

Ichijo, Atsuko. "Food and Nationalism: Gastronationalism Revisited." *Nationalities Papers* 48, no. 2 (March 2020): 215–23.
Ichijo, Atsuko, and Ronald Ranta. *Food, National Identity and Nationalism: From Everyday to Global Politics*. Cham, Switzerland: Palgrave Macmillan, 2016.
"Jabugo, the Town That Knows Cinco Jotas." *Cinco Jotas Blog*, November 22, 2018.
Janer, Oriol. "Correspondence with Catalunyam Info." September 15, 2019.
Johannes, Venetia. *Nourishing the Nation: Food as National Identity in Catalonia*. New York: Berghahn, 2020. See also Congdon, Venetia.
Junta Directiva, La. "Editorial - Amb 'Gras i Magre,' Una Nova Etapa de La Revista Gremial." *Gras i Magre: Portaveu Del Gremi Provincial de Cansaladers i Xarcuters de Barcelona* 26, no. 37 (September 1986).
"Un Llibre Recommanable: Els Embotits a Catalunya." *Gras i Magre* 38 (October-December, 1986).
Luján, Néstor. "Editorial." *La Cuina: revista mensual de gastronomia i vins* 1, no. 1 (1982).
———. *La Llonganissa de Vic: del rebost del pagès a la taula del rei*. Vic, Spain: Casa Riera Ordeix, 1992.
Luján, Néstor, and Tin Luján. *La cocina moderna en Cataluña/La cuina moderna a Catalunya*. Madrid: Espasa-Calpe, 1988.
Luján, Nestor, and Juan Perucho. *El libro de la cocina española: gastronomía e historia*. Barcelona: Tusquets Editores, 2003.
Mercer, Leigh K., and H. Rosi Song. "*Catalanidad* in the Kitchen: Tourism, Gastronomy and Identity in Modern and Contemporary Barcelona." *Bulletin of Spanish Studies* 97, no. 4 (January 2020): 1–22.
Mercaconsumo. "El Comercio Que Viene." *La Industria Tocinera* 35 (March–April 1985).
"Mesa Revuelta: estudio sobre embutidos catalanes." *Club de Gourmets* 116 (December 1985): 14–15.
Miller, Montserrat. *Feeding Barcelona, 1714–1975: Public Market Halls, Social Networks, and Consumer Culture*. Baton Rouge: Louisiana State University Press, 2015.
Moreno, María Paz. "Discurso Ideológico e Idea de España En *El Cocinero Español* de 1898 y 1938." *Bulletin of Spanish Studies* 97, no. 4 (April 2020): 635–58.
Noticias y Documentales. February 16, 1981.
Parker, Thomas. *Tasting French Terroir: The History of an Idea*. Berkeley: University of California Press, 2015.
Ponce i Vivet, Santi. *Embotits Espina: 1911-2011, Cent Anys*. Barcelona: Embotits Espina, 2011.
Pratdesaba, Pere. "Vic nomena Josep M. Solà i Sala cronista oficial de la ciutat." *Nació Digital*, May 7, 2012.
"Profesionalidad, Hoy." *Gras i Magre* 38 (October–December 1986).
Raviv, Yael. *Falafel Nation: Cuisine and the Making of National Identity in Israel*. Lincoln: University of Nebraska Press, 2015.
Ribalta, Marta, et al. *Gastronomy in Catalonia*. Barcelona: Generalitat de Catalunya, Departament de Comerç, Consum i Turisme, Servei d'Informació, Documentació i Publicacions, 1993.
Ribera Gabande, Enrique. "Editorial - Un nuevo formato." *Santa Marta hostelera* 3, no. 11 (1980).

Sabater i Mecre, Francesc. "Editorial - Salutació." *Girona gastronòmica revista de turisme, viatges i gastronomia* 1, no. 0 (May 1986).
Salgot, Pere, ed. *Embotits Salgot, 75 Anys d'història*. Barcelona: l'Empresa, 2003.
Sassatelli, Roberta, editor. *Italians and Food*. Cham, Switzerland: Palgrave Macmillan, 2019.
Simón Palmer, María del Carmen. "Ignacio Doménech, Editor y Autor Culinario." *Cincinnati Romance Review*, no. 33 (2012): 4–26.
Skey, Michael. "The National in Everyday Life: A Critical Engagement with Michael Billig's Thesis of *Banal Nationalism*." *The Sociological Review* 57, no. 2 (May 2009): 331–46.
"Societat i Cultura – Els Embotits a Catalunya: Una Tradició, Un Art, Una Indústria." In *La Industria tocinera: órgano oficial del Gremio Provincial de Industriales Tocineros Detallistas de Barcelona: revista técnica - especializada al servicio de la industria chacinera*, edited by Gremi Provincial de Cansaladers-Xarcuters de Barcelona, Consell de Cent, 80, l'entitat, 1960.
Solanilla, Laura, and F. Xavier Medina. "Gastronomy and Social Networks: Heritage and Foodblogging in Catalonia." In *Food and the Internet: Proceedings of the 20th International Ethnological Food Research Conference, Department of Folklore and Ethnology, Institute of Ethnology and Cultural Anthropology, University of Lódz, Poland, 3.–6. September 2014*, edited by Violetta Krawczyk-Wasilewska and Patricia Lysaght. Frankfurt, Germany: Peter Lang, 2015.
Song, H. Rosi, and Anna Riera. *A Taste of Barcelona: The History of Catalan Cooking and Eating*. Lanham, MD: Rowman and Littlefield, 2019.
Spain Gourmetour. "Editorial." *Spain Gourmetour: Food, Wine and Travels Magazine*, September 1985.
Torrado, Llorenç. *Els Embotits a Catalunya: una tradició, un art, una indústria*. Barcelona: FECIC, Federació Catalana d'Indústries de la Carn: Generalitat de Catalunya, Departament d'Agricultura, Ramaderia i Pesca, 1985.
———. "El Porc: Miscellània." *La Cuina: revista mensual de gastronomia i vins* 1, no. 3 (January 1983).
Valencia García, Antonio, and José Ros Mayor. "ElPozo: Una Decisión Firme Por La Innovación y La Diferenciación. Plan de Marketing Para La Gama de Productos BienStar de ElPozo." UCAM-Universidad Católica San Antonio, 2014.
Vázquez Montalbán, Manuel. *L'Art del Menjar a Catalunya*. Barcelona: Edicions 62, S. A., 1977.
Weiss, Jeffrey. *Charcuteria: The Soul of Spain*. Evanston, IL: Surrey Books, 2014.

◆ AFTERWORD

Future Directions on Food Studies and Politics in Spain Today

Carolyn A. Nadeau

In today's headlines, numerous articles surrounding food politics, policies and regulations inundate the media. Articles ranging from international food aid to local food markets; from ethical and cultural food production to biofuel, GMO, and pesticide usage; from water rights, to animal cruelty, and to migrant labor rights are at the forefront of news, social and web medias, as well as academic presses. Thus, the timing of *Digestible Governance: Gastrocracy and Spanish Foodways* could not be more perfect for scholars today to gain a more informed understanding of the deep-seated relationship that exists between food and politics. This contribution will join the ranks of other celebrated works such as Atsuko Ichijo and Ronald Ranta's *Food, National Identity and Nationalism*; Katharina Vester's *A Taste of Power: Food and American Identities*; and Michaela DeSoucey's *Contested Tastes: Foie Gras and the Politics of Food* to shed light on food and food politics in Spain today.

From start to finish this volume of collective essays is a thoughtful and compelling exploration of the history of and current debates on food and politics in Spain. Each of the eleven essays in this stimulating volume offers thought-provoking ideas about the sourcing, preparation, distribution and/or consumption of food and how those practices and perspectives relate to or interact with affairs of the state. The grouping into four sections provides an effective structure to help make sense of the different ways in which food, culture and politics intermingle. As the editors state: "Gastronomy has always been gastrocracy.... What happened to the Spanish economy, also and first happened to Spanish gastronomy."[1] What follows in these final pages are some reflections on and contextualization of the insights each author shares, several key takeaways from each of the essays, and where readers can go from here as we continue to consider the value of Spanish food studies today.

In the spring of 2017, the three editors, Eugenia Afinoguénova, Lara Anderson, and Rebecca Ingram, and I presented work in the joint panel, "Food Studies Finds Iberia," at the MACHL conference in Saint Louis. In the post-presentation discussion, we (with the audience) engaged in a rich exchange of the state of food studies in Spain today and I remember that in that lively dialogue, the editors brought to light some of the gaps in Spanish food studies that demanded attention. Since then Afinoguénova has published both books and articles on Spanish culture more broadly, including her insightful article, "De la carta a la papeleta: El 'menú del día' entre la dictadura y la democracia en España, 1964–1981" (*Bulletin of Hispanic Studies*, 2020). In this latter work she explores the transnational origins of the *menu del día* (daily lunch special) and how the government invested in that model to promote tourism. She further argues that it was the middle-class Spaniard who played a critical role in establishing the *menu del día* as a quintessential facet of Spanish cuisine because the middle class began to consume outside the home and explore tourism within their own country.

Anderson and Ingram went on to co-edit the special issue "Transhispanic Food Cultural Studies" for the *Bulletin of Spanish Studies* (2020). This volume brought together a series of groundbreaking articles on the conditioning of food culture and discourse from critical transnational and national frameworks, and, as such, definitively established food as a central praxis within the field of transhispanic cultural studies. Anderson also authored *Control and Resistance: Food Discourse in Franco Spain*. This monograph focuses on both overt and subtle ways in which food becomes an instrument of the state to invent and maintain a nationalist cuisine and conversely examines food texts that resisted Francoist ideology. This landmark study takes on how food was turned into a "biopolitical tool" that privileged patriotism manifested through autarky, prescriptive gender roles, and monolithic nationalism. Anderson writes, "food instructions, preparation procedures, domestic manuals, descriptions of meals in literature and the media, images of dishes, accounts of national or regional food habits, and information about food in official reports and domestic magazines made explicit to Spaniards what was expected of them in a totalitarian and ultra-conservative Spain."[2] It also delves into points of resistance, specifically, she explores more autonomous authors whose work provided alternatives to state-controlled food narratives. Additionally, Ingram wrote the exceptional book *Women's Work: How Culinary Cultures Shaped Modern Spain*, in which she examines how specific women writers challenged hegemonic discourses via culinary culture in the early part of the twentieth century. Her meticulous research incorporates feminist thought and political activity in the first decades of the twentieth century and broadens those claims to complicate debates on how foodscapes, haute cuisine chefs, and the institution of culinary tourism have shaped and continue to shape contemporary Spain.

Knowing their respective research agendas, one can better understand how well-positioned these scholars were to bring together this timely volume of collected essays and what an outstanding contribution they make once again to food studies, cultural studies, Catalan and Spanish studies. In their introduction, the editors bring to light current debates surrounding food and politics and draw on key critical sources. They contextualize the volume by providing necessary background on gastronationalism (of the early twentieth century); food discourse as a site of control and resistance under Franco, the rise of peripheral nationalisms, and the influence of minority populations in fostering a multicultural and multiethnic presence in the twenty-first century.

They clearly state the goal of this collection: to examine the ways in which food is a political tool. Gastrocracy, as they explain, the "power produced and reproduced by appropriating the discourses and practices related to the sourcing, preparation, distribution, and consumption of food," is at the center of each essay.[3] Throughout, authors expose how governance is inextricably linked to food systems, how food-related discourses and culinary practices, found even in everyday practices push up against state interests, and what role food performances take on in the relationship between food systems and the government. As the editors state early on, the core idea examined here is that "food systems and governance so visible in contemporary foodscape have a long history of connections underpinning Spain's nation-building."[4] Each author returns to this key idea in unique ways. While this volume is divided into four sections that focus on politics, identity, institutions, and political resistance all studied through the lens of gastronomy, the comments that follow are based on a holistic reading of the text and seek to tease out commonalities that cut across these topics. I will begin with food history and food heritage, and then continue with observations on regionalism, gastronationalism, and culinary xenophobia that recur throughout the study.

As an early modern scholar, one of the recurring commonalities I observed throughout the collection is the role history plays in current gastropolitical discussions. Knowing the patterns, challenges and achievements that surround food practices and perspectives historically, helps to provide necessary context to unpack current issues surrounding food. In the very first essay, "Public Control over Private Trade: Barcelona's Market Hall Food Retailing System," Montserrat Miller provides an outstanding example of how the history of the market, its role in urban social order, in modernization, and in providing women a historic space in the market-based trade, is fundamental to understanding the market place today. We learn how at key moments in the twentieth century, the market served as a site of control for tamping down rebellions, policing not only social control but also public health codes. Miller's impeccable research opens doors for future comparative studies. Among the questions her essay provokes is why

Barcelona's open-air/market-hall food retail system has largely succeeded while in other urban centers it struggles to compete with supermarket chains. How can small business owners and local government negotiate the balance of market halls and locally run stalls with supermarket chains? How can Barcelona's successes translate to other cities? What are the issues particular to Barcelona that would frame what is happening there within a broader Spanish or European context?

Silvina Schammah Gesser and Susy Gruss also provide readers today with an important historical exploration of the role of religion in dietary laws. Their impeccable study "*Kashrut* in Spain: Religious Observance, State Tolerance or Niche Market Entrepreneurship?" provides a foundational understanding of how Jewish food practices were affected by and affected government laws and economic practices. This type of inquiry, which includes significant interviews with rabbis and historic Jewish figures, serves as a model for further explorations of minority groups and their role in better understanding gastrocracy today. In the case of Spanish regionalism, *kashrut* practices vary from region to region thus highlighting nuances within the country. For example, Schammah Gesser and Gruss analyze the different dietary practices among Jewish communities of continental Spain and the Spanish enclaves in North Africa and how these differences shed light on larger cultural nuances. Bringing to light the complex history of dietary practices among minority groups in Spain helps to better understand the larger cultural contributions that diverse groups have brought and continue to bring to Spain.

In "Ideology 'à la Carte': Food Politics in Franco's Spain," Suzanne Dunai provides another provocative example on why the history of food is so important to understanding food and politics today. She maps out mechanisms the Franco regime used to impart its ideology (patriotism, patriarchy and Catholicism) into common practices of everyday life as banal as eating. At each historic stage, Dunai exposes how ideology was converted into policy and then into practice. She brings to the discussion an excellent series of primary texts to provide evidence of food policies regarding nutrition.

Likewise, in his essay "The Institutionalization of the Asturian *Espicha* during the Franco Regime," Luis Benito García Álvarez offers impeccable research into how Franco first controlled and restricted historic Asturian cider celebrations, specifically the *espicha* events when producers would open the cider barrel, and later appropriated the same celebrations to construct a narrative of harmonious social order. His essay is a brilliant reminder of the power of regional archives to understand more fully the history of food politics and food culture.

In these essays, and others in this collection, studying the history of food practices allows us to consider how food has historically engaged government, private businesses, ethnic and religious groups, and other entities. Understanding decisive and historic food moments helps us address contemporary issues because it provides us with a deeper awareness and more informed context. Additionally, in discussing food heritage and its stake in the tourist industry in his article, "Food, Heritage, and Tourism: On the Uses of Food Heritage and Its Relations with Culture, Politics, and Socioeconomic Development," F. Xavier Medina emphatically states that "the recognition of food-related heritage needs to be constantly redefined and honed, ensuring more specific analysis of how heritagization affects—both positively and negatively—different assets. He distinguishes between history and heritage, the latter being something that comes from the past but is always part of the present, and go on to affirm that "on-the-ground analysis must be as critical as possible, detecting any points of friction and fostering practical debates and proper, speedy solutions to problems."[5] Further developmental studies like Medina's that reach back to previous centuries and historic food issues could provide new perspectives on food's relationship with culture, the economy and politics today.

Medina's essay also brings to the forefront the role of the outsider in shaping both regional and national food identities by way of the tourist industry. He reminds readers that tourism alone in no way accounts for systemic changes when he states, "From our standpoint, tourism is just one further aspect in the processes of cultural evolution within a much broader framework of globalization and, under no circumstance, is an isolated factor that can be regarded as solely responsible for any process. There are no 'pure' trajectories, either in society or in culture."[6]

And yet, his essay does inspire scholars to consider how voices external to one's region or country influence the evolving definition of food identity. Within the complex network that forms part of food practices and perceptions, how does tourism affect food culture? And, he rightly notes that restaurants are not the only food players in the tourist industry that have a bearing on how gastronomy evolves. He firmly states that "the concept should be as broad as possible, covering the entire agri-food chain, from production and productive landscapes to forms of preparation, consumption, dishes, restaurants and even the use of resources."[7] Without repeating what Medina has already so compellingly argued in his essay, I will only add that he has clearly identified the need to further investigate the economics, the politics, and the ever-evolving cultural impact the role food plays in the tourist industry.

Another common theme developed in several of the essays relates to regional foods and nationalistic discourse. In fact, three of the essays explore identity formation through Catalan cuisine. In "Regenerating Catalan Culinary Identity," H. Rosi Song traces the development of Catalan cuisine and ties it to the land.

They acknowledge the scholarship already published on the role food plays in Catalan identity politics, and turn to a singular cookbook to further explore the roots of Catalan identity. Song astutely demonstrates how a single cookbook, in this case Ferran Agulló's *Llibre de la cuina catalana*, not only defined a nationalist cuisine but also set in motion the cooking and eating practices that shaped Catalan nationality.

Equally fascinating are the two essays on specific Catalan food and beverage: "Cava's Place" by Bob Davidson and "Creating a 'Land of Charcuterie': Cured Meat Producers, Culinary Marketing, and the Construction of Gastronationalist Discourses in Twentieth-Century Catalonia" by Alejandro J. Gómez del Moral. In the former essay, Davidson leads us through the incredibly complex history of cava's production and reception (and resistance to it) in these past twenty plus years. He explains the recent break some local producers have made from the regulatory *Denominación de origen* system to create a new brand of sparkling wine, Corpinat, that insists on a strict land connection, its *terroir*, that is the wine grown and produced exclusively in the Penedès region and with organic practices. A similar *terroir* approach is highlighted in Gómez del Moral's essay. Here, the author deftly delineates the social, cultural and political implications that have developed (and continue to develop) in the production of Catalan cured pork products in recent years. The author does an outstanding job contextualizing the case of Catalan cured pork products within the larger framework of gastronationalism as each section of the essay builds upon the previous one to make compelling arguments that support the historic trajectory of cured pork and its larger social and political ramifications.

These essays serve as models for future studies of regional food and gastronationalist discourse and prompt a series of further research. Similar studies to Song's that bring to light the role of historic cookbooks in the formation of culinary and, more broadly, cultural and political identity, would continue to enrich our understanding of food's role in the affairs of the state. Regarding viticulture, another line of interdisciplinary scholarship could include partnering with botanists involved in projects like Etnobiofic, who seek to recover traditional knowledge of plants, diversity of agroecosystems and their relation to the urban marketplace. In keeping with specific food products such as cured meats and wines, similar studies would open up nuances of microclimates, farming practices, and regional perspectives to better inform current debates on food, identity and politics in Spain today. For example, when considering cured pork products, how has the rise of animal rights activism and awareness of plant-forward diets drawn attention to how pigs (and other animals) are bred and raised? Gómez del Moral asserts that "meat production and processing is now Spain's fifth largest industry, ... and Spain has become the European Union's foremost pork exporter by volume, and fourth-biggest worldwide."[8] In what conditions are these animals living? Might animal husbandry practices also be part of an expression of national identity that sets Catalonia apart from Spanish practices found elsewhere?

Food has the power to unite people through a common gastronomic identity. It allows those from a specific area involved at any level of production to take pride in who they are and what their land produces. I am reminded of Lara Anderson's eloquent conclusion in her essay, "Francoist Food Culture in Post-Authoritarian Spain: Culinary Maps, Centralism, and Food Memories," when she writes: "We must find new ways of thinking about food that alert us to its inherently political nature and capacity to bring us together."[9] Yet, this collection of essays also alerts us to the use of food as a divisive instrument, particularly in cases of culinary xenophobia and nativism as teased out in Aitana Guia's essay, "Food Fights: Nativism and Culinary Xenophobia in Europe." Guia states, "Gastronationalism refers to a mechanism mostly deployed by the state to defend violations or threats to the symbolic boundaries of national food."[10] Her essay points to instances across Europe in which political directives have undermined the rights of minority populations via restrictions of food practices: in Spain and Denmark, a denial of Halal menu options in the public-school system; in Italy, blocking the establishment of small kebob shop businesses; and in Valencia, Spain; the opposition to build arches designating Chinatown, where food establishments define much of the area. I was particularly drawn to the distinction between nation building and normalization of culture, as Guia asserts, the uses of food "are not as important during nation-building project as they are during its period of normalization."[11] Her essay also serves as a model and inspiration for future research on the role of food at different stages of shaping nationalism. In considering the power of food, these essays led to future research questions, for example, whose responsibility is it to protect children's rights when the government does not? What role do families, teachers, school administrators and school associations play in the decision-making process?

Guia's essay also shares similar concerns with those in Jessica Boll's essay, "Culinary Conflict or *Convivencia*?: *Halal* Food Practices, Perceptions, and Promotion in Spain." As the title states, the author cogently presents the state of halal practices, perceptions and promotion and the current debates surrounding them. Her essay also presses readers to consider the *halal* market in a global context as it is such a fast-growing industry and has become a food trend of sorts, which in turn makes readers consider both the changing face of Spain's culinary identity and also the growing tourist industry related to Spain's Muslim history. Future research could explore how the issues in Spain are playing out in other European countries.

Perhaps a response to the rise of *halal* food in Spain has been the instances of Neo-Franco restaurants dotting the landscape of central Spain. To return to "Francoist Food Culture in Post-Authoritarian Spain," Anderson brings to the attention of scholars the role food plays in conservative political agendas at many social junctures, including populist restauranteurs. Owners nostalgic for the Franco era create menu items such as "bacalao grande y libre" (great and free cod) or "chuletillas del Valle" (lamb chops from the Valley) to evoke Spain's former dictator.[12] This food nostalgia is also seen in other countries, for example, in Texas restaurants selling "Trump burgers." Additional research along these lines could explore how populist culture uses food sovereignty as a mobilizing tool.

Anderson's article also brings to the forefront the role of the media in the formation of gastrocracy as she examines the Spanish TV show, "Un país para comerselo" (A country good enough to eat), a popular series that ran from 2010–2014. Anderson deftly explains that "although it purports to celebrate regional diversity, the show in fact plates up a Spain that is primarily imagined as a singular, unified whole."[13] In this way, food is used as an instrument of the state to create a national culinary culture. Returning to Boll, she too notes that when film and TV cover immigrant culinary culture, it is usually defined as a marker of cultural difference and "the familiar motif of a majority host sampling minority food underscores the hierarchical relationship between the two populations."[14] In both cases, the dominant sources minimize the role of the other. How then can we think of food media, particularly the roles of the state and the private sector, in representing food practices as part of a larger social identity? Also, what role may social and web-based media play in shaping food policy? Within food media, how may state-controlled or privately-owned sources differ in their positions? In what ways might state-configured structures be taken up in the private sector to perpetuate certain politic statements through foodways?

This volume also inspired me to think of the issues raised in a primarily Spanish context within the larger European framework. For example, how are ongoing food debates, alliances, and controversies that are playing out in Spain relevant within a broader European context? What are the current halal practices and perceptions in other countries? Davidson's study of cava and its "deterritorialized indeterminancy" is a wonderful case study that can be used as a model for other foodstuffs and territorial identities.[15] Are there, for example, comparable debates surrounding cheeses, condiments, honey, and meats in other regions of Spain and, more generally, Europe? In what ways are national food identities shifting with food fusions that immigrant communities have successfully transplanted as they settle in a new country? In what ways are other movements like animal rights activism or ecotourism shifting food practices and their political framework? How do practices of food nostalgia and food fusion play out in the shaping of regional and national cultures? By informing and stimulating readers on both historic and contemporary food practices and how they affect and provide meaning to the larger cultural, political, social and economic landscape, this volume of collected essays is a significant contribution to Food Studies and Cultural Studies. It inspires us all to consider, investigate, and share with others the many and varied ways that foodways and politics intersect at all levels of society.

NOTES

1. This book, 10.
2. Anderson, *Control and Resistance*, 5.
3. This book, 1.
4. This book, 4.
5. This book, 231.
6. This book, 223.
7. This book, 226
8. This book, 281.
9. This book, 93.
10. This book, 103.
11. This book, 103–4.
12. This book, 92.
13. This book, 88.
14. This book, 156.
15. This book, 198.

WORKS CITED

Afinoguénova, Eugenia. "De la carta a la papeleta: El 'menú del día' entre la dictadura y la democracia en España, 1964–1981." *Bulletin of Hispanic Studies* 97, no. 4 (2020): 515–38.
Anderson, Lara. *Control and Resistance: Food Discourse in Franco Spain*. Toronto: University of Toronto Press, 2020.
"Biosistemàtica, filogènia & citogenètica moleculars de plantes: Etnobotàntica dels Països Catalans." Etnobiofic, accessed Feb. 1, 2022. http://www.etnobiofic.cat.
DeSoucey, Michaela. *Contested Tastes: Foie Gras and the Politics of Food*. Princeton, NJ:

Princeton University Press, 2016.
Ichijo, Atsuko, and Ronald Ranta. *Food, National Identity and Nationalism: From Everyday to Global Politics*. New York: Palgrave Macmillan, 2016.
Ingram, Rebecca. *Women's Work: How Culinary Cultures Shaped Modern Spain*. Nashville, TN: Vanderbilt University Press, 2022.
Vester, Katharina. *A Taste of Power: Food and American Identities*. Berkeley: University of California Press, 2015.

◆ CONTRIBUTORS

EUGENIA AFINOGUÉNOVA is professor of Spanish language and culture at Marquette University (USA) specializing in tourism, museum history, and visual culture. She is the author of *The Prado: Spanish Culture and Leisure, 1819–1939* (Penn State University Press, 2018; winner of the 2019 Eleanor Tufts Award from the American Society for Hispanic Art Historical Studies) and a coeditor, with Silvina Schammah Gesser and Robert Lubar Messeri, of the forthcoming *Edinburgh Companion to the Spanish Civil War and Visual Culture* funded by the National Endowment for the Humanities Collaborative Grant Award. Afinoguénova's current research project explores the intersections of gastronomy and visuality.

LARA ANDERSON is associate professor in Spanish and Latin American studies at the University of Melbourne (Australia), specializing in nineteenth-century Spanish cultural history, Spanish food studies with an emphasis on food and nationalism, food and gender, and food and authoritarianism. She is the author of numerous articles in leading journals, and has authored three books, including *Control and Resistance: Food Discourse in Franco Spain (1939–1959)* (University of Toronto Press, 2020) and *Cooking up the Nation: Nineteenth Century and Twentieth Century Culinary Nationalization* (Tamesis, 2013).

JESSICA BOLL is associate professor of Spanish at Carroll University (USA), specializing in early modern Spanish-Ottoman relations and the dynamics between Christians and Muslims in contemporary Spain. She is author of numerous articles on the legacy of al-Andalus, the controversies surrounding the Mosque-Cathedral in Córdoba, and the depictions of Istanbul in early modern Spanish literature. Her current project focuses on the increasing presence of *halal* food in Spain and the representations thereof in cultural texts.

BOB DAVIDSON is professor of Spanish and Catalan studies at the University of Toronto, faculty at the Culinaria Research Centre, and director of the Northrop Frye Centre, Victoria College. He is the author of *Jazz Age Barcelona* (2009) and *The Hotel: Occupied Space* (2018) and is currently researching a new project entitled *The Scent of Spain: Fragrance, Odour and Culture*. Professor Davidson is founder and coeditor of the Toronto Iberic book series at University of Toronto Press, where he also serves as chair of the Manuscript Review Committee. In 2022, he was accorded the Josep Maria Batista i Roca-Memorial Enric Garriga Trullols Award for the promotion of the Catalan language and culture abroad.

SUZANNE DUNAI is assistant professor of history at Southwestern Oklahoma State University (USA), specializing in modern European history, food history, and women and gender studies. She is the author of numerous publications on consumer rationing, food policies, and the social consequences of food crises in urban Spain during the 1940s, a time known as the "hunger years." She is currently working on transforming her dissertation on food strategies and everyday life in Francoist Spain into a monograph.

LUIS BENITO GARCÍA ÁLVAREZ is the chair of Asturias Cider at the University of Oviedo (Spain), specializing in the history of beverages and the sociability developed around their consumption, food history, and socio-cultural history. He is the author of numerous articles and monographs on these topics. He is the lead researcher responsible for the candidacy of Asturian cider culture for recognition as an Intangible Heritage of Humanity by UNESCO.

ALEJANDRO J. GÓMEZ DEL MORAL is university lecturer in economic and social history at the University of Helsinki (Finland), specializing in the history of consumer cultures, transnational flows of social and political ideas, fascisms, and national identity, most especially in modern Spain. He is author of *Buying into Change: Mass Consumption, Dictatorship, and Democracy in Franco's Spain, 1939-1982* (University of Nebraska Press, 2021), as well as several articles examining the socio-political changes that a boom in mass consumption helped catalyze in Spain during the Franco dictatorship. His current project focuses on the development of the Spanish cured pork industry, and how Spain's famed pork charcuterie became a national symbol as private actors and public authorities together constructed and marketed a Spanish culinary nation-brand globally during the twentieth and twenty-first centuries.

SUSY GRUSS is a lecturer at the Salti Institute, in the Department of Literature of the Jewish People, Bar Ilan University (Israel), specializing in modern Sephardic culture and literature with special emphasis on contemporary Sephardic writers such as Michael Molho and Judah Haim HaCohen Perahia. She is a member of the Israel National Academy of Ladino and *Académica correspondiente* (Current member) in the Spanish Royal Academy (RAE). She has written extensively in major academic journals. Her book *Las novelas de Juda Haim Perahia* was published in Barcelona, Spain, in 2020. Her current project focuses on new comparative readings of texts in Yiddish and Ladino, Judeo-Spanish texts about the Holocaust in the Balkans, and the image of the Spanish Civil War in the Ladino press.

AITANA GUIA is associate professor of history at California State University, Fullerton (USA), specializing in migration, nationalism, and minorities in postwar Europe. She is author of *The Muslim Struggle for Civil Rights in Spain: Promoting Democracy Through Migrant Engagement (1985–2010)* (Sussex Academic Press, 2015), "The Concept of Nativism and Anti-Immigrant Sentiments in Europe," and "Political Muslim Women: Embracing Citizenship and Feminism in Democratic Spain." She was awarded the City of Alzira's literary nonfiction book award for *La rebel·lió dels vianants: El Jardí del riu Túria al centre d'una nova València* (Bromera, 2022), a book about the fight of environmental and neighborhood movements to build a large urban park in the old Turia riverbed in Valencia, Spain, against the freeway that Francoist authorities had planned (1957–2022).

REBECCA INGRAM is professor of Spanish at the University of San Diego (USA) and affiliated faculty with the Women's and Gender Studies Program, specializing in food studies and Iberian cultural and gender studies. She is author of *Women's Work: How Culinary Cultures Shaped Modern Spain* (Vanderbilt University Press, 2022) and co-editor, with Lara Anderson, of the special issue "Transhispanic Food Cultural Studies" of *Bulletin of Spanish Studies* (2020). Her current research focuses on Mediterranean foodscapes and ideas of racialized citizenship.

F. XAVIER MEDINA is professor of the anthropology of food at the Universitat Oberta de Catalunya / Open University of Catalonia (UOC) in Barcelona (Spain) and the UNESCO chair on Food, Culture and Development at the UOC. He is also president of the International Commission on the Anthropology of Food and Nutrition (ICAF). His main fields of research are food, culture, heritage, tourism, and migrations. He is the author of numerous articles and a dozen books related to those fields.

MONTSERRAT MILLER is professor of history and executive director of the John Deaver Drinko Academy at Marshall University (USA), specializing in Modern European, Spanish, and food history. Her book *Feeding Barcelona: 1714–1975: Public Market Halls, Social Networks, and Consumer Culture* (Louisiana State University Press, 2018) was awarded the Phi Alpha Theta Best First Book Award. She has published extensively in English, Catalan, and Spanish on topics including symbolic iconography of market women, public rituals associated with market modernization initiatives, and retail associationism and civic life under dictatorial rule. Her current research focuses on the intersection between gastronomy and governance in modern Spain.

CAROLYN NADEAU is the Byron S. Tucci Professor of Spanish at Illinois Wesleyan University. Carolyn is fascinated by the role food played in Spain's social and cultural development. Her monograph *Food Matters: Alonso Quijano's Diet and the Discourse of Early Modern Food in Spain* (University of Toronto Press, 2016) contextualizes the shifts in Spain's gastronomic history at many levels of society and in the process, explores the evolving social and cultural identity of early modern Spain. Her critical edition and translation of Francisco Martínez Montiño's *Arte de cocina, pastelería, vizcochería y conservería* (1611; University of Toronto Press, 2023) unpacks Martínez Montiño's sophisticated culinary experiences and explains the trends and complexities that constitute Spain's culinary practices during the early modern period. Her current project, "Artistic Visions of the Transatlantic Exchange," explores how painters and poets, playwrights, and storytellers represented New World foodstuffs.

SILVINA SCHAMMAH GESSER lectures at the Salti Institute of Ladino Studies at Bar Ilan University and is a researcher at the Truman Institute of the Hebrew University of Jerusalem (Israel). She specializes in the intellectual and cultural history of early twentieth-century Spain and has written widely on otherness, memory, museum studies, and Jewish presence in Iberia. Among her publications are *Madrid's Forgotten Avant-garde. Between Essentialism and Modernity* (Sussex Academic Press, 2015) and *Jewish (In) Visibility in Iberia: A View from the Margins*, edited for Contemporary Jewry, 2020-21. Her current projects focus an intellectual biography of the Argentine Sephardic playwriter Ricardo Halac and the co-edition with Eugenia Afinoguénova and Robert Lubar Messeri of the *Edinburgh Companion to the Spanish Civil War and Visual Culture* funded by the National Endowment for the Humanities Collaborative Grant Award.

H. ROSI SONG is professor of Hispanic studies at Durham University (UK) specializing in twentieth- and twenty first-century Spanish culture and literature. She is the author of *Lost in Transition: Constructing Memory in Contemporary Spain* (Liverpool University Press, 2016) and the co-editor of *Towards a Cultural Archive of* la Movida: *Back to the Future* (Farleigh Dickinson University Press, 2013). Her most recent book, co-written with Anna Riera, *A Taste of Barcelona: The History of Catalan Cooking and Eating* (Rowman and Littlefield, 2019), received the North American Catalan Society Award for Outstanding Work in the Field of Catalan

Studies in 2021. She is one of the series editors for Culinaria, a new book series from the University of Toronto Press on food studies and serves on the editorial board for Toronto Iberic Series. She's currently working on a project on recipes.

INDEX

Page numbers in *italic* indicate figures.

acculturation, 9, 129
activism, 14, 58
administration, 43, 52–53, 78, 230, 260–61
Adrià, Ferran, 19, 65
advertisement, ads, 66, 181–84, 190, 193, 203, 251–52, 256, 274
aesthetics, 4, 37
agrarian, 179, 201
agroecosystems, 298
agroindustry, 229
Agulló, Ferran, 11, 58–62, 64–80, 272, 287, 298
Alcampo grocery stores, 207–8, 218
alcohol, 134, 157, 160, 164, 192, 242
Alicante, 129, 147, 208
allergies, 105–6
Almería, 154, 244
Alzira, 105, 122
ambivalence, 155, 251
Andalucía, 14, 112, 137, 156, 159, 163, 167, 271
al-Andalus, 149, 159–60, 163, 168, 170, 303
animal rights, 121, 159, 293, 298, 301
anonymity, 45, 157, 207
antibiotics, 166
anticlerical, 34–36, 104
anti-Kebab, 114, 116, 119
Antiquity, 47
antisemitism, 133

Arab, 12, 160
Arab Jews, 132
Aragón, 28, 210, 215, 273, 277
architecture, 36, 41, 160, 203
Argentina, 136, 248
Arms, armed, 34, 40, 240
artisanal, artisans, 32, 220, 226, 267, 275–76, 278
artists, 32, 60–61, 116, 187
assimilation, 1, 9–10, 59, 68, 104, 129, 137
Athens, 28, 133
austerity, 181, 242, 253
Australia, 68, 121, 162
Austria, 129–30
autarky, 7–8, 44, 186, 244, 246, 248–49, 251, 294
authenticity, 10, 61, 68–69, 78–79, 186, 228–30, 233
authoritarianism, 81, 303
autochthonous, 5
Autonomous Communities, 9, 14, 143
autonomy, 133, 206, 208, 241–42, 266, 281
Ávila, 92

bagpipes, 183–84, 187–89
Balearic Islands, the, 277
Balkans, 130, 305
ban, 32, 52, 108–9, 114, 158, 249
banalization, 229, 269

banal nationalism, 2, 15, 54, 77, 103, 124, 268, 283, 291
banquet, 70, 81, 86–87, 94, 147, 150, 189
barrels, 12, 179–85, 189
Basque Country, 8, 14–15, 85, 106, 160, 205, 243
bastardization, 278
beef, 111–12, 153–54, 163
Belgium, 113, 140, 143, 149, 165, 171
beliefs, 87–88, 90, 110, 254, 258, 266, 271
    dietary, 254
    popular, 269
    religious, 102, 107, 253–54
beverages, 213–14, 298, 304
biopolitics, 3, 16, 19–20, 82–84, 94, 96, 241, 294
biopower, 3, 83
biscuits, 134, 148, 246
body, 5–6, 32, 38, 41, 82–83, 91, 273, 276
    body politic, 6
borders, 68, 92, 113, 142, 156, 203, 273
boundaries, 65, 103, 266, 299
bourgeois, 5, 41, 59, 180
bourgeoisie, 42, 59, 180, 214
boycotts, 168, 173, 205–10, 216–18
branding, 2, 10–14, 166, 173–74, 217–18, 228–29, 284, 287
bread, 31–33, 182, 254, 280
buñuelos, 113
burgers, 111–12, 124
business-owners, 102, 116, 141, 179–80, 185, 266, 296, 299
butcheries, 27, 131, 135–36, 138, 146

Cáceres, 139, 187
café, 160, 253, 262
calendar, 135, 270
    religious, 243, 253–54
Canada, 115, 155
Canary Islands, the, 14, 244
cartoons, 111, 122, 126
Casablanca, 135
Castile, Castilian, 63, 91, 131, 193, 243, 273, 278

Catalan
    gastronomy, 58, 60, 67–69, 73, 77, 80, 275–78
    identity, 62, 69, 276, 282, 288, 298
    nationalism, 59, 74, 206, 208, 213
Catalan Pyrenees, the, 270
Catholic, Catholics, 34, 103, 129, 186, 240, 243, 252–55, 257
Catholicism, 133, 183–84, 240, 253, 257, 296
cattle, 131–32, 146
cava, 13, 17, 87, 198–99, 203–19, 300
celebrate, celebration, 70, 88, 118, 133, 187–88, 190, 244, 256
cemeteries, 107, 134, 136, 145
censorship, 83–84, 251
centralism, centralist, 11, 81, 83, 85, 87, 299
centralization, 86, 272, 277
ceremonies, 13, 34–36, 41, 43, 87, 131, 136
Ceuta, 129, 131–32, 134, 137, 146, 150
chains
    agri-food, 211, 226, 280, 297
    supply and distribution, 115, 123, 296
champagne, 13, 87, 198–99, 201, 204, 214, 216, 218
charcuterie, 264, 267, 269, 271, 274–76, 278–81
cheese, 86, 134, 180, 247, 256, 279
chef, 5, 10, 14, 68, 71, 73, 136, 160, 169, 174
chicken, 111–12, 120, 257
child, children, 44, 75, 105–10, 121, 126, 133, 201, 252
Chinatown
    Barcelona, 102, 115–19, 126, 299
    Valencia, 125
Chinese, 117–18, 247
chocolate, 33
cholesterol, 106
chorizo, 103, 277–79, 282
Christianity, Christian, 102–3, 157–58, 167, 170–74, 248, 253, 266, 270
Christians, 147–48, 158, 163, 170, 172, 303
Christmas, 113, 207, 209, 256–57
churros, 113
cider, 12–13, 179–84, 186–93

civic, 5, 185, 229, 306
civil society, 220–21, 225
Civil War, Spanish (1936-1939), 44, 90, 93, 192, 239–40, 242–48, 251, 258
climate, 11, 59, 81, 136, 213, 246, 272, 280
coalition, 118, 180, 239, 243
coasts, 60–61, 65–67, 73, 76, 188, 200
Coca-Cola, 138, 217
cod, 92, 256, 300
coffee, 33, 62
coloniality, colonial, 9, 89, 309
colonies, 130, 248
comfort food, 113
commemoration, 36, 91, 184
commerce, 26, 28, 32, 47, 63, 139, 165
commercialization, 180, 187, 229
commodities, commodification, 6, 26, 33, 36, 155, 229, 233, 240–43
common good, 5, 11, 49, 55
communal, 134, 155
communication, 232–33, 268, 284, 287
communions, 189, 255
communities
    Autonomous. *See* Autonomous Communities
    contemporary Muslim, 154
    diasporic, 9, 46, 83, 104, 115–16, 155, 301
    local, 229–30
    national, 281
    native, 104
    religious, 143
    rural, 63
competition, 39, 42, 75, 189–90, 192, 195, 268, 279
complaints, 114, 255
condiments, 69, 71, 300
conquest, 28, 89, 247–48
conservation, 220, 229–30
conservatives, 36, 40, 59, 243
constitutional, 94, 96, 206
Constitution of Spain, 137, 206
consumer cosmopolitanism, 155, 165, 174
consumer culture, 44, 159, 181, 240, 244, 283, 290, 304–5

consumer ethnocentrism, 155, 165, 174
consumerism, 33, 39, 57, 140, 256
contracts, 40, 107, 200, 214–15, 221, 224
    social, 215, 221, 224, 230
control
    municipal, 28, 40, 46
    public, 11, 25, 27–57, 295
    social, 37–38, 295
Convivencia, 12, 153–74, 299
cook, 73–74, 119, 144, 224, 242, 246–47, 256–57
cookbook, 58–65, 68–75, 86, 95, 243, 246–57, 264, 270–75
Córdoba, 137, 160–61, 169, 303
Corpinnat, 210–13, 217–18
cosmopolitan, 28, 71–72, 227
Costa Brava, 60, 64, 66–67, 69, 75–76, 79–80
countercultures, 243
COVID19 pandemic, 113, 161, 210, 217–18, 228
crafts, 62, 222, 275
crisis, 10, 14, 16, 20, 29, 33–34, 40, 54, 68, 228, 232–33
crustaceans, 147
Cuelgamuros, 95
culinary
    cultures, 16, 20, 69, 78, 166, 294, 302, 305
    maps, 11, 81, 93, 299
    multiculturalism, 17–18, 167, 171
    nationalism, 7, 86–87, 89, 266
    nostalgia, 90–91, 282, 287
    traditions, 14, 58, 68, 70, 74, 285
    xenophobia, 11, 101, 104, 119, 155, 295, 299
cultural
    heritage, 12, 117, 220–22, 225, 228, 230, 248
    identity, 7, 253, 268, 306
    movements, 60, 67, 73
    patterns, 26, 37, 47
    practices, 1, 3, 83
    texts, 155, 167, 303
    tourism, 142, 227, 230, 232–33

dairy, 138, 140
dances, 186, 188–89, 273
democracy, 45, 81–85, 93–94, 137, 188, 206, 274, 304
Denmark, Danish, 102, 110–12, 119, 121, 123, 126, 299
designations, 118, 204, 225, 228
desserts, 86, 148, 253
deterritorialization, 129, 198, 300
dictator, 85, 90, 133, 300
diet, 33, 40, 109–12, 120, 241–45, 250–52, 254, 258
discourse
    food-related, 5, 12, 295
    gendered, 7
    hegemonic, 84, 294
    nationalistic, 58, 248, 297
    nativist, 111
    patriarchal, 250
discrimination, 44, 106–7, 115, 167, 171
disparities, 154, 243, 247, 251
diversity, 8–9, 121–24, 129, 162, 172, 249, 277, 298
    regional, 88, 300
domesticity, 38, 70, 73, 77, 80
dough, 113, 146
drinking, 142, 190, 192, 198

eateries, 135–36, 154, 159–62, 164, 241
eating habits, 77, 102–3, 113, 132, 158, 241, 250, 256
economic development, 2, 7, 44, 221, 275
education, 71–72, 78n76, 83, 105–6, 185–86, 250
eggs, 40, 92, 105–6, 112, 148, 180, 256, 282
Egypt, 142
elite, 7, 31, 33, 82, 85, 199–200, 211, 241, 268–69
empire, 247–48, 259, 261, 309
employment, 30, 73
enclaves, 27, 130, 138
environment, 17, 19–20, 65, 101, 103, 160
Environmental Cultural Studies, 14, 18
espicha, 12, 179–93, 296
Esquerra Republicana de Catalunya (ERC), 205, 207, 215, 218

ethnic, ethnicity, 9, 104, 113, 115, 156
European, 11, 36, 102, 139, 165, 246, 296, 300
European Economic Community (ECC), 186, 204, 275, 279, 281
European Union (EU), 11, 121, 143, 198, 211, 268, 281, 299
euros, 116, 141, 158, 167, 172, 208
exceptionalism, 246
exotic, 113, 161
exploitation, 14, 225
export, exporters, 28, 112, 139–41, 144, 148, 200, 209–10, 241
Extremadura, 14, 205, 210, 215

fabada, 182, 184, 193, 273
Facebook, 158, 161, 169, 171
faith, 165, 173, 247, 253
falafel, 109
famine, 251–52
farm, 14, 136, 245
farmers, 69, 157, 200, 245
farming, 200, 229, 298
fascism, fascist, 42, 81–82, 92, 94–96, 260, 262, 273, 304
fast food, 123, 125, 159
fasting, 122, 253–56
fat, 275
feast, 134, 253
festival, 77, 146, 182–83, 185, 190, 227
finger food, 182
fiscal, 7, 28, 30
fish, 28–29, 62, 110–12, 120, 132, 190, 242–44, 255–56
folklore, 185–86, 283, 291
food
    comfort, 113
    fast, 123, 125
    finger, 182
    forbidden, 107
    foreign, 114, 246
    local, 8, 228, 267
    ready-made, 138
    regional, 58, 264, 297–98
    subsidized, 244
    taboo, 144, 152, 255
    vegetarian, 254

food and food politics, 293
food commodity, 257
food communities, 12
food crises, 41, 249, 304
food disparities, 158
food distribution, 272
food factories, 73
food fusions, 301
food gentrification, 14
food heritage, 2–3, 6, 13, 220, 223–26,
    228–31, 295, 297
food history, 8, 295, 304–5
food hygiene, 143
food identities, 9, 297
food ideologies, 240, 243, 245, 258
food industry, 155, 164
food intolerances, 105–6
food markets, 25–27, 29, 40, 47, 49, 153, 241
food media, 83, 300
food memories, 11, 81, 90–91, 93, 299
food multiculturalism, 155
food nostalgia, 300–301
food packaging, 166
food policies, 240, 244–45, 254–55, 262, 285,
    289, 293, 296
food production, 103, 141, 157, 222–23,
    293
food provisioning, 7, 250, 254
food purity, 166
food rationing, 35, 42, 251
food retailing, 25, 36–37, 46–47
food riots, 30–31
food safety, 37, 40, 122, 143, 153, 227
foodscapes, 2, 4, 12, 86, 154, 158, 163, 294–95
food sovereignty, 14, 300
Food Studies, 2–3, 103, 293, 301
foodstuffs, 7, 28, 91, 243, 248, 250, 257, 306
food subcultures, 242–43
food supply, 25, 27, 42, 239–40, 243, 245, 251
food systems, 1, 4, 6, 10, 26, 36, 69, 295
food texts, 43, 84, 88, 294
foreign, 5, 113, 119, 246, 277, 279
foreigners, 35, 66, 70, 76, 119, 122, 125,
    275–76
France, 5, 19, 32–33, 50, 107–10, 129, 158,
    171–72

Franco, Francisco, 8, 13, 76, 82–86, 90–93,
    239–40, 243–45, 295–96
Francoism, 43, 81–82, 85, 91–92, 243, 245,
    253, 258
French Revolution, 5, 31
fruits, 28, 86, 147–48, 199, 248

Galicia, 14, 19
gastrocracy, 1–6, 8, 10–11, 13–14, 82, 293,
    295, 300
gastronationalism, 13, 103–4, 121, 166, 266–
    69, 283–84, 298–99
gastronativism, 104, 121, 126
gastronomic tourism, gastrotourism, 9, 11,
    228, 230–31
gaze, 39, 208, 224
gender, 17, 19, 29, 38, 47, 70, 250–51, 303
gendered, 38, 40, 71, 256, 294
Girona, 59, 65, 78–80, 151, 215, 282, 284, 288
globalization, 9, 17, 223, 266, 297, 309
governance, 1–4, 6, 10, 14, 82, 93, 295, 306
grapes, 142, 199–201, 204, 211–12, 244
Great Britain, 33, 37, 50, 111, 122, 127, 246

habits, 135, 145, 167, 191, 242
halal, 107–10, 121–22, 126–27, 143–44, 153–
    66, 168–74, 299–300, 303
halal jamón, 154, 164
ham, 91, 103, 112, 140, 154, 180, 270–71, 280
hamburgers, 111, 123, 127
haute cuisine, 69, 71, 124–25, 294
health, 110, 114, 153, 158, 166, 250–51, 254,
    257–58
hegemony, hegemonic, 7, 83–84, 188, 225,
    242–43
heritage, 8, 13, 69, 77, 220–31, 233–34, 283,
    291, 297, 305
    food, 231, 297
    intangible, 77, 195, 222, 304
heritagization, 224–25, 228–29, 231, 297
Hispanidad, 248
Historical Memory Law, 84, 90–91
home cooking, 37, 69, 73, 132, 146
homogeneity, homogeneous, 89, 102, 227
honey, 163, 300
households, 29, 72, 112, 146, 250–51

housewives, 45, 72, 241–42, 250, 256
hunger, 16, 20, 34, 42, 245, 247, 251, 304
hybridity, 1, 9, 17, 19–20, 188, 310
hygiene, 37, 40, 114, 153

imaginaries, 15–16, 19, 67, 228, 248
immigrant cuisines, 155, 300
immigrants, 9, 102, 115–16, 119, 156–57, 159, 165, 167
    Chinese, 117–18, 155
    Muslim, 154, 159, 163–64
immigration, 8, 123, 126, 156–57, 167, 170–73, 282, 288
inaugurations, 136, 213
incentives, 38, 154, 242, 272
industrialization, 25, 33–34, 74, 80, 200–201, 267, 279
industry, 66, 139, 154, 157, 161, 165, 179, 184
    cured-pork, 265
    fishing, 66, 268
    local, 201
ingredients, 65, 69, 142, 163, 181, 241–42, 250, 256
    forbidden, 142
    foreign, 246, 249
    local, 69, 71
    seasonal, 78
    state-promoted, 245
innovations, 10, 36, 45, 192, 200–201
investment, 29, 40, 45, 140, 142, 182
invisiblization, 10
Islam, 103, 106, 111, 123, 126, 143, 156–60, 168–73
Islamophobia, 107, 158, 162, 164, 167, 171–72, 174
Italians, 268, 278, 283, 291
Italy, 115, 119, 155, 250

jamón, 91, 103, 112–13, 124, 140, 154, 278–80, 287–88
Japan, 162, 268
Jewish, 107, 129–31, 135, 137–39, 143
Jews, 102, 107, 112, 128–31, 133–34, 136–37, 142
journalists, 14, 61, 91, 271, 273–74
Judaism, 103, 128, 135, 137, 143

kebab, 102, 114, 120, 123, 154, 159, 168
Kentucky Fried Chicken, KFC, 158, 168, 172
kosher, 12, 108, 128–52, 296

labels, 91, 128, 166, 173, 204, 208, 210–11, 213
labor, 6, 9–10, 34, 41, 95, 137, 199
lamb, 92, 112, 153–54, 215, 270, 300
land, 64, 113, 204, 224, 247, 277–78, 299
landscape, 62, 64–69, 77, 80, 119, 222, 300
Latin America, Latin American, 136–37, 140, 248, 280, 303, 309–10
laws, 26, 59, 63, 115, 120, 128, 137–40, 206
    appellation, 204
    dietary, 128, 131, 296
    local, 64
    zoning, 159
legislation, 107, 115–16, 215, 239, 251, 257–58
legitimacy, legitimize, 2, 35, 43, 137, 143, 185, 192, 221–22
lent, 30, 46, 243, 254, 256
Lombardy, 114
lunch, 86, 105, 110, 121, 138, 294
luxury, 198, 241, 253

magazine, 73, 111, 131, 245, 248, 250, 274, 279
Majorca (Mallorca), Majorcan (Mallorcan), 28, 61, 94, 147, 277
Málaga, 129, 137
malnutrition, 252
management, 38, 83, 220–21, 223, 230
maps, 89, 296
Marca España, 142, 167
marketing, 264
marriage, 252–53, 310
mass consumption, 55, 181, 285, 289, 304
Mataró, 31, 109, 200
meal plans, 73
meat, 108–21, 131–32, 135, 138, 146, 154, 254–56, 272
    cured, 13, 163, 274, 276, 298
meatballs, 110

medical conditions, 109, 250
medieval, 27–28, 75–76, 114, 147, 160, 270, 272, 309–10
Mediterranean, 25, 47, 60, 131, 168, 207, 289, 309
Mediterranean Diet, 15, 19, 231, 233
Melilla, 129, 131–32, 134, 137–38, 147
memory, 15, 60, 82–83, 90–91, 138, 221–22, 229, 306
menú del día, 16, 18, 282, 287, 294, 301
menu, 86, 105–7, 109–11, 120–21, 131, 138, 154, 193, 294
middle classes, 59, 70, 72, 74, 180, 188, 193, 204, 215, 294
Middle East, Middle Eastern, 114, 161
migrant labor rights, 293
migrants, 6, 9–11, 130, 155–56, 167, 171
migrations, 9, 30, 39, 129, 138, 305
military, 8, 32, 35, 136, 164, 240, 243, 268
milk, 39, 106, 112, 163, 244, 278
minorities, 9, 12, 129, 136, 254, 296, 305
mobility, product's, 70, 199, 201
Modernisme, 60, 67, 77, 203
modernity, 7, 25, 40, 73, 199, 306, 309
modernization, 10, 26, 33, 46, 67, 137, 188, 295
modified crops, 14, 166
money, 6, 50, 57, 115, 209, 213, 253
Moorish, 159, 170, 173
moriscos, 102, 149, 158
mosques, 104, 121, 303
mothers, 35, 109, 138, 250
multicultural, multiculturalism, 9, 154–56, 295
multiethnic, 8–9, 295
music, 139, 164, 180, 182, 184, 187, 189
Muslim, 102, 106–12, 141, 147n49, 157–61, 163–64, 165n8, 166nn15–16, 169n60

Naples, 28
nation building, 4, 7, 14, 58, 70, 104, 250, 295, 299
nation state, 3, 11, 67, 86, 198
nativism, 11, 103–4, 119–20, 125, 299, 305

neighborhoods, 43, 115–19, 147, 184–85
Netherlands, the, 104, 134, 170
NGOs, 95, 220
non-Muslim, 107, 154–55, 158, 164–66, 172, 174
norms, gender, 38, 239
nostalgia, 11, 68, 71, 85, 90–91, 95, 97
nutrition, 40, 73, 250, 272, 296
nutritionists, 251–52

obesity, 106, 250–52
oil, 28, 31, 62, 91, 101, 148
omelets, 62, 180, 255
one-plate program, 253, 255
Orientalism, 12, 160

paella, 112, 273
pasta, 78, 111–12, 268
patriarchy, 240, 250, 257, 296
patriotism, patriotic, 70, 88, 241–42, 244–45, 257, 294, 296
peasants, 29, 226
Penedès, 201, 204, 211–13, 298
peripheries, 1–2, 26, 43, 85
pesticides, 14, 166
Philip V, 32, 48
phylloxera, 66, 201, 215
pigs, 14, 101, 120
pilgrimages, 166, 174, 180–81, 184, 187
plants, 120, 148, 298
poet, 60, 72, 75, 306
policing, 30, 37–38, 251, 295
policymakers, 13, 268–69
politician, 61, 64, 72, 92, 110, 184
politicization, politicize, 109, 112, 119
popular culture, 73, 77, 79, 87, 102, 186, 251–52, 264
populist, 102, 104, 107, 114–15, 119, 300
pork, 101–13, 119, 153–54, 157–58, 266–68, 278–80, 298
potatoes, 62, 78, 92, 112, 256
poultry, 28–29, 131–32, 134–35
preservatives, 40, 166
prestige, 58, 67, 142, 209, 231

price-setting, 31, 240, 247
Primo de Rivera, Miguel, 7, 16, 18, 40, 88, 95
private sphere, 145, 239, 241, 245
private trade, 11, 25, 27–57, 295
progress, 34, 51, 96, 155, 259
prohibitions, 111, 140, 156, 242, 254
prosecco, 199–201
prosperity, 44–45, 50, 92, 130, 138
prostitution, 38, 116
protein, 8, 40, 243
protests, 31, 41, 111, 158, 210, 280
provisions, 9, 30, 40–42, 45, 66, 115, 136, 253
public sphere, 38, 83, 101–2, 119, 221, 239–41, 245

racialization, 9–10, 248
radio, 4, 118, 190, 250–51
rationing, 247, 250, 257
recipes, 16, 18, 64–65, 78, 163, 241–42, 255–56, 270
reconciliation, 164, 167, 172
Reconquista, 158, 163
recreational activities, 135, 161, 181, 188
referendum, 58, 206, 210
refugees, 3, 130–31, 133
Regeneration, 11, 61–79, 297
regional food cultures, 8, 81, 86, 273
regionalism, 7, 16, 18, 76, 273, 295
regions, 46, 75, 105, 137, 199
religion, 109–10, 145, 151–52, 156, 166, 173, 252–55, 258
religious
    minorities, 102, 104–8, 111–12, 119, 133, 137
    slaughter, 143, 149, 151
repression, 31, 34, 82–83, 239, 243–44
Republic, 109, 281
Republicans, 93, 95, 207
restrictions, 102, 131, 140, 180, 241–42, 299
retail, 29, 36, 39, 41–42, 117, 187, 228, 278
revival, 12, 26–27, 56, 60, 167, 199
rhetoric, 35, 62, 68, 187, 247, 268–69
rites, 105, 131–32, 139, 190, 192, 309
rituals, 35, 45, 102–3, 131, 136, 142, 144, 179–80, 191
roasting, 179, 242

Romans, 270
Rome, 26, 101
Royal Academy of Gastronomy, the, 2, 10

sacrifice, sacrificial, 147, 244, 253, 256
sales, 28, 30–32, 141, 180, 208–10, 272
salt, 242, 282
sausages, 113, 180, 182, 265, 270–71, 275–77, 281
scarcity, 7, 65, 146, 162, 181, 250, 257, 266
schools, 105–11, 113–14, 121, 145, 164, 215
seafood, 14, 112, 147, 183–84, 190, 193, 243
secularism, 108–9, 136, 143, 145, 148
security, 82, 85, 227, 246
Sephardic, 130, 132, 135, 306
shellfish, 180
shopping, 30, 45, 73, 113, 257
shortages, 31, 34, 40, 162, 242, 247
slaughtering, 121, 137, 143, 153
smells, 101–2, 113–14, 116, 119
smoked paprika, 277, 282
snacks, 113, 115, 120, 138, 180, 182, 184, 191
snails, 112
sobrasada, sobrassada, 103, 277
sociability, 38, 47, 179, 192, 304
social practices, 6, 69, 73
soil, 65, 201, 204–5, 213
sovereignty, 63, 67, 95, 198, 204, 206, 269
Spain
    Civil War in, 42, 52, 92–93, 132, 239–40, 244–58, 263, 305–6
    contemporary, 11, 18, 93, 168, 170–71, 294, 303, 306, 309
    continental, 129–30, 133, 135, 137, 296
    Democratic, 94–95, 129, 137, 143, 305
    during the Franco regime, 12–13, 43–44, 82–86, 179–80, 239–44, 274, 296, 303–4
    early twentieth-century, 15, 18, 77, 79, 94–95
    Medieval, 170, 172, 174
    post-Franco, 11, 81, 90, 299–300
    twentieth-century, 40, 94–96, 306, 310
    twenty-first century, 15, 19
    under the Bourbon rule, 30, 32, 36

Spanish cuisine, 70, 81, 84, 101, 103, 155, 246–47, 273–74
   standard, 92
   traditional, 13, 87
   unified, 85
Spanish nationalism, 7, 85–87, 244
Spanish omelet. See *tortilla española*
Spanish-style food, 86, 92, 246–47
sparkling wine, 198–201, 203–5, 212–13, 217–18, 298
sport, 117, 188, 205, 250, 260, 262
starvation, 42
statement, 59–64
stew, 182
subjectivities, 6, 9, 81–84, 93, 156
sub-nationalisms, subnations, 8, 86
sugars, 106, 148, 201
supermarkets, 13, 40, 45–47
supranational, 198, 225
surplus, 26–28
surveillance, 38, 254
survival, 38, 42, 73, 131, 133, 185, 201, 278
sustainability, 46, 227
sweet, 113, 166, 173

taste, 4–5, 17, 21, 77–78, 96, 213, 278, 285
television, 4, 11, 81, 86–87, 156, 190, 210, 229
territoriality, 8, 69, 95, 198, 225, 227, 229, 300
terroir, 13, 68–69, 77, 79–80, 198, 204–5, 218–19, 298
testimonies, 42, 131–35, 138, 179, 222
textiles, 29, 272
theater, 41, 61, 186
Torremolinos, 129, 147
tortilla española, Spanish omelet, 4, 112–13, 120, 123, 127
tourism, 13, 17, 66, 74, 168–71, 188, 220–34, 305
   gastronomic, 226–28, 230, 232–34
tourists, 8, 90, 116, 142, 159, 227–28, 230
tradition, 13, 65, 147, 150, 181, 192–93, 221–22, 276–77
   food-related, 132, 190, 199, 201, 244, 279, 281
trains, train stations, 36, 114, 116–17, 182, 245

transition to democracy, 8, 45, 81–82, 84–85, 93, 137, 206
translation, 74, 120, 229, 306
transnational, 134, 294, 304
travelers, 66, 88, 162
turkey, 169, 256–57
Tuscany, 114–15

UNESCO, 12, 115, 117, 195, 304
unified gastronomic space, 7, 86, 273
United Kingdom, the 108, 111, 142
United Nations, 15
United States, 8, 104, 111, 142, 248, 271, 280, 310
urbanization, 18–19, 272
Uruguay, 248

Valencia, 28, 105–6, 113, 116–18, 120, 200, 277
varieties, 2, 139, 201, 212, 226, 277
vegans, 106, 112, 140–41, 254
vegetables, 28–29, 42, 111, 255
vegetarian, 106–7, 109–12, 147, 160, 243, 254–55
Veneto, 114, 123, 126
villages, 26, 35, 47, 65–69
vineyards, 139, 149, 199–201, 204, 211–12, 214, 217
violence, 33–35, 82–83, 92–93
viticulture, 199–200, 207, 214, 298
Vox (political party), 107, 112, 167–68, 172

waffles, 113, 116
wages, 33, 35, 214
war, 32, 48, 71, 73, 130, 133, 181–82, 245, 251
water, 37, 216, 293
weather, 215, 228
websites, 12, 15, 89–90, 149, 160–61, 169, 215, 293
weddings, 87, 189
Western Europe, 26–27, 29, 31, 33, 47, 119
wheat, 28, 32–33
whisky, 269
wine, 28, 131–32, 148–49, 199–201, 210–12, 218–19, 274–75, 298

winemaking, 69, 200, 205, 212
wineries, 139, 143, 201, 203, 211, 228
women, 5–7, 29–31, 40–44, 50–57, 71–73, 183, 241–42, 250–52
workers, 9, 35, 40, 62, 188, 215, 250, 254

xenophobia, 11, 109, 155, 158

Zaragoza, 105, 121, 126, 154, 200

◆ VOLUMES IN THE HISPANIC ISSUES SERIES

47   *Digestible Governance: Gastrocracy and Spanish Foodways*, edited by Eugenia Afinoguénova, Lara Anderson, and Rebecca Ingram
46   *Améfrica in Letters: Literary Interventions from Mexico 46   Améfrica in Letters: Literary Interventions from Mexico to the Southern Cone*, edited by Jennifer Carolina Gómez Menjívar
45   *Rite, Flesh, and Stone: Cultures of Death in Contemporary Spain, 1959–2021*, edited by Antonio Córdoba and Daniel García-Donoso
44   *Iberian Empires and the Roots of Globalization*, edited by Ivonne del Valle, Anna More, and Rachel Sarah O'Toole
43   *Cartographies of Madrid*, edited by Silvia Bermúdez and Anthony L. Geist
42   *Ethics of Life: Contemporary Iberian Debates*, edited by Katarzyna Beilin and William Viestenz
41   *In and Of the Mediterranean: Medieval and Early Modern Iberian Studies*, edited by Michelle M. Hamilton and Núria Silleras-Fernández
40   *Coloniality, Religion, and the Law in the Early Iberian World*, edited by Santa Arias and Raúl Marrero-Fente
39   *Poiesis and Modernity in the Old and New Worlds*, edited by Anthony J. Cascardi and Leah Middlebrook
38   *Spectacle and Topophilia: Reading Early (and Post-) Modern Hispanic Cultures*, edited by David R. Castillo and Bradley J. Nelson
37   *New Spain, New Literatures*, edited by Luis Martín-Estudillo and Nicholas Spadaccini
36   *Latin American Jewish Cultural Production*, edited by David William Foster
35   *Post-Authoritarian Cultures: Spain and Latin America's Southern Cone*, edited by Luis Martín-Estudillo and Roberto Ampuero
34   *Spanish and Empire*, edited by Nelsy Echávez-Solano and Kenya C. Dworkin y Méndez
33   *Generation X Rocks: Contemporary Peninsular Fiction, Film, and Rock Culture*, edited by Christine Henseler and Randolph D. Pope

32 *Reason and Its Others: Italy, Spain, and the New World*, edited by David Castillo and Massimo Lollini
31 *Hispanic Baroques: Reading Cultures in Context*, edited by Nicholas Spadaccini and Luis Martín-Estudillo
30 *Ideologies of Hispanism*, edited by Mabel Moraña
29 *The State of Latino Theater in the United States: Hybridity, Transculturation, and Identity*, edited by Luis A. Ramos-García
28 *Latin America Writes Back: Postmodernity in the Periphery (An Interdisciplinary Perspective)*, edited by Emil Volek
27 *Women's Narrative and Film in Twentieth-Century Spain: A World of Difference(s)*, edited by Ofelia Ferrán and Kathleen M. Glenn
26 *Marriage and Sexuality in Medieval and Early Modern Iberia*, edited by Eukene Lacarra Lanz
25 *Pablo Neruda and the U.S. Culture Industry*, edited by Teresa Longo
24 *Iberian Cities*, edited by Joan Ramon Resina
23 *National Identities and Sociopolitical Changes in Latin America*, edited by Mercedes F. Durán-Cogan and Antonio Gómez-Moriana

www.ingramcontent.com/pod-product-compliance
Lightning Source LLC
Chambersburg PA
CBHW020327240426
43665CB00044B/721